THE RURAL TRADITION

W.J. KEITH

The Rural Tradition

A STUDY OF THE NON-FICTION PROSE WRITERS
OF THE ENGLISH COUNTRYSIDE

UNIVERSITY OF TORONTO PRESS

© University of Toronto Press 1974
Toronto and Buffalo
Printed in Canada
ISBN 0-8020-5294-0
LC 73-81754

In our depths we are a country, not an urban, people.
H.J. MASSINGHAM, *The English Countryman*

CONTENTS

PREFACE

Rural writing is a curiously neglected topic. Although we possess numerous studies of individual authors, no scholarly attempt has been made to consider the literature of the countryside as a definable and legitimate field of study. No one has set out to survey the whole subject, to trace significant continuities between one rural writer and another, to examine the critical problems inherent in such writing, to test the cogency of thinking in terms of a possible 'rural tradition.' Naturally no single volume can hope to cover such a broad and uncharted area, but the present study is an attempt to clear the ground – or, to be more circumspect, part of the ground. In order to keep my subject within manageable limits I have confined my attention to those writers whose main literary productions belong to the area of non-fiction (hence the omission of certain figures such as Thomas Hardy who might otherwise be considered central). As a consequence the book tries in addition to offer an original if modest contribution to that most neglected of literary topics, the critical appreciation of non-fiction prose.

After an introductory discussion of the basic principles involved, the book contains eleven chapters devoted to individual studies of the most important and influential rural writers from Izaak Walton to modern times. While I hope that these chapters provide useful and reasonably self-sufficient discussions of their respective subjects, I should like to emphasize the fact that the book is intended to be read as a whole. Its most important feature consists in the examination of these authors within the specific context of rural writing. It is based on the belief that such works are not seen at their best within the whole panorama of literary history, or even within studies of particular periods, since in both cases they tend to get set aside as awkward misfits 'out of the main stream.' When studied together, however, each throws fascinating light on the the others and will be seen to fit into a loose but none the less discernible 'line.'

Such an approach might well result in an excessive rigidity, but I have tried to avoid this. While I consider it helpful to see these writers as part of a 'rural tradition,' I have not attempted to force them all into a common mould. In each chapter the emphasis falls according to the nature of the writer in question. Sometimes thematic rather than stylistic aspects are accentuated, sometimes the reverse. In certain cases (Borrow and Williamson in fiction, Thomas in poetry) I have made excursions into other literary areas when the situation demanded it. While biographical information has generally been kept to a minimum, this rule has been broken whenever, as in the case of Massingham, important biographical facts are little known. Yet despite the variety to be found in the writers under examination, and despite the different approaches demanded as a consequence, I believe that the study hangs together as a whole and that each writer appears more impressive and coherent when discussed within the context of his own kind.

Just as this book was going to press, and too late to acknowledge in the body of the text, Raymond Williams's long-awaited *The Country and the City* was published (London: Chatto & Windus, 1973). Many of the problems raised briefly in my opening chapter are explored by Williams in detail, and, although his subject is much broader than mine and his approach very different, I regret that my own study was not able to benefit from his stimulating discussions of several of the writers treated here.

It is a pleasure at this point to acknowledge with gratitude assistance that made the publication of this book possible: a grant from the Humanities Research Council of Canada, using funds provided by the Canada Council, and a grant to University of Toronto Press from the Andrew W. Mellon Foundation. And for technical help and advice in the preparation of the manuscript I am particularly indebted to Miss Jean C. Jamieson and Miss Joan Bulger, both of University of Toronto Press.

In the course of writing the book I was helped by a number of friends, colleagues, and students too numerous to be mentioned individually. There are, however, four persons who deserve special acknowledgment. My colleague, Professor Michael Kirkham, read the whole manuscript with a keen eye for factual inaccuracies and stylistic inelegancies. Professor Lucille Herbert read an early version of the chapter on Borrow and made a number of helpful and stimulating suggestions. Similar services were performed by Mr Peter Simpson (for the chapter on Thomas) and by Mr Marvin Hays (for those on Sturt,

Williamson, and Massingham). I am particularly grateful to these four; whatever the faults of the book as it now stands, I know that it is indisputably the better for their generous encouragement and firm scrutiny.

W.J.K.
University College, University of Toronto, October 1973

ACKNOWLEDGMENTS

Acknowledgments are due to the following publishers for permission to quote from copyright material: to B.T. Batsford Ltd, for quotations from the following works by H.J. Massingham: *Chiltern Country, Cotswold Country, The English Countryman, English Downland, Remembrance*; to Cambridge University Press, for quotations from the following works by George Sturt: *The Journals of George Sturt, 1890–1927* (ed. E.D. Mackerness), *A Small Boy in the Sixties, The Wheelwright's Shop*; to Jonathan Cape Ltd, for quotations from *A Farmer's Life* by George Sturt / 'George Bourne'; to Chapman & Hall Ltd, for quotations from the following works by H.J. Massingham: *The Fall of the Year, Genius of England, Shepherd's Country, The Tree of Life*; to Collins Publishers, for quotations from the following works by H.J. Massingham: *The Curious Traveller, An Englishman's Year, This Plot of Earth, Where Man Belongs, The Wisdom of the Fields*; to Gerald Duckworth & Co Ltd, for quotations from the following works by George Sturt / 'George Bourne': *The Bettesworth Book, Change in the Village, Lucy Bettesworth, Memoirs of a Surrey Labourer*; to Faber & Faber Ltd and A.M. Heath & Company Ltd, for quotations from the following works by Henry Williamson: *The Children of Shallowford, A Clear Water Stream, A Dream of Fair Women, The Labouring Life, The Linhay on the Downs, Norfolk Life* (with Lilias Rider Haggard), *The Pathway, Richard Jefferies, The Story of a Norfolk Farm, The Sun in the Sands, The Village Book, The Wild Red Deer of Exmoor*; and to The Society of Authors as the literary representative of the Estate of H.J. Massingham, for quotations from *An Englishman's Year, The Curious Traveller, This Plot of Earth, The Wisdom of the Fields, Where Man Belongs*.

THE RURAL TRADITION

ONE

Rural Literature and the Rural Tradition

The truth is that to enjoy the country, pure and simple, is not the easiest thing in the world: perhaps an art is necessary to-day to give scope even to our deep ancient instincts.   EDWARD THOMAS[1]

In 1910 E.M. Forster predicted in *Howards End* that 'the literature of the near future will probably ignore the country and seek inspiration from the town.'[2] His prophecy has been dramatically fulfilled – so completely, in fact, that we are in danger of forgetting the extent to which urban values dominate our thinking. It is sometimes difficult to understand that assumptions which to the majority of us seem obvious and undeniable may to the traditional countryman appear, in the most literal sense of the word, unnatural. And even if we recognize a difference of viewpoint, we are only too likely to see the disagreement in prejudiced terms, as reactionary rural stubbornness in ignorant opposition to the march of a sophisticated and inevitable progress. We tend unconsciously to think of the countryman as a quaint survivor of an earlier stage in the world's evolution – as Hodge, the rustic 'clown,' the yokel with a straw in his mouth. Once the point is made in these extreme terms, of course, its absurdity becomes immediately apparent, but it is important that we recognize this temptation to think in stereotypes. Any serious discussion of rural life and literature must begin by isolating and analyzing our conventional attitudes to the subject.

Although the deep and seemingly irreparable split between urban and rural viewpoints is comparatively recent, a distinction between town and country is, of course, as old as literature and recorded history. Without it, for example, a pastoral convention would be unthinkable, and it is vital to this study that 'rural' and 'pastoral' should be distinguished forthwith. Despite superficial similarities the two are opposed rather than related. Although we may at first think of the pastoral tradition as a mouthpiece for the rural view, it is in fact predominantly urban in character. While it generally presents the country in positive terms as a retreat from care, it is a highly sophisticated form originating in the town and invariably for urban consumption; in William Empson's terms it is about countrymen but neither by nor for them.[3] Theocritus, for example, wrote his idylls for the cultivated townsmen of his day; Virgil, though of yeoman origin, was educated in fashionable centres including Milan and Rome, and his eclogues presuppose a sophisticated society. Their verse was smooth, allusive, and urbane. It is therefore not altogether surprising to find W.H. Auden listing pastoral verse together with basilicas, divas, and dictionaries among 'the courtesies of the city.'[4]

The basic distinction between rural and pastoral literature is clearcut; none the less, by virtue of a common setting the two share certain characteristics, and even overlap to some extent. In Walton's *Compleat Angler*, for instance, the earliest important example in English of non-fiction rural writing, we find the same tendency to view country and town in terms of simple and complicated that is a prime feature of pastoral. Again, since its productions are 'artificial,' even if its subject matter is 'natural,' a tradition of rural writing is almost certain to be dependent, economically, upon an urban readership. To adapt Empson's requirements for pastoral to the rural, it will be 'about' but not necessarily 'by' and not primarily 'for' countrymen. Granted these similarities, however, the two traditions ultimately veer off in different directions. Despite Spenser's attempt in *The Shepheardes Calender* to naturalize classical pastoral by adapting it to the conditions of the English countryside, the form proved surprisingly intractable, save for the more limited purposes of satire or burlesque. Pastoral has tended more and more to represent either an allegorical setting or an ideal. As Alexander Pope noted in his 'Discourse on Pastoral Poetry,' it offers 'an image of what we call the golden age'[5] and is thus deliberately opposed to realistic accuracy. Indeed Pope has stressed the need for 'some illusion to render a Pastoral delightful; and this consists in exposing the best side only of a shepherd's life, and in concealing its miseries.'[6] By contrast, although an idealizing tendency is often pronounced, rural writing depends for its effectiveness on a verifiable connection with an existing countryside.

Another point of departure is the relation between style and subject matter. In pastoral, as Empson has insisted, a clash between the theme and the language in which it is expressed is an important ingredient in the total effect. In particular, praise of simplicity is wittily communicated in an ornate and complicated style, and appreciation of natural beauty conveyed in the language of urban elegance.[7] In rural writing, on the other hand, style has always been much more intimately related to content, and the tension between natural and artificial, which offers opportunity for sophisticated pastoral effects, is here reduced to a minimum.

At this stage in the argument, however, we should remember that Virgil wrote georgics as well as eclogues, and, although the tradition of the georgic is now so neglected that many dictionaries of literary terms fail to define or describe it, there is reason to suppose that it may have had a considerable influence, not so much in the sphere of verse as in that of prose. Historically, of course, pastorals took shepherding and grazing for their subject matter, georgics the manifold duties of agricultural husbandry. The following description by Addison is informative:

> [The Georgic] fall[s] under that class of Poetry, which consists in giving plain and direct instructions to the reader ... [It] addresses it self wholly to the imagination: It is altogether conversant among the fields and woods, and has the most delightful part of Nature for its province. It raises in our minds a pleasing variety of scenes and landscapes, whilst it teaches us, and makes the dryest of its precepts look like a description. A Georgic, *therefore, is some part of the science of husbandry put into a pleasing dress, and set off with all the Beauties and Embellishments of Poetry.*[8]

Thus the georgic comprises a realistic and generally didactic account of husbandry (appealing, however, to 'the imagination'), and we may add to Addison's definition by noting that 'digressions arising from the theme'[9] are a characteristic feature. If we substitute prose for poetry in Addison's account, we are presented with a remarkably faithful description of rural prose writing. The emphasis on rustic crafts and the traditional customs of the past represent another possible continuity, and Virgil's insistence on stressing the arts of peace in time of war might also be seen as analogous to the nineteenth-century interest in the countryside at a time of increasing industrialization.

I do not wish to argue for any rigid or necessary connection between the georgic tradition and the writers I shall be considering in this book, but it may be helpful to suggest that non-fiction rural writing in prose fulfils a similar need in recent literary experience to that of the georgic in earlier times. At all events the tradition of the georgic is manifestly closer to the spirit of the rural tradition than is that of the pastoral. The rural writing that is the main concern of this study certainly did not arise suddenly out of a void, and this discussion is merely intended to indicate, however briefly and inadequately, the literary complex of attitudes and assumptions concerning town and country out of which works like *The Compleat Angler, The Natural History of Selborne,* and *Rural Rides* eventually emerged. Whatever its ultimate historical origins, the important point which I want to establish in the following chapters is that non-fiction rural prose should be recognized as a distinct tradition that deserves serious attention from literary critics.

Throughout the period to be covered, from Izaak Walton to the present, the relation between town and country has been uncertain and uneasy. Often, as almost any restoration comedy demonstrates, the town is regarded as the ultimate in wit and civilized amusement while the country is the home of vulgar, ignorant, and drunken boors. But the advantage is even more frequently on the side of the rural. Indeed 'the Countries sweet simplicity,' as Herrick calls it, is continually being contrasted disparagingly with Tennyson's 'dust and din and steam of town,'[10] and around this basic opposition develops a number of convenient literary myths. Prominent among these, of course, is the myth of rural innocence; one remembers in *Tess of the D'Urbervilles* the sophisticated Angel Clare's thinking that he could secure 'rustic innocence as surely as ... pink cheeks.'[11] Even more commonly the town is presented as the place of activity, worry, and fatigue, the country as the home of peace, health, and rest. We may well be tempted to accept this as a truism, but it requires only a moment's reflection to realize that the myth itself must have been a product of the town – or, at least, of a leisured society affected by urban presuppositions. Certainly no one with an experience of agricultural labour could have had a hand in its making. Stephen Duck's account of threshing and Richard Jefferies' observation that 'gleaning – poetical gleaning – is the most unpleasant and uncomfortable of labour, tedious, slow, back-aching work'[12] are but two examples that demonstrate the inadequacy of this view as a general statement. This in itself should be sufficient to make us re-examine our assumptions about the relations of town and country.

Although the attempt to graft the pastoral mode onto the English literary tradition was not generally successful, the myth of rural peace and content, well established in *The Compleat Angler*, became an accepted convention in Augustan verse, and these are the terms in which rural life appears most conspicuously in eighteenth-century literature. Joseph Warton in *The Enthusiast: or, The Lover of Nature* (1744) offers a succinct example:

> Happy the first of men, ere yet confined
> To smoky cities; who in sheltering groves,
> Warm caves, and deep-sunk valleys lived and loved
> By cares unwounded.   (ll. 78–81)

By contrast urban values are seen as both decadent and potentially destructive:

> O taste corrupt! that luxury and pomp
> In specious names of polished manners veiled,
> Should proudly banish Nature's simple charms.   (ll. 111–13)

If we confine ourselves to this theme (a tactic defensible for present purposes, though obviously inadequate within the larger context of literary history), the step seems but short to the age of Rousseau and Romanticism.

It would be a mistake, however, to see the romantic cult of Nature as a mere continuation and intensification of an age-old conventional attitude. Had it been no more than this, it would have had little impact on the history of taste. What gives it its strength and impetus is that, for the first time, the attitude becomes more than a mere convention. With the beginning of the Industrial Revolution 'Nature's simple charms' were visibly threatened, and the quest for peace and solitude took on a new urgency. Our own period has seen such a proliferation of city expansion and suburban sprawl that the fears of the late eighteenth century may seem, to say the least, premature. Wordsworth seemed extreme to his contemporaries when in 1802 he listed 'the increasing accumulation of men in cities' as one of a number of causes 'acting with a combined force to blunt the discriminating powers of the mind.'[13] But the importance of this rural declaration of independence can hardly be overemphasized. For Wordsworth himself, though urban and rural are clearly separated, there is still no necessary distinction between townsman and countryman. He chooses 'humble and rustic life' for the subject matter of his poems because he believes it to be closer to the fountain-head, which is nature; the townsman, although further away from this healthful source, is still subject to its influence. But we are on the threshold of a new myth; once we have admitted, as Wordsworth seems to do, the possible debilitating effect of urban living, it will not be long before we regard the countryman as inheritor of the good life and the townsman as banished from the rural Eden, hopelessly cut off from the springs of natural grace. Soon townsman and countryman will be seen as essentially different – in outlook, in upbringing, in values.

It would seem, therefore, that the distinction between urban and rural, though present from the earliest times, does not become crucial until the Industrial Revolution. Even Raymond Williams, who is healthily sceptical of any specific date for pinpointing rural decline, admits that the rise of a commercial society, with all its consequences to the rural way of life, was 'immensely quickened in the late eighteenth century.'[14] For men like Thomson and Pope it had been easy to retire into rural solitude and yet remain close to the amenities of London. For Cobbett and Miss Mitford this is still possible but much more difficult; and improved communications, instead of facilitating such movement, tend to urbanize all the more quickly the countryside which they 'open up.' Since their time, of course, the breach has widened with alarming rapidity. At the beginning of the nineteenth century a considerable majority of Englishmen still lived on the land and depended for their livelihood upon agriculture; before its close an even larger majority lived in cities and were employed in industry. It is scarcely surprising that townsmen and countrymen no longer thought in the same way. By the time that E.M. Forster made his literary prophecy, town values had already triumphed. Galsworthy documents the change with bitter though humorous irony in the opening chapter of *The Man of Property*, when James Forsyte goes to see the place 'down in Devonshire' where the family, only a few generations before, had originated. His report is briefly expressed yet packed with significant meaning: '''There's very little to be had out of that,'' he said; "regular country little place, old as the hills.'' '[15] At the turn of the century the point had been made with greater force by Rider Haggard:

> In this twentieth century England we seem to have grown away from the land; we have flocked into cities, and are occupied with the things of cities; we have set our hearts on trade, and look to its profits for our luxury. But the land is still the true mother of our race, which, were it not for that same land, would soon dwindle into littleness. ... Though to-day they be so poor, yet the might of England is in her villages, those villages so many of whose homes are crumbling, and whose arable fields go back daily to the wasteful and unproductive grass out of which our forefathers reclaimed them.[16]

To the countryman, faced every day by these same crumbling cottages and untilled fields, they represent not merely a historical change but a blatant betrayal. Evidence of this frustration sometimes occurs in the most unlikely places, like the Hampshire tombstone upon which is carved the couplet

> England made her choice years ago –
> Wealth, great cities, industry – all countrymen know.[17]

Within the context of literature we find the point fully articulated by William Cobbett, whose whole crusade was dedicated to the threatened rural interest. Even the generally sunny Miss Mitford, a contemporary of Cobbett, protests in a letter that 'our wise legislators never think of the rural districts – *never*'.[18] Political statements of this kind now become so frequent that I can only pick a few, almost random, instances as indicative of the general and apparently inexorable trend. Arthur Young claimed of one proposed bill that it lost because 'it was a measure well calculated to favour the agriculture of the kingdom ... and such measures never can pass our manufacturing, trading and shopkeeping legislature.'[19] After the urban enfranchisement of 1867 the split became even more pronounced. The situation was described in much stronger terms when Sir George Otto Trevelyan moved the second reading of the Household Franchise Counties Bill in 1875: 'We draw a distinction almost unknown in any constitutional country or in our own colonies ... between the inhabitants of towns and those of rural England. We brand our village population as if they were political pagans.'[20]

For the most part, however, the voice of rural dissent, whether against enclosure in the eighteenth century or industrialism in the nineteenth, was ignored in its own time, and only rarely recorded for the judgment of posterity. The village Hampdens and Miltons have generally been mute, inglorious, and defeated; there have been pitifully few Cobbetts. Consequently when a countryman raises his voice and insists strongly on the rural viewpoint, our reaction is likely to be one of shocked surprise. One such outburst was made in 1912 by Alfred Williams, the Wiltshire 'hammerman poet' who had earned his living both as agricultural labourer and in the railway factories of Swindon. Straddled between two hostile cultures, well aware that the battle was hopelessly lost, he was none the less determined to state the facts as he saw them:

> Parliaments are elected by the towns; armies and navies are raised and built to protect the towns; wages, rights, privileges, arts and crafts, and everything else, are for the same. The dweller in the country – the humble agriculturist, the most honourable and most necessary of all workers, the alpha and omega, the beginning, end, and middle, the very backbone and support of every industry and all society, is forgotten, spurned, despised, and ridiculed.[21]

The passage seems strained, yet, although we may legitimately recall the opposite situation just before the First Reform Act when the rural aristocracy held inequitable power, it is difficult to deny its justice. Even more significant, however, is the impression it conveys of the countryman's impassioned bitterness.

But we should not be justified in seeing the process as a calculated rejection of the country on the part of the town. The nineteenth-century townsman still retained a vision of Nature, however sentimental or inadequate it may have been. As W.E. Houghton has pointed out, this image 'had its basis in memory, for every Victorian in the city had either grown up in the country or in a town small enough for ready contact with the rural environment.'[22] Although thoroughly urbanized, he still yearned for the open air. This countermovement was noted at the time by no less a countryman than Richard Jefferies. He admits that urban influence has been victorious over the traditional rural ways; but at the same time he detects a reverse factor:

> The town has gone out into the country, but the country has also penetrated the mind of the town. No sooner has a man made a little money in the city, than away he rushes to the fields and rivers, and nothing would so deeply hurt the pride of the nouveaux riches as to insinuate that he [sic] was not quite fully imbued with the spirit and the knowledge of the country.[23]

Ironically enough, as the agricultural labourer was setting out from a depressed countryside in search of a new and more prosperous life in the industrial town, he was likely to be passed by the middle-class urban dweller making a temporary but no less significant journey back into the country seeking the pastoral goals of rest and health.

We are consequently faced with the paradox, to be elaborated a little later, that the nineteenth century, which saw the decline of the English countryside, is also the great age of nature writing. The Victorian reading public found its rural writers congenial. Not only is this the century in which the majority of the works to be discussed in this book were written, but even the popularity of the earlier writings of Walton and White dates from this period. The explanation lies, of course, in the counter-movement which Jefferies describes. Nostalgia for the countryside was still strong, and, just as the diehard sportsman considered that the next best thing to otter-hunting was reading about otter-hunting, so the Victorians found reading about the countryside an acceptable (often, indeed, a preferable) substitute for a visit to the country itself. But this taste was comparatively short-lived. The new generation that had been born in the city did not necessarily share this rural interest. The Leonard Bast of *Howards End*, whom Forster characterizes 'as the third generation, grandson to the shepherd or ploughboy whom civilization had sucked into the town; as one of the thousands who have lost the life of the body and failed to reach the life of the spirit,'[24] was probably untypical in his rural enthusiasm. Most of his generation, like the suburban villa people who so irritated George Sturt, were unconscious of any lack. With them the urban trend found its final and logical culmination in the loss of any significant awareness that an outlook or way of life different from their own had ever existed. Informed dissidents were uncommon; a Massingham in the early twentieth century was as rare as a Cobbett in the nineteenth. Moreover the minority who dimly recognized the heritage of which they had been dispossessed – the hikers and ramblers – were often ignorant of what they might find or even of what they were seeking. They returned to the countryside as aliens, bringing with them all the urban characteristics from which they were vainly trying to escape. They were in danger of killing the thing they loved: what C.E.M. Joad has called 'the Untutored Townsman's Invasion of the Countryside'[25] had begun.

Not until the split between town and country has been recognized and accepted does the emergence of a specifically rural literature become possible. This need not be, and indeed has rarely been, a conscious tradition, but historical circumstances inevitably tend to force rural writers into their own company. For instance, a writer like Edward Thomas in the opening years of the twentieth century is likely to have more in common with, say, Cobbett in the 1820s or Jefferies in the 1880s than with the majority of his contemporaries. Such writers are linked by common interests, common values, and even a common enemy. They tend to see themselves as 'second-class citizens' in a continual state of siege against further encroachment of their heritage. At best, they are tolerated as eccentrics, read and appreciated for the wrong reasons, but invariably neglected or misunderstood when, in their own view, they have something really important to say.

The townsman, however, can hardly be condemned as wrong-headed if he persists in noting the paradoxes inherent in any conception of a rural literary tradition. He will note first that townsmen must be credited with creating an interest in the material that the rural writer claims as his own. As we have seen, it is no coincidence that the romantic cult of wild nature flourished just at the time when the Industrial Revolution was gaining momentum; the countryside is cherished only when it is seriously threatened – and it is cherished most by those who threaten it. This is a paradox that can be argued from both sides. The rural Wordsworth knew that popularity can be self-destructive, and he therefore supported what any townsman would consider a reactionary position on the proposed Kendal and Windermere Railway. He insisted that 'opening up' the Lake District would destroy the very beauty that the visitors were seeking, and likened the idea to 'the child's cutting up his drum to learn where the sound comes from.'[26] A century later the urban and urbane Aldous Huxley offers the same argument for the sake of its witty absurdity: 'It's a pity the English love the country so much,' he makes one of his characters exclaim, 'they're killing it with kindness.'[27] In spreading his message the rural writer finds himself in the odd position of both protesting against and contributing to this paradoxical situation.

This is but one example of the rural writer's habitual embarrassment at his dependence upon an urban readership. Cobbett may have thundered against 'the Wen' but his books and newspapers generally bear a London imprint. Jefferies and Hudson both yearned for the country life, but they were forced to live in or near London for the sake of their writing. Moreover the taste for rural literature depends upon its urban counterpart; it is welcomed as a refreshing change, as an escape into the unfamiliar, but its very remoteness from the circumstances of urban experience forces it into a place of secondary importance. For it can never rely upon a sufficient number of country readers – and this leads to yet another paradox: the rural writer may crusade in favour of the natural life, but if he were successful he would destroy his own livelihood. When Henry Williamson went 'back to the land' and began farming in Norfolk, he found, not unexpectedly, that he had no time for reading 'literature.' As

George Sturt came to realize, in the traditional countryman the literary and artistic impulses are channelled into other areas. As a result the countryman shows little interest in having his surroundings recreated in print. Rural literature – at least in the townsman's sense of the term – serves almost by definition as a pleasant substitute for 'the thing itself.'

Yet despite all these anomalies it is by no means absurd to talk in terms of a rural tradition, particularly if, as here, we confine ourselves to writers whose work for the most part comes under the category of non-fiction prose. It will admittedly be a loosely knit confraternity. There is probably no single quality or characteristic – besides love of the countryside – that must inevitably distinguish a rural writer. More often than not he will be a countryman by birth, but he can be born in London like Edward Thomas and H.J. Massingham, or even abroad like W.H. Hudson. He may confine himself to a limited geographical area, like Gilbert White or Mary Mitford or George Sturt, or he may be a wanderer over the length and breadth of the land, like William Cobbett or George Borrow. He may limit himself to a single study like Izaak Walton, or take as his province the whole field of natural history – human, animal, vegetable, mineral – like Richard Jefferies or Henry Williamson. Politically he may belong to any party, but his attitudes will usually be, in the non-party sense, conservative; this, however, in no way precludes a challenging radicalism. He is generally religious in the broad sense of the term, but the orthodox like Walton and White are balanced by those who prefer to worship the 'god of Nature' in the open air. Again a rural writer's approach to nature can be infinitely varied. At one extreme we find White's *systema naturae* in which everything is neatly categorized, at the other the deliberately rambling essays of Hudson which hold the mirror up to an unsystematized nature. He may, like Cobbett, produce his best work in immediate response to the present, or, like the later Jefferies, through the recreation of past memories.

At this point, however, we encounter a major problem. What Llewelyn Powys has called 'the magical mirror or retrospective memory'[28] is a common feature of rural writing. We find it in most of the writers under discussion, especially in Borrow, Sturt, and Williamson. But how reliable are such memories? The question is notorious with reference to Borrow, yet it may be considered crucial wherever it occurs. Even when, as in Cobbett, the focus is on the present, there is generally a standard assumed in the past against which the contemporary situation is judged. And if the assumptions concerning the past prove inaccurate, the judgments concerning the present may well be rendered suspect. The whole question of truth and accuracy is one that we shall have to consider in more detail. Lament and nostalgia are popular literary modes; adults are always prone to look back to the days of their childhood through rose-tinted spectacles. Add to this the fact that the natural conservatism of the countryman makes him suspicious and critical of any innovations, that imagination, as George Eliot writes, 'does a little Toryism by the sly, revelling in regret,'[29] and we cannot help raising the question: to what extent does the literature of the countryside reflect a genuine historical situation? For the modern reader all these descriptions belong to the past. How can we gauge the reliability of any individual witness to a past countryside? Do such descriptions communicate an undeniable truth or are they merely imaginative constructs of a hypothetical earthly paradise?

The historical accuracy of the rural tradition has been challenged most recently by Raymond Williams. 'Country life,' he insists, 'has ... been seen, repeatedly, as the life of the past, of the writer's childhood, or of man's childhood, in Eden and the Golden Age.'[30] He goes on to postulate 'a kind of historical escalator' upon which, the further we go back into history, the further the vision of a peaceful, unchanging rural community recedes into the past. He moves from George Sturt back through Hardy and George Eliot to Cobbett, Clare, and Bewick, to Goldsmith's *Deserted Village*, and eventually through the seventeenth and sixteenth centuries to the middle ages, and so on. The result is to throw doubt on the literal truth of much rural writing: 'Clearly we need the sharpest scepticism against the sentimental and intellectualised accounts of an unlocalised "Old England."'[31] There is considerable force in this argument. Indeed it would not be difficult to extend Williams's list. To confine ourselves to the writers discussed in this book, we may note Henry Williamson's backward look to 'the beautiful years,' the 'dandelion days' before the First World War, Borrow's 'happy days for Englishmen in general' during 'the latter part of the seventeenth and the whole of the eighteenth century,'[32] even Izaak Walton's regret for the old pre-Cromwellian age. To look back longingly to the days that are no more is a constant and doubtless natural human instinct, though one should remember that this is a trait by no means confined to the rural tradition. It would certainly be wrong to overlook the temptation to idealize; on the other hand, it would be equally wrong to allow it an exaggerated emphasis.

The first point that needs to be made is that the most distinguished rural writers have for the most part been fully aware of this danger. For instance, because of his surroundings and temperament we might expect William Cowper to be unusually susceptible to an idealizing myth, and indeed we find him exclaiming in the fourth book of *The Task*:

> Would I had fall'n upon those happier days
> That poets celebrate, those golden times
> And those Arcadian scenes that Maro sings
> And Sidney, warbler of poetic prose.   (IV, 513–16)

But Cowper does not allow this feeling to pass unchallenged. He recognizes it as a daydream, and soon comments: 'Vain wish! those days were never' (IV, 525). Though many writers are prepared to indulge in this kind of lament, most of them know, with Tennyson, that 'the past will always win / A glory from its being far.'[33] It is certainly no unconscious trait for the writers I am considering here, including those mentioned in Williams's argument. Sturt, for example, is continually reminding himself and his readers of the danger of the backward view; 'The Golden Age,' he writes in his journal, 'is less an outward environment, than a state of inward being.'[34] In works like *Change in the Village* he risks the charge of being repetitious in his concern to avoid the charge of being reactionary. He is suspicious of 'that almost festive temper, that glad relish of life, which, if we may believe the poets, used to characterize the English village of old times.'[35] And the last paragraph of the book, summing up his conclusions, looks to the future rather than to the past: 'The old system had gone on long enough ... I do not think the end of that wasteful system can be lamented by anyone who believes in the English.'[36] Indeed Sturt even goes so far as to admit in his journals that he deliberately suppressed some of his beliefs concerning the satisfactions of the peasant life 'for fear of providing "gentlemen" with an excuse for preserving the present economic system.'[37]

Sturt is probably the rural writer most conscious of the dangers of nostalgia, but examples can readily be found in the work of the others. Edward Thomas shows himself aware of the problem when he writes: 'As mankind has looked back to a golden age, so the individual, repeating the history of the race, looks back and finds one in his own past.'[38] And Richard Jefferies, in *Round About a Great Estate*, gathering together records of 'the former state of things before it passes away entirely,' immediately qualifies his statement: 'But I would not have it therefore thought that I wish it to continue or return. My sympathies and hopes are with the light of the future, though I should like it to come from nature.'[39] To see all rural writers as favouring an imaginary past, to cast doubt on any positives that have been recorded in their observations, is clearly to oversimplify.

None the less Raymond Williams is certainly right in pointing out that the decline of the countryside is one of those trends, like the rise of the middle classes, that seem to be demonstrable from the evidence of virtually any period one cares to select. But we may grant all this without denying the accuracy – let alone the sincerity – of the individual writers. Rural values, like all others, are continually in a state of flux; every generation encounters new changes and challenges. It can hardly be denied, however, that the foundations of rural society have been gradually whittled away over recent centuries, just as the number of acres under cultivation has declined, sometimes slowly, sometimes rapidly, over recent generations. Once we relate this situation to the natural conservatism of the rural mind, the constant stress on deterioration becomes readily explicable. At the same time the countryside has remarkable powers of assimilation. The startling invention, bitterly opposed as fatal to the rural order, is soon accepted as traditional practice. Thus the threshing-machine, at first a flagrant example of technological intrusion, quickly established itself as a characteristic feature of the rural scene. As Jefferies noted in the early 1880s, it 'has already grown old. It is so accepted that the fields would seem to lack something if it were absent. It is as natural as the rocks; things grow old so soon in the fields.'[40]

We should do well to remember that each individual accepts the existing practice in his own childhood as standard. Changes – particularly those for the worse – are recorded with regret. But for the next generation they will no longer be new; indeed they will have become part of the standard. We may therefore recognize the transitional nature of that apparently fixed and eternal way of life experienced in childhood without casting doubt on the reports of particular changes. We should remember, too, that such reports are likely to be especially frequent in the Victorian period, not only because of the increased rate of change which is one of its most important characteristics, but also because the nineteenth century was so much more historically minded than preceding ages. All these factors combine to create the sad, elegiac tone of much rural writing, a tone that caused Forster to sum up the whole movement in a succinct, witty, but unkind phrase as 'Borrow, Thoreau and sorrow'.[41]

But there is another, perhaps more cogent, reason for qualifying Williams's argument – the premium put on truth and accuracy by most rural writers. By the normal standards of literary criticism (itself predominantly 'urban' in origin), these are qualities which are considered not so much unnecessary as irrelevant to creative writing. The poet, as Sidney said, never affirmeth; it is usually sufficient if a writer's portayal is imaginatively credible, if in the experience of reading we are prepared to give ourselves up to Coleridge's 'willing suspension of disbelief.' But the situation of the rural writer seems somehow different. Even in a novelist like Hardy we may well be concerned about the accuracy of the portrayal – if Flintcombe Ash is 'real,' how about Talbothays or the Mellstock of *Under the Greenwood Tree?* Such a question is crucial or irrelevant depending upon one's critical approach. To take *Tess of the D'Urbervilles* as an example, the historical accuracy of the novel is central for a socially committed critic like Arnold Kettle: 'It is a novel with a thesis – a *roman à thèse* – and the thesis is true.'[42] For the more literary, aesthetic approach of Dorothy Van Ghent, however, it is unimportant: 'Whether Hardy's "folk," in all the attributes he gives them, ever existed historically or not is scarcely pertinent; they exist here.'[43] But in the case of the non-fiction writer the problem cannot be disposed of so lightly. What right has anyone to offer us a

detailed description that cannot be accepted as 'true'? Even with the realization
that this is a standard we are less likely to insist on in a landscape painter, our
doubts are by no means allayed.

The majority of those who take the countryside as their subject matter
clearly share this concern – the poets as much as the prose writers. Goldsmith's
dedicatory preface to *The Deserted Village*, addressed to Sir Joshua Reynolds,
insists upon the accuracy of what he has portrayed: 'I sincerely believe what I
have written; ... I have taken all possible pains, in my country excursions, for
these four or five years past, to be certain of what I allege; ... all my views and
inquiries have led me to believe those miseries real, which I here attempt to
display.'[44] And Crabbe, while attacking the falsity of the conventional pastoral,
asserts that 'What form the real Picture of the Poor / Demand a song' and
promises to 'paint the Cot / As Truth will paint it, and as Bards will not.'[45] The
bards in question are presumably adherents of the pastoral convention. Here
once again it is important to distinguish the pastoralists, whose works make no
pretensions to literal truth, from the genuinely rural writers. When we turn to
the novelists, we find similar statements. Hardy insists in his 'General Preface'
to the Wessex Edition of his works that 'at the dates represented in the various
narrations things were like that in Wessex.'[46] The remark is echoed by numerous regional novelists. We may also remember that it is in *Adam Bede*, the
closest of all her novels to the rural tradition, that George Eliot most eloquently
stresses her determination 'to tell my simple story, without trying to make
things seem better than they are; dreading nothing, indeed, but falsity ...
Falsehood is so easy, truth so difficult.'[47]

The last sentence might well have been taken as an epigraph by scores of
non-fiction rural writers. For many of these, of course, truth is the sole *raison
d'être* of their work. They are crusaders for a fair deal for the agricultural
community, and they see their writings not as literature so much as social
politics. J.W. Robertson Scott, founder and editor of the *Countryman*, may be
taken as representative of this group. He subtitles his *England's Green and
Pleasant Land* 'The Truth Attempted,' and throughout his work he is concerned
to establish this truth against the romantic temptation to select or idyllicize. Even
more than most countrymen he is suspicious of literary frills, but he is forced to
make an important – and ultimately artistic – distinction: 'I have tried hard to
write – oh, how difficult it is! – not the literal but the *essential* truth.'[48] This is
surely the crux of the matter, and it is a distinction that affects not only the
propagandist like Robertson Scott himself, but also the more ambitious writers
we shall be discussing in subsequent chapters. For these truth has an aesthetic
appeal in addition to its moral force. Jefferies is a seeker after *'essential* truth'
not only in his phase as rural reporter but in the more lyrical final essays. So is
Hudson, whose role as field naturalist is dedicated to truth, and Thomas, whose

concern for 'the life of the farm as it is lived, not as it is seen over a five-barred gate,'[49] is an important variation on the basic theme. We may even be able to say the same of Borrow, the rural writer who most obviously exploits for artistic purposes the shadowy ground between the true and the imagined.

The conflict that most often presents itself, however, is not between the true and the false but between the realistic and the sentimental. Here we are brought back yet again to the paradox of the rural writer's urban audience, for it is probably true to state that, whenever rural writing lapses into sentimental idyllicism, the writer has been too anxious to satisfy the supposed desire of his townsmen readers. John Britton, the self-educated topographer who began life as an agricultural labourer and was therefore in a position to speak with some authority, is adamant on this point: 'Many poets and essayists have eulogized rustic life and manners, as being replete with sylvan joys, arcadian scenes, primeval innocence, and unsophisticated pleasures. Alas! they are but the closet-dreams of metropolitan poets and visionary enthusiasts, for I fear that all these pleasing pictures are wholly drawn from imagination, and not from nature.'[50] This tendency to overlook the harshness of country life is admittedly widespread, but it is continually being exposed by the rural writers themselves. W.H. Hudson relates two anecdotes especially relevant to this subject; they may stand as representative of evidence that could be culled from most rural writers in most periods. In the first Hudson encounters a tramp in Hampshire, who remarks:

'Very fine, very beautiful all this' – waving his hand to indicate the hedge, its rich tangle of purple-red stems and coloured leaves, and scarlet fruit and silvery old-man's-beard. 'An artist enjoys seeing this sort of thing, and it's nice for all those who go about for the pleasure of seeing things. But when it comes to a man tramping twenty or thirty miles a day on an empty belly, looking for work which he can't find, he doesn't see it in quite the same way.'[51]

The second concerns a Cornish farmer:

One day last summer a lady visitor staying in the neighbourhood came to where he was doing some work and burst out in praise of the place, and told him she envied him his home in the dearest, sweetest, loveliest spot on earth. 'That's what you think, ma'am,' he returned, 'because you're here for a week or two in summer when it's fine and the heath in bloom. Now I think it's the poorest, ugliest, horriblest place in the whole world, because I've got to live on it and get my living out of it.'[52]

These anecdotes are healthy reminders that so much depends upon our 'way of looking,' that the townsman is likely to bring his own urban and not necessarily appropriate values to bear on the conditions he observes in the country. His prejudices will naturally tend towards the extremes. He may be charmed by the quaint and determined, like the lady in Hudson's story, to find in the real countryside the idyllic paradise of his dreams. It is against this attitude that Robertson Scott is wittily reacting when he quotes the verse by Mrs Hemans,

> The cottage-homes of England!
> By thousands on her plains,
> They are smiling o'er the silvery brooks
> And round the hamlet fanes,

only to add the deflating footnote to the third line: 'And are therefore damp.'[53] On the other hand, he may choose to see nothing but the dampness. This extreme is perhaps the more disturbing since it is so much more difficult to expose. It depends, however, on a standard of life and luxury that is the prerogative of the town. An example of the false judgments which may result is offered by Hardy in his essay 'The Dorsetshire Labourer':

> The happiness of a class can rarely be estimated aright by philosophers who look down upon that class from the Olympian heights of society. Nothing, for instance, is more common than for some philanthropic lady to burst in upon a family, be struck by the apparent squalor of the scene, and to straightway mark down that household in her note-book as a frightful example of the misery of the labouring classes. There are two distinct probabilities of error in forming any such estimate. The first is that the apparent squalor is no squalor at all ... The second probability arises from the error of supposing that actual slovenliness is always accompanied by unhappiness.[54]

That this argument could be employed and exaggerated by the forces of reaction is no denial of its validity. It bears witness to an important fact: that the rural way of life may be hard and devoid of refinements, but is not to be condemned out of hand for that reason. We may well have doubts when Mary Mitford writes too glibly of 'an industrious and light-hearted proverty'[55] but the same point is made by Cobbett, who despised urban elegance, and similar arguments may be found in such writers as Jefferies and Williamson. The rural cottage is not necessarily deprived because it lacks items which commercialism has encouraged us to regard as necessities instead of luxuries. At the same time no true countryman has ever claimed that the rural life is easy.

The rural tradition in literature is clearly beset with many pitfalls. It must avoid the idyllic and sentimental, but in acknowledging the harsh and ugly it should not present these as the norm. Inaccuracy, and therefore untruth, will result from a bias towards either extreme. But Robertson Scott, in attacking the distortions of the enthusiasts, is not denying the admirable and positive aspects of the country scene; indeed he is sensitive to what he calls 'the daily miracle of natural beauty.'[56] Jefferies gets to the heart of the problem in the final sentence of 'One of the New Voters,' which represents a succinct but perfect summing-up: 'The wheat is beautiful, but human life is labour.'[57] Most rural writers follow him in making a conscious attempt to hold the two sides in balance.

We have still to discuss one of the most important artistic challenges confronting writers on the countryside: the problem of form. This is a subject with widespread ramifications. The struggle between man and the forces of nature has always been a major theme in literature, but this generally presupposes an inscrutable and even hostile power that has to be overcome. As Edward Thomas points out, until human ingenuity has tamed these natural forces, a love of nature (and, therefore, a rural literature) is hardly possible: 'Sea, mountain, "bad weather," inconvenient solitude, are unlikely to be much admired until the man who is to admire them is free from fear and in every way practically safe from them.'[58] Once these requirements are met, however, and the literary appreciation of nature develops, the struggle is renewed on a different level. The battleground is transferred to the writer's study. He it is who tries to bring order to what Thomson calls 'rural confusion';[59] he it is who attempts the mammoth task of recreating nature and presenting her, contained and subdued, upon his page.

'Who has not felt,' asks Newman, 'the irritation of mind and impatience created by a deep, rich country, visited for the first time, with winding lanes, and high hedges, and green steeps, and tangled woods, and every thing smiling, but in a maze?'[60] It is typical of Newman's yearning for order and design that he should feel irritation at this prospect; others might well react with pleasure and delight. One of the charms of the countryside, it could be argued, is that, although its basic features are determined by such unalterable facts as geological structure or the pattern of the seasons, it always offers the possibility of surprise. Certain objects, like Arnold's signal elm, are fixed and, one hopes, eternal; but others, like his cuckoo, are free to come and go with the bloom of the year. We are never quite sure what may confront us around the next corner, and this is an important ingredient in the satisfaction that we derive from a rural walk. Again, nature, as the eighteenth century discovered, abhors a straight line, and although we may grant the extent to which England's is a manmade countryside, the forms in which we take delight in the world of nature are still not the same as those we are accustomed to admire in art. All these factors add to the formal and structural problems of the rural writer.

This is no place to embark upon an involved discussion of artificial and 'organic' form – country writers are rarely stimulated by the abstractions of aesthetic theory – but the relevance of these matters to the craft of nature writing can hardly be disputed. For instance, Hudson has described the typical English hedgerow as 'that wild disordered tangle of all the most beautiful plants in these islands.'[61] Yet how does a writer, intent upon recreating the experience of nature in words, find the verbal equivalent for that 'wild disordered tangle'? And if, as Newman suggests, a stretch of country is like a maze, how can the writer contain it in his work? If he reveals the hidden plan of the maze, he thereby falsifies it and destroys its interest; if he presents it as it presents itself to him, in a series of distinct but unrelated images, his work will be condemned as arbitrary and formless.

This is, indeed, the criticism that rural writing has continually provoked. An early example is the eighteenth-century reaction to Thomson's *Seasons*. Pope observes that 'it is a great fault, in descriptive writing, to describe everything,' and Dr Johnson complains: 'The great defect of *The Seasons* is want of method; but for this I know not that there was any remedy. Of many appearances subsisting all at once, no rule can be given why one should be mentioned before another; yet the memory wants the help of order, and the curiosity is not excited by suspense and expectation.'[62] The same kind of criticism has persisted into our own time, and much of it could apply to rural writing in general. Here, for example, is the verdict of Thomson's biographer, Douglas Grant: '*The Seasons* is in fact a collection of many poems. It is a poetic repository into which Thomson tumbled at haphazard a host of subjects which were only slightly connected to each other by the style. The reader is consequently bewildered by their rapid and unordered succession, and his memory cannot retain any distinct impression of the whole poem.'[63] Formlessness is undoubtedly the greatest weakness of the rural tradition. In Ruskin's terms rural writers are men of facts rather than men of design.[64] At worst – in some of Jefferies' run-of-the-mill articles produced under the stress of daily journalism, for example – a rural essay can deteriorate into the random jottings from a notebook.

Responses to the charge of formlessness have generally been of two kinds. Some have questioned the need for formal niceties; even the traditionalist Crabbe considers that 'the love of order' should be ranked 'With all that's low, degrading, mean and base.'[65] Others, more positively, have promoted formlessness as if it were a virtue. In fact rural writing has often been praised for the same reason that it has most encountered criticism. Elizabeth Barrett Browning's reaction to *Our Village* is typical: 'If read by snatches, it comes on the mind as the summer air and the sweet hum of rural sounds would float upon the senses through an open window in the country, and leaves you for the whole day a tradition of fragrance and dew.'[66] In other words, rural writing is successful in so far as it reproduces the effect of experiencing the random sights and sounds of the countryside. This is the kind of reaction that most rural writers will welcome. They are suspicious of set forms which suggest, like straight macadamized roads and regular railway timetables, the forces of urban intrusion. At the same time Mrs Browning's opening phrase, 'if read by snatches,' is a significant qualification. It is no coincidence that most of the classics of the rural tradition (one thinks of *Rural Rides*, *Our Village*, and the essay gatherings of Jefferies, Hudson, and Thomas) are collections of smaller items. Rural writing, particularly when offered primarily for urban consumption, seems more acceptable in small doses.

The rural writer, it appears, is searching for a way of expression that will combine, in Northrop Frye's terms, the encyclopaedic and the episodic, that will contain the vastness of nature yet reflect the response of the individual. The principle of the *pot-pourri*, though often imitated, is rarely successful. While one can certainly sympathize with the decision of Thomas Hughes, in *The Scouring of the White Horse*, 'to follow the example of a good housewife in the composition of that excellent food called "stir-about,"'[67] it represents too plainly an admission of defeat; in fact it bears indirect witness to the importance of artistic methods by its drastic effort to dispense with them. There are, of course, numerous formal conventions available, many of them arising directly out of the rural writer's subject matter. Seasonal changes can conveniently be invoked, and diary-style narratives that follow the cycle of the year are understandably popular; regional divisions also provide an obvious but useful means of limitation, while focus on a particular rural individual, like Sturt's Bettesworth or Hudson's Caleb Bawcombe, is another frequently employed device. But perhaps the most important convention of all, as we shall see in the ensuing section, is the sense of unity achieved by the revelation, through attitude and style, of the writer's own distinctive self. All these conventions, it will be noted, have the merit of flexibility. They do not prevent the introduction of legitimate digressions, nor do they give the false impression of exhausting their material. One might even suggest that the best rural writing, while staking out its recognizable plot of ground, always indicates the presence of an expanding countryside beyond its own boundaries.

Before examining the work of the most distinguished rural writers of non-fiction prose, it may be helpful to offer some generalizations concerning the qualities requisite for such writing. We have already seen that one of the most important features is a concern for truth and honest clarity, but, however strongly we may admire these qualities, they are hardly sufficient in themselves. Wordsworth once complained that 'nineteen out of twenty of Crabbe's pictures are mere matters of fact, with which the muses have just about as much to do as they have with a collection of medical reports,'[68] and, although we need not agree with the specific criticism, its general validity may be accepted. Literature has a higher function than that of the mere camera or recorder, and this is as true of rural literature as of any other variety. 'It is not sufficient,' writes Ruskin, 'that the facts or the features of Nature be around us if they are not within us.'[69] But the question remains: how does the rural writer change 'around' to 'within'?

A related point is made, somewhat obliquely, by Edmund Blunden in discussing the relation between nature and English literature. 'I am not wholly certain,' he writes, 'that I would rank Richard Jefferies' *Story of My Heart* beside Miller on *Gardening* for the truth about our intercourse with Nature.'[70] I presume that Blunden is not placing Miller above Jefferies here. He is merely demonstrating that 'truth about our intercourse with Nature' is one thing while creative writing is another, that the truth of the gardener is not necessarily the same as that of the artist. He is, however, taking up a characteristically rural viewpoint in putting so high a premium on the informative aspects of non-fiction. We must never underestimate the widespread suspicion of the 'artistic' and the 'literary' among commentators on the rural scene – and, indeed, among countrymen in general. Blunden's sense of discomfort when faced with a text as transcendental and 'mystical' as *The Story of My Heart* is a case in point. It doubtless arises from fear that artistry will falsify by presenting the unique or the imaginary as if it were commonplace or actual. Sentimentality, such writers believe, is most likely to enter through the door of art. Thus Robertson Scott warns: 'It is a sad snare for writers, who are not of "the two or three men and women of a generation," to think too much of artistry. It is surely a fatal snare for writers about the country.'[71]

The potential dangers of an excessively literary approach to the rural were cogently discussed as early as 1902 by John Burroughs, the American naturalist, in the course of an appreciation of Gilbert White:

> When one reads the writers of our own day upon rural England and the wild life there, he finds that they have not the charm of the Selborne naturalist; mainly, I think, because they go out with deliberate intent to write up nature. They choose their theme; the theme does not choose them. They love the birds and flowers for the literary effects they can produce out of them. It requires no great talent to go out in the fields or woods and describe in graceful sentences what one finds there, – birds, trees, flowers, clouds, streams; but to give the atmosphere of these things, to seize the significant and interesting features and to put the reader into sympathetic communication with them, that is another matter.[72]

The growing problems that confront the rural writer will be amply demonstrated, I hope, in the course of the following chapters. Burroughs' last requirement becomes more and more difficult to achieve as the years go by. With increasing urbanization the general reader becomes less ready – indeed, less able – to enter into 'sympathetic communication' with natural objects, and, as previous examples multiply and something fresh and original is demanded, the law of diminishing returns seems almost bound to set in. As D.H. Lawrence remarked in a poem, 'There is nothing to look at any more / everything has been seen to death.'[73] One obvious solution is to move from an outer to an inner landscape, to concentrate on the subjective response rather than the objective fact. But the result is another example of dissociation of sensibility, in which content and treatment become separated, in which the artistic qualities of form and style work against rather than for the subject matter they are supposed to be presenting.

The importance of Burroughs' comment lies, however, in his distinction between artistry as gilding or veneering and art as a means by which the writer can 'give the atmosphere of these things.' Any rigid separation of the observer from what he observes is obviously simple-minded. The atmosphere that Burroughs demands resides in the beholder. A comment by Mary Mitford on the writing of *Belford Regis* may be helpful here: 'I am firmly of opinion that were twenty writers to sit down at once to compose a book upon the theme, there would not be the slightest danger of their interfering with each other. Every separate work would bear the stamp of the author's mind, of his peculiar train of thought, and habits of observation.'[74] The all-important factor, however, is the way in which 'the stamp of the author's mind' is revealed. The example of Cobbett is worth invoking at this point. If the value of *Rural Rides* lay solely in its information about farming conditions in the 1820s, it would be a dead text today. We read it, not primarily for the subject matter, but for Cobbett himself – or, to be more exact, for Cobbett's individual viewpoint; yet we can be sure that Cobbett did not write it to reveal or express his inner self. One might argue, indeed, that as soon as a rural writer begins to regard his work as 'literature,' as soon as he becomes acutely conscious of his own artistry, he is likely to cross the elusive boundary between 'rural writing' and urban *belles-lettres*.

None the less, whatever the dangers to the writer of a preoccupation with artistry, this should not deter us, as readers and critics, from examining rural prose with special reference to its literary qualities. If we accept Burroughs' argument, as we surely must, we are making a distinction remarkably similar to that which Pater made, in his essay on 'Style,' between 'the prose of fact' and 'the prose of the imaginative sense of fact';[75] and, however insidious Paterian influence may have been on the rural tradition in literature (as Edward Thomas, somewhat tardily, was to discover), it at least encourages us to focus on the literary means by which this imaginative sense of fact is communicated. What has recently been described as 'the increasingly appealing doctrine that style is above all a function of self'[76] is essential here, for it provides a needful bridge between self-revelation and too narrow a preoccupation with verbal niceties. Cobbett's pre-eminence is due, primarily, to the way in which his vigorous personality is conveyed through the 'hammer-blows' of his language, but stylistic power is equally important in less dramatic instances – in the ordered simplicity of Walton, the colloquial familiarity of Mary Mitford, the quiet introspection of Sturt, or the easy, comprehensive naturalness of Hudson. The writers to be considered here are memorable, quite simply, by virtue of their language. They have succeeded in establishing on the printed page a verbal image which fuses themselves with the life around them.

Above all the rural writer must initiate a response (Burroughs' 'sympathetic communication' again) on the part of the reader. When we turn to the literature of the countryside, we go in search, not of 'nature,' but of a way of looking at nature; we seek a guide, not a subject. What distinguishes rural writing that belongs to literature from that belonging to natural history, agricultural history, etc, is, as Richard E. Haymaker has observed, the writer's 'means of revealing Nature as well as describing her.'[77] To emphasize pictorial and descriptive qualities is not enough – indeed any attempt to employ the imagery of the fine arts is misleading. In the final analysis the rural essayist paints neither landscapes nor self-portraits; instead he communicates the subtle relationship between himself and his environment, offering for our inspection his own attitudes and his own vision. We may be asked to look or to agree, but more than anything else we are invited to share. Ultimately, then, the best rural writing may be said to provide us, in a phrase adapted from Robert Langbaum, with a prose of experience.

TWO

Izaak Walton

1593–1683

As no man is born an artist, so no man is born an Angler.[1]

The Compleat Angler, first published in 1653, may be chosen as an appropriate starting-point for a survey of the English rural tradition, not because it represents the *actual* starting-point, but because it is the earliest work to survive as a living part of our rural literature. It has long been acknowledged, of course, that Walton borrowed freely from earlier sources, and the comparatively recent discovery of a hitherto unknown work, *The Arte of Angling* (1577), has made this even more evident.[2] But Walton's traditionalism is not merely a matter of appropriating material from older writers (a practice no more reprehensible, of course, than Shakespeare's borrowing of the majority of his plots); it extends to a whole series of conventions and genres that he has inherited from the past. These have now been skilfully disentangled and discussed by John R. Cooper in his book *The Art of 'The Compleat Angler.'* They include the pastoral, the georgic, and the philosophical dialogue. Cooper has indisputably demonstrated that Walton was not the 'honest old Izaak' of the nineteenth-century commentators but 'a conscious artist, shaping his materials to make them conform to his own desired meaning.'[3] Moreover he has clearly traced the evolution of the book through the five editions that appeared in Walton's lifetime, pointing out that there is a development 'in the direction of the didactic and discursive, and away from the imaginative and dramatic.'[4]

Those who are interested in the traditional elements that go to make up Walton's book can do no better than turn to Cooper's expert study. My own concern here is to examine *The Compleat Angler* not as the climax of an ancient tradition but as the beginning of a new one. Unlike its predecessors, it is widely known; indeed it has been claimed as 'second only to the Bible in popular fame,'[5] and this continued popularity alone would render it significant irrespective of its quality. It has now been reprinted in at least three hundred editions, and no bookshelf of rural literature is complete without it. Above all, it has been read and loved by nearly all later rural writers. To Mary Mitford it was 'that great pastoral,'[6] and those who praise it include John Clare, Thomas Bewick, W.H. Hudson, Edward Thomas, and Henry Williamson. Like White's *Natural History of Selborne*, it has attained the venerable (and deserved) status of an established classic.

Since the bibliography of *The Compleat Angler* is a highly complex subject, it is important that I explain my own practice at the outset. Because most modern editions reprint the text of the enlarged edition of 1676, which has thus become the most familiar version, I have for convenience followed suit. As is well known, however, Walton appended to this edition, in the interests of utility and completeness, a second part written by Charles Cotton and a reprint of Colonel Robert Venables' *Experienc'd Angler* (1662). Venables' contribution is now rarely printed; Cotton's sequel is as often as not omitted. Because I am interested in the book as a work of literature rather than as a comprehensive fishing manual, I have confined myself to Walton's own text.

If we set aside the dedications and commendatory verses, *The Compleat Angler* begins – and therefore, to all intents and purposes, the English rural tradition begins – with three men, Piscator, Venator, and Auceps, meeting on a road leading out of London 'this fine, fresh May morning' (*CA*, 19). The setting is at one and the same time familiar and original. Inevitably we recall the congregation of pilgrims at the Tabard Inn at the opening of *The Canterbury Tales*, but, whereas Chaucer presents us with a journey from the secular city to the sacred cathedral of God, Walton shows us three men leaving London for the enjoyments of the countryside. True, the river Lea may at first sight appear a trivial goal compared with the shrine at Canterbury, yet the overall tone of Walton's book is more sober and, despite the Parson's concluding and comprehensive sermon (interestingly parallelled by Piscator's speech in the final chapter), more pious than that of Chaucer's poem. While the Canterbury pilgrims turn a holy duty into a diverting recreation, Piscator converts a secular hobby into a contemplation and celebration of God's gifts to man on earth. Implicit here, I suggest, is the idea later to be expressed with memorable conciseness by William Cowper that 'God made the country, and man made the town.'[7]

In subsequent writing about the countryside we shall frequently encounter variations on this basic theme. Wordsworth, for instance, opens his autobiographical but tightly constructed personal epic *The Prelude* with a description of a journey out of London as emblematic of freedom from care. He pictures himself

> escaped
> From the great city, where I long had pined
> A discontented sojourner: now free,
> Free as a bird to settle where I will.[8]

In *Rural Rides* we find Cobbett, forced by circumstances to live close to his hated Wen, gladly setting off at every opportunity for a new rural tour. George Borrow, though originally going to London with the romantic dream of seeking his fortune, eventually leaves on his wanderings with eagerness and relief, and the account forms one of the most memorable chapters in *Lavengro* (chap. LIX). Edward Thomas, himself urban-born, opens several of his books, including *The Heart of England* and *In Pursuit of Spring*, with descriptions of 'Leaving Town.'

It is worth noting that Piscator, Walton's mouthpiece, is also a townsman. Moreover, for all the catalogues of rural delights, *The Compleat Angler* ends by coming full circle, thus completing what Cooper calls 'the pastoral plot of withdrawal and return.'[9] As Piscator says, 'we are now almost at *Tottenham*, where I first met you' (*CA*, 215), and the book ends appropriately with thanks for *'the innocent mirth and pleasure, we have met with since we met together'* (*CA*, 222), before master and scholar part for their respective urban duties. They return refreshed but not unhappy; there is no suggestion that they see themselves as re-entering a dreaded prison. It would therefore be a mistake to make too much of the urban-rural division at this time. In the first chapter, when Piscator delivers his apologia for angling, he is defending his sport not against urban diversions but against the rival country pursuits of hunting and falconry. We hear many references in the book to the simple as opposed to the complicated life (a dichotomy taken over directly from the pastoral tradition), but none to pleasant as opposed to unpleasant conditions. At this stage London has clearly not yet taken on the character of Cobbett's Wen, and Piscator seems in no way conscious – let alone self-conscious – of any incongruity between his urban residence and his rural recreation.

The three travellers are leaving London to practise their respective rural sports, but at the same time Walton makes no secret of the fact that 'escape' is a strong motive. It is not, however, escape purely for its own sake. Its effect is therapeutic, and it results, like rest on the Sabbath, in renewed health and vigour. In the dedication Walton praises angling as an art that often enables his patron to 'give rest' to his mind and to divest himself of his 'more serious business' (*CA*, 3). This is a comparatively modest quality, and, although

Walton clearly views the angler's life as ideal, he is aware that in a fallen world it can provide a rest that is only temporary. It is emblematic, even exemplary, in its contrast to the pursuits of others: 'No life, my honest Scholar, no life so happy and so pleasant, as the life of a well governed *Angler*; for when the *Lawyer* is swallowed up with business, and the *Statesman* is preventing or contriving plots, then we sit on *Cowslip-banks*, hear the birds sing, and possess our selves in as much quietness as these silent silver streams, which we now see glide so quietly by us' (*CA*, 113). Passages such as this have probably contributed greatly to the book's appeal for later generations, but it is easy to read into them much more than Walton intended. I suspect that Leslie Stephen falls into this trap when he claims that Walton's fishing-rod 'was the magic wand to interpose a soft idyllic mist between his eyes and such scenes as were visible at times from the windows of Whitehall. He loved his paradise the better because it was an escape from pandemonium.'[10] This observation may well reveal more about Stephen and his age than about Walton. Although Peter Oliver is undoubtedly justified in observing that 'its pleasant pages are still a solace for the cares of too practical lives,'[11] he is noting what is in fact, if not a misinterpretation, at least an exaggerated emphasis.

Leslie Stephen's remark is based, however, not only on the restful tone of the book, but on the historical factors that led to its composition. Walton, we know, was both a Royalist and a staunch supporter of the Church of England, the church into which his son was ordained. Yet *The Compleat Angler* was first published during Cromwell's Commonwealth; it appeared, in fact, within a few weeks of the dismissal of the Long Parliament. B.D. Greenslade has persuasively argued that the book had a particular meaning for the 'sequestered clergy' of Walton's time. Not only did he write a book which 'praised the virtues that flourished in adversity,'[12] but he also conjured up an ideal world of peace and security that at the time of writing might well have been considered as lost for ever. This is acceptable enough, but we should be careful not to link it with any sentimentalized 'backward view.' Stephen tends to do this when he insists that Walton's landscape represented a past Utopia 'before English fields had been drenched with the blood of Roundheads and Cavaliers.'[13] In such an interpretation Piscator would become the first spokesman in the rural tradition to lament the passing of the 'good old days.'

This is a tempting idea, but I do not think it can be accepted without considerable qualification as an accurate portrayal of Walton's attitude. There are, to be sure, a number of passages in the book that suggest a somewhat reactionary nostalgia. When Venator accuses anglers of being 'simple men,' for example, Piscator accepts the charge, but converts it into a compliment by applying the reference to 'such simple men as lived in those times when there were fewer Lawyers [;] when men might have had a Lordship safely conveyed to them in a piece of Parchment no bigger than your hand (though several sheets will not do it safely in this wiser age)' (*CA*, 23). Elsewhere we find praise of 'our honest Forefathers' (*CA*, 85) and a preference for 'old-fashioned Poetry' over 'the strong lines that are now in fashion in this critical age' (*CA*, 80). Similar sentiments occur in Walton's other work; examples include a reference to 'the very happy days of our late and Good Queen Elizabeth' and his lament concerning 'the decay of common honesty, and how the former piety and plain dealing of this now sinful nation is turned into cruelty and cunning.'[14] But these passages are comparatively few in number in *The Compleat Angler*, nor are they confined to his writings during the period of 'Oliver the tyrant.'[15] Besides, we find frequent references to the lives of the primitive Christians, where simplicity of manners is also stressed, but not the circumstances of their lives which, of course, involved danger and adversity. These allusions obviously refer to the beleaguered situation of the sincere Christian in an imperfect world, and are clearly at odds with any conception of an ideal past.

Therefore it seems evident that, although Walton may occasionally offer some indirect (and, in the early editions, necessarily muted) political comment, this constitutes an additional rather than a primary meaning. As for Cooper's observation that 'both *The Compleat Angler* and Virgil's *Georgics* were written in a period of civil war and the break-up of the old order,'[16] this is indisputable, but it is not altogether clear whether Walton echoed Virgil in order to allude to the civil war or whether he reminds us of Virgil because of the context of civil war. Personally I would go no further than the guarded suggestion that, as I indicated in my introductory chapter, comparison with the georgic tradition seems fruitful. We can assert with confidence, however, that *The Compleat Angler*, as its name implies, is above all else a handbook on fishing. We know too that a pious tone had been characteristic of angling books long before Walton's time. His book should certainly not be read as anything approaching 'naive allegory.' If it offers advice that transcends the immediate limits of angling, it recommends not a passive lament for the past but a peaceful and contemplative state of mind that is valuable at all times. The main appeal is not back but within. Although Walton's religious and political attitudes were diametrically opposed to those of his contemporary John Milton, both men agree in seeking a paradise not limited by time but ever present, through God's grace, in the Christian soul.

Stapleton Martin is undoubtedly correct in observing that 'it is impossible to dissociate Walton from his religion.'[17] In concentrating on *The Compleat Angler* we should not forget that Walton's other claim to fame – and one that was primary in his own time – was as biographer of distinguished Anglican divines, including John Donne, George Herbert, and Richard Hooker. Indeed R.B. Greenslade would argue that *The Compleat Angler* was as relevant to the clergy of his time as his *Lives*. 'Angling,' he insists, 'was a sign of grace, of membership in a "brotherhood" of pious and peaceable men,'[18] and the tone of simple piety that pervades the book, however traditional it may have been, is certainly conducive to this view. Douglas Bush has gone so far as to remark that 'it would not have strained seventeenth-century etymology to identify "angler" and "Anglican."'[19] Be that as it may, it would perhaps be more accurate to suggest that Walton enjoyed a unified sensibility in which his religious and secular interests were one and indivisible. Certainly a quotation from St John's Gospel appears on his title page, and the book ends with a formal but obviously sincere tribute to 'the goodness of the God of *Nature*' (*CA*, 229), followed by the text from the First Epistle to the Thessalonians which Walton has made his own: '*Study to be quiet.*'

Walton's religious beliefs are of interest here not only for their own sake but because an intimate connection between religous piety and the rural tradition is discernible throughout the period in which that tradition is at its strongest. Gilbert White, of course, is the most distinguished in a long and honorable line of parson-naturalists. Cobbett may at first appear the epitome of the secular, but he conspicuously labelled himself as 'a Protestant of the Church of England' and could legitimately ask: 'Do I not *make Sermons* myself?'[20] Like Langland and many others, his quarrel was not against the Church but against individual and unworthy churchmen. Mary Mitford, despite private doubts, supported the Church as a pillar of strength and stability, and Borrow's championship of Anglicanism bordered on the fanatic. With Jefferies, Sturt, Hudson, and Thomas, religious orthodoxy declines with the increasing agnosticism of the late nineteenth century, but all acknowledge the strength of religious belief in rural people. This religious consciousness naturally takes many forms. The spectrum is wide and the possible combinations innumerable, but the intimate relation between the recurring rural cycles and the rhythms of the church year which impressed so independent a mind as D.H. Lawrence is an important factor in the rural tradition, and one which it would be folly to ignore.

Walton's piety is closely linked with his political conservatism, and here too he is the advocate of a position that we shall find characteristic of many later country writers. His political and moral positives are by no means simple, however. Although he was a confirmed Royalist, his high standards of morality and his hatred of the vulgar and the licentious – indeed, of excess of any description – are qualities which are popularly, if erroneously, considered the hallmark of Puritanism. Thus we find Piscator objecting to the behaviour of their host on the first evening: 'To speak truly, he is not to me a good companion: for most of his conceits were either Scripture jests, or lascivious jests; for which I count no man witty, for the Devil will help a man that way inclined, to the first; and his own corrupt nature (which he always carries with him) to the latter' (*CA*, 62). The entertainments and relaxations offered in the course of the book are specifically presented as wholesome examples, and he is continually stressing 'harmless mirth' and 'innocent pleasure.' For we should be on our guard against the assumption that Walton disapproves of mirth and pleasure as such. He is no enemy of cakes and ale, but his position is well summed up by Piscator: 'I love such mirth as does not make friends ashamed to look upon one another next morning' (*CA*, 89). What he objects to is excess, blasphemy, and uncleanness of any description. Moreover he is the confirmed enemy of luxury, the pressures of social ambition, and what we have come to know as urban morality – for the very reason that they fail to result in genuine pleasure. '*Let me tell you* [,] *Scholar,*' says Piscator: '*I have a rich Neighbour that is always so busie, that he has no leisure to laugh; the whole business of his life is to get money, and more money, that he may still get more and more money; … but he considers not that 'tis not in the power of riches to make a man happy*' (*CA*, 219). This too is a strain that we shall encounter frequently in the rural tradition – in Cobbett's belief in plain fare and regular habits and his contempt for the excesses of luxury, in Borrow's passionate invective against genteel fashion and decadent weakness.

All these qualities clearly place Walton in a tradition that it is customary to regard as characteristically English. There is a confirmed loyalty, a stolid patriotism evident in these passages that is all the more impressive since it does not need to be specifically asserted. It is so clearly *there*, woven into the very texture of the work. We find none of the bludgeoning patriotism so prominent in parts of Cobbett and Borrow, and no signs of the jingoism (mercifully rare in the rural tradition) of the latter part of the nineteenth century. But this quieter and wholly legitimate form is an important ingredient that is carried down into later writers. It is perhaps significant that Edward Thomas, writing at the end of the tradition, found Walton particularly endearing at the time of the First World War. He was writing specifically of *The Compleat Angler* in the following passage: 'Since the war began I have not met so English a book, a book that filled me so with a sense of England as this, though I have handled scores of deliberately patriotic works. There, in that sort of work, you get, as it were, the shouting without the crowd, which is ghastly. In Walton's book I touched the antiquity and sweetness of England – English fields, English people, English poetry, all together.'[21] When Thomas came to compile his wartime anthology *This England*, a book which he wished to be 'as full of English character and country as an egg is full to meat,' when he was concerned to exclude 'professedly patriotic writing' but to emphasize the 'indirect praise [that] is sweeter and more profound,'[22] it was *The Compleat Angler* that immediately came to his mind.

There is no doubt that Walton, like Piscator, was keenly appreciative of natural beauty; as Margaret Bottrall notes, 'he was a genuine lover of country sights and sounds.'[23] But the reader who comes to *The Compleat Angler* from the detailed natural description of later rural writing is likely to be disappointed. He will find no elaborate word-pictures here; indeed one has to search the book with some care to find passages specifically concerned with the natural environment. And when one is found, it may well sound perfunctory and artificial. The longest descriptive passage occurs when Piscator suggests that they retire out of a shower:

> But turn out of the way a little, good Scholar, towards yonder *honysuckle hedg*; there we'll sit and sing whilst this showr falls so gently upon the teeming earth, and gives yet a sweeter smell to the lovely flowers that adorn these verdant Meadows.
>
> Look! under that broad *Beech-tree*, I sate down, when I was last this way a fishing, and the birds in the adjoyning Grove seemed to have a friendly contention with an Eccho, whose dead voice seemed to live in a hollow tree, near to the brow of that Primrose-hill; there I sate viewing the silver streams glide silently towards their center, the tempestuous Sea; yet, sometimes opposed by rugged roots, and pebble-stones, which broke their waves, and turned them into foam: and sometimes I beguil'd time by viewing the harmless Lambs, some leaping securely in the cool shade, whilst others sported themselves in the chearful Sun; and saw others craving comfort from the swoln Udders of their bleating Dams.   (*CA*, 79)

Passages like this go a long way towards vindicating Cooper's comment that, 'like most English pastoral poets, Walton draws the details of his natural description more from classical tradition than from direct observation.'[24] We must be on our guard, however, against exaggerating the point. We may well be surprised by the lack of particularity, and disturbed by the stiffly conventional adjectives ('the lovely flowers,' 'the verdant Meadows,' 'the silver streams'), but we should remember that in Walton's time neither poet nor prose writer was expected to number the streaks of the tulip. It would be wrong to require from Walton adherence to a convention which he neither recognized nor observed. To quote Cooper once again, 'Walton is more concerned to celebrate certain traditional pastoral values by means of description of nature than to re-create a dramatic moment or sensuous experience.'[25] Walton's intention is not to reproduce the exact features of a particular landscape (like the scenes we can identify 'in the field' in the work of Jefferies or Hardy or D.H. Lawrence); he aims rather at conveying a general impression. He gives us, therefore, the basic elements to be found in any rural scene instead of the special details that distinguish one scene from another. We certainly receive the effect of an English landscape, but it is not localized. The stretch of the river Lea between Ware and Waltham will never become known as 'Walton's Country' since he is at pains to recreate not *a* countryside but *the* countryside.

As a result, although the passages of rural description are few in number, we are none the less offered a clear if generalized picture of the natural world. For the most part, Walton takes it for granted – and this is no small part of his success. It is not that he fails to react to the beauty of the natural scene, but merely that he has no reason to find it unusual. He is never guilty of trying to work up a reaction to it either in himself or in his readers. In the passage just quoted, we may occasionally find him wrestling with the rhythms of English prose – a matter which will be discussed later – but he is never forcing his own responses.

Walton's lack of self-consciousness in face of the natural world has resulted in an acceptance of the harsher aspects of nature which to many modern readers borders on the unfeeling. The otter-hunting is not only pursued with enthusiasm as sport, but with positive enjoyment at the destruction. Piscator, so gentle at other times, argues that 'in my judgment all men that keep *Otter-dogs* ought to have pensions from the King, to encourage them to destroy the very breed of those base *Otters*, they do so much mischief.' As 'a Brother of the *Angle*,' he continues, he is 'therefore an enemy to the Otter' (*CA*, 21), and, after enjoying the sport in the company of Venator, he takes his leave with the words: 'God keep you all, Gentlemen, and send you meet this day with another Bitch-Otter, and kill her merrily, and all her young ones too' (*CA*, 60). Moreover, although he says elsewhere that he loves 'to kill nothing but Fish' (*CA*, 62), his attitude to worms as bait, together with his detailed instructions on how to pierce the living worm on a hook (see *CA*, 94–5), has shocked later, more sensitive souls like John Cowper Powys, who goes so far as to call him a 'cold-blooded wretch.'[26] But, as Leslie Stephen pointed out long ago, Walton 'is simply discharging his functions as a part of nature, like the pike or the frog.'[27] His attitude is tough but realistic. Otters are rivals, and enemies; worms are inferior creatures over whom man has natural rights. Like most later writers in the rural tradition, Walton is close enough to the realities of nature not to have any sentimental scruples. Cobbett's support of 'manly sports' like boxing and single-stick and Jefferies' delight in pheasant-shooting are two instances among many of the countryman's harsh but honest acceptance of the consequences of what D.H. Lawrence called 'blood-intimacy.'

The modern reader is also likely to be surprised when he encounters Walton's presentation of country people. At first sight, what with his ballad-singing milkwoman and a shepherd named Coridon, we appear to be firmly set in the never-never-land of sophisticated pastoral; but, while Walton is obviously using the literary tradition, he is by no means a slave to it. If, remembering *As You Like It*, we observe that his Maudlin is no Audrey, it is worth noting that she is no Phebe either. That there is little differentiation between the rustic speech and that of Piscator and Venator may be partly attributable to Walton's indifference to realistic dialogue, but it is also due to the lack of any patronizing, class-conscious attitude on Walton's part. The rustics are presented as neither 'quaint' on the one hand nor 'inferior' on the other. There is, of course, no question of democratic equality. The social hierarchies are unchallenged; servants are servants – but they are not yet wage slaves. Piscator's conversations with the milkwoman and the inn-hostess are polite and considerate; their replies are courteous but never servile. Walton's presentation tends indirectly to bear out H.J. Massingham's contention that, by suppressing rural festivals (thereby discouraging regional differences) and, above all, by separating economics from ethics, 'it was the Puritan who was the bridge in the transition from a rural to an urban England.'[28] Here we catch a glimpse of the earlier world. Without denying the presence of an idyllic element in *The Compleat Angler*, it is none the less reasonable to conclude that the dignity of Walton's countrymen and countrywomen was at least in part a reflection of the contemporary situation. The English peasant had not yet been degraded.

Much has been written about Walton's prose style, though commentators are in curious disagreement concerning its qualities. Some, including Leslie Stephen and Margaret Bottrall, find it clear and lucid – 'that lucent, dewy, rain-sweet prose,' to quote Walter de la Mare's poetic tribute;[29] others, including James Russell Lowell and H.J. Oliver, consider it complex, and even clumsy. Oliver, who has explored the problem in detail, notes that 'Walton's style is not altered even after the changes in prose style during his lifetime ... He is struggling with the more ornate, balanced prose of a previous age.'[30] The two positions are not, however, as incompatible as might appear at first sight. Once again the problem is one that tends to recur within the rural tradition. We become aware of this when we find Oliver detecting 'a certain lack of polish' in Walton's prose.[31] The point may be granted, but is is difficult to see how stylistic polish would be appropriate either to Walton's subject or to his sentiments.

A crucial statement on this matter may be found in *The Compleat Angler* itself – crucial not only for its viewpoint but for its example. Piscator has been quoting references to fishing in the Old Testament (and it is worth remembering at this point that Walton was considerably influenced by the King James Version which had appeared some forty years earlier). He ends his discussion as follows:

> Concerning which last, namely the prophet *Amos* I shall make but this Observation, That he that shall read the *humble, lowly, plain style* of that *Prophet*, and compare it with the *high, glorious, eloquent style* of the prophet *Isaiah* (though they be both equally true) may easily believe *Amos* to be, not only a shepherd, but a good-natur'd, plain *Fisher-man*.   (*CA*, 50)

We do not need the parenthesis to remind us that the pious Walton is not likely to make any value judgments concerning the inspired mouthpieces of God's wisdom, but his personal preference is clearly on the side of Amos. It would seem as if a 'humble, lowly, plain style' were Walton's ideal for a discourse on angling. Yet the passage itself scarcely qualifies for such a description. Its ungainly construction and bumpy rhythms bear out James Russell Lowell's charge that 'Walton too often leaves his sentences in a clutter.'[32] Although he admires the virtues of smooth-flowing simplicity – he praises a poetic description of a spring by Sir Henry Wotton because 'it glided as soft and sweetly from his pen, as that river does ... by which it was ... made' (CA, 54) – he appears unable to achieve it himself. Indeed manuscript evidence from the *Lives* suggests that he composed with difficulty. At the same time Cooper does well to remind us that Walton's prose 'at its clumsiest and most garrulous' is firmly within the traditional practice of his own time.[33]

What we can say is that Walton certainly shows no pretensions towards 'the high, glorious, eloquent style,' which would in any case have been unsuitable. As Leslie Stephen pointed out, Walton was 'far too much in earnest to be aiming at literary ornament,'[34] and he even appears unconcerned about the distinctions between kinds of prose. H.J. Oliver has shown that there is little stylistic difference between the dialogue of *The Compleat Angler* and the 'written' prose of the *Lives*, while his revisions, whatever the reasons for them, can rarely be claimed as stylistic improvements. What in fact we find in *The Compleat Angler* is a leisurely, 'natural' style with no self-conscious frills – one that reads better than it sounds, thereby vindicating Oliver's insistence that the dialogue form is not intended to be in any way dramatic. Cooper makes a similar point by asserting that Walton creates 'the illusion of speech' without achieving 'the artlessness of transcribed conversation.'[35] Perhaps Lowell describes it best when he observes that Walton 'attained, at least in prose, to something which, if it may not be called style, was a very charming way of writing, all the more so that he has an innocent air of not knowing how it is done.'[36] This 'amateur' quality, like Gilbert White's, is both attractive and useful. It enables him to move freely from colloquial discourse through formal address (as in the set speeches in favour of falconry, hunting, and fishing in the opening chapter) to the direct instruction which, whether we like it or not, is obviously the main motive of the book. Walton's prose, therefore, for all its ostensible clumsiness, is an admirable vehicle for his subject. Indeed its success may be judged by the ease with which it combines the heterogeneous materials out of which the book is moulded.

So we arrive at the final characteristic by which *The Compleat Angler* looks forward to later rural writing – its composite form. For, despite its title, the book is much more than a discourse on fishing. Not only are we offered supposed facts about fish (which include a large number of 'vulgar errors' alongside much legitimate natural history) and instructed how to catch them and how to cook them, but these details are interspersed with songs and poems, passages of description and moralizing, and apparent digressions like the anecdote of the gypsies and the beggars.[37] It is clearly a work compounded of many simples. Such a mixture may well have been traditional; H.J. Oliver has noted that Henry Peacham, in *The Compleat Gentleman* (1634), produces a similar medley of stories, proverbs, history, and mythology.[38] We shall certainly be encountering such medleys again and again in the rural tradition. But instead of accepting it as a *pot-pourri* ('a kind of anthology of his delights,' as Margaret Bottrall calls it[39]) or dismissing it as a hodge-podge, according to taste, it is more useful to follow Northrop Frye (who should know) and classify it as an anatomy:

> *The Compleat Angler* is an anatomy because of its mixture of prose and verse, its rural *cena* setting, its dialogue form, its deipnosophistical interest in food, and its gentle Menippean raillery of a society which considers everything more important than fishing and yet has discovered very few better things to do.[40]

This is not a familiar form, and the present-day reader may be additionally inhibited by what Cooper calls 'the modern distinction between imaginative and didactic writing.'[41] The seventeenth century would not have recognized such a division, and it seems clear that one reason for Walton's choice of the form of the anatomy was his dislike of unalloyed instruction. At one point he makes Piscator say: 'But Scholar, have you nothing to mix with this discourse, which now grows both tedious and tiresom?' (*CA*, 167). Many of his digressions are obviously intended as breaks between passages of concentrated didacticism. But Walton has another, more important reason. For him the art of angling is not merely a set of skills by which fish can be caught. It is a many-sided experience that includes appreciation of natural surroundings, quiet contemplation, and congenial fellowship. Piscator's observation that 'there is more pleasure in Hunting the *Hare* than in eating her' (*CA*, 183) extends in meaning to include all sport and takes in all the associated satisfactions to be derived from the countryside. Consequently Walton makes his book more than a useful fishing manual; it becomes an imitation and re-creation of the comprehensive experience of angling.

To create this effect requires art, but an art (like that of angling itself) which, though possessing its own rules, is above all leisurely and open. It should attempt neither a false sophistication nor a false modesty. *The Compleat Angler*, by moving at ease between the pastoral and the real, the didactic and the recreational, the pious and the mirthful – above all, between polished verses and rough prose rhythms – maintains an artistic balance that even manages to contain and harmonize the diverse qualities which we now identify (and thereby separate) as urban and rural. In Piscator the cultures of town and country are united; to put it briefly, he can compose poety and prepare a tempting bait. The combination is at once natural and deliberate. Cooper is right to note that Walton's book reflects a 'more literary world' than *The Arte of Angling*, whose 'sense of earthy realism' he stresses,[42] but this in no way detracts from its presentation of a 'rural' way of life. The idea of angling as 'the contemplative man's recreation,' to quote Walton's subtitle, goes back at least to the fifteenth century,[43] and we should be on our guard against dissociating the rural from the cultivated. There is in Walton no strain between the world of learning and the practical skill of the angler. At the same time, though *The Compleat Angler* may contain the fruits of artifice, any attempt to impose an overall sophistication would destroy the all-important balance and prove fatal alike to the form of the book and to its atmosphere.

Once again Walton's transparent honesty is his saving grace. He is so disarmingly frank in acknowledging his lack of an artificial design. Thus one abrupt transition is introduced with the comment: 'But whither am I going? I had almost lost my self' (*CA*, 138). And a little later Piscator is made to say: 'These, my honest Scholar, are some observations told to you as they now come suddenly into my memory' (*CA*, 203). Not only do these passages disarm by their blunt directness; they do much to justify the variety of the ingredients by the very act of drawing attention to it. They display, indeed, a sly but disguised artifice that gives the impression of casualness to what is by no means casual.[44] Above all they clearly reveal Walton himself.

And this, indeed, gives us the clue to the most crucial formal device of all – and one which many later practitioners in the rural tradition will, consciously or unconsciously, imitate. In *The Compleat Angler*, as Leslie Stephen remarks, we see 'Walton at full length.'[45] His knowledge of fishing, his delight in 'old-fashioned Poetry,' his firmness of character, his genuine but unostentatious piety, all these come together in the total design. More than the formal frame (beginning and ending in London), more than the dialogue form, more even than the interest of his subject matter, it is Walton himself who combines the diverse materials out of which the book is made. As he tells us clearly enough in his Epistle to the Reader, '*the whole Discourse is, or rather was, a picture of my own disposition*' (*CA*, 6). He acts, indeed, as the touchstone for his book. And once we have realized this, a number of superficial difficulties resolve themselves. Arguments concerning Walton's prime interest, whether angling, love of countryside, or religious teaching, literary questions about his use of dialogue or his theories of prose, all become peripheral as soon as we appreciate the fact that Walton himself provides the central focus. Fishing is not an occasional activity, a mere pastime; it is a way of life to which the whole man contributes. Walton is supreme among fishermen because of his instinctive awareness of this; only in him, we might say, is the angler 'compleat.'

THREE

Gilbert White

1720–93

All nature is so full, that that district produces the greatest variety which is most examined.[1]

James Russell Lowell observed in 1889 that 'there are two books which have a place by themselves and side by side in our literature – Walton's "Complete Angler" and White's "Natural History of Selborne."'[2] Athough separated by well over a century, the two books have many points in common. Lowell himself has listed a number of these:

> [They] have secured immortality without showing any tincture of imagination or of constructive faculty ... They neither stimulate thought nor stir any passionate emotion ... They cannot be called popular, because they attract only a limited number of readers, but that number is kept full by new recruits in every generation ... Theirs is an immortality of affection, perhaps the most desirable, as it is the rarest of all ... They are companionable books, that tempt us out-of-doors and keep us there.[3]

But these are for the most part negative – and arguable – characteristics. More positively, one can point to the straightforwardness and sincerity of the two books, their quiet, genuine, but unassuming love for the countryside, their blending of rural instruction with homely pleasure. Although one is written in dialogue and the other in the form of letters, they partake of a similar atmosphere, partly attributable to the simple, unquestioning faith of their authors. Above all, Walton's statement in *The Compleat Angler* that 'the whole Dis-

course is, or rather was, a picture of my own disposition' (*CA*, 6) could have been made by White with equal appropriateness to *The Natural History of Selborne*.

On the other hand, while their books may be considered similar, there are many differences to be noted between the two writers. Walton was an urban tradesman of apparently humble origins; White was a country clergyman who asserted at the time of the French Revolution: 'I was born and bred a Gentleman, and hope I shall be allowed to die such.'[4] Walton, while an expert on fishing, claims no authority in other areas of natural history; White is clearly an all-round naturalist, but specifically admits that he is 'no angler' (*NHS(P)*, xxii). Their aims were also very different. While it is incumbent on Walton to demonstrate that angling is an art, White is under no necessity to prove the obvious fact that natural history is, or should be, a science. But they are most clearly at opposite extremes in their treatment of locality. Whereas Walton, as we have seen, concentrates on the general features of a countryside, the most important contribution of Gilbert White is his demonstration of the value and interest of a detailed and particular description of a limited area. To the rural tradition he bequeaths the varied possibilities of the microcosm.

Gilbert White was born, lived for most of his life, and died in the small and, in the eighteenth century, isolated Hampshire village of Selborne – 'the Mecca of countryminded Englishmen,' to quote H.J. Massingham.[5] The names of White and Selborne are now so intimately associated that it is virtually impossible to mention one without immediately recalling the other. Like the connection between Jefferies and Coate, and that between Hardy and 'Wessex,' the bond linking White and Selborne was forged by an early attachment that lasted, in White's case, to the end of his days. It should be emphasized, however, that although Selborne was the residential centre of White's life, he was a considerable traveller by the standards of his time, and knew a great deal, at first hand as well as through correspondence, about other parts of England, particularly in the south. As E.M. Nicholson has noted, 'within the limits Lincoln-Derby-Shrewsbury-Gloucester-Plymouth there was not much country that he did not know, except in East Anglia' (*NHS*, 23; see also 32–3). Indeed his lifelong friend John Mulso went so far as to write in a letter: 'We have great faith in your Topography, as if in fact you had been everywhere' (*WLL*, I, 114). One is forced to stress this point, not only because the myth still persists that White lived a hermetically sealed existence within self-erected boundaries around Selborne parish (a myth perpetuated by his own modest reference to 'the narrow sphere of my own observations at home' [*NHS(P)*, xxvii]), but because the facts are essential for an accurate assessment of his contribution to natural knowledge. Had his observations been confined to Selborne, they would have been of only minor interest; it was because he was able to compare the flora and fauna of Selborne with those of other areas that his observations are so valuable.

Because of the fame of White's book, Selborne has become known as the epitome of the sleepy, eighteenth-century village. In his time the local roads were so inadequate as to give the village the elusive quality of Hardy's fictional Little Hintock. Its particular associations suggest seclusion and tranquillity. The 'Plestor' or playing-place which recalls Blake's 'Echoing Green,' the Hanger, the Church, Gilbert White's own home 'The Wakes,' above all, the association with a quiet, celibate parson-naturalist – all these enable Selborne to fit neatly into the idealized picture of a 'haunt of ancient peace.'

Such, perhaps, was the world of Gilbert White the curate – a world with its roots firmly imbedded in the past. But Gilbert White the naturalist inhabited another world – one that looked towards the future. Nothing could be more erroneous than the assumption that White's interests and studies were either old-fashioned or out of touch with contemporary trends. *The Natural History of Selborne*, with its record of correspondence with two of the distinguished scientists of his day, is itself evidence of his ready contact with current intellectual interests. Through his brother Benjamin, a London publisher, White was able to keep abreast of up-to-date contributions to his field of study, and through another brother, John, who was a garrison chaplain in Gibraltar, he was enabled to exchange observations and even specimens. White was, in fact, a pioneer in a highly fashionable study. It is extremely misleading for H.J. Massingham to call him 'a naturalist in the age of villas, pump-rooms, coffee-houses, country mansions and improved Gothic ruins.'[6] He was, rather, a naturalist in an age of natural history. Horace Walpole remarked in 1770 that 'Natural History is in fashion,'[7] and another of White's contemporaries, Peter Collinson, wrote to Linnaeus: 'We [English] are very fond of all branches of Natural History; they sell the best of any books in England.'[8] Even White himself, for all his reputation for otherworldliness, attested to this interest by observing to his brother John that 'anything in the naturalist way now sells well' (WLL, 1, 279). It is worth remembering that *The Natural History of Selborne* was published in the same year as Erasmus Darwin's 'Loves of the Plants' and a year before the founding of the Society for Promoting Natural History. Far from hiding himself in a parochial backwater, White was in the mainstream of his century's scientific and intellectual pursuits.

As early as 1776 John Mulso had shown unusual foresight in remarking: 'No Man communicates the Pleasures of his Excursions, or makes the world partake of them in more Usefull Manner, than You do ... Your work ... will immortalize your Place of Abode as well as Yourself.'[9] It was not wholly coincidental, of course, that the earliest significant example of 'local' natural history should originate in a village like Selborne. Or, to approach the point from another angle, White was remarkably fortunate in his place of birth. Walter Johnson has drawn attention to the 'extraordinary diversity of terrain within small compass' around Selborne, 'its topographical features including in pleasant proximity open moor, downs, farmland, woods, ponds, and streams, with all the resultant varieties of soil and vegetation.'[10] He might also have added that the village's southern position less than thirty miles from the English Channel renders it a favoured spot for the observation of migrants and birds of passage. White was, of course, acutely aware of his good fortune, as he notes in the following remark to Barrington: 'In a district so diversified with such a variety of hill and dale, aspects, and soils, it is no wonder that great choice of plants should be found. Chalks, clays, sands, sheep-walks and downs, bogs, heaths, woodlands, and champaign fields, cannot but furnish an ample *Flora*' (*NHS(B)*, XLI). The parish of Selborne had the variety and complexity of a self-contained world in miniature, and the same methods could be adopted there that were applied on the larger scale. As Richard Haymaker has expressed it, 'from a scientific point of view, the terrain around Selborne is described in the manner employed by explorers for a whole continent.'[11]

White's own attitudes and theories can best be demonstrated by bringing together three important passages in the writings that clearly express his overall intention:

> The Author of the following Letters takes the liberty, with all proper deference, of laying before the public his idea of *parochial history*, which, he thinks, ought to consist of natural productions and occurrences as well as antiquities. He is also of opinion that if stationary men would pay some attention to the districts on which they reside, and would publish their thoughts respecting the objects that surround them, from such materials might be drawn the most complete county-histories.[12]

> If people that live in the country would take a little pains, daily observations might be made with respect to animals, and particularly regarding their life and conversation, their actions and oeconomy, which are the life and soul of natural history. (*WLL*, I, 176–7)

> Men that undertake only one district are much more likely to advance natural knowledge than those that grasp at more than they can possibly be acquainted with: every kingdom, every province, should have it's own *monographer*. (*NHS(B)*, VII)

This emphasis on detailed examination of a limited area is so obvious as to require little or no comment. At the time, however, it was a new idea, and its importance can hardly be exaggerated – whether in the field of natural history or of rural literature. One recalls an equally significant comment in the nineteenth century by Thoreau: 'I cannot but regard it as a kindness in those who have the steering of me that, by the want of pecuniary wealth, I have been nailed down to this my native region so long and steadily, and made to study and love this spot more and more. What would signify in comparison a thin and diffused love and knowledge of the whole earth instead, got by wandering?'[13] Less obvious, but equally noteworthy, is White's concern for what we should now call the interdisciplinary range of these studies. The 'natural knowledge' that he mentions in the third of the quoted extracts can include historical and antiquarian records as well as observations in the field of natural history. Despite his title (which is admittedly more accurate when quoted in its original form as *The Natural History and Antiquities of Selborne*), White is interested in the interlocking relevance of all studies, whether zoology, botany, geology, or human history. As C.S. Emden has well expressed it, 'the *whole* Selborne captivated him, and it is the *whole* Selborne that he pictures for the perennial pleasure of numberless readers.'[14]

White describes natural history as 'a kind of information to which I have been attached from my childhood' (*NHS(P)*, x); he was a naturalist first and a writer second. Consequently, although our prime concern in this study will be with the literary quality and influence of his work, we cannot properly discuss the subject until we come to a clear understanding of his particular capacity as a naturalist. How far was he an innovator? What did he contribute to the study of natural history? What aspects of his subject did he consider most important? Unless we know the answers to such questions, we shall not be able to appreciate the intentions behind the writing.

According to W.H. Hudson 'Gilbert White lived in an age which had its own little, firmly-established, conventional ideas about nature, which he, open-air though he was, did not escape, or else felt bound to respect.'[15] That White was a 'man of his age' can hardly be denied, and his continual debates concerning the migration or hibernation of swallows and his frequent references, derived partly from John Ray and partly from the clerical side of his nature, to 'the wisdom of God in the creation' are obviously aspects of his eighteenth-century heritage. This is natural and to be expected. It is hardly surprising that many of his paragraphs have been rendered obsolete by subsequent discoveries, but it is worth pointing out that White is no more the prisoner of his period than Hudson was of his own.

Indeed one of the most significant characteristics that enabled White to become an important natural historian was the healthy scepticism which he derived from his century, and perhaps from his Church. 'There is such a propensity in mankind,' he writes, 'towards deceiving and being deceived, that one cannot safely relate any thing from common report; especially in print, without expressing some degree of doubt and suspicion' (NHS(P), xxi). This is an attitude, incidentally, that clearly distinguishes the eighteenth-century White from the seventeenth-century Walton, whose trust in the printed word is notorious. Although White has been laughed at for his refusal to dismiss the possibility of swallows and martins hibernating instead of migrating, his conduct on this subject was, in fact, admirably scientific. Unlike Dr Johnson ('Swallows certainly sleep all winter'[16]) and Cobbett ('How ridiculous it is to suppose, that these frail birds [nightingales], with their slender wings and proportionately heavy bodies, *cross the sea*, and come back again!'[17]), White refused to accept reports of hibernation on hearsay, and went to considerable pains to secure evidence for himself. His conclusion (like that of Sir Roger de Coverley on another occasion) that there was much to be said on both sides, was the only proper one, given the state of ornithological research in his time. He frequently speculated on the matter – and we now know that he often speculated wrongly – but he was undoubtedly justified in declaring it an open question. As he wrote to Pennant, 'candour and openness [are] the very life of natural history' (NHS(P), xxv).

Another of White's impressive qualities as a naturalist was his capacity to build upon the new foundations that had just been laid for a more scientific study of living creatures. He was quick to apply the new and improved system of natural classification worked out by the Swedish botanist Carl Linnaeus, who was still alive when the earlier Selborne letters were written, and who was described by White himself as 'the greatest naturalist in Europe' (WLL, I, 261). White would have heartily endorsed Linnaeus's statement that 'the first step in science is to know one thing from another.'[18] In White's time the Linnaean system was still making its way against the earlier nomenclature associated with the name of John Ray. Indeed, as Walter Johnson has noted, White's two correspondents differed in their allegiances to the systems, and he altered his references according to the taste of the recipient: 'Knowing that Pennant preferred the Linnaean nomenclature, he employs that system when writing to him about the birds of Selborne. Barrington, on the other hand, liked the older system of Ray, hence White fell in with his convenience, or prejudice.'[19] It is clear, however, that despite his tribute to Ray as 'our great countryman' (WLL, I, 166), White himself favoured Linnaeus, and it seems likely that he was considerably influential in popularizing Linnaeus's system in England.[20]

But it would be a serious mistake to assume that White was a rigid systematizer. *The Natural History of Selborne* would never have attained classic status had that been the case. On the contrary, he has been hailed as a 'pioneer in the popular treatment of natural history,'[21] a distinction that may be granted so long as it is not seen as detracting in any way from his continued concern with natural history as a scientific discipline. Our best guide here is the modern naturalist James Fisher. 'In the middle of the eighteenth century,' Fisher writes, 'there were already signs of two distinct trends in natural history. These can widely be described as Classification and Observation.' Of these, Gilbert White was 'the greatest, and the type' of the latter. 'Being sensible men, these observers did not neglect the names and arrangements provided for them by the classifiers, but they were concerned more with how the animals lived than with where they should be put when they were dead.'[22] Add to this the lifelong devotion which White gave to his subject, and we begin to realize the extent to which he differed from earlier naturalists.

In his first letter to Barrington White describes himself as 'an *out-door naturalist*, one that takes his observations from the subject itself, and not from the writings of others,' and the necessity for observation in the field is a point he returns to again and again. The remark that Richard Jefferies made about Linnaeus, that 'he touched nature with his fingers instead of sitting looking out of window,'[23] can with equal justice be applied to White. In a later letter to Barrington, for example, he elaborates on the theme himself:

> *Faunists*, as you observe, are too apt to acquiesce in bare descriptions, and a few synonyms: the reason is plain; because all that may be done at home in a man's study, but the investigation of the life and conversation of animals, is a concern of much more trouble and difficulty, and is not to be attained but by the active and inquisitive, and by those that reside much in the country.   (*NHS(B)*, x)

This needs to be emphasized since it is a requirement continually stressed by writers in the rural tradition. Jefferies and Hudson, in particular, insist upon the importance of personal observation in the field, and this is the area in which White's example has been most influential and beneficial. John Burroughs remarks that White 'seems to have been about the first writer upon natural history who observed things minutely,'[24] and R.M. Lockley, a modern outdoor naturalist of some distinction, considers him 'unequalled as a field observer.'[25] Until the last few years of his life White was fortunate in possessing remarkably fine eyesight, a factor extremely important in the period before binoculars. This enabled him, as C.S. Emden has noted, 'to see what no naturalist had seen before, that swifts mate in the air.'[26] All this may seem, by modern scientific standards, elementary, but there is no better way of demonstrating White's particular genius than by contrasting him with the two more traditional naturalists to whom the Selborne letters are addressed – Thomas Pennant, who despite his widely publicized but superficial tours was essentially an indoor scholar, and Daines Barrington, who may be fairly described as an enthusiastic but amateur dilettante.

But it is not sufficient, of course, for the naturalist merely to be out of doors. Records must be kept clearly and continually over a number of years if the observations are to be of scientific value. White would doubtless have considered Barrington's invention of 'The Naturalist's Journal,' a diary designed for the outdoor observer, as his correspondent's greatest contribution to the subject. White himself used it over an extended period of time, and also devised his own notebooks for special purposes. 'For many months,' he tells Barrington, 'I carried a list in my pocket of the birds that were to be remarked, and, as I rode or walked about my business, I noted each day the continuance or omission of each bird's song' (NHS(B), III). His outdoor observations were further extended by the fact that, as a sufferer from coach sickness, he rode on horseback wherever possible – one of the few points of resemblance between White and his very different rural near-contemporary, William Cobbett.

One of Cobbett's few references to White is, indeed, highly relevant in this context. 'By the bye,' he writes, 'if *all the parsons* had, for the last thirty years, employed their leisure time in writing the histories of their several parishes, instead of living, as many of them have, engaged in pursuits that I need not here name, neither their situation nor that of their flocks would, perhaps, have been the worse for it at this day.'[27] White's vocation as a country curate proved, in fact, a noteworthy advantage for his natural history interests. Not only did he enjoy the necessary leisure for such work, but, as he rode out regularly to preach at neighbouring parishes, he had ample opportunity to add to his observations and, even more significantly, to visit localities regularly throughout the year. Barrington once paid White the compliment of describing him as 'one of the few naturalists who not only observe but think' (NHS, 30). The tribute is just. Much of the interest of *The Natural History of Selborne* derives from the fact that White thinks, and thinks hard, about the observations he has made. He is always seeking reasons, offering general statements to explain recorded phenomena. Richard Jefferies remarked that the book 'reads as if it had been compiled in the evening,'[28] and he is doubtless referring to the meditative, discursive method of the letters, which sum up the significant observations of the previous few days, attempting to fit them into what is already known, always probing deeper into the mysterious but fascinating ways of God as manifest in his creation.

White has been credited with a number of significant discoveries in the field of natural history. He is best known for being the first naturalist to distinguish the three English species of willow warbler, and he also provided the first descriptions in England of the lesser whitethroat, the harvest mouse, and the noctule bat. In addition, he was the first to claim earthworms to be hermaphroditic, anticipated Darwin in isolating the ancestral prototype of domestic pigeons, and made original contributions to our knowledge of protective coloration. Moreover, as James Fisher notes, 'he anticipated the modern theories of bird territory, and the effect of the holding of territory by birds upon their population.'[29] His references to sexual selection and the struggle for existence were also notably ahead of his time. R.M. Lockley pays him a fine and justified tribute by stating: 'No modern naturalist can fail in reading him to remark his originality, shown in the number of occasions Gilbert White anticipates a now commonly recognized concept or theory of animal behaviour or ecological consequence.'[30]

It is this last contribution that merits most attention here, since it has implications that extend far beyond the limits of 'pure' natural history. The currently fashionable science of ecology is that part of biology which studies the relationship between organisms and their environments, and this is the relationship (upon which Darwin's contribution to science depends) that White continually emphasized. For him, though it had profound consequences for his scientific attitude, it was probably an innate awareness rather than a developed mode of inquiry. But whatever its origin in White's own case, the ecological approach is certainly the true centre of his contribution to natural history; it combines his stress on direct observation, his study of individual species against the background of the area they inhabit (in this case, Selborne), and the premium that he places upon disciplined, rigorous thought based upon the insights gained out of doors. For the purposes of our present study the importance of White's insistence on the intimate connection between an organism – whether human or animal – and the environment in which it is found can hardly be overemphasized.

Natural history, John Henry Newman tells us, is one of the sciences which 'has before now been treated by an author with so much colouring derived from his own mind as to become a sort of literature.'[31] He might well have had *The Natural History of Selborne* in mind. One of the questions that invariably arises in any discussion of Gilbert White is: does the effectiveness of the book stem from art or artlessness? Modern commentators have been curiously reluctant to place too much stress on White's art – for reasons, however, that are not far to seek. The difficulty involves the expectations aroused by later developments in rural writing – perhaps, too, by an unconscious inheritance from romanticism. We have learnt to expect more 'atmosphere' from our outdoor writers, and more recognizable 'fine writing.' This may explain why W.H. Hudson, who first encountered the book as a youth on the pampas, while fascinated by its revelations of natural history, none the less felt that 'it did not reveal to me the secret of my own feeling for Nature – the feeling of which I was becoming more and more conscious.'[32] In his impetuous zeal for natural knowledge Hudson overlooked the artistic virtues of simplicity. As Jefferies noted so acutely in the last century, 'the simple character of the writings of Gilbert White have, perhaps, in these latter days somewhat deterred people from reading him. They seem so very simple, just as a boy might snatch a bloom of horse-chestnut and bring it home; so very easy to do that.'[33] But, as Jefferies himself recognized, it is *not* easy. Indeed, without White's contribution the later writings would hardly have been possible.

One thing is certain: *The Natural History of Selborne* is no hasty compilation. Although it conveys a tone of freshness and spontaneity, its writing was a long and arduous process, and, before proceeding to the literary aspects of the book, it will be as well to consider briefly what we know about its genesis. It seems that, not long after the correspondence with Barrington had begun, the latter suggested the possibility of White's publishing some of his findings. As early as 1770 we find White commenting:

> When we meet, I shall be glad to have some conversation with you concerning the proposal you make of my drawing up an account of the animals in this neighbourhood. Your partiality towards my small abilities persuades you, I fear, that I am able to do more than is in my power: for it is no small undertaking for a man unsupported and alone to begin a natural history from his own autopsia! (NHS(B), v)

(It must be pointed out that White is almost certainly using the word 'autopsia' in its original sense of 'seeing with one's own eyes'; it does not, in this context, imply scientific dissection, a practice which White employs when necessary but not indiscriminately. Here White is simply asserting that his work would depend upon personal observation.) It is scarcely surprising that he should be reluctant to embark upon what, undertaken single-handed, would be an extremely ambitious piece of work. Ironically, however, the finished book, while not claiming any comprehensive coverage, is actually broader in range than Barrington's original suggestion. White goes further to include plant life, local superstitions, the geology and meteorology of Selborne, as well as 'the animals in this neighbourhood,' and at the same time presents a detailed historical commentary in the *Antiquities*.

Less than a year later, we find that the suggestion has had some effect, but that the plan has been altered. Most of these references, however, have been omitted from the published version of the letters, and we have to depend on other sources. In January 1771 he writes to his brother John in Gibraltar: 'As matter flows in upon me I begin to think of composing a Natural History of

Selborne in the form of a journal for 1769' (*WLL*, I, 197). This is elaborated in a suppressed paragraph from the ninth letter to Barrington, quoted by Nicholson in his introduction:

> In obedience to yr. repeated injunctions I have begun to throw my thoughts into a little order that I may reduce them into the form of an *annus-historico-naturalis* comprizing the nat. history of my native place. As I never dreamed 'til very lately of composing anything of this sort for the public inspection, I enter on the business with great diffidence, suspecting that my observations will be deemed too minute and trifling. However if I ever finish it I shall submit it to yr. better judgment. (*NHS*, 30)

What is of particular interest here is the assumption, even at this early stage, that the book will be, not a transcription of a diary, but the composite creation of one. White is thinking in terms of a model rather than an example, a work of art rather than an authentic document.

A few months later he is still doubtful of his abilities for such a project ('I ought to have begun it twenty years ago') and still pondering the form that such a volume might take. To a year's diary is added the idea of 'large notes and observations' (*WLL*, 201), and these are, of course, destined to oust the diary as the central text. The diary lingered on as a possibility, only rejected on the last page of the published work because 'something of this sort' had recently appeared. It seems likely, however, that White had realized at an early stage that a reproduced (if highly altered and edited) correspondence provided him with a more appropriate form for his subject and for his own particular talents.

By 1774 the form of the book becomes much clearer. He is again writing to his brother John, and for the first time *The Natural History of Selborne* as we know it is recognizable.

> Out of all my journals I think I might collect matter enough, and such a series of incidents as might pretty well comprehend the Natural History of this district, especially as to the ornithological part; and I have moreover half a century of letters on the same subject, most of them very long; all which together (were they thought worthy to be seen) might make up a moderate volume. To these might be added some circumstances of the country, its most curious plants, its few anti-quities; all which together might soon be moulded into a work, had I resolution and spirits enough to set about it.   (*WLL*, I, 250)

We learn here that, if White has not already decided to incorporate additional material from his journals into the revised and rewritten letters, it is an inevitable step that is to be taken very shortly. The 'circumstances of the country' suggest the first nine letters to Pennant (later additions that might better be described as short chapters), while we also note the first mention of the important but less popular *Antiquities*. Only the 'soon' in the last sentence needs qualification – the *Natural History* was still fifteen years away from publication.

Once White had firmly decided upon his task, we hear comparatively little about its progress. We know that he began collecting material for the *Antiquities* as early as August 1775, but that he had not yet 'entered upon' them (*WLL*, I, 289). There are also various references to the difficulties of the work. 'Were it not for the want of a good amanuensis,' he writes to Samuel Barker in 1780, 'I think I should make more progress; but much writing and transcribing always hurts me.'[34] He is continually being encouraged, and even prodded, by his friends, but he is curiously evasive about the state of his work. We are therefore forced back upon various forms of detection and speculation to gain an adequate picture of his creative methods. There are, however, a few clues. Perhaps the most interesting occurs in a letter as late as March 1788, when presumably only a few finishing touches remain to be made. It is clear that his correspondent has questioned the consistency of the whole scheme. 'As to the Antiq. letters being addressed to somebody, I cannot well tell what to say: though I think if to any, it should be to Dr Chandler; ... but ... I think it may be best to let the letters go as they are, addressed to *no one*' (*WLL*, II, 182). This provides a fascinating glimpse into White's 'workshop.' Clearly he approaches the epistolary medium in natural history in much the same way as one of his contemporaries might have approached it in fiction. The use of letters is, in fact, no more than a convention – a literary method that appeals not so much to the naturalist in White as to the creative artist. It is a ready way of communicating not only his material but his attitude towards his material. This leads us conveniently to a consideration of White's inconspicuous but subtle art.

As Henry C. Shelley has pointed out, 'Gilbert White began to write a book without knowing it. What he thought he was doing was something quite different from the serious work of authorship.'[35] No consideration of White's art is valid which does not continually remind itself of this obvious but none the less crucial fact. At the same time, it is clear to anyone who examines the book with care that White has paid more attention to artistic matters than we might expect from a superficial reading. We have already seen that he was considering publication while the correspondence with Pennant and Barrington was still in progress. We find, indeed, that after 1774 White's prose in these letters becomes somewhat self-conscious, and we may reasonably assume that from this time onward he was aware of the likelihood of a wider audience. It is also clear that when he got down to the actual work of gathering and presenting material he must have realized that all sorts of artistic problems had to be considered and solved before the finished work emerged.

His materials consisted of the manuscripts of his natural history journals and copies of the letters he had already written to Pennant and Barrington and also to some of his relatives and other friends. The epistolary method, once thought of, must have seemed peculiarly attractive. It would avoid a dull species-by-species presentation – the sort of museum tour in words which White would have been the first to recognize as unsuitable for his own particular purposes. It would also avoid the need for comprehensive coverage which he knew from the outset would be impossible to achieve. More positively, it could provide a convenient means of dividing the book into small sections, allow a desirable informality of style and treatment, and above all emphasize the human element which was so important a part of White's intention. For the book is not merely a volume containing facts of natural history; it is itself a demonstration of how the study of natural history can be enjoyably and usefully organized.

At this point, however, additional difficulties, necessitating a certain amount of editorial action, would become visible. Although the greater part of the letters was devoted to natural history, there were certain irrelevant passages that would have to be omitted. E.M. Nicholson has stressed White's strict selectivity: 'To read the *Natural History*, and then to go through his private letters on the same subjects, or even the original letters to Pennant and Barrington, is an education in restraint. Exclamations, personal comments, irrelevancies, humorous remarks, and anything approaching sarcasm are ruthlessly extirpated' (*NHS*, 34–5). Repetition was also a problem. Even in the book as it now stands the careful reader will notice the repetition in letters to Barrington of material that has already been discussed with Pennant. Had the correspondence been reproduced in full, such instances would be multiplied.

But White's editorial problems were by no means confined to omissions. He was in many respects a perfectionist and could rarely resist the temptation to tinker with the originals in order to improve them. As he read over his earlier letters, he would frequently be reminded of a later observation that strengthened or qualified the original. Reasons in favour of adding sentences, and even whole paragraphs, could easily be mustered – hence the numerous instances of dated passages that are demonstrably anachronistic according to the dating of the actual correspondence. At the same time, White had no wish to endanger the element of spontaneity, however much the interests of scientific knowledge might be served. It is impossible, of course, to decide how consciously this process of reasoning was followed through, but we may be sure that the difficulties White encountered derived from this tension, evident in almost all the writings in the rural tradition, between the claims of exactitude on the one hand and the human element on the other.

Willy-nilly, then, White was destined to encounter problems that required answers in essentially literary terms. In fact, however, he was acutely interested in such matters, as may be seen by numerous references in his private letters (see *WLL*, I, 246, 258–9, 276–7; II, 18, etc). It would seem from the available evidence that White ultimately chose the epistolary form because it allowed him the greatest possible variety in both style and presentation. That the book remains a classic almost two centuries after its first publication is no small indication of the rightness of his decision.

The best way to explore the artistic variety of the book is simply to proceed through it, noting any stylistic and formal features as we come upon them. The opening letter begins abruptly. There is no place or date indicated, and no salutation. This is true, we find, of the first nine letters, which together provide a detailed and ordered introduction to the area around Selborne that is to be the centre of attention in the rest of the correspondence. As Virginia Woolf has noted, 'no novelist could have given us more briefly and completely all that we need to know before the story begins.'[36] It is obvious, as soon as we stop to consider the point, that no genuine letter series could have presented the material in such economical and orderly fashion. This is clearly an artificial device. It is true that White occasionally inserts brief sentences intended to give the illusion of actual correspondence – thus the fourth letter begins: 'As in a former letter the freestone of this place has only been mentioned incidentally, I shall here become more particular' – but these insertions are, to say the least, perfunctory, and no one is likely to be deceived. None the less, we accept the convention. These opening letters in fact constitute a clear, well-written essay of scientific description, employing a clarity of diction and smoothness of development that is in the best tradition of eighteenth-century plain prose.

Letter x, dated 4 August 1767, exists in its original form, so this can confidently be called the beginning of the correspondence proper. It has, however, been adapted, and in his *Life and Letters of Gilbert White* Rashleigh Holt-White has reproduced passages that do not appear in the final text. None the less, it reads like a genuine letter, and in its content and tone it is characteristic of the greater part of the book. There are paragraphs on White's favourite subject, the winter habits of swallows, on black-caps, water-rats, and an unfamiliar *falco* which White had found hanging on a barn door and was sending to Pennant for identification. The letter ends suddenly with the isolated sentence: 'The parish I live in is a very abrupt, uneven country, full of hills and woods, and therefore full of birds.' This reads strangely in its context, now that the nine introductory letters have been concocted. One would have expected White to omit it as no longer relevant, but he is by no means consistent on these matters. There are a number of loose ends scattered through the book. One hesitates to conjecture whether White was aware of these inconsistencies or not, though he was so meticulous about other details that it is difficult to believe that he could have overlooked them. Whatever the reason may have been, however, such oddities help to convey the impression of a real correspondence. If the book's ragged edges were all smoothed out, it would lose much of its interest.

Letter xɪ opens with another reference to the unfamiliar falcon: 'It will not be without impatience that I shall wait for your thoughts with regard to the *falco* …' This introduces us to one of the perennial qualities of the book – the sense of interested discovery which White conveys so well. We share with him the suspense, and, although we know that White hopes it will prove a 'nondescript,' we none the less share his more limited pleasure when he writes at the opening of letter xɪɪ: 'It gave me no small satisfaction to hear that the *falco* turned out an uncommon one. I must confess I should have been better pleased to have heard that I had sent you a bird that you had never seen before; but that, I find, would be a difficult task.' The advantages of the epistolary form are never more evident than here. The straight scientific record would merely show that a peregrine falcon, then a rarity in Hampshire, had been shot near Selborne. But White achieves more than this; he is at pains to communicate the experience of a natural observer in action, and the successful identification of an unfamiliar species is one of the humble but genuine pleasures of the outdoor naturalist. As Walter Johnson writes, 'this unobtrusive naturalist can make us undergo in our own persons the experiences through which he himself has passed.'[37]

The letters continue in this fashion for some time. White sends any notable observations to Pennant, discusses his replies, and offers his own thoughts on subjects that his correspondent has raised. He does not jolt our responses again until the close of letter xxɪv when we are suddenly confronted, without any introduction or subsequent comment, with one of his poems, 'The Naturalist's Evening Walk.' Similarly a well-known fragment of White's verse is found attached, again without comment, to the end of letter xlɪ to Barrington. It is interesting (because potentially revealing) to note that a bibliographical oddity is involved in this last instance. In the first edition this verse-fragment and a preceding paragraph were included in a sort of appendix at the end of the book under the title 'Additions to Letter xlɪ …'; it appears in its correct place only in the second edition of 1802. Apparently, then, this was a later interpolation that was accidentally omitted when the first edition went to press. The matter is of some interest here, since it may throw light on White's literarary intentions. I suggest that the insertion of the two poems at well-placed intervals in the book was intended to lend artistic variety to the whole. Despite White's scientific footnotes for 'The Naturalist's Evening Walk,' both poems are obviously literary in inspiration – that is to say, they show the influence not of the scientific versifying best known in Erasmus Darwin's *Botanic Garden* but of Thomson's *Seasons*, which White greatly admired. So far as natural history and 'parochial history' are concerned, the poems are an irrelevance; in literary terms they succeed in communicating White's personal, subjective response to his surroundings.

The epistolary style continues for several more letters. References to White's journals occur more frequently, however, and in letters xxxix and xl we are faced with another change of approach. Here, under the guise of offering Pennant a series of remarks concerning his revisions to his *British Zoology*, White presents the reader with a collection of random observations, many of which consist of a single, bald statement, such as: 'Crows go in pairs the whole year round' (*NHS(P)*, xxxix). These may well have been culled from his annotations to an earlier edition of Pennant's book, but the effect on the reader is not unlike that of reading Walter Johnson's selection from White's *Journals*, save that the remarks are more generalized and undated. There is no sign of any particular ordering – observations concerning eels are sandwiched in between notes on sparrow-hawks and hen-harriers, for example (*NHS(P)*, xl) – and the reader may be forgiven for wondering why these letters were not omitted. They do serve, however, to demonstrate not only the wide-ranging scope of the true naturalist's interest, but also the apparently commonplace observations that, when properly recorded, can contribute to natural knowledge. While the 'moral' is relevant to natural history, White is once more employing a literary device to draw attention not so much to a fact as to the human means of discovering the fact. John Burroughs is certainly justified in describing *The Natural History of Selborne* as 'a treatise on the art of observing things.'[38]

In the final letter to Pennant we may note a significant stylistic change within the letter. It begins genuinely enough, and White is evidently answering specific points raised in a previous communication from Pennant. Towards the end, however, we detect White bracing himself for a more formal conclusion. One paragraph begins: 'It will by no means be foreign to the present purpose to add that ...' – which one finds difficult to accept as spontaneous phrasing. And White ends by quoting Virgil and appending the equivalent in Dryden's translation. This is obviously a final flourish explicable as the close to the book's first section, but hardly appropriate to an informal correspondence.

The letters to Barrington, which may be dealt with more briefly, show evidence of a similar concern for stylistic and formal variety. In the first two White offers some useful ornithological statistics. These include lists of winter and summer birds of passage, and groupings of birds according to their habits of singing and breeding. Obviously experimental in nature, they demonstrate the way in which ordered classifications can emerge out of the random observations hitherto recorded. White then returns to the basic pattern of chatty correspondence until, at the end of letter xv, he interrupts the epistolary form to write a brief preface to the succeeding letters on swallows and martins which, in somewhat different form, had been read to the Royal Society and published in its *Philosophical Transactions*. Here, then, we are confronted with a brief scientific monograph embedded in the otherwise exploratory and 'amateur' observations.

I have already noted the fragment of verse at the end of letter xLi. This, together with a number of quotations from earlier poets, both classical and English, which are considerably more numerous in the letters to Barrington, helps to maintain a just balance between the literary and the scientific. The correspondence ends with a series of letters about the weather of the district in which White generalizes from his earlier records. Like the opening letters to Pennant, they are undated, impersonal, and, save for the final signature, lacking any form of salutation; together, these two organized series of concocted letters at the beginning and at the end provide an orderly and dignified framework for the correspondence as a whole. (The *Antiquities*, which display few literary characteristics, are best seen not as a third section but as a historical appendix to the main text.)

The Natural History of Selborne is a work whose quality and attractiveness are extraordinarily difficult to isolate or explain. Indeed the mystery of the book's appeal may be seen as one aspect of its fascination. In Virginia Woolf's words, 'it is one of those ambiguous books that seem to tell a plain story, ... and yet by some apparently unconscious device of the author's [it] has a door left open.'[39] What is the secret of its success? Why has it gone through edition after edition, while other apparently similar works have been forgotten within a year or two of publication? It certainly lacks all the obvious marks of popularity. An unsympathetic reader will be at a loss to understand the charm that it clearly exercises over others. John Burroughs has written well about the difficulties of approaching the book:

> There is indeed something a little disappointing in White's book when one takes it up for the first time, with his mind full of its great fame. It is not seasoned quite up to the modern taste. White is content that the facts of nature should be just what they are; his concern alone is to see them just as they are. When I myself first looked into his book, many years ago, I found nothing that attracted me, and so passed it by.[40]

In his modesty White himself feared that the public would 'laugh at an old country parson's book' (*WLL*, II, 184), but *The Natural History of Selborne* is now established as an enduring if somewhat uncertain classic. Like *The Compleat Angler*, its interest is not confined to its informative qualities as a handbook; this is clearly demonstrated by its popularity in North America, where few of its observations can be verified in the field. Every commentator feels obliged to account, in some way or other, for its continued fame. The most common explanations include its evocation of locality, its style, the geniality of White's own character, and (inevitably) its escapist charm. Occasionally champions of different aspects clash head-on. Thus Grant Allen finds it 'essential to insist upon the point that the interest of these Letters is now chiefly literary,'[41] while Henry C. Shelley can retort: 'To affirm that it is read to-day only as literature – for its manner and not for its matter – is to woefully miss the mark.'[42] This should be enough to convince us that, whatever our own attitude may be, it is a mistake to look for *the* explanation. There is no single solution. *The Natural History of Selborne* has survived because it is so many things to so many men. White's care to include numerous varieties of style and approach within his book is rewarded by its proven capacity to appeal to a wide range of readers. To the poet Coleridge it is 'this sweet delightful book,' while Charles Darwin, who read it in his youth, reacts by wondering 'why every gentleman did not become an ornithologist';[43] the spectrum is obviously broad.

None the less, while it would be foolish to insist on one aspect at the expense of others, it is reasonable to concentrate in this study on those qualities of White's book which ensure its place within the rural tradition. Here, as in *The Compleat Angler*, we find traces of the old georgic tradition. White is on record as considering Virgil's *Georgics* to be 'the most beautiful of all human compositions' (*WLL*, I, 212), and the didactic and moral elements of White's book, linked so surely with an approval of retirement and rural simplicity, all bear witness to a latent if not necessarily conscious connection. According to Virginia Woolf, 'it was with Virgil in his mind that Gilbert White described the women making rush candles at Selborne.'[44] But White is 'of' as well as 'in' the country. The usual classical education that he received at school and at Oxford, the polished and sophisticated manners that were an intrinsic part of his age, these did little to temper his essentially rustic attitudes. As Burroughs has noted, he was 'a born countryman – one who had in the very texture of his mind the flavour of rural things.'[45] We should not allow the eighteenth-century suspicion of emotional response to suggest that White was unnaturally cold or aloof. Though he might not have been prepared to admit the fact, White *loved* Selborne, and C.S. Emden is right to describe him in a chapter-title as 'A Very Human Naturalist.'

A common criticism of White's book (though to some readers it is an important part of its charm) is the general absence of references to international events. He is similarly charged with neglecting the humbler local inhabitants. We are asked to believe that White was narrow in his interests and lacking in a true sense of community. Both charges are exaggerated. The first is particularly unfair, and it is surprising to find even so knowledgeable and sympathetic an editor as E.M. Nicholson observing with complacent irony that 'we find him cross-questioning a woman about night-jars on the day that the Bastille was stormed' (*NHS*, 22). But there is nothing foolish in continuing one's own specialist studies at a time of crisis, and we know from his letters and journals that he was by no means uninformed about what was happening in the world. (On one occasion, indeed, his awareness of current developments impressed itself dramatically upon his neighbours when he correctly forecast the time of an early balloon flight over Selborne in 1784 [see *WLL*, II, 134–6].) But his omission of political references from *The Natural History of Selborne* is a deliberate artistic decision. Like the similar controversy concerning the novels of Jane Austen, it is fully explicable in terms of literary decorum.

The second charge is more forceful. It has been expressed gently and convincingly by Richard Jefferies in his introduction to White's book:

> If the great observer had put down what he saw of the people of his day just as he has put down his notes of animals and birds, there would have been a book composed of extraordinary interest. Walking about among the cottages, he saw and heard all their curious ways, and must have been familiar with their superstitions ... He knew the farmers and the squires; he had access everywhere, and he had the quickest of eyes. It must ever be regretted that he did not leave a natural history of the people of his day.[46]

This is acceptable because it presupposes White's familiarity with the people of his neighbourhood. Unacceptable is the deduction that, because White rarely mentions the villagers, he is therefore uninterested in them. All the available evidence militates against this view. Indeed it seems likely that one of the reasons why he took so long to complete the book is that he devoted so much of his time and energy to parish duties. Rightly or wrongly, White believes that his readers will find little interest in his observations on village life. C.S. Emden, who has stressed White's sociability and the co-operation that he enjoyed from the villagers for his natural history records, proves his case, but is forced to draw his material more from the journals and private letters than from *The Natural History of Selborne* itself. More crucial, perhaps, are George Sturt's deductions on this matter, since he derives his views not from private evidence but from a rigorous examination of the published text. He points out that White must have depended for his opening description of Selborne in the first letter upon the 'primitive knowledge,' as he calls it, of his local and probably illiterate neighbours. He quotes specific passages – 'a vein of stiff clay (good wheat-land),' 'a kind of white land, neither chalk nor clay, neither fit for pasture nor for the plough, yet kindly for hops' – that involved communal experience rather than a single man's observation, and comments: 'Thus to learn their country, field by field, has been one among the many studies of the English for fourteen hundred years.'[47] This helps to account for the earthy solidity of the book that has often been praised – by Mary Mitford, for instance, who wrote: 'There is an air of reality in [White's] descriptions which I meet nowhere else.'[48]

None the less, he naturally maintains his position as clergyman and gentleman in the traditional hierarchy of village life. Even if we grant H.J. Massingham's argument in his edition of White's writings that the Selborne of his time was essentially a medieval village, with all that that implies concerning the close connection of the pastor with his flock, he could never have known the countryside in the way that John Clare or even Cobbett knew it. We become keenly aware of this difference when we encounter the reaction of George Sturt's peasant-labourer Bettesworth to *The Natural History of Selborne*. He is ultimately prepared to grant that 'it seems a nice sort o' book,'[49] but his initial reaction goes straight to the present point: 'What's the sense o' they bits of aristocracy we comes to – a line or two of English and then a lot of Latin? Is that put there, so's nobody should understand it?'[50] Sturt himself, while admiring White's knowledge of Selborne, admires his uncle's knowledge of Farnborough or Frensham even more because it is 'closer, like a peasant's.'[51]

Although White certainly knew more about the local community than he includes in his book, it is doubtful if he were fully aware of the developments that were going to shatter the calm of Selborne within a generation or so of his own death. In the last year of his life, soon after the commencement of the Reign of Terror in France, we find him writing to Robert Masham, the Norfolk naturalist: 'You cannot abhor the dangerous doctrines of levellers and republicans more than I do! ... The reason you have so many bad neighbours is your nearness to a great factious manufacturing town. Our common people are more simple-minded and know nothing of Jacobin clubs' (*WLL*, II, 255). The reference to 'our common people' recalls his earlier description of the human inhabitants of Selborne in the fifth letter to Pennant: 'We abound with poor; many of whom are sober and industrious, and live comfortably in good stone or brick cottages, which are glazed, and have chambers above stairs: mud buildings we have none.' The passage is open to various interpretations. Virginia Woolf, in a foolishly imperceptive paragraph, quotes the first four words which read, she claims, 'as if the vermin were beneath his notice,'[52] but the objective, almost clinical description, like that of Jefferies in his *Times* letters on the Wiltshire labourer, is clearly deliberate and at one with the tone and approach of the whole book. E.V. Bovill, more to the point, picks up the last clause of the quoted passage and comments: 'The poor of Selborne were lucky.'[53]

One may assume that, at least by the standards of the times, the state of the poor in White's Selborne was fairly good. White was an honest and conscientious man, and, if any extreme hardship had existed, we can be sure that it would not have passed unrecorded. None the less, his own account of the 'riotous' insistence of the poor on their rights of 'lop and top' (*NHS(P)*, IX) suggests that conditions left much to be desired. And in 1775 he acknowledges a donation from his sister Mrs Barker for the poor of the parish as very acceptable 'in these hard times' (*WLL*, I, 286). The situation of the poor, though apparently stable, seems in fact to have been precarious – and it was on the brink of rapid deterioration.

The extent of deterioration may be gauged by the situation as Cobbett found it when he visited Selborne on 7 August 1823. He was impressed by the outward appearance of the place, but goes on to report: 'As I was coming into this village, I observed to a farmer who was standing at his gateway, that people ought to be happy here, for that God had done everything for them. His answer was, that he did not believe there was a more unhappy place in England: for that there were always quarrels of some sort or another going on. This made me call to mind the King's proclamation relative to a reward for discovering the person who had recently *shot at the parson of this village*.'[54] This is no exaggeration on Cobbett's part. Selborne was soon to be one of the centres of disturbance during the labourers' riots of the 1830s, the story of which may be found in W.H. Hudson and the Hammonds.[55] It is a sad decline from the days of Gilbert White; although less than forty years later, it belongs to another age – the age of which Cobbett himself is the supreme spokesman.

FOUR

William Cobbett

1763–1835

What signifies it who I am? The only question is, *am I right*?[1]

William Cobbett may be called the first spokesman and representative of the rural poor. It is true, of course, that talented men had risen from humble life in the past. Some, like Stephen Duck, author of 'The Thresher's Labour' (1730), had been able to describe the peasant way of life in realistic terms; others, despite the supposedly rigid class divisions of England, had attained positions of importance and influence in various professions and callings. But Cobbett alone became the mouthpiece of the toilers of the field. In him the small farmers and particularly the agricultural labourers found a voice so powerful and persistent that it could not readily be ignored.

This was all the more important since at no time in the agricultural past had the need for such a voice been so urgent. England was becoming more and more centralized. What Cobbett called (with a probable excess of nostalgia) 'the old and amiable parochial governments of England'[2] were losing their influence. The enclosure movement and the simultaneous tendency towards large farms and more scientific and businesslike farming were breaking down the old rural patterns. Improved communications (including the stagecoaches that Cobbett loved and the turnpike roads that he detested) were having a similar effect. Power was concentrating on London, and on the parliament in London; the rural interest was in danger of being overwhelmed, particularly since the country members spent more and more of their time in the city and came increasingly under the influence of urban values. The traditional split between urban and rural was now further complicated; country society was itself divided and came to be seen in terms of an educated land-owning class and an ignorant, unsophisticated, and (through enclosure) landless set of tenants and dependants. Cobbett observed with scorn that 'the general notion in London has been, that the country labourers are ignorant creatures' (OWC, 246). The rural squires, who were tending more and more to represent their own interests rather than those of the constituencies from which they came, did nothing to correct this impression. To as devoted a countryman as Cobbett, they could no longer be seen as acting for the good of the rural areas. No one spoke up for the small farmers or the labourers, and Cobbett, who saw himself an 'one of those, whom the spirit-stirring circumstances of those awful times drew forth from his native obscurity,'[3] strove valiantly and tenaciously in his speeches and writings to break this barrier of silence.

Cobbett's is perhaps the most remarkable and unexpected contribution of all the rural writers to be discussed here. It is both ironic and significant, of course, that the circumstances which brought him into the limelight also required his frequent presence in 'the Wen' that he despised and away from the countryside that he loved. He is himself conscious of this, regretting 'that a heart and mind so wrapped up in every thing belonging to the gardens, the fields and the woods, should have been condemned to waste themselves away amidst the stench, the noise and the strife of cities.'[4] But although this saddened him, it never affected his outlook. Indeed the most remarkable quality of Cobbett's genius may well lie in his preservation of the stance and attitude of the class into which he was born. 'A great misfortune of the present day,' he writes in his *Advice to Young Men*, 'is that every one is, in his own estimation, raised above his real state of life.'[5] The 'every one' did not include Cobbett. Less than a year before his death he noted with justifiable pride: 'I was born and bred a farmer, or a sort of labourer; and I have never desired to have any rank, station, or name, or calling, more and other than that of a farmer' (AWC, 226). In the course of a long public life he frequently changed his mind, but never his viewpoint. The Member of Parliament for Oldham in the post-Reform Bill House of Commons spoke with the same accents as the young countryman who had been 'bred at the plough-tail' (AWC, 9).

Cobbett's range was as wide as his output was prolific. Works on grammar, contemporary politics, economics, and religious history flowed as readily and rapidly from his pen as the surveys of rural life and skills for which he is best known today. It is particularly appropriate, however, that he should be considered within the context of the rural tradition, for this is where his effective centre is to be found. No study of his work and opinions is acceptable if it does not emphasize that Cobbett was, first and foremost, a countryman. Indeed Edward Thomas has called him 'one of the few thorough-going countrymen in our literature,'[6] and he insists himself that 'my natural taste, my unsubdueable [sic] bias for the country, has never been, and never can be overcome as long as I have life' (*RR*, 568). This chapter is intended to demonstrate the central importance of this statement. It will make no attempt to provide a full-scale survey of his biography or writings; it will focus upon the way in which the countryside moulded his ideas and upon the vividness with which he has delineated the rural life of the first three decades of the nineteenth century.

Cobbett was born in 1763 in Farnham, Surrey, one of the great hop-growing centres of southern England, little more than ten miles from White's Selborne. It seems to have been a more than usually prosperous area in mid-eighteenth-century England, and Cobbett looked upon it with deep affection throughout his life. He loved it partly for its natural beauty, calling it 'the neatest [place] in England, and, I believe, in the whole world' (*AWC*, 9), but more significantly for the traditional rural life which it had preserved. Farnham was a genuine part of the ancient agricultural past, and Cobbett was making no idle claim when he wrote: 'All that I can boast of in my birth is that I was born in old England' (*AWC*, 10). His grandfather, George Cobbett, had been a labourer, and William records with satisfaction that 'he worked for one farmer from the day of his marriage to that of his death, upwards of forty years' (*AWC*, 10). While his grandfather died some three years before William's own birth, his grandmother, 'who lived to be pretty nearly ninety,'[7] was well known to him, and provided a tangible link with the early eighteenth-century peasantry whose way of life was to seem untroubled and ideal in the dark, disturbed years of the early 1800s. William's father, also a George Cobbett, had succeeded, through a capacity for hard work that was inherited by his third son, not only in obtaining a farm but also in becoming landlord of an inn with the appropriate name of 'The Jolly Farmer.' (When he passed through Farnham in 1913, Edward Thomas noted with wry amusement that the inn 'was labelled "Cobbett's Birthplace," in letters as big as are usually given to the name of a brewer.'[8]) His father's talk, William tells us nostalgically, was 'chiefly about his garden and his fields,' and he goes on to describe him as 'learned for a man in his rank of life, ... honest, industrious and frugal' (*AWC*, 10, 11). In other words, he was a living example to his son of the ideal countryman – hardworking, independent, content.

Cobbett's own early life would, by our standards, be considered harsh:

> I do not remember the time when I did not earn my living. My first occupation was, driving the small birds from the turnip seed, and the rooks from the peas. When I trudged afield, with my wooden bottle and my satchel on my shoulders, I was hardly able to climb the gates and stiles, and, at the close of day, to reach home was a task of infinite labour. (*AWC*, 11)

None the less, Cobbett loved the world of his childhood, and throughout his life he never tired of stressing the importance of love for one's native place. It was, tor one thing, the bedrock of patriotism: 'He who is not more attached to the spot on which he was born than to any other spot of his country, will very easily bring himself to like any other country as well as his own' (*RR*, 845). Again, on one of his rides in the north, he grants of the pitmen that 'their work is terrible,' but is consoled by the thought that 'though they live not in a beautiful scene, they are in the scene where they were born' (*RR*, 737). But he considered himself particularly fortunate. Farnham and its environs become a fixed standard for comparison in *Rural Rides* and elsewhere, and we frequently encounter in such passages a warm, almost passionate response to natural beauty which is an important though seldom noticed quality in Cobbett's writings. Here, for example, is a passage which originally appeared in *Advice to Young Men*:

> When I was a little boy, I was, in the barley-sowing season, going along by the side of a field, near Waverley Abbey; the primroses and bluebells new spangling the banks on both sides of me; a thousand linnets singing in a spreading oak over my head; while the jingle of the traces and the whistling of the plough-boys saluted my ears over the hedge; and, as it were to snatch me away from the enchantment, the hounds, at that instant, having started a hare in the hanger on the other side of the field, came scampering over it in full cry, taking me after them many a mile. I was not more than eight years old; but this particular scene presented itself to my mind every year from that day.   (*AWC*, 99–100)

The tenderness with which this scene is described might seem closer to Mary Mitford than to the popular conception of Cobbett. It is a strain, however, that should not be overlooked. He portrays himself elsewhere as one who 'seems to have been born to love rural life, and trees and plants of all sorts' (*AWC*, 38). As G.K. Chesterton has noted, when in North America 'he remembered England as a great green nursery.'[9] This love, though rarely stated, is the force behind such works as *The English Gardener* and *The Woodlands*, books that may legitimately be described as labours of love. He observes: 'I never set myself down in any spot in my whole life, without causing fruits and flowers and trees (if there was time) and all the beauties of vegetation to rise up around me' (*AWC*, 134–5). In later life he derived great satisfaction 'from the reflection, that I caused millions of trees and shrubs to be planted in England, that would never have been planted in England, for ages yet to come, had it not been for me' (*AWC*, 204).

Rural life, Cobbett knew, could be an unfailing delight. On this point he is obdurate:

> If the cultivators of the land be not, generally speaking, the most virtuous and most happy of mankind, there must be something at work in the community to

counteract the operations of nature. This way of life gives the best security for health and strength of body. It does not teach, it necessarily produces early rising; constant forethought; constant attention; and constant care of dumb animals. The nature and qualities of all living things are known to country boys better than to philosophers. The seasons, the weather, the causes and effects of propagation, in cultivation, in tillage, are all known from habit, from incessant repetition of observation ... Rural affairs leave not a day, not an hour, unoccupied and without its cares, its promises, and its fruitions. (AWC, 234)

This was the message he learnt from his childhood glimpse of the old rural life of Farnham, and it provided an inspiration that never failed. John W. Osborne is surely being unduly cynical in pointing out that 'despite later glowing accounts of early life in the country and the deep impression which it made upon him, young William ran away from home three times.'[10] It would be more to the purpose to note that he returned, a sadder and a wiser man, with the appreciation of his early life strengthened rather than weakened. Indeed, since Cobbett was only too well acquainted in later life with the facts of agricultural poverty, his looking back to these early years at Farnham with gratitude and envy should carry even greater authority. They were, quite simply, 'happy days';[11] they reflected a natural life and a perfectly possible one. While it is true that the young Cobbett was blissfully ignorant of the economic worries that may well have existed in the village of his childhood, it is difficult to believe that his picture is hopelessly distorted. We should always remember that he claimed it to be a good and satisfying life, not an easy one. He records that on visits with his brothers to their grandmother, 'she used to give us milk and bread for breakfast, an apple pudding for our dinner, and a piece of bread and cheese for supper' (AWC, 10). This is clearly no golden age, but Cobbett finds it acceptable. Even if Farnham had been more fortunate than other parts of England, which may well be the case, this does not prevent its serving as a model for what could be more generally achieved. Throughout his life, which took him not only to the great Wen of London, but to France, to North America, to Ireland, and even to prison, that early vision of the good life remained. It was something for which he fought in print, and to which he returned whenever he had the opportunity.

For, despite his extraordinarily prolific literary output, his agricultural ventures were numerous. In 1804, weary of London and the toils of political journalism, and insistent that his children should experience the same rural upbringing that he had enjoyed, he obtained a farm at Botley, Hampshire, and forthwith attempted to recreate his vision. Here, for a little while, the old ways of the eighteenth century flourished once more. Yet again we find him responding with enthusiasm to its beauty: 'Botley is the most delightful village in the

world. It has everything in a village, that I love; and none of the things I hate. It
is in a valley. The soil is rich, thick set with wood, the farms are small, the
cottages neat ... "Would I were poetical," I would write a poem in praise of
Botley' (*AWC*, 258). Mary Mitford reports that on the Botley farm 'everything
was in accordance with the largest idea of a great English yeoman of the old
time.'[12] Sir Richard Phillips also visited Cobbett's farm and claimed never to
have seen ' such excellent cottages, gardens, and other comforts appropriated to
the labouring classes as those which he erected and laid out on his estate.'[13] It
would be wrong to assume, however, that Cobbett was a 'soft' or easy master.
We gain a fascinating glimpse into his principles and methods in the following
passage from *The Woodlands*:

> The best, and in the end, the *cheapest* way is to employ men by the day, to have a
> really good and trusty man to *work with them* (example is better than scolding); to
> see them *begin well* yourself; to visit them often, to repeat, at *every visit* (for
> memories are short), your orders as to the manner of doing the work, and to insist
> on their keeping steadily at work, for if men *keep on*, they will almost always do
> work enough. The straight back and the gossip are the great enemies of the
> progress of the labours of the field. But the great things of all (next after sufficient
> pay) are your own *presence* on, or near, the spot, and a conviction in the minds of
> the men, that *you understand the whole of the business well*.[14]

The economic success of Botley is uncertain, for Cobbett's eighteenth-century
practice extended into what we should now call an unbusinesslike attitude
towards accounts. G.D.H. Cole notes that from 1807 onwards 'he was sinking
money heavily in his farming and probably did not know whether it was paying
or not; for as fast as he got money from the land he put it back into the land.'[15]
He continued, however, for a number of years, even while in prison (for alleged
sedition) from 1810 to 1812, during which period he directed the farm affairs by
word and letter from his confinement in Newgate. We know, at any rate, that
his bankruptcy, which took place in 1820 and which saw the end of the Botley
farm, was attributable to other causes. We also know that, despite numerous
attempts on the part of his enemies to prove the contrary, he was popular with
the men he employed. Alexander Somerville, rural advocate of free trade in the
1840s, interviewed one of Cobbett's farm servants, who declared that he 'would
never wish to serve a better master';[16] other reports tell a similar story.

Botley was his most ambitious experience of farming, but there were
others. When in America in 1817, to escape prosecution and censorship, he
immediately bought a farm on Long Island – a venture which came to an
unfortunate end when the farmhouse burned down in 1819. Much more
successful was his next experiment, a seed farm which he opened in Kensington

in 1821. This was not only financially satisfactory but artistically rewarding. *The English Gardener* and *The Woodlands* were both products of these years, and the comparatively small amount of supervision involved left Cobbett free to embark on his famous series of rural rides in which his love for the countryside and wide knowledge of agriculture combined to produce his most characteristic and best-known book. Finally, in 1831, he was able to obtain a farm at Ash within a few miles of his native Farnham. He was therefore able to fulfil his wish to pass the close of his life 'amongst that class of society that I have always most loved and cherished, the people employed in the cultivation of the land' (*AWC*, 233–4). Though still intimately involved in politics, taking his seat in the first reform parliament, he had returned to the place of his birth, and upon his death in 1835 he was buried in Farnham churchyard.

Once we accept Cobbett's rural viewpoint as central, many of the difficulties surrounding his opinions and attitudes can be resolved. Too often in the past his career has been seen as inconsistent, confused, contradictory. This is particularly true of his political allegiances, but the same problems may be encountered even in his response to rural affairs. Yet the mote is not necessarily in Cobbett's eye. The problems themselves are frequently urban constructs, and customary responses to them are more often than not urban-oriented. Cobbett's reactions, which may at first sight appear quixotic, almost invariably reflect his rural upbringing; his thinking refuses to fit itself into an urban mould. In approaching his ideas we should keep the rapidly increasing split between rural and urban values firmly in mind.

Nowhere is this confusion more conspicuous than in Cobbett's relations with the major political parties. To talk of a political evolution from Tory through Whig to Radical is an absurb oversimplification and involves serious distortion. This viewpoint has unfortunately been encouraged (though at a far more sophisticated level) by G.D.H. Cole, Cobbett's most scholarly biographer, whose own political position has led him to place Cobbett on what he believes to be the side of the angels. But on this subject G.K. Chesterton's subjective and impressionistic study of Cobbett is by far the more acceptable. 'It is not true,' Chesterton writes, 'that he belonged successively to two parties; it is much truer to say that he never belonged to any.'[17] Cobbett certainly supported different governments at different times, but this does not imply that he was an unreliable turncoat. Party policies change, as well as individuals, and Cobbett's chopping and changing is best seen as a vain search for a party that would firmly uphold both rural interests and honest principles. Again one can do no better than quote Chesterton:

Cobbett had only supported Pitt because he thought the Pitt rule stood for Old

England; but it did not. Cobbett never supported the Pitt party after he had discovered that it did not. It is true that as he drifted further from Pitt and the Tories he necessarily appeared to be drifting nearer to Brougham and the Radicals, who also did not. But the slightest acquaintance with what he said about Brougham and the Radicals will show that it was almost always a movement of repulsion and not of attraction.[18]

This argument can be backed up from Cobbett's own statements. As early as 1806 he claims that 'the words Tory and Whig now excite ridicule and contempt at the bare sound of them' (OWC, 253), and the following year we find him exhorting the people to reject 'the appellation ... of Whig or Tory' and to be 'influenced by principles and not by names.'[19] But this had been his original point, from his complaints against corruption in the army onwards. In his earlier years his patriotism may have led him close to the attitude of 'my country, right or wrong,' but he could never be seduced by the heresy of 'my party, right or wrong.' Even when he was closest to the Tories, he firmly rejected a proposal that seemed to limit his freedom to speak his mind. He soon learned that political promises differed from subsequent actions, and sadly realized that, when it came to the reformation of deep-seated abuses, no party was to be trusted. In 1807 we find him writing to Dr Mitford: 'As to our fellows at Whitehall and Westminster, we shall be sure to do right if we hate them all.'[20] His only resource was to throw his weight behind whichever party seemed least unsatisfactory at any given time, and to attack it with all his might when it proves itself unworthy. In consequence, he was persecuted – and prosecuted – by both Tory and Whig governments. Even in his brief career as Member of Parliament at the close of his life, he adopted the same practice, accepting and rejecting successive governments of either party according to his two basic yardsticks: the honesty of their principles and the effect of their actions on the agricultural poor. His position is best expressed, perhaps, by his assurance to the electors of Preston in 1827: 'I will be under no control of anybody' (OWC, 235). Politically Cobbett could never have been anything but independent.

The difficulty in discussing Cobbett in terms of the usual political assumptions is well illustrated by his attitude to the Corn Laws. We tend to assume that in this controversy the Tories and the rural interests advocated protection, while the liberals and the urban middle class were champions of free trade. Where does Cobbett stand in this instance? In Rural Rides he quotes from a speech that he made at Battle in 1822: 'I am decidedly of opinion, Gentlemen, that a Corn Bill of no description, no matter what its principles or provisions, can do either tenant or landlord any good.' This appears 'liberal' and 'progressive' until he goes on to give his reasons: 'A law to prohibit or check the importation of human food is a perfect novelty in our history, and ought, therefore, independent of the reason, and the recent experience of the case, to be received and entertained with great suspicion' (RR, 55). The argument could hardly be more 'conservative.' This is typical of the way in which Cobbett's reasoning cuts across what we have come in a later age to consider the conventional party boundaries.

None the less, Cobbett's early Tory connections clearly point to where his instinctive allegiances lay. He was radical in the sense that he wanted notorious existing abuses removed, but not in any democratic, levelling sense. Cobbett was no enemy to authority so long as that authority was just and dutiful, and in this he once again reflects a rural attitude which is apparently difficult for the urban mind to comprehend. The malicious attacks on Cobbett in his own time (always originating in 'the Wen') reflect the basic fears of the period rather than any clear understanding of his position. The following statement of 1833 is only one of many that could be quoted. 'I have known for many years, and have been a strict observer of all classes of men in this country, and I never heard amongst common tradesmen, little farmers, artisans or labourers, anything indicating a wish to see the nobility pulled down' (AWC, 212). Indeed many of his views can be labelled reactionary. He even goes so far as to grant that 'there must always be, and shall be poor people; that is, people in extreme poverty' (CLL, 80). This, for Cobbett, is a realistic as well as a divinely ordained fact of existence; he is concerned only that the labourers should be 'happy in that state of life in which it has pleased God to place them' (RR, 886). No wonder Chesterton describes him as 'more Tory than most Tories' as well as 'more Radical than most Radicals'![21] One is tempted, in fact, to view his whole work as an appeal from the new to the old Tories. All this will seem neither puzzling nor paradoxical once we have examined Cobbett's attitude to the various classes that comprise rural society.

The assumption that Cobbett is automatically on the side of the poor farmers and labourers against the rich farmers and landlords is one that will not survive any forthright examination of his writings. He would doubtless see it himself as a typically urban simplification of what is in fact a complex issue. Such abstract classifications have no relevance for him. We cannot isolate his opinion of 'the landowner,' only of individual landowners; hence his contempt for

> the shallow fool, who cannot duly estimate the difference between a resident *native* gentry, attached to the soil, known to every farmer and labourer from their childhood, frequently mixing with them in those pursuits where all artificial distinctions are lost, practising hospitality without ceremony, from habit and not on calculation; and a gentry, only now-and-then residing at all, having no relish for country-delights, foreign in their manners, distant and haughty in their

behavior, looking to the soil only for its rents, viewing it as a mere object of speculation, unacquainted with its cultivators, despising them and their pursuits, and relying, for influence, not upon the good will of the vicinage, but upon the dread of their power.   (*RR*, 34)

The sentimentalist might expect every country squire to belong to the first category; the urban progressive (including many of Cobbett's commentators) is only too likely to take the second as the norm. But Cobbett is well aware of the folly of generalization. He judges a landowner, as he judges anyone else, not by what he is but by what he does. And he is quite clear about what a landowner should be doing: 'It is the *first* duty of all rulers to watch over the happiness of *the people at large*, civil society having been formed for the good of the whole of the people, and not for the profit, or honours of a few.'[22] Cobbett approves of rulers so long as they carry out their duties, and the verdict on any individual landowner is often favourable. Thus on one of his rides through Sussex he observes:

I suppose, that every inch of land, that I came through this morning, belongs either to the Duke of Richmond, or to Lord Egremont. *No harm* in that, mind, if those who till the land have fair play; and I should act unjustly towards these noblemen, if I insinuated that the husbandmen have not fair play, as far as the landlords are concerned; for every body speaks well of them.   (*RR*, 166)

Later Mr Chamberlayne of Netley is presented as an ideal landlord, who recognizes his social duties and does not make excessive profits at the expense of his labourers (see *RR*, 505). Cobbett invariably gives credit where credit is due; as he says, he is never afraid 'of being accused of flattering a rich man' (*RR*, 506).

His contempt is reserved for two varieties of landowner. First, of course, there are 'those Fundlords who retire to be country-'squires' (*RR*, 3), the *parvenus* who 'have risen suddenly from the dunghill to the chariot.' These are 'the very worst species of aristocracy,' possessing 'all the *pride* and none of the *liberal sentiments* of the nobility and great gentry' (*OWC*, 87). This distinction recurs again and again. 'An aristocracy of *title and privilege*,' he writes elsewhere, 'when kept within due and constitutional bounds, brings none of the oppression upon the people which is always brought upon them by a *damned aristocracy of money*.'[23] But he reserves his greatest venom for those members of the rural aristocracy who had thrown in their lot with the urban 'tax-eaters,' those who were not only betraying their responsibilities to the rural order but were also in a position to see what they were doing. It is this wilful betrayal, the exchange of a good life for a bad, that Cobbett finds unforgivable. He never fails to record their downfall with an almost apocalyptic gratification.

His attitude towards farmers is similar. For those who attempt to ape the fashions and standards of the gentry he has an unrelenting hatred. 'When farmers become *gentlemen*,' he observes, 'then labourers become slaves' (*OWC*, 48). But Cobbett was a farmer himself 'by taste as well as in fact,'[24] and he is well aware of the difficulties and burdens under which they work. We are reminded at this point that Cobbett was first attracted to Ann Reid, whom he later married, by seeing her in New Brunswick at dawn 'out on the snow, scrubbing out a washing tub' (*AWC*, 37). Here for Cobbett was the perfect farmer's wife. His rural rides gave him insight into the variety of farmers as well as the variety of farms, and he was appalled at the number of those who were failing through no fault of their own:

> The accounts which my country newspapers give of the failure of farmers are perfectly dismal ... I cannot help feeling for these people, for whom my birth, education, taste, and habits give me so strong a partiality. Who can help feeling for their wives and children, hurled down headlong from affluence to misery in the space of a few months! (*RR*, 8)

Doubtless there is some journalistic heightening at work here, but the basic situation can hardly be disputed. It is Cobbett's determination to gather the facts and inquire into their causes that results in *Rural Rides*.

But Cobbett's main concern is, properly, with the condition of the labourers. It is a subject upon which he speaks with authority. He claims, indeed, to 'know more of their toils, their sufferings, and their virtues, than any other man' (*OWC*, 244). This being so, it is all the more significant that his use of the word 'poverty' should be carefully defined. Unlike some outside observers, he refuses to see the labourers as by definition under-privileged. 'I despise the man that is poor and contented,' he writes, but continues:

> Let it be understood, however, that, by poverty, I mean real want, a real insufficiency of the food and raiment and lodging necessary to health and decency; and not that imaginary poverty, of which some persons complain. The man who, by his own and his family's labour, can provide a sufficiency of food and raiment, and a comfortable dwelling-place, is not a poor man. (*CE*, 3)

In the early eighteenth century, he claims, the labourer had been able to command the necessities of life — and Cobbett has no interest in frills and luxuries. He speaks longingly of the time when 'each had his little home,' when labourers lived in the same cottage and worked for the same master all their lives,[25] of 'the days when they had meat dinners and Sunday coats' (*CE*, 144). As I have already noted, Cobbett does not claim that the old rural life was easy; on the contrary, it was often hard and harsh, but there was no reason why it should not be both healthy and satisfying. Indeed he has no doubt that 'the labourers were happy.'[26]

Thus Cobbett offers no high-flown plan for the extermination of poverty, but is adamant in insisting that contemporary conditions were not only disgraceful but unendurable: '*All*, all, the labourers, having families, are now *paupers*!' And this, he stresses, 'is new: it was not so in former times: it was not so even till *late* years' (*OWC*, 120, 121). This was written in 1806, and in 1807 he is even more forceful:

> I challenge contradiction when I say, that a labouring man, in England, with a wife and only three children, though he never lose a day's work, though he and his family be economical, frugal, and industrious in the most extensive sense of these words, is not now able to procure himself by his labour a single meal of meat from one end of the year to the other. Is this a state in which the labouring man ought to be?[27]

To Cobbett this was the most pressing problem facing the England of his time: 'A full belly to the labourer was, in my opinion, the foundation of public morals and the only source of public peace' (*AWC*, 187). Set against this, the contemporary myth of progress ('*vast improvements, Ma'am*' [*RR*, 116, etc.]) had no meaning. It was time to put back the clock. Thus Cobbett is the chief petitioner in 1815 in a letter which calls for 'the restoration of the labouring classes to their former state of comfort, of independence of mind, and of frankness and boldness of manners' (*OWC*, 74).

But however much he may champion the rights of the labourers, it is never at the expense of the rights of the other classes. He is, for instance, a defender of property – we find him proudly telling Dr Mitford in 1808 that he now owns 'one hundred and fifty acres of woods and cornfields, into which no one but myself has a right to enter'[28] – but he insists, of course, that a labourer's property rights are as sacred as a lord's. He has nothing against the often criticized 'master-and-man' relationship, so long as the rights, duties, and privileges of both sides are maintained. He will even emphasize these rights when addressing the labourers themselves:

> Many of the *farmers* are not able, in the present state of things, with all these taxes and monopolies arising out of them, to give the wages that I give, without being *ruined themselves*; theirs is, in many cases, a life of greater hardship than that of the labourer ... Then the *landlords*: why should their *rents* not be paid? Not to get their rents is to lose their estates; and why should they have their estates taken away? Those estates are as much *their right* as good living in exchange for your labour, and as parish aid in case of inability are *your* rights.   (*RR*, 888)

Such sentiments are so often discounted as the prejudices of the ignorant or the partisan that it is both refreshing and enlightening to encounter them in the writings of the 'radical' Cobbett.

But Cobbett's radicalism, though a fact, has been exaggerated. It is of a kind that bears little or no resemblance to modern revolutionary ideals. It looks to the future not for any new dispensation but for restoration of the liberties of the past. 'It would give me as much pain as it would give to any man in England,' he writes, 'to see a change *in the form of the government*. With *King, Lords* and *Commons*, this nation enjoyed many ages of happiness and of glory.'[29] His attitude to the monarchy is an impressive blend of the deferential and the sturdily independent: 'I think much of the office of the King; I think much of my DUTY towards him; I have always inculcated due obedience to his authority: but favours from him I want none' (*OWC*, 237). An appreciation of the rationale behind that statement might be considered an ultimate test in the understanding of Cobbett. He envisages nothing that he does not believe had once existed. If he must be seen as a revolutionary, his aims should be appreciated not in terms of modern, predominantly urban reform movements but as a latter-day version of the 1381 Peasants' Revolt which, as H.J. Massingham has insisted, was essentially a conservative revolution, 'not a revolution on behalf of abstract rights and Utopian conceptions but a battle for the restoration of the ancient custom.'[30] Perhaps the clearest statement of Cobbett's position may be found in the following extract from 'An Address to Journeymen and Labourers' (November 1816):

> I know of no enemy of reform and of the happiness of the country so great as that man, who would persuade you that we possess *nothing good*, and that all *must* be torn to pieces. There is no principle, no precedent, no regulations (except as to mere matter of detail), favourable to freedom, which is not to be found in the Laws of England or in the example of our ancestors. Therefore, I say, we may ask for, and we want, *nothing new*. We have great constitutional laws and principles, to which we are immoveably attached. We want *great alteration*, but we want *nothing new*. Alteration, modification to suit the times and circumstances; but the great principles, ought to be and must be, the same, or else confusion will follow.[31]

What need to be destroyed are not the old laws and customs but '*innovations*, ... the monstrous encroachments of the aristocracy and of the usurers, within the last fifty years especially' (*CLL*, 2). In 'A Letter to the People of Hampshire' (February 1817), a list of recent and bad innovations is given; it includes licensed printing houses, special juries, newspaper stamps, the Game Laws, the Excise Laws, Paper Money, the Debt, etc., etc. (see *CPW*, v, 130–5). The Jerusalem to be built in England's green and pleasant land must be based on the firm foundations of the past, established long before the dark satanic mills of the industrial 'Thing.' Cobbett's aim is quite explicit – 'to bring my country back to something like the government which existed when I was born' (*CLL*, 2).

Rural Rides might well be considered the central text in this study, since it contains within itself, and in conspicuous fashion, nearly all the varied qualities possible within the rural tradition. In the first place there is a concentration on facts. Cobbett's express aim is 'to see the *country*; to see the farmers at *home*, and to see the labourers in the *fields*' (*RR*, 85) – and to report back upon what he sees. His contemporaries read the accounts as they appeared in the *Political Register* primarily in order to find out the condition of agricultural England, to hear from a reporter 'on the spot' what life was like in the different rural areas. But if this were all that Cobbett had to offer, we should not, of course, be reading his work today. What makes *Rural Rides* of permanent interest is not so much its description of the early nineteenth-century landscape (though naturally this is valuable) as the eyes through which this countryside is seen. Here we encounter, in an extreme form, the paradox at the heart of the rural tradition – the necessity for objective and subjective to meet and conjoin. *Rural Rides* contains perhaps the most vivid and 'realistic' descriptions of country life, but this becomes possible only through the all-pervading personality of the observer. As Chesterton puts it, 'the *Rural Rides* are a landscape, but they are also a portrait.'[32]

For the unity of the book is provided not by its subject so much as by Cobbett himself. Pages which from the pens of other writers would be considered unwarranted digressions are here fully acceptable because it is Cobbett who makes the connection and we are prepared to follow the unorthodox but stimulating convolutions of his mind. This is why, as G.D.H. Cole has pointed out, attempts to abridge *Rural Rides* by omitting the supposedly irrelevant or obsolete passages of political tirade invariably fail;[33] the political comments and rural descriptions are firmly connected through Cobbett's own personality, and without the former the latter lose most of their force. There is an inextricable link (heightened in degree but not different in kind from that of other observers) between what Cobbett sees and what he is. For instance, he is no naturalist like Gilbert White; if he mentions birds, they are likely to be either game-birds or, from the farmer's point of view, pests; the flowers mentioned in *Rural Rides* are not things of beauty by the side of the hedgerow, but weeds in the corn. And he is not interested, like such later writers as Edward Thomas, in the actual process of wandering about the countryside: 'I never could go out "to take a walk" in the whole course of my life; nor to take a ride: there had to be something to make me take either one or the other' (*AWC*, 203–4). His chief concern is the nature of the land itself – its suitability for agriculture, its present condition, the state of those who depend upon it for a livelihood, and, perhaps most important, its function as paradigm of the social health of the country as a whole.

None the less, it is probable that too much has been made of Cobbett's practical approach to the countryside. Mary Mitford offers an admirable corrective when she writes of 'the poetry that we trace in his writings, whenever he speaks of scenery or of rural objects.'[34] Cobbett has chosen his words precisely when he writes: 'I have, for *my part*, no idea of *picturesque beauty* separate from *fertility of soil*' (RR, 881). It is a matter of 'both-and,' not 'either-or.' Admittedly he continues, 'If I must have *one* or *the other*, any body may have the *picturesque beauty* for me,' but he considers this a false choice. In other words, he follows the true countryman's instinct in acknowledging what H.J. Massingham has called 'the marriage between use and beauty which husbandry has joined together for thousands of years in the service of God and man.'[35] Cobbett's appreciation of natural beauty is, in fact, strong; he is certainly no Peter Bell. His practicality is of the common-sense variety, and he is by no means blind to other considerations. Thus he writes of the keeping of pigeons: 'It is not to be supposed that there could be much profit attached to them; but they are of this use; they are very pretty creatures; very interesting in their manners; they are an object of delight to children' (CE, 138). And of *The English Gardener*, he asserts: 'I do not write for the curious in botany, but for the use of those, for the practical application of those, who have the means and desire to make pretty spots for their pleasure.'[36]

But it is, of course, in the countryside itself that Cobbett finds most satisfaction. One cannot read far in *Rural Rides* without becoming aware of his intense but never sentimental response to natural beauty. 'What, in point of *beauty*,' he exclaims, 'is a country without woods and lofty trees!' (RR, 40). And again: 'Large sweeping downs, and deep dells here and there, with villages amongst lofty trees, are my great delight' (RR, 297). One is continually encountering the enthusiastic exaggeration that becomes a hallmark of Cobbett's writing – a park, a pasture, or a tree is sure to be described as 'the finest I ever saw in my life.' With Cobbett, however, the country is a whole; it cannot be separated into watertight compartments. He is incapable of appreciating natural beauty in places where human conditions are poor. He is properly blind to what William Morris was later to call the 'tumbledown picturesque.'[37] The morally acceptable and the aesthetically pleasing are for Cobbett inseparable.

If we wish to go further in a discussion of *Rural Rides*, however, we are immediately faced with a difficulty. Any deeper exploration will inevitably be concerned with the artistry of the book; yet to consider Cobbett as anything so grandiose as an artist seems somehow incongruous. We imagine him writing up his reports at first light in a dingy rural inn before riding a dozen miles or so to the next market town in time for breakfast. He had no concern, surely, with the niceties of literary criticism which he would readily leave to the over-educated dunces inhabiting the universities (cf *RR*, 93). Yet *Rural Rides* is now established, however freakishly, as an English classic, and, if we want an explanation for its survival as a living document, it is to literary criticism that we must turn. We shall find that Cobbett was far more concerned with questions of formal and stylistic artistry than is generally recognized.

George Woodcock has recently reminded us of Cobbett's formal preoccupations. He observes that Cobbett 'appears to have been conscious of a unified structure emerging from the *Rides*, however journalistic their original intent may have been, since he set quite deliberate limitations to his book when he prepared it for publication in 1830.'[38] This has usually been blurred for modern readers by the publication of enlarged texts. In 1853 an edition prepared by Cobbett's third son, James Paul Cobbett, contained a number of new rides (particularly in the Midlands and the north of England) reprinted from the *Political Register*, and this version has now become the norm for modern texts. Furthermore the three-volume edition of G.D.H. and Margaret Cole, which appeared in 1930, printed additional material, including Cobbett's tours in Scotland and Ireland, and proudly claimed that 'these additions lengthen the complete work [by which they mean James Paul Cobbett's already enlarged text] by more than one-third' (*RR*, ix).* The formal virtues of the original are, as Woodcock insists, considerable. They include confining the area involved to the counties of southern England, limiting the time to the four years between 1822 and 1826, and choosing those rides that were accomplished on horseback rather than by stage-coach.

Another formal device which is worth mentioning is that each ride, like *The Compleat Angler*, begins and ends in London. Some are subdivided, but it will be found that in these cases they are continuous. There is even one instance in which Cobbett deliberately telescopes two rides into one, suppressing the difference in dates, in order to create what is in fact an artificial continuity in his narrative.[39] There can be little doubt that the position of London within the scheme of *Rural Rides* – alpha and omega, the first and the last – has a considerable effect on the whole book. Cobbett cannot have been unaware of the irony (and it is an effect that had surely become an irony since Walton's time) that the book which most directly communicates, in G.D.H. Cole's words, 'the smell and feel and look of the English country'[40] should be almost symbolically framed by 'the Wen.'

The mention of symbolism in a discussion of Cobbett may appear even more

---

*   In the Penguin English Library (1967) George Woodcock reprints Cobbett's original text. Although for convenience of reference I have quoted here from the Cole edition, I thoroughly agree, for artistic reasons, with Woodcock's choice of the first edition of 1830.

incongruous than that of artistry. Yet Cobbett is continually employing what we might call a naturally symbolic speech as a kind of stylistic shorthand and also as a way of heightening the emotional effect of his words. What are 'the Wen' and 'the Thing' but highly potent symbols, the first suggesting a malignant growth spreading cancerously across the fair face of the countryside, the second deriving from the Old Testament[41] and emblematic of an evil that is threatening but itself doomed by a mysterious curse? Many of Cobbett's phrases work in this way. Thus 'the Pitt-system,' another name for at least part of 'the Thing,' may well contain a suggestive but generally overlooked pun, and Chesterton has demonstrated the way in which Cobbett elevates Old Sarum to symbolic significance. It was already well known as a rotten borough, but 'for him alone Old Sarum was a place ... He called it the Accursed Hill. That single title, compared with the terms used by pamphleteers and politicians, has in it something of the palpable apocalypse.'[42] At times he is not forced to invent a symbol – he finds it. The famous notice 'PARADISE PLACE. *Spring guns and steel traps are set here'* (RR, 234), which he discovered in Kent, had only to be written down to take on momentous significance within the context of *Rural Rides*.

It will now be clear that an artistic inquiry into Cobbett's work is by no means inappropriate. True, it has its attendant dangers, the most important of which is the kind of literary study that neglects aim and content in the intricacies of stylistic analysis. Cobbett criticism has not escaped this pitfall. Indeed Chesterton complained that 'he has only been admired in the way in which he would have specially hated to be admired. He who was full of his subject has been valued only for his style.'[43] But a literary study that demonstrates how Cobbett's argument is strengthened and communicated by the apt use of verbal devices should avoid this dilemma. Moreover Cobbett himself has a good deal to say on the subject. When he claims to 'listen to nothing about *style* as it is called' (OWC, 42), he must be understood to be referring to the kind of detachable ornament which, both before and after Cobbett's time, has frequently inhibited an intelligent discussion of prose. Writing, for Cobbett, is an essentially practical thing. 'My style,' he writes, 'was such as to please all those who read with a desire of acquiring knowledge' (AWC, 130). But he is too intelligent a man to underestimate the power of rhetoric. Towards the end of his *Grammar of the English Language* he sets down many of his own rules, and it is worthwhile picking out those statements that are obviously applicable to his own work:

Strength must be found in the *thought*, or it will never be found in the *words*.

Sit down *to write what you have thought*, and not *to think what you shall write* ...

Never stop to *make choice of words*. Put down your thoughts in words just as they come.

If you use figures of rhetoric, you ought to take care that you do not make nonsense of what you say.

He who writes badly thinks badly. Confusedness in words can proceed from nothing but confusedness in the thoughts which give rise to them.

The best writing is that which is best calculated to secure the object of the writer.[44]

The advice is both sensible and curiously 'modern.' 'He who writes badly thinks badly' might well have been a 'practical criticism' motto of our own century.

He has also told us something of the development of his own style. It did not, as we might easily assume, come naturally and without effort; it had to be tempered in the heat of controversy, consciously moulded to conform to his needs. 'When I began to write,' he observes, 'I was as modest as a maid, and dealt in qualifications, and modifications, and mitigations to the best of my poor powers of palavering; [but,] when I was unprovokedly assaulted, I instantly resolved to proceed in the very same way, giving three, four, or ten blows for one' (*AWC*, 232). This remark is of special interest, of course, because it is written in the later style, complete with jagged rhythms and explosive alliteration. It is the style which forced Hazlitt to fall back continually upon the imagery of pugilism in order to convey its effect, and led Edward Thomas almost a century later to write: 'The movement of his prose is a bodily thing.'[45]

The physical immediacy of Cobbett's prose, which I take to be its most conspicuous feature, is in perfect accord with the whole cast of his mind. His enemy, in literature and in life, is abstraction. Cobbett never offers us discourses on poverty; we are presented instead with vivid pictures of starving labourers. As G.D.H. Cole points out, 'he was not a man who theorised easily; he needed actual sights and experiences to stir his mind to thought.'[46] The article which led to his imprisonment was a concrete protest against a real scandal; but he was punished for an abstract offence. His overwhelming hatred of the 'new' systems of finance and economics is heightened by their cold abstraction. 'The Thing' is a bold attempt to force this system into concrete terms; only then can Cobbett fight it: while it remains abstract, without form or limit, it is elusive. Finally *Rural Rides* provides particular examples and experiences which can stimulate his mind into action. The roads are hard, but so are the facts. Every scene that he describes becomes for Cobbett an emblem of the times. Every modern barrack symbolizes the 'Thing' that built it; every empty pre-Reformation church is a reminder of bygone days that he believes to have been happier than his present; every dilapidated labourer's cottage calls up an angry vision, not of the landowner's estate, but of the stock-jobber's town house. A half-clad peasant child tells him more about the crisis in agriculture than a whole volume of statistics. Within his prose these images take on the significance of symbols, but they never fail to remain themselves. Even those scoffers who claimed that he was merely tilting at windmills had to admit that the windmills in question were undoubtedly real.

Cobbett thinks clearly and rapidly in concrete terms. We can hardly doubt that he is following his own practice in advising his son to 'put down [his] thoughts, in words as they come.' The result is, perhaps, the most natural-sounding, spontaneous, zestful prose in our literature. Edward Thomas has called his style 'the nearest thing to speech that has really survived,'[47] and one of its most pleasing features is the simple imagery drawn naturally and without effort from the rural experience in which he was saturated. When he measures himself not in terms of stones and pounds but as 'just the weight of a four-bushel sack of good wheat' (RR, 28), he is speaking with the expert knowledge of a farmer on market day. When he describes his family as 'having for years been scattered about like a covey of partridges that had been sprung and shot at,'[48] we are listening to Cobbett the sportsman. Many examples could be cited of the indisputably right image that suddenly appears to clinch Cobbett's point. Here are three:

A sudden blowing up of the Debt would scatter [the inhabitants of 'the Wen'] as a whirlwind scatters a haycock.   (OWC, 90)

The government newspapers have been recommending the Parliament to pass a law to put an end to these [trade] unions. Better call for a law to prevent those inconvenient things called spring-tides.   (OWC, 303)

The publications [set up to counter the Political Register] dropped off one by one, like blighted apples in a summer's storm.   (CPW, 1, 322)

It should be noted that these images are more than rhetorical tricks of style. They constantly refer us back to natural occurrences and natural conditions. The world of winds and tides is Cobbett's yardstick against which he measures and condemns the un-naturalness of the system.

Such effects are not confined to the single clause or sentence. Often enough they are themselves but parts of a larger pattern. This, for example, is a more extended passage:

I have done my best to prevent these calamities. Those farmers who have attended to me are safe while the storm rages. My endeavours to stop the evil in time cost me the earnings of twenty long years! I did not sink, no, nor *bend*, beneath the heavy and reiterated blows of the accursed system, which I have dealt back blow for blow, and, blessed be God, I now see it *reel*! It is staggering about like a sheep with water in the head: turning its pate up on one side: seeming to listen, but has no hearing: seeming to look, but has no sight: one day it capers and dances: the next it mopes and seems ready to die.   (*RR*, 8)

The image of the storm, carrying an apocalyptic suggestion, sets the tone here. We think in terms of rain and thunderbolts. But Cobbett goes on to point out that he did not sink in the storm-floods nor bend under the blows from above. He has returned the blows and seen the system reel and stagger. The image has apparently changed from storm to prize-ring, but in a moment a third image emerges – the sheep with water in the head, a specifically rural image (one that Hardy was later to use with effect) which, while different, none the less recombines the imagery of water and staggering. It would, of course, be absurd to suggest that Cobbett consciously worked out the relation between these images; analysis does show us, however, the way in which his mind tended to work. It can also help to explain his effectiveness. This succession of simple images ultimately forms an elaborate pattern that can be experienced subliminally; by such means Cobbett communicates to his readers not merely facts but a way of thought.

Cobbett, whom H.J. Massingham has called 'the most English of Englishmen,'[49] witnessed in his lifetime the transition from the 'old' England to the new. He was born into an England practically indistinguishable from that of *Tom Jones*; at his death he was within two years of qualifying as a Victorian. At the time of his birth the principles of steam were in the process of being discovered; in his last years he was to complain bitterly about the spread of railways. The dramatic nature of these developments is brought home to us when we find Cobbett remarking as late as 1830: 'I never was induced to go into a factory, in England before' (*RR*, 598), and admitting a few years later: 'I never liked to see these machines lest I should be tempted to endeavour to understand them' (*AWC*, 217).

Noting this, and linking it with the fact that, in the post-Reform parliament, Cobbett was usually in a tiny minority, commentators have often been tempted to regard his later years as a period of failure. We are told that he failed to understand the new age, that he 'did not "move with the times."'[50] But there is all the difference in the world between misunderstanding and rejection. That Cobbett *did* understand the trends of the times may be seen from the following shrewd comment on the mercantile system: 'Now-a-days, all is looked for at *shops*: all is to be had by *trafficking*: scarcely any one thinks of providing for his own wants *out of his own land* ... To buy the thing, *ready made*, is the taste of the day ... The fair and the market bring the producer and the consumer in contact with each other ... The shop and the trafficker *keep them apart*' (*RR*, 508,511). This shows considerable insight into the facts of sociological change. It is not enough to comment, like Osborne, that Cobbett 'was out of touch with a society which was changing politically as well as in other respects' and that this disqualified him as a popular leader;[51] one is not necessarily 'out of touch' if one disapproves of the circumstances of one's own time. Cobbett was well aware of what was going on – and he was in violent opposition to it. Even if he were defending a lost cause, he maintained both his intelligence and his integrity. He saw no merit in moving with the times if they were headed in the wrong direction. Nor did he desire to be a popular leader at any cost – he wanted to lead the people back to what he considered the true way.

In evaluating Cobbett's career from the rural viewpoint we have to consider not his demonstrable success but, some peripheral idiosyncracies excepted, his essential rightness. This is a principle that holds good throughout his life. In attacking corruption in the Army in the 1790s Cobbett was unsuccessful, but he was right. In the United States he accused Benjamin Rush of being a quack and was found guilty of libel, but there is little doubt that Rush *was* a quack. Later, in England, he was imprisoned for protesting against military brutality – and it is to his eternal credit. Similarly his protests against the trends of the 1830s, whether in or out of parliament, may well have been doomed, but that is irrelevant. To take but one example, it may have seemed absurd in 1834 to oppose the New Poor Law (the Poor Man's Robbery Act, as Cobbett called it), but history, when it has not been distorted in the interests of city-dwellers, has vindicated Cobbett. The importance of being on the winning side would have escaped him, and he would probably have condemned it as the product of an urban and false system of values. Once again, one feels, he would have been right.

I began this chapter by describing Cobbett as the first fully articulate spokesman and representative of the rural poor. His career as farmer and politician has often obscured his proximity to the traditions and attitudes of the eighteenth-century English peasantry. The connection is, I believe, close, and the last word on the subject may be left, appropriately, to George Sturt, Cobbett's fellow-townsman and a lifelong student of peasant life and culture. Writing in his journal in 1910, Sturt offered the following assessment:

Cobbett, it may be said, did not use his brains as his peasant or folk ancestors used theirs. Yet really he was nearer to them than to me. True, in going about the country, he too saw a significance behind the obvious appearances of the land-scape: he too traced causes and effects, with a sagacity far exceeding that of the 'folk'; and he, if you like, was concerned with the fate of common people. But always it was on the 'materialistic' side that his ideas were active. He saw the labouring classes as a section of the nation, not as a species of living things dwelling under the sky and working out a mysterious fate: and the laws he thought of were acts of parliament, not the mysterious processes of life. In short, the ideas which the landscape called into activity in him seem to have lingered still in the peasant world, the folk world, of material success; and it may be doubted if he ever strayed into that other world of emotion, passion, or peace, of the spirit. In those respects, was he not still at the folk level?[52]

FIVE

Mary Russell Mitford

1787–1855

> There is an atmosphere of love, a sunshine of fancy, in which objects appear
> clearer and brighter, and from which I sometimes paint.[1]

To turn from William Cobbett to 'merry Miss Mitford,' as Ruskin called her,[2]
seems at first sight to be a move from the central to the peripheral, from the
important to the trivial, from the pugnaciously real to the coyly sentimental.
Any linking of the two figures, one might reasonably assume, could only be
made by means of obvious contrasts; though they were contemporaries, there
seems no likelihood of association. In fact, however, a poem addressed to
Cobbett will be found in Miss Mitford's first published volume, and the two
were at one time acquainted. Mary Mitford had visited Cobbett at Botley in the
company of her father in 1808, and she generally writes of him with affection.
Indeed, when commenting on the way that the reviewers of her poems explained her friendships by the political influence of her father, 'a zealous and
uncompromising Whig,'[3] she goes so far as to say: 'They would have been more
correct if they had asserted a directly contrary opinion, for Cobbett is your
favourite because he is mine.'[4] But, despite this statement, the acquaintance
apparently began through Dr Mitford's coursing interests. Elsewhere she states
that 'sporting, not politics, brought about our present visit [to Botley] and
subsequent intimacy' [*RLL*, 199]. This intimacy, however, failed to develop
into lasting friendship. According to Miss Mitford's biographer and editor, Rev.
A.G. L'Estrange, 'a dispute between Mr. Cobbett and another gentleman, in
which Dr. Mitford became involved, separated the families' (*FM*, 36), and as a
result the two writers never met after Cobbett's imprisonment in 1810. In later

years Miss Mitford regretted what she called 'the coarseness and violence of his political writings,' but at the same time acknowledged that 'with all his faults, he was a man one could not help liking.'[5] All this should remind us that it is a mistake to approach Mary Mitford as if she were one of the ladies of Mrs Gaskell's Cranford. Even a brief account of her life will reveal a toughness – both intellectual and physical – that is at odds with her popular reputation.

Like her beloved Jane Austen, Mary Mitford could claim Hampshire as her native county; she was born in Alresford (the 'Cranley' of *Our Village* and *Belford Regis*) on 16 December 1787. The Mitfords belonged socially, 'by birth, and habits, and old associations,'[6] to the gentry, and in the normal course of events she might have grown up to take her place in the fashionable society of the regency. For the first few years she enjoyed a happy though solitary childhood and displayed a tendency to the precocious. The Mitfords' days of leisure were numbered, however, and Mary was only a girl when her improvident and financially irresponsible father had spent all the fortune that he had gained through his marriage. The house at Alresford was sold, and there followed an uncertain period of changed addresses, one of which (for the father) was the King's Bench debtors' prison. But a lucky lottery ticket, chosen by Mary, repaired the family fortunes, and the Mitfords were soon installed in Reading, the 'Belford' of the prose writings. In 1802, while Mary was at a London boarding school, the foundation-stone was ceremoniously laid for the grandiose and even ostentatious 'Bertram House' at Grasely, a few miles outside Reading. In later life she was to look back with some regret to 'its spacious lawn, its extensive paddock, and noble piece of water' (*ATH*, 278). This was the Mitfords' home until yet again, Dr Mitford had run through his fortune.

Had it not been for his financial negligence, however, we should probably have known his daughter, if at all, only as a poet of minor or even minimal importance. Her début in literature, appropriate to her social standing, was the publication of a slim volume of elegant but unexceptional verse. And it is doubtful if, in normal circumstances, her other talents would have developed. As she has said herself, 'our family losses made me an authoress' (*MLL*, II, 118). In 1820, after years of ruinous litigation, the Mitfords were forced to leave Bertram House; they settled in a small hamlet called Three Mile Cross, between Reading and Basingstoke, and it was here that most of Mary Mitford's prose work was written. Three Mile Cross, indeed, was destined to become famous as the model for 'our village.'

After the stateliness of Bertram House, the cottage in which they now found themselves must have seemed ridiculously small. One of Mary's early descriptions of it, in a letter to Sir William Elford, is well known:

Our residence is a cottage – no, not a cottage – it does not deserve the name – a messuage or tenement, such as a little farmer who had made twelve or fourteen hundred pounds might retire to when he left off business to live on his means. It consists of a series of closets, the largest of which may be about eight feet square, which they call parlors, and kitchens, and pantries; some of them minus a corner, which has been unnaturally filched for a chimney; others deficient in half a side, which has been truncated by the shelving roof.   (*MLL*, I, 331)

Although she refers to it at this time as 'a mere *pied à terre* till we can suit ourselves better,'[7] this cottage remained her home for thirty years. And she soon came – sincerely, no doubt, but partly through necessity – to love it. Less than three months after moving in she writes once more to Sir William Elford, in a very different strain: 'I have grown exceedingly fond of this little place. Did I ever tell you I disliked it? I love it of all things – have taken root completely – could be content to live and die here' (*MLL*, I, 335).

At Three Mile Cross Mary Mitford wrote 'as hard as a lawyer's clerk' (*MLL*, I, 356) in an uphill struggle to make ends meet. Encouraged by the financial profit enjoyed by some indifferent playwrights, she embarked upon the writing of poetic tragedies and enjoyed considerable, if ephemeral, success with the productions of *Julian* (1823), *Foscari* (1826), and *Rienzi* (1828). In addition to her dramatic work, however, she had also been contributing short stories and sketches of village life to periodicals, particularly the *Lady's Magazine*. The first series of these was collected and published as *Our Village* in 1824, and so successful was this venture that subsequent collections appeared at regular two-year intervals until 1832.

Mary Mitford was now established as a writer. But personal circumstances were always pressing, and for the rest of her life she was by necessity engaged in writing and editing. Her later works include the play *Charles the First* (1834), *Belford Regis* (1835), *Country Stories* (1837), *Recollections of a Literary Life* (1852), and *Atherton* (1854). Yet, despite the fact that she was able to describe herself as a 'high-priced' writer (*MLL*, II, 165), none of these successes was able to make her secure from the threat of poverty; they did not even allow her to keep her cottage in proper repair. Consequently the friends of her later years painted a very different picture of her home. To Henry Chorley, for example, it was an 'insufficient, meanly furnished labourer's cottage' with a 'shabby greenhouse parlour' (*LMM*, I, 4), and even Miss Mitford herself was forced to recognize its dilapidation. Her final description of it makes sad reading:

All above the foundation seemed mouldering, like an old cheese, with damp and rottenness. The rain came dripping through the roof and steaming through the walls. The hail-stones pattered upon my head through the casements, and the small panes rattled and fell to pieces every high wind ... The poor cottage was crumbling around us, and if we had stayed much longer we should have been buried in the ruins.   (RLL, 514)

By this time, moreover, both her parents were dead. Miss Mitford consequently moved to a cottage a few miles away in Swallowfield in 1850. This new home she describes to Elizabeth Barrett Browning as 'not pretty, yet too unpretending to be vulgar, and abundantly snug and comfortable' (MLL, II, 300–1). Swallowfield itself is called 'this prettiest village' (RLL, 516), but she was not destined to enjoy its beauties for long. After several years of general ill-health she died there on 10 January 1855.

Miss Mitford saw herself and her household as occupying 'a sort of middle station between the gentry ... and the country people, almost our equals in fortune' (ATH, 283). It is important to be clear about her social status – and that of her readers – since a misapprehension on the subject can easily inhibit our appreciation of the aims and assumptions behind her work. The evidence, moreover, is by no means straightforward. Occasionally the memory of her family traditions leads her to overestimate her actual position. Thus, when she describes herself as 'a country lady who lives almost literally in the open air, in green fields or flowery gardens' (MLL, I, 375), it is only too easy to imagine her enjoying the carefree leisure traditionally associated with the rural life of the upper classes. On the other hand, when she calls attention to the smallness of her home at Three Mile Cross, we need to bear in mind the implied contrast with Bertram House. Differing reports give the number of bedrooms in the cottage as between four and six (which casts doubt on Henry Chorley's account of the 'labourer's cottage'), while the number of servants, though modest by aristocratic standards, indicates a position well above the poverty line.

This middle position was advantageous when she came to present her 'Sketches of Rural Character,' to quote part of the secondary title for Our Village. She was able to move out with comparative ease towards both extremes of rural society, for she was accepted with equal readiness in the big house and the humble cottage. Her readership, too, belonged for the most part to the middle class. It was an audience which shared the attitudes, interests, and standards of the writer, and one which consequently allowed her to achieve the intimacy of tone that is so intrinsic and successful a feature of her work. It was an audience, then, in which she could confide – and she certainly needed an outlet beyond her own family and the society of Three Mile Cross; conversely, she was a writer for whom the individual reader could react with particular affection and warmth, since her sketches read not as literary essays but as personal letters. No subsequent rural writer was to enjoy so trustworthy and appreciative a public.

Though her original publication in the *Lady's Magazine* suggests a primarily female audience, it was by no means exclusively so, and her village sketches reached a wide range of classes and age groups. It is probable, indeed, that Miss Mitford attracted a kind of readership similar to, and often overlapping with, that of Jane Austen. Miss Mitford never attains, of course, to the intellectual and artistic subtlety of the novelist; she was content in her prose with what may be described, without implying too patronizing a stance, as 'pure' entertainment. Nor am I suggesting that Miss Mitford had either the ability or the inclination to rival Jane Austen's undermining satire; but her gentler approach, combining generosity and tolerance with a firm awareness of individual quirks and failings, invites a response far removed from the sentimental or parochial. We should not imagine her in any way cut off from social and intellectual contacts. Though a spinster, she was no solitary. Three Mile Cross may have been a secluded backwater, but its position on a turnpike road meant that it was readily accessible. Miss Mitford herself made frequent visits to London, and her letters and autobiographical writings show that she knew many if not most of the literary, artistic, and fashionable people of her day. It is worth remembering that her contemporary admirers included Wordsworth, Ruskin, Landor, and Elizabeth Barrett Browning.

She is, in fact, a far more complex figure than is usually recognized. We must remember that, although her twentieth-century reputation rests largely – and, I think, properly – on *Our Village*, she was known in her own time as much for her poetic tragedies as for her prose. Her ability to move easily and without apparent strain between Three Mile Cross and the sophisticated theatrical life of London is remarkable. Not only does this show the resilience of her own character, but it also suggests that the rural writer was not nearly as isolated in this period as he was later to become. It is pointless to try to categorize Mary Mitford as either townsman or countryman, and she is certainly less conscious of the separation of urban and rural than Cobbett. Though 'born and bred in the country,'[8] she is, with the exception of Izaak Walton, the least countrified of the writers to be considered in this book. Neither by temperament nor by attitude is she confined to the rural context. Her education provided her with an entrée into urban culture, and we feel that, under slightly different circumstances, she would have been equally successful – and equally happy – living in the city. Indeed she admits at one point: 'I am something of a Cockney in my tastes, in spite of my rural habits. I like no other great town, but I like London and all that comes from it' (*MLL*, I, 354). Moreover she is (if only by necessity) a decidedly professional writer. Of all the contributors to the rural tradition, only Miss Mitford could have written her memoirs as recollections of a *literary* life.

After the publication of her first volume of poems Miss Mitford became known by the newspapers as 'the poetess of Nature' (see *MLL*, I, 126), and, despite her lack of sympathy for Wordsworth's work, she certainly shares much of the Wordsworthian feeling for nature that was characteristic of her time. Her writings offer the same kind of nature solace. 'The grass beneath our feet,' she writes, 'the trees above our heads, the birds that flutter around us, all tend invisibly to soothe and cheer' (LMM, II, 164). Similar effects can be experienced, albeit at second-hand, through the invigorating quality of her rural sketches. Thus Ruskin claimed to receive from a reading of *Atherton* 'the same kind of refreshment which I do from lying on the grass in spring.'[9] Ideally, however, her writings are intended as advocates rather than substitutes for the rural life, which she continually presents as both civilizing and uplifting: 'To live in the country is, to my mind, to bring the poetry of Nature home to the eyes and heart' (MLL, II, 248).

None the less, though her love for the countryside was unbounded, her knowledge of natural things was unremarkable. Her father is presented in *Our Village* as 'a dabbler in natural history' and the keeper of a 'Naturalist's Calendar' (OV, I, 204, 205), and from him she must have derived a general interest in wild life. But just as Wordsworth's knowledge of the natural world was superficial compared with that of John Clare, so Miss Mitford's compares unfavourably with that of Gilbert White, and she certainly has no claim to be considered even in the same category as Jefferies or Hudson. This may be partly a matter of physical disability; in a letter to Sir William Elford she admits: 'I am no naturalist – not for lack of inclination, but from a real want of physical powers; for though I have, to be sure, two ears and two eyes like other people, so miserably defective are these organs, that neither of them would serve me to distinguish a tomtit from a robin-redbreast' (MLL, I, 148). This may explain W.H. Hudson's acute comment on *Our Village* that 'it is about the country, and she has so little observation that it might have been written in a town, out of a book, away from nature's sights and sounds.'[10]

But the real reason lies deeper than this. It is revealed more clearly in an earlier letter to Elford: 'You are quite right in believing my fondness for rural scenery to be sincere, and yet one is apt to fall into the prevailing cant upon these subjects ... There is no trouble or exertion in admiring a beautiful view, listening to a murmuring stream, or reading poetry under the shade of an old oak; and I am afraid that is why I love them so well' (MLL, I, 91). When nature can be enjoyed passively, Miss Mitford is enthusiastic, but she desires no active part in rural labour. Though she proudly claims that in the years around 1830 she was 'the best walker of my years for a dozen miles around' (RLL, 171), she keeps to the lanes and bridle-paths. She fails to pass Leslie Stephen's test for a rural writer – 'Our guide may save us the trouble of stumbling through farmyards and across ploughed fields, but he must have gone through it himself.'[11] Like Stephen, she has no desire to get her feet wet. This is made quite explicit in an early letter to her mother, where she observes that 'the scenery, though extremely beautiful, by no means compensated me for all the mud I was forced to wade through' (*MLL*, I, 41). Similarly, in her description of haymakers in *Our Village*, her role is decidedly that of the spectator. Haymaking can be enjoyed because, of all rural occupations, it is most readily dissociated from the harsher realities of the labouring life: 'One looks on it, pretty picture as it is, without the almost saddening sympathy produced by the slow and painful toil of the harvest field' (*OV*, II, 469). And, a little later: 'I have been used all my life to take a lively interest, and even so much participation as may belong to a mere spectator, in this pleasant labour; for I cannot say that I ever actually handled the fork or the rake' (*OV*, II, 470). One has only to compare this with Jefferies' essay 'One of the New Voters,' in *The Open Air*, to appreciate the difference in outlook and in intensity. Not that Jefferies was an active worker among the toilers of the field – far from it; but his deeper commitment to the rural life enabled him to enter the world of the agricultural labourer, and to communicate it, if not from the inside, at least with the suggestion of inwardness. Where Miss Mitford gives us, in her own words, a 'pretty picture,' Jefferies offers us an actual experience.

Despite all this Miss Mitford is extremely knowledgeable within the confines of her own interest. First among these were flowers – particularly wild flowers; it is clear from numerous passage in *Our Village* and *Recollections of a Literary Life* that she was no mean botanist. She was certainly an accomplished gardener, and although she modestly claims that 'it [is] a pretty proof of the way in which gardeners estimate my love of flowers, that they are constantly calling plants after me' (*MLL*, II, 159), we can reasonably assume that this was as much a tribute to her ability as to her love. None the less, she cannot help admitting: 'I try to like the garden, but my heart is in the fields and woods' (*MLL*, II, 247).

Her countryside, like her natural history, has its limits, but within them she is supreme. Though her attitude towards scenery is characteristically romantic in its enthusiastic sensitivity, she has no desire for the rugged or the sublime. The gentler contours of 'this rich and lovely but monotonous county' of Berkshire (*OV*, I, 61), reminiscent of Cowper's Olney, are completely appropriate to her taste and temperament: 'I have always had a preference for close, shut-in scenes, both in a landscape and in nature, and prefer the end of a woody lane, with a porch, and a vine, and clustered chimneys peeping out among trees, to any prospect I ever saw in my life' (*MLL*, I, 366). *Our Village* offers many such scenes, and received praise on its first publication for its 'convincing air of locality.'[12] Indeed it set a fashion for what Edward Thomas was later to call the literary pilgrim. William and Mary Howitt were early and enthusiastic pioneers of this new taste, and both attest to the peculiar fascination of *Our Village*.[13] Visitors to Three Mile Cross became common in the late 1820s, and the vivid reality of the scenes which Miss Mitford describes seems to have been as much a cause as the congenial atmosphere which she evokes. The reaction of the contemporary reader is well caught by Mrs Hemans in a letter to Miss Mitford: 'There are writers whose works we cannot read without feeling as if we really *had* looked with them upon the scenes they bring before us ... Will you allow me to say that *your* writings have this effect upon me' (*FM*, 125). Miss Mitford's talents are for describing not the unknown, but the familiar that is rarely recognized. Though specific, her scenes are generally representative. One reason, indeed, for the book's continuing popularity is that she finds the quiet, unassuming beauty so often celebrated as characteristic of the whole country in 'this shady and yet sunny Berkshire, where the scenery, without rising into grandeur or breaking into wildness, is so peaceful, so cheerful, so varied, and so thoroughly English' (*OV*, I, 108).

Her chief interest, however, lies not so much in the countryside itself as in the people who inhabit it. Descriptions of deserted nature are rare; her landscapes almost invariably contain figures. And curiously enough, she exhibits a greater range when portraying her countrymen than when describing the country. Although her chief models were 'Nature and Miss Austen' (*MLL*, II, 39), her social range is considerably broader than Jane Austen's famous 'little bit (two inches wide) of ivory,' even if it lacks the breadth of what Chesterton has called 'the long, rolling panorama of *Rural Rides*.'[14] When, after completing *Our Village*, Miss Mitford contemplated novel-writing, she believed that she had an advantage over her mentor: 'I shall be able to go higher and lower than Miss Austen, and to embrace all ranks of English life, as Scott did of Scottish' (*MLL*, II, 161). *Our Village*, unexpectedly perhaps, tends to justify this statement.

In the twentieth century we are less likely to be impressed by this achievement, and may even fail to recognize it. She may seem to idyllicize the poor and be over-impressed by the elegances of the great. But it is worth while remembering that at least one contemporary reviewer had reservations about her 'coarseness of expression' and her tendency to identify too closely with 'uneducated society';[15] moreover at least one of her sketches was rejected by an annual because it was too 'daring' (*FM*, 152). It is true that her extremes are less successful, that her poor seem excessively literate and urbane (they never speak in dialect), and that her rich are rarely more than stereotypes; they are, none the less, adequate for her modest purposes. We can agree, however, that her favourite class – at least, that in which she is most at home – is not so much the middle class as what she calls 'the middling classes, emphatically the *people*' (*MLL*, II, 160), a class deliberately embodied in the character of Stephen Lane, the John-Bullish radical butcher in *Belford Regis*. This is reflected in the modest setting for *Our Village*. It consists of 'a small neighbourhood, not of fine mansions finely peopled, but of cottages and cottage-like houses, ... with inhabitants whose faces are as familiar to us as the flowers in our garden' (*OV*, I, 1). The following passage is typical:

> This rustic dwelling belongs to what used to be called in this part of the country 'a little bargain:' thirty or forty acres, perhaps, of arable land, which the owner and his sons cultivated themselves, whilst the wife and daughters assisted in the husbandry, and eked out the slender earnings by the produce of the dairy, the poultry yard, and the orchard: – an order of cultivation now passing rapidly away, but in which much of the best part of the English character, its industry, its frugality, its sound sense, and its kindness might be found. (*OV*, I, 81–2)

Another idealization of the ever-vanishing yeoman? Perhaps, but the emphasis on a mean between riches and poverty is important. In this respect Miss Mitford looks not so much back to Jane Austen as forward to George Eliot. It was a most important contribution to her time, and Ruskin was later to praise her for just this, for 'finding history enough in the life of the butcher's boy, and romance enough in the story of the miller's daughter.'[16]

In the preface to *Our Village* Miss Mitford takes pains, like so many rural writers, to insist on the accuracy of her presentation of country life:

> The following pages contain an attempt to delineate country scenery and country manners, as they exist in a small village in the south of England. The writer may at least claim the merit of a hearty love of her subject, and of that local and personal familiarity which only a long residence in one neighbourhood could have enabled her to attain. Her descriptions have always been written on the spot, and at the moment, and in nearly every instance with the closest and most resolute fidelity to the place and the people.

On the original publication of the first series, when her friend Sir William Elford queried this accuracy, she was adamant on the point – '"Are the characters and descriptions true?" Yes! Yes! Yes! As true as is well possible' – but she goes on to make a slight but significant qualification: 'You, as a great landscape painter, know that in painting a favourite scene you do a little embellish, and can't help it; you avail yourself of happy incidents of atmosphere, and if anything be ugly, you strike it out, or if anything be wanting, you put it in. But still the picture is a likeness; and ... this is a very faithful one' (*MLL*, II, 26). As her work continues, such qualifications become stronger. Indeed by 1835, when she publishes *Belford Regis*, she appears to have made an almost complete *volte-face*, and begs her readers '*not* to believe one word of these sketches from beginning to end. General truth of delineation I hope there is; but of individual portrait painting, I must seriously assert that none has been intended.'[17] None the less, it is clear that she lays great stress on faithful portraiture and needs the stimulus of actual incidents and living models.

But the question of specific accuracy is less important than that of general truth. How far, we want to know, is the village a just representation of Three Mile Cross or any other village in the decade before the First Reform Act? One almost exact contemporary, John Britton, the topographer who worked his way up from agricultural labourer to respected man of letters, made such a striking challenge to Miss Mitford's claim to 'general truth of delineation' that it must be quoted at some length:

> It is with great regret that I differ from Miss Mitford, the eloquent and fascinating author of 'Our Village,' in her florid description of rural scenery and society in the places wherein she resided for many years ... Aided by a vivid fancy and a graphic pen, that gifted writer had painted cottage-life and cottage-inmates in such glowing colours, and with such pleasing characteristics, as to make her varied pictures full of innocence, cheerfulness, and social happiness. She describes the local scenery as fine and beautiful; the homes of the poor labourers as clean and comfortable; and their domestic manners and morals as devoid of guile and vice ... 'My Village,' however, was so unlike Miss Mitford's, that it might be regarded as belonging to a different part of the world, and occupied by a distinct class of the human race.[18]

Similarly it is difficult to reconcile Miss Mitford's report with John Clare's description of his native Helpston at about the same time, where he claims to have been surrounded with 'partners whose whole study was continual striving how to get beer,' whose standards were reflected by the fact that 'such as had got drunk the oftenest fancied themselves the best fellows.'[19] We may remember that this was also the age of George Crabbe – above all, perhaps, that it was the period painted in such dark colours by J.L. and Barbara Hammond in *The Village Labourer*. With all this contrary evidence we may well be tempted to doubt if 'our village' ever existed outside Miss Mitford's idealizing daydreams.

We have already heard her making the admission, as if as a matter of course, that 'if anything be ugly, you strike it out.' Even the contemporary reviews, we discover, had some doubts on this point, one of them describing the sketches in *Belford Regis* as 'a trifle too sunny and too cheerful to be real,'[20] and William Howitt, whose own descriptions of rural life verge on the enthusiastic, refers to her 'sunshiny pictures of an English village.'[21] As we read through her books, we become more and more aware of corners unexplored and doubts unanswered. Too many of her stories end in a peal of marriage-bells with an implied fairy-tale ending of 'all lived happily ever after'; the historical evidence would often suggest harsher probabilities. Thus if we come to Miss Mitford after a reading of Crabbe, we shall doubtless suspect that the numerous 'unattached' village boys (in the chapter on cricket, for example) are illegitimate, but this is only occasionally hinted as a possibility. She often appears insensitive – and perhaps unaware – of hardships that must have been not uncommon in her immediate vicinity. Complacency is sometimes explicit. 'It is delightful,' she writes in *Belford Regis*, 'to see the gratitude of these poor people' (*BR*, III, 147n), and the adjective is revealing. When poverty is presented at all, it is more often than not 'an industrious and light-hearted poverty' (*OV*, I, 20), and in her description of Joe Kirby we feel that she dismisses the problem with too easy a shrug of her shoulders: 'But why should I lament the poverty that never troubles him? Joe is the merriest and happiest creature that ever lived twelve years in this wicked world' (*OV*, I, 41). But is he?

We may legitimately ask, for instance, if Joe is ever hungry. *Our Village* can be searched in vain for any means of checking Cobbett's statements about the diet of the contemporary labourer. As Britton pointed out, she presents the cottages as 'clean and comfortable,' and it is perhaps noteworthy that her descriptions are almost invariably exteriors. We rarely get a close-up, inside view of a poor cottage, and, even when we do, the focus is generally on the inhabitants, not on the conditions in which they live. Indeed we learn curiously little from Miss Mitford concerning rural economics. Her weakness for ignoring the unpleasant comes quite clearly to the surface in her description of the parish workhouse:

> That is the parish workhouse ... I always hurry past that place as if it were a prison. Restraint, sickness, age, extreme poverty, misery which I have no power to remove or alleviate, – these are the ideas, the feelings, which the sight of those walls excites; yet, perhaps, if not certainly, they contain less of that extreme desolation than the morbid fancy is apt to paint ... There may be worse places than a parish workhouse – and yet I hurry past it.   (*OV*, I, 25)

The desire not to see all that might be seen is transparent here. We suspect a reluctance to think out the implications of what she says to their logical ends. Even when she rejoices that she lives in 'an unenclosed parish' (*OV*, I, 24), we find that this satisfaction is for the most part an aesthetic one, with little concern for the social and economic state of the people. After all this we are not surprised to discover that, while at first impressed by Crabbe's *The Borough*, Miss Mitford later decides that it 'contains too gloomy a picture of the world.'[22] She appears to sum up her basic attitude in the observation that 'despair is not in my nature.'[23]

None the less, it would be unfair to Miss Mitford to 'write her off' as a hopeless sentimentalist intent on viewing the world through rose-coloured spectacles at all costs. Her own life, we know, was by no means easy, and, although W.J. Roberts may be right in describing *Our Village* as 'a deliberate glorification of the simple life which had been forced upon her,'[24] this need not imply a blatant distortion of the facts. At its worst, the case against Mary Mitford is that she occasionally distorts by omission, and even this fault can be exaggerated. We have already seen that, though she may admit to hurrying past the workhouse, she does not omit it entirely; indeed she tends to draw attention to it by the very discomfort with which she views it. The passage occurs in a sketch entitled 'Violeting,' and it is interesting to note that the beauty and delight connected with the violets are deliberately juxtaposed not only with the workhouse but also with an old farmhouse whose 'very walls are crumbling to decay under a careless landlord and ruined tenant' (*OV*, 1, 26). Because she does not burst into a bitter denunciation of 'the system,' we should not assume that she lacks insight into the conditions of her time. The club is not her weapon, but she has others. It seems clear that she is creating a deliberate artistic effect in 'Violeting' by offering these obviously discordant elements in a single sketch and then refraining from direct comment. At all events she certainly does not confine herself to listing 'the common blessings of Nature' (*OV*, 1, 27).

The closer we read her work, the more we shall become aware of the darker side of her rural picture; there are plenty of indications, however lightly touched, that there is shadow as well as sunshine in Three Mile Cross. The period in which she writes is described as 'this declining age, when the circumstances of so many worthy members of the community seem to have "an alacrity in sinking"' (*OV*, 1, 44). The opening sentence of 'A Great Farmhouse,' a sketch in which Miss Mitford takes great care to note that the greatness belongs to the past, runs: 'These are bad times for farmers' (*OV*, 1, 126). The old house at Aberleigh, which gives its name to one of the sketches, is picturesque and romantic, but significantly in ruins, and this is only one of a veritable succession of deserted and decaying mansions. One large farmhouse 'has become a very genteel-looking residence' (*OV*, 1, 250), a fact which would have infuriated, but not surprised, Cobbett; more often, however, we are told of 'ample but disused farm-buildings' (*OV*, 11, 24) or an old manor house that has 'dilapidated into its present condition' (*OV*, 1, 466). One of the most vigorous and effective descriptions occurs in *Country Stories*. Of a farm vacated by 'the absentee tenant of an absentee landlord' she writes:

> Barns half unthatched, tumble-down cart-houses, palings rotting to pieces, and pigsties in ruins, contributed, together with a grand collection of substantial and dingy ricks of fine old hay – that most valuable but most gloomy-looking species of

agricultural property – to the general aspect of desolation by which the place was distinguished.   (*CS*, 27–8)

In such reports we can clearly recognize the physical and moral landscape of *Rural Rides*.

The social relevance of Miss Mitford's work is not confined, however, to passages of straightforward description. The short stories, which, whatever their factual basis, clearly belong to the realm of fiction, similarly suggest that all is not well in rural society. Despite the numerous happy endings we find, when we start counting them, that the number of stories that end in death or disaster is remarkably high. One thinks of 'Tom Cordery,' 'The Chalk Pit,' 'The Vicar's Maid,' 'Jessy Lucas,' to name but a few. Again the fortunes of many of the characters have sociological implications. The village boys who run away to seek their fortune in London are representative of a pattern that is to become even more conspicuous as the nineteenth century advances; similarly Miss 'Gusta Brookes, the well-to-do farmer's daughter in *Belford Regis*, with her expensive tastes and lack of practical skill in the farmhouse, is a living symbol of a significant trend (see *BR*, II, 214). Moreover Miss Mitford is scrupulous in recording the evidence of meaningful rural change. In 'A Parting Glance at Our Village,' the concluding paper in the first series, she lists the changes that have occurred since she began writing. These are few but ominous. They include the knocking-down of a wall by the stage-coach and the macadamizing of the road, of which she comments: 'I do not know what good may ensue' (*OV*, I, 230). With the advantage of hindsight we can appreciate that, in these references to developing means of transportation, Miss Mitford has put her finger upon precisely those changes that will have the most radical effect not only upon her village but upon all villages.

In the later series the results of change – generally for the worse – are seen even more clearly. Three Mile Cross, Miss Mitford tells us, 'had a trick of standing still, or remaining stationary, unchanged and unimproved in this most changeable and improving world' (*OV*, I, 241), but (and the 'buts' get more and more assertive in *Our Village*)

this little hamlet of ours is much nearer to [the local town] than it used to be ... Our ancient neighbour, whose suburbs are sprouting forth in all directions, hath made a particularly strong shoot towards us ... The good town has already pushed the turnpike-gate half a mile nearer to us, and is in a fair way to overleap that boundary and build on, till the buildings join ours, as London has done by Hampstead or Kensington. What a strange figure our rude and rustical habitations would cut ranged by the side of some staring red row of newly-erected houses, each as like the other as two drops of water, with courts before and behind, a row of poplars opposite, and a fine new name! How different we should look in our countless variety of nooks and angles, our gardens and arbours, and lime trees, and pond! But this union of town and country will hardly happen in my time. (*OV*, I, 242–3)

This is, in fact, a remarkable if depressing vision of the future. When W.H. Hudson visited Miss Mitford's countryside at the beginning of this century, he found Three Mile Cross much changed, spoilt by the development of what he calls 'the hated biscuit metropolis' – i.e., Reading or 'Belford.'[25] This suburban mixture of town and country, working to the detriment of both, is the gloomy landscape that Edward Thomas and George Sturt were to describe in Hudson's own time. One feels that Miss Mitford's consolation – that this 'will hardly happen in my time' – is, even for her, a cold comfort. The 'sunny side of Berkshire' (*OV*, II, 317) is not without its threatening shadows.

Despite her apparent avoidance of 'issues,' Miss Mitford succeeds in presenting virtually all the major factors that are changing the rural life of her time. Her attitude towards absentee rural landowners is hardly less contemptuous than Cobbett's:

> The people of the higher classes in this neighbourhood are as mutable as the six-months denizens of Richmond, or Hampstead – mere birds of passage, who 'come like shadows, so depart.' ... All our mansions are let, or to be let. The old manorial Hall, where squire succeeded to squire from generation to generation, is cut down into a villa, or a hunting-lodge, and transferred season after season from tenant to tenant, with as little remorse as if it were a lodging-house at Brighton. The lords of the soil are almost ... universally absentees ... The spirit of migration possesses the land.   (*OV*, I, 253–4)

This is both forthright and acute. In *Belford Regis*, perhaps as a result of the Reform Bill controversy, we find a number of socio-political discussions, including a protest against the enclosure system which, besides lamenting the aesthetic effects, insists that 'an enclosure bill is a positive evil to the poor' (*BR*, III, 273). We gradually come to realize that Mary Mitford's understanding of the basic problems of the countryside is by no means superficial. In *Country Stories* there is even a curt reference to 'that fertile source of crime and misery, the game laws' (*CS*, 42), and a change in the occupancy of one of the large farmhouses allows her to to comment on the changes in agricultural practice in a passage that anticipates Jefferies' *Hodge and His Masters*:

> The quiet respectable old couple, who had resided there for half a century, had erected the mossy sun-dial, and planted the great mulberry-tree, having deter-

mined to retire from business, were succeeded by a new tenant from a distant county, the youngest son of a gentleman brought up to agricultural pursuits, whose spirit and activity, his boldness in stocking and cropping, and his scientific management of manures and machinery, formed the strongest possible contrast with the old-world practices of his predecessors.   (*OV*, II, 79)

The survivors of the older period seem more and more out of place. Miss Mitford herself belongs to this group; in her memoirs she refers to herself as 'an anachronism in this locomotive age' (*RLL*, 515), and, although the tone is revealed by its context to be flippant and 'tongue-in-cheek,' it is at the same time deeply felt.

But the most important shadow to be cast over the 'sunny side of Berkshire' was undoubtedly that of the machine riots that reached their climax in 1830, and it is a remarkable fact that, for the most vivid contemporary description of these disturbances, one must turn to the supposedly unalloyed sunshine and sentiment of the pages of *Our Village*. We should not expect Miss Mitford to have the same kind of sympathy for the insurgents as that displayed by Cobbett – and, indeed, it is a healthy and necessary corrective to Cobbett's testimony (see, particularly, *AWC*, 207–10) to read of the anarchy and terror the rioters caused as well as of the causes that motivated them – but this is counterbalanced by the dramatic immediacy which Miss Mitford communicates. Although Three Mile Cross remained, in her own partisan word, 'uncontaminated' (*OV*, II, 319), it was situated 'in the midst of the disturbed districts' (*OV*, II, 186). The first paper of the fifth series (a melodramatic short story entitled 'The Incendiary: A Country Tale') opens with the following remarkable account:

No one that had the misfortune to reside during the last winter in the disturbed districts of the south of England, will ever forget the awful impression of that terrible time. The stilly gatherings of the misguided peasantry amongst the wild hills, partly heath and partly woodland, of which so much of the northern part of Hampshire is composed, – dropping in one by one, and two by two, in the gloom of evening, or the dim twilight of a November morning; or the open and noisy meetings of determined men at noontide in the streets and greens of our Berkshire villages, and even sometimes in the very churchyards, sallying forth in small but resolute numbers to collect money or destroy machinery, and compelling or persuading their fellow-labourers to join them at every farm they visited; or the sudden appearance and disappearance of these large bodies, who sometimes remained together to the amount of several hundred for many days, and sometimes dispersed, one scarcely knew how, in a few hours; their daylight marches on the high road, regular and orderly as those of an army, or their midnight visits to lonely houses, lawless and terrific as the descent of pirates, or the incursions of banditti; – all brought close to us a state of things which we never thought to have witnessed in peaceful and happy England.   (*OV*, II, 318–19)

The obvious sincerity of this is deeply impressive, however much we may question the underlying social position that it represents. It is clear that these few months had a deep, almost traumatic effect on Miss Mitford's general assumptions. She realizes, perhaps for the first time, that her own reports of village life, while doubtless true, do not contain the whole truth. She receives 'letters of condolence and fellow-feeling' from correspondents who, she is acute enough to notice, 'wrote far too well to feel any thing,' and this forces upon her the melancholy reflection: 'How often, not intending to feign, or suspecting myself of feigning, I myself had written such' (*OV*, II, 319). It is typical of Miss Mitford's honesty and integrity that she should admit this at once; it is also consistent with her artistic purpose that she should introduce this new note into the final series of her sketches. What had been only delicate water-colours are now interspersed with strong and disturbing oils. When it would be most tempting to omit the ugly, Miss Mitford does not flinch. As a result, *Our Village* (and, to a lesser extent, the rest of her country writing) can confidently take its place as a significant milestone in the rural tradition.

And, strangely enough, the honest inclusion of this darker view causes us to return to the earlier and happier pictures with a greater tolerance and sympathy. Granted that she may have overemphasized the idyllic circumstances of village life in her time, this does not justify a corresponding overemphasis on the injustices and the suffering. She is certainly selective, but never misleading. Even Cobbett admitted that conditions varied considerably in different parts of the country, and it is, indeed, always a mistake to assume that any single view of rural conditions, however just, is generally applicable or representative. In painting the harsh, bitter landscapes of *Tess of the D'Urbervilles* and *Jude the Obscure* Hardy did not deny the validity of the society he had portrayed in *Under the Greenwood Tree*. Nor, in Miss Mitford's own time, did Wordsworth's pathetic stories of the agricultural poor contradict his general faith in the goodness of the rural life. We need Miss Mitford's presentation of Three Mile Cross to balance the view we derive from Cobbett on the one hand and Crabbe on the other. Elizabeth Barrett Browning described her as 'a sort of prose Crabbe in the sun';[26] a superficial reading of Miss Mitford makes any comparison with Crabbe seem almost perverse, but the foregoing discussion has, I hope, demonstrated the essential justice of this description.

It is time now to emphasize the sun rather than Crabbe. 'The country,' remarks one of the characters in *Atherton*, 'accounts for the spread of all news, false or true. As there are certain districts to which typhus seems indigenous, so gossip springs up spontaneously in the country, – it is indeed its natural product' (*ATH*, 111). Here, as so often, the author is deliberately making a joke against herself, for Mary Mitford is surely the gossip *par excellence*. She is garrulous but never boring. Nothing is too trivial to mention, no one too humble to be ignored. Although her own personality is essential for maintaining the tonal unity of her work, for subject matter she looks outward. With Cobbett the speaker is everything; his observations, anecdotes, interviews are all presented to strengthen his own viewpoint and further his own goals. With Miss Mitford, though her interests and enthusiasms reveal her on every page, it is the scenes and characters that are dominant. In brief, *Rural Rides* leaves us with an unforgettable portrait of Cobbett, *Our Village* with a memorable impression of Three Mile Cross. One can easily understand why Miss Mitford was deluged with inquiries about the developing fortunes of the inhabitants of 'our village,' from the shoe-maker to Lucy the maid, from Ben Kirby to May the greyhound. Her own all-embracing curiosity is infectious. Through the impact of her personality – and, I think, through the vigorous enthusiasm of her prose – we learn to share her attitudes. In W.H. Hudson's words, 'her pleasure in everything makes everything interesting.'[27] A century and half after her time, in a world so different as to be virtually unrecognizable, this is still true. It is no small tribute to her creative strength.

But if Miss Mitford is, to some extent, a busybody, she is also busy in the literal sense. Nowhere, perhaps, in the literature of the countryside is there so much emphasis on movement and bustle. The rural life may produce a peace of spirit, but it is certainly not quiet. Miss Mitford emphasizes its vigorous activity: 'They who talk of the quiet of the country can hardly have been in a great farm-yard, towards sunset on a wintry day, when the teams are come back from the plough and the cattle from the field, and the whole population is gathered together for the purpose of feeding. I would match it for noise and dirt and jostling against Cheapside' (*ATH*, 17–18). And Miss Mitford herself is always on the move. As late as 1853 she claimed to be 'two years ago the most active woman in Berkshire' (*MLL*, II, 332), and it is a statement one is reluctant to challenge. Sketch after sketch of *Our Village* involves movement and action – walks, visits, such rural activities as violeting, wheat-hoeing, haymaking, nutting, even 'Going to the Races.' The individual doings may be trivial, but they are certainly positive. This is reflected in the almost breathless quality of much of Miss Mitford's prose ('Mayflower is out coursing, too, and Lizzy gone to school. Never mind. Up the hill again! Walk we must' (*OV*, I, 17). Later writers like George Sturt will give us detailed and authoritative accounts of country crafts and labours that are utterly beyond her sphere, but for a picture of countrymen at work, moving and doing, hustling and bustling, no one can equal her.

If such claims for the importance of Miss Mitford's achievement seem exaggerated, if it appears incongruous to think of her as a serious artist, this may well be because her work gives the impression of being artless. A paradoxical statement of this kind is unlikely, however, to quell all doubts. Are we not in danger, it may still be asked, of crediting her with subtleties of approach which she would not even have comprehended, let alone have used? Perhaps, though we should guard against the temptation – itself richly ironical in this context – to confuse the writer with a possible persona. The true Mary Mitford is much more complex a figure than the rather scatter-brained 'implied author' of *Our Village*. At this point, however, an example is needed. Here is a representative extract, selected more or less at random, from 'The Visit.' Once more the emphasis is on movement. Miss Mitford and a friend have sent their servant on ahead and are making a short journey in a one-horse cart:

> But we must get on ... We must get on up the hill. Ah! that is precisely what we are not likely to do! This horse, this beautiful and high-bred horse, well fed, and fat and glossy, who stood prancing at our gate like an Arabian, has suddenly turned sulky. He does not indeed stand quite still, but his way of moving is little better – the slowest and most sullen of all walks. Even they who ply the hearse at funerals, sad-looking beasts who totter under black feathers, go faster. It is of no use to admonish him by whip, or rein, or word. The rogue has found out that it is a weak and tender hand that guides him now. Oh, for one pull, one stroke of his old driver the groom! How he would fly! But there is the groom half-a-mile before us, out of ear-shot, clearing the ground at a capital rate, beating us hollow. He has just turned the top of the hill; – and in a moment – aye, *now* he is out of sight, and will undoubtedly so continue till he meets us at the lawn gate. Well! there is no great harm. It is only prolonging the pleasure of enjoying together this charming scenery in this fine weather. If once we make up our minds not to care how slowly our steed goes, not to fret ourselves by vain exertions, it is no matter what his pace may be. There is little doubt of his getting home by sunset, and that will content us.   (*OV*, I, 53)

Our first reaction may well be to underestimate the effectiveness of such writing. The complacent chattiness, the free use of exclamation marks, the emphasis on trivia, can easily blind us to its very real virtues. Above all the prose is remarkable for its immediacy. The reader is drawn into the subject, feels himself actually present ('and in a moment – aye, *now*'). Indeed we are not all that far removed from the supposedly modern and sophisticated technique of the stream-of-consciousness. We do not feel that she is describing something to us but rather that, in some obscure way, we are overhearing her inner thoughts. It is at one and the same time a remarkably vivid portrayal of an actual situation and a dramatic view of an individual mind. The amused good humour, the abrupt shifts of emphasis (from foreground to background, from internal to external), particularly the optimistic readiness to make the best of it in the final sentences – all these bring us closer to the speaker and enable us to partake of the all-embracing mood. The writer of such a passage is by no means unskilled in the art of prose.

In fact, Miss Mitford places a greater importance upon prose than any of her predecessors in the rural tradition, and however aware we may be that the illusion of facility in writing is often the result of intense, painstaking labour, it is still something of a shock (particularly after Cobbett) to discover her accounts of the difficulties of composition. 'Easy writing,' she notes, 'is very rarely easy reading. Remember, that prose requires higher finish than verse. It is more difficult to do' (LMM, 1, 16). And in a letter to Elford she reveals both the hardships of writing and the seriousness with which she approached her task: 'You would laugh if you saw me puzzling over my prose. You have no idea how much difficulty I find in writing anything at all readable. One cause of this is my having been so egregious a letter-writer I have accustomed myself to a certain careless sauciness, a fluent incorrectness, which passed very well with indulgent friends, ... but will not do at all for that tremendous correspondent, the Public' (MLL, 1, 356–7). This statement – an excellent embodiment, incidentally, of the qualities which it describes – is at the same time revealing and puzzling. This may be explained by its date, 1821, before the scheme of Our Village was finally clear in her mind. It offers a perfect capsule description of her literary effect ('a certain careless sauciness, a fluent incorrectness') but implies a distinction between her public writing and her private correspondence which is hardly borne out by the evidence.

In fact, one of the chief qualities of Miss Mitford's prose style is its colloquial directness, the ease with which it reproduces the casual rhythms of an individual speaking voice. As early as 1812, at which time she had published only her early verses, Elford complimented her on her letter-writing, asserting: 'I would a thousand times rather see what falls from your pen naturally and spontaneously (that is, in a letter) than the most polished and beautiful composition that ever went to the press' (FM, 66). Apparently Miss Mitford took some time to appreciate the possible implications of this statement, though Our Village is itself testimony that the lesson was eventually well learnt. One of her correspondents, Mrs Franklin, writing about the first series of sketches in 1824, remarks on 'the exact accordance between your printed and epistolary style' (FM, 110). That she devoted more care to her professional writings is both obvious and proper, but in them the virtues of her informal letters are fortunately preserved.

Miss Mitford is, indeed, a connoisseur of the art of letter-writing. We find her speaking authoritatively about the letters of Walpole, Gray, and Cowper, remarking of the last that his letters 'would have immortalized him had "The Task" never been written' (MLL, I, 121). Her generalizations on the subject are often profoundly applicable to her own letters. 'Letters,' she writes, 'should assimilate to the higher style of conversation, without the snip-snap of fashionable dialogue, and with more of the transcripts of natural feeling than the usage of good society would authorize' (MLL, I, 122). In her own case, however, a matter of decorum is involved. The naturalness of such discourse (be it real or assumed) is peculiarly appropriate to her homely subject matter. It seems inevitable to use natural imagery in characterizing them. Thus W.H. Hudson, who appears to have preferred her letters to her more ambitious work, speaks of 'the little friendly letters which came from her pen like balls of silvery down from a sun-ripened plant, and were wafted far and wide over the land to those she loved. There is a wonderful charm about them; they are so spontaneous, so natural.'[28] And towards the end of her life she came to realize the connection herself. Writing to Digby Starkey in 1852, she observes: 'I never could understand what people found to like in my letters, unless it be that they sprang direct from the soil, that they have a root to them – the sort of quality that makes one sometimes prefer a wild plant alive and growing in its woodland nook to a fine cut flower in a rich vase' (FM, 366).

But what is perhaps Mary Mitford's most endearing literary trait has not yet been mentioned. When James Agate wrote his eulogy of her, he was contributing to a collection of essays entitled *English Wits*, and, although this is the last place one would look for any discussion of a rural writer, she undoubtedly justifies her inclusion there. Hers is not the sharp, piercing wit of a Sydney Smith or an Oscar Wilde, but its epigrammatic quality – her ability to find legitimate likenesses in the most unexpected objects – makes up in tautness for what it lacks in piquancy. We find it sometimes in a single phrase– 'that windmill of a walk' (OV, I, 18), 'this boiled lobster of a house' (OV, I, 58) – or in a brilliantly apt descriptive clause – 'ladies cased inwardly and outwardly in Addison and whalebone' (OV, I, 118), 'my grandfather, faithful to his wives, but not to their memories' (OV, I, 220). As with all wits, each individual reader will collect his own favourite examples. The following illustrate something of her variety: 'The white nuisance of snow ... subsided into the brown nuisance of mud' (OV, II, 134); 'the baker ... eminent for his loaves, which are crusty, and his temper, which is not' (OV, II, 136); 'she was as unfit as a two-year-old cabbage' (OV, I, 504). Miss Mitford's continual reference to Jane Austen as a literary model may now seem, if still over-ambitious, at least less inappropriate. The connection is not so much in their presentation of country manners as in shrewd understanding linked with verbal dexterity. Of course, Miss Mitford is, compared with Jane Austen, a decidedly minor figure, but she deserves a place not only in the rural tradition but in English literature as a whole. Certainly no judgment of her writing is adequate if it fails to take her wit into account.

W.H. Hudson's tribute to her in *Afoot in England* provides an excellent summing-up, since he makes no attempt to overlook her literary weaknesses. He criticizes her characters, her dialogue, and the artificial quality of her romantic invention. For most writers all this might appear damning, but in Miss Mitford's case there are compensations. As Hudson admits, 'one might go on poking it all to pieces like a dandelion blossom. Nevertheless it endures, outliving scores of in a way better books on the same themes, because her own delightful personality manifests itself and shines in all these little pictures.'[29] This is a defence that has a familiar ring. Walton, White, and Cobbett have all been defended in much the same terms, for the individual personality that imposes unity on otherwise recalcitrant subject matter. The important factor, however, is the appropriateness of this personality for the particular aspects of rural life to be conveyed. Walton's patient resignation, White's constant but unimpassioned curiosity, Cobbett's earthy vitality are all profoundly suitable to their subjects. And, similarly, Mary Mitford's combination of garrulous enthusiasm with gentle wit and a sincere interest in all the inhabitants of her village provides the perfect tone for communicating the humble chronicles of Three Mile Cross.

SIX

George Borrow

1803–81

I am never happier than when keeping my own company.[1]

Lavengro and *The Romany Rye*, though published in the age of Dickens, belong historically to the age of Cobbett. While Mary Mitford was recording the peaceful, unhurried life at Three Mile Cross, while Cobbett was collecting his evidence for agricultural depression in *Rural Rides*, George Borrow was tramping the roads, living rough in dingles, and associating with gypsies, prize-fighters, road-girls, and tinkers. This fact has been obscured by the passage of time between Borrow's early wanderings and the publication of his imaginative recreations of them in the 1850s. It is important, however, that his record should be set in its proper historical context. There is no better way of demonstrating the variety existing in rural England at a particular moment in time than to show how these three writers, following the guides of their own interests and personalities, produced works which, though legitimately representing the societies in which they lived, offer surprisingly few grounds for comparison. Seton Dearden has pointed out that, if we can trust his own chronology, Borrow visited Old Sarum within a few months of Cobbett,[2] yet their accounts have little or nothing in common. Again it is difficult to connect the gypsies who make occasional appearances in *Our Village* with the tribe of Mrs Herne and Jasper Petulengro.

Borrow's world is less familiar than those of Cobbett or Miss Mitford; it is also, I suspect, a considerably more complex creation, though this may not be apparent at first sight. Historically this complexity stems from the strange combination of qualities derived, according to our unsatisfying but convenient categories, from the Augustan and romantic periods. In Cobbett we feel the eighteenth-century mode of no-nonsense realism to be dominant; in Mary Mitford a disciplined sense is blended with a no less disciplined sensibility. In the case of Borrow, however, the cult of the romantic hero, with all its accompanying trappings of mystery and rebellion, is yoked to a subject matter and an attitude of mind that smack strongly of the rougher world of the eighteenth century. The result, at least on a first reading, is highly incongruous, though I hope to demonstrate in the course of this chapter that it is a deliberate effect on Borrow's part which, if we are prepared to judge according to his own standards, will be found thoroughly successful.

Initially the rural England of Borrow will seem very limited, as if its main virtue were the negative one of not being a bustling city. As the name-character comments in *Lavengro*: 'The Great City does not agree with me. Should I be so fortunate as to earn some money, I would leave the Big City, and take to the woods and fields' (*LAV*, II, 40). Yet when he eventually acts upon his resolution, we hear surprisingly little, either from him or from his creator, about the world of nature, and this has led some commentators to underestimate Borrow's concern for the external scene. Edward Thomas, for example, has described *Lavengro* as 'pure inward Borrow,' as a book which 'does not depend on anything outside itself, but creates its own atmosphere and dwells on it without admitting that of the outer world,' and he goes on to observe that 'his England is strange, I think, because it is presented according to a purely spiritual geography.'[3] This, however, is only part of the truth. It responds to the romance but not to the balancing realism in Borrow's work. On the one hand, we are tempted to agree with Thomas's later statement that 'it would be difficult for one describing a journey to give a less realistic account of the country, the roads, and the conditions of travel.'[4] On the other hand, we recall scenes and incidents which leave an impression of immediacy upon the memory that no other rural writer (least of all, Thomas himself) can equal.

It seems that Borrow was not, at least in his early years, a great admirer of landscape for its own sake. He may exclaim rhetorically about the beauty of England, but he rarely presents it. Though he claims on a number of occasions to have responded to the loveliness of nature – 'from my earliest recollection, sunshine and the song of birds have been dear to me' (*LAV*, I, 254) – there are few details provided. A passage of formal landscape description in Borrow will generally be found to have an ulterior purpose, as in the description of alpine scenery in the first chapter of *Lavengro* (praised by J.H. Shorthouse as reminiscent of Ruskin[5]) which turns out to be an emblem illustrating the differences in character between Lavengro and his brother. When Borrow does single out the details of a landscape for comment, they will usually be those features that are generally ignored. As his friend Egmont Hake remarks, 'his enthusiasm for nature was peculiar; he could draw more poetry from a wide-spreading marsh with its struggling rushes than from the most beautiful scenery, and would stand and look at it with rapture.'[6] As always, he is attracted by the unfamiliar and the neglected.

The reasons for Borrow's preferences will be found not only in the obstinacy of his character but also in the historical influences under which he wrote. Contemptuous of cant and humbug as he was, Borrow would naturally be reluctant to show his feelings on subjects that had been praised to the point of exhaustion by his immediate literary predecessors in the romantic period. Enthusiasm for nature, as he shows in the wickedly iconoclastic twenty-second chapter of *The Romany Rye* about Wordsworth, can be so boring as to be soporific. Yet this is no proof of any lack of response on Borrow's part. We may even suspect that his love of the countryside was genuinely too deep for words. He would certainly have appreciated a story Theodore Watts-Dunton tells of accompanying a 'Romany chi,' Sinfi Lovell, up Snowdon. Since she offered no comment on the view from the summit, he accused her of not enjoying it. '"Don't injiy it, don't I?" said she, removing her pipe. "*You* injiy talking about it, *I* injiy lettin' it soak in."'[7] Borrow's appreciation is similarly unostentatious. R.A.J. Walling has written well of *Lavengro*: 'It stirs the deepest emotion of those who have the sub-conscious love of Nature – the instinct for nature which manifests itself not in petty eulogies of the fine things of the world, but in silent, ecstatic content with Earth.'[8] Here, as in so many aspects of his work, we find Borrow linked with the preromantic tradition. The backgrounds in *Lavengro* and *The Romany Rye*, like those in Fielding's novels, are for the most part taken for granted.

There is a similar lack of detail concerning the flora and fauna of the countryside. Borrow was clearly no naturalist. Horses and snakes excepted, he shows little interest in the non-human world; as Brian Vesey-Fitzgerald (himself a distinguished naturalist) has noted, 'You can read all his books, and you will find scarcely a mention of a bird or a butterfly or a flower or a mammal.'[9] The fact is that, for Borrow, man is always primary. He seems to be consciously paraphrasing Pope when he announces in *The Bible in Spain* that 'my favourite, I might say my only study, is man' (*BS*, I, 70). Landscapes and the non-human world are relevant only as settings for human action. When present they should either be dramatic – like the violent thunderstorm on Mousehold Heath or the story of the King of the Vipers – or decorously inconspicuous. He has little patience for the charming or (until *Wild Wales*) for the picturesque.

Although little or nothing about wild life is to be learnt from Borrow's pages, when he turns his attention to the gypsies he displays all the qualities of a field naturalist. Like the birds in Gilbert White or W.H. Hudson, the gypsies are observed lovingly and faithfully in their natural surroundings. It is obvious that the gypsy race exerted an acute fascination upon him throughout his life. As he writes in his introduction to *The Zincali*, 'I can remember no period when the mentioning of the name of Gypsy did not awaken feelings within my mind hard to be described' (*BZ*, 1). Gypsies, in fact, bring out all his latent romanticism. They are free, independent spirits wandering about the countryside, ignoring formal ties or stuffy conventions. They reject all that Borrow hates in the Victorian world, obstinately maintaining the traditions of an older 'merrie England.' The mystery of their origins and the antiquity of their language fascinate him, but he does not allow his enthusiasm to betray him into either whitewashing or idealization. There is no sentimentality about Borrow's gypsy portraits. As we might expect, they are intensely vital, but he makes no effort to disguise their failings. Though he insists that the gypsies have their own ethical and moral standards, they are frequently associated with such dubious practices as counterfeiting and 'drabbing baulor' (poisoning pigs). They strike hard bargains as horse-traders, hit hard in the prize-ring, and are given to lying. But the great merit of Borrow's presentation is that they are always credible. From an academic viewpoint Borrow is decidedly imperfect as an authority on the gypsies and their language, but his enthusiastic honesty more than compensates for his lack of expertise, and even Francis Hindes Groome, who was infinitely his superior in Romany lore, praises him for communicating 'a subtle insight into gypsydom.'[10] In this Borrow is supreme. His impressionistic presentation of the gypsies resembles his impressionistic portrait of himself – and is equally effective.

It would be a mistake, however, to assume that his outdoor interests were confined to the life of the gypsies. Indeed, as Arthur Rickett has stressed, he 'can delight in the garrulous talk of a country inn, understand the magic of big solitudes, ... appraise the points of a horse and feel the impalpable glamour of an old ruin.'[11] This is both true and important. It draws attention once more to Borrow's strange blend of romanticism and realism, his curious combination of the mysterious and the earthy. Where Cobbett was interested in hard facts, and Miss Mitford intent, like Wordsworth, on the attractions of the commonplace, Borrow seeks out the neglected and the unusual. Although Lavengro leaves London to get away from Londoners, he certainly makes no attempt to get away from people. Indeed Borrow's books might well be described as anthologies of interviews; they leave the impression, like some of Dickens's novels, of a motley array of eccentrics and oddities who threaten at times to break the narrative thread of the story. Just as he makes a point of neglecting the details that most writers give, so Borrow delights in including incidents and characters that are usually omitted. As early as 1841, when *The Bible in Spain* was being written, his friend Richard Ford offered Borrow the following constructive suggestions: 'My advice again and again is to avoid all fine writing, all descriptions of mere scenery and trivial events. What the world wants are racy, genuine scenes, and the more out of the way the better.'[12] In contrast to his reactions to most other pieces of gratuitous advice, Borrow seems to have taken this very much to heart – probably because it coincided with his own taste. Its effect, I suggest, is to be found not only in *The Bible in Spain* but in most of his subsequent work. As a result, he seeks out the byways and unexplored paths, the deserted dingles, and all the nooks and crannies 'off the beaten track,' and it is in such places that he finds the human waifs and strays, the innocents and the law-breakers, the eccentrics and the knaves, the oppressors and the oppressed, who appear, in suitably heightened form, in his writings.

Moreover his passionate hatred of 'gentility' leads him, in an increasingly bourgeois world, to choose his human subjects from those who are either above or below the conventionally respectable. The Armenian merchant, the man with the 'touch,' the student of Chinese poetry, the cultured Hungarian are, by virtue of their wealth and leisure, above the common standard – as is Lavengro himself on account of his unusual knowledge of languages. Murtagh, the apple-woman, the jockey, and above all the gypsies inhabit a world beyond the pale of 'polite society' and are praised for the bluff, masculine qualities lacking in the decadent genteel. (And, as Martin Armstrong has pointed out, Borrow gives himself the best of both worlds in his role as Romany Rye; he is both gypsy – outcast – and gentleman.[13]) Similarly the memorable scenes in Borrow are either intensely 'romantic' and elevated, like the 'wind on the heath' passage and the visit to Stonehenge, or blatantly 'low,' like the descriptions of prize-fighting and the doings of the gypsies.

As I have already touched on Borrow's hatred of 'gentility,' it is essential at this point to distinguish his concept of 'the gentleman.' The two similar words mean, for Borrow, two very different things. This is a subject that has frequently confused both readers and critics of Borrow, though the distinction should be easier to understand in the present context, since Borrow is nowhere closer to 'fierce old Cobbett' (*LAV*, 1, 278) than on this vexed topic. It would be fair to state that, while never confusing the two in his mind, Borrow was careless in his verbal discrimination. To all intents and purposes, 'gentleman' is a term applied to a natural aristocracy of talent and intelligence, though it may also refer to the traditional, uncorrupted rural squirearchy. 'Gentility,' on the other hand, is an opprobrious term reserved for the commercial *nouveaux riches* and Cobbett's tax-eaters. The distinction is not, of course, an uncommon one in Victorian literature, and it creates some interesting links between Borrow and writers with whom one might not otherwise have associated him. He is, no less than Tennyson, a champion of

The grand old name of gentleman
Defamed by every charlatan,
And soil'd with all ignoble use,[14]

while his contempt for false gentility is as relentless as that of Dickens in *Great Expectations*. Borrow's protest, however, is specifically focused on the situation in the countryside. His main contempt for 'Gentility Nonsense' stems from the fact that its upholders have, in his view, 'contributed enormously to corrupt the rural innocence of England' (*RYE*, II, 225).

By 'rural innocence' he is making no sentimental reference to an idealized golden age. Though he can occasionally be betrayed into an excessively rhetorical flourish, as when, in *Lavengro*, he refers to 'a bygone time, when loyalty was in vogue, and smiling content lay like a sunbeam on the land' (*LAV*, I, 35), his general stance is conspicuously different from most nostalgia for the past since he looks back, not to a more peaceful world, but to a rougher one. The 'sickly odours' of gentility are contrasted with 'the wholesome smell of the stable with which many of these pages are redolent' (*RYE*, I, 238). Borrow's defence of prize-fighting, like Cobbett's crusade for single-stick and other 'manly sports,' is at one with his longing for a less sophisticated world that was harsher, tougher, yet in Borrow's view more straightforward and honest. Above all it was free from 'unmanly cant' (*RYE*, II, 267), as he insists in the notorious appendix to *The Romany Rye*: 'The use of the fist is almost lost in England. Yet are the people better than they were when they knew how to use their fists? The writer believes not ... Is polite taste better than when it could bear the details of a fight? The writer believes not' (*RYE*, II, 274). Borrow's ideal gentleman has a well-developed sense of honour and integrity – and packs a strong right-hook.

Borrow offers, in fact, for the first time in serious rural writing, a tramp's-eye view of the English countryside. Cobbett had toured England on horseback, but Borrow, with a few exceptions (particularly in *The Romany Rye*), prefers to go on foot. Blessed, as he puts it in *Wild Wales*, with 'the health of an elephant' (*WW*, I, 378), he is never happier than when out of doors. One of his Cornish acquaintances reports of his visit to Cornwall that 'he almost lived in the open air, though it was in the depth of a bitter winter.'[25] He is described at the age of sixty by another acquaintance as 'a tireless walker, with extraordinary powers of endurance.'[16] Like the gypsies who fascinate him, he is essentially nomadic – a wanderer. 'The like of us,' says Jasper Petulengro, 'don't find it exactly wholesome to stay in towns; we keep abroad' (*LAV*, I, 167), and the same applies to Lavengro – and, by implication, to Borrow himself. Lavengro's year in London was constricting and tedious not only because of his wretched life as a hack-writer but because his movements were circumscribed.

He felt shut in, imprisoned. Consequently, as soon as he has earned money by writing *Joseph Sell*, he resolves: 'I would go forth into the country, travelling on foot, and, by exercise and inhaling pure air, endeavour to recover my health' (*LAV*, II, 57). This statement should not be interpreted as just another expression of the 'escape into Nature'; Lavengro becomes, not a nature lover, but a tramp. He may meditate philosophically in the loneliness of Mumper's Dingle, but only after a day of intense physical exertion. He goes out in search of health, not peace. Indeed he embarks in quest of adventures like an Arthurian knight from Camelot. That he goes on foot or with a tinker's pony-and-trap may make the comparison superficially absurd, but this should not disguise the fact that the impulse is essentially the same. His 'rescue' of Isopel Berners from the Flaming Tinman, albeit at an ironic remove, belongs to the same archetype. His adventures involve not knights and dragons but gypsies and eccentrics, and through them all we can feel the breath of an authentic rural tradition. To Eileen Bigland Borrow is 'the Ulysses of the Nineteenth Centrury,'[17] but it might be even more appropriate to see him as a Galahad of low life, a rustic Don Quixote.

Borrow's somewhat unusual interests led, as we might expect, to a varied reaction to his work on the part of the Victorian reading public. *The Bible in Spain* (1843) was a tremendous success. The fact that Borrow had gone to Spain as a servant of the Bible Society cast an air of respectability over his exotic adventures. It is true that he associated with some very strange characters, but he was, after all, converting the heathen, so that his mingling with outcasts and disreputables could be regarded as meritorious. Moreover, as several commentators have noted, a book with such a pious (in fact, misleading) title might legitimately be perused on the Sabbath, and the exciting adventures that it contained, resembling picaresque fiction rather than the usual Sunday fare, were hallowed since they were undertaken for the greater glory of God. Although at least one Victorian who had met Borrow, William Mackay, suspected that the book was 'chiefly lies,'[18] the possibility of Borrow's romancing on a sacred topic would never have crossed the minds of his more pious readers.

But *Lavengro* was a different matter. Here the talk was more about gypsies than about Jesus; there was more pugilism than preaching. Despite Borrow's own statements, however, it is not true that *Lavengro* and *The Romany Rye* were unanimously rejected by critics and public alike.[19] This is all part of Borrow's portrait of himself as neglected genius. In fact, many who had fallen under his earlier spell were still open to his influence. The world of gypsies, grooms, and horse-traders had its attractions for those who found the Victorian atmosphere claustrophobic – particularly in view of the fact that it was a world little known and fast disappearing. Thus a writer in the *Saturday Review* praised *The Romany Rye* because 'it is a pleasant thing to find a man who, in these days of railways and enclosures, can still tell us stories about the old heaths where highwaymen often robbed and were sometimes gibbeted, ... where gypsies talk about stealing poultry and poisoning pigs.'[20] On the other hand, many were shocked by Borrow's preoccupation with the 'low.' *Lavengro* was published in the year of the Great Exhibition, and its reminder of the rough world of the past seemed both inappropriate and in doubtful taste. The wind on the heath was not blowing in the direction of progress.

But the controversy over Borrow's writings was not confined to his subject matter. His love for the strange and the fantastic, his violent juxtapositions of the mysterious and the prosaic, led many (not without cause) to express doubts concerning his truthfulness. And it was an age, as Robert R. Meyers has observed, where 'the question, Is it Truth or is it merely Fiction? came with great moral significance.'[21] In reviewing *Lavengro* for *Fraser's Magazine*, William Stirling summed up the puzzlement of many a contemporary reader: 'The story of *Lavengro* will content no one. It is for ever hovering between Romance and Reality, and the whole tone of the narrative inspires a profound distrust.'[22] The Victorians wanted their fiction and autobiography in separate compartments; any mixture was irksome and seemed dishonest. There were few precedents for any mingling, and no criteria with which to judge it. Borrow never really understood that the air of mystery and puzzlement that delighted him could be a source of irritation for others. Whitwell Elwin tried to explain this to him in a letter of 1852:

> You must remember that the bulk of readers have no personal acquaintance with you, or the characters you describe. The consequence is that they fancy there is an immensity of romance mixed up with the facts, and they are irritated by the inability to distinguish between them. I am confident, from all I have heard, that this was the source of the comparatively cold reception of *Lavengro*. I should have partaken the feeling myself if I had not the means of testing the fidelity of many portions of the book, from which I inferred the equal fidelity of the rest.[23]

This is a sincere and valid digest of the Victorian reaction, though we can imagine Borrow smiling over Elwin's naivety. But even to Murray, Borrow's long-suffering publisher, the mixture of fact and fiction was clearly a 'defect,' and he requested Borrow to 'dissolve the mystery'[24] – only to be answered by the even greater mystification of *The Romany Rye*.

Half a century later, however, we find D.H. Lawrence praising Borrow for the very quality that the Victorians had mistrusted. Jessie Chambers reports: 'Lawrence greatly admired George Borrow ... He said that Borrow had mingled autobiography and fiction so inextricably in *Lavengro* that the most astute critics could not be sure where the one ended and the other began.'[25] Certainly an age that has accustomed itself to the artistic moulding of personal experience in *Sons and Lovers* and *A Portrait of the Artist as a Young Man* should have no difficulty in responding to *Lavengro* and *The Romany Rye*. Classification is still a problem, and the books still tend to elude the traditional categories; as Northrop Frye has pointed out, Everyman's Library lists *Lavengro* under 'fiction,' the World's Classics under 'travel and topography.'[26] But this is a problem for librarians; as literary critics we should now be in a position to approach the essential artistry of George Borrow.

Unfortunately most of the critical attention that Borrow has received has focused not so much on his work as on his biography. This is both understandable and regrettable – understandable because Borrow has deliberately presented Lavengro as a mysterious character with a 'secret' to be solved, regrettable because this approach merely attempts to unpick (or often to cut through) the strands that Borrow has woven together with such skill. In fact, the biography of Borrow is an extremely difficult subject, since in all its most interesting details we are forced to rely upon the clearly untrustworthy evidence of Borrow himself. Most biographies consist in the retelling (with greater or lesser gullibility) of the events described in his books, to which is added an explanation in the terms which most interest the individual writer. For R.A.J. Walling, for example, the key to Borrow lies in his Celtic ancestry, for Seton Dearden in his supposedly abnormal psychology, for Brian Vesey-Fitzgerald in the unproven hypothesis that Borrow was a full-blooded gypsy.

To treat him primarily as countryman may be no less partial, but it has a number of merits. First of all, it provides him with an understandable context that makes him appear less eccentric and isolated. Borrow's interests and attitudes are often very different from Cobbett's, but his rather prickly individualism is clearly similar. His indignant patriotism and somewhat bull-headed loyalty to the Church of England are other qualities to be met with elsewhere in the rural tradition. His fascination with the gypsies, as we have seen, may be explained by his admiration for a life without civilized shackles, self-sufficient, unregulated, free as the wind on the heath itself. In his later life he assumed the role of country gentleman, and he was, according to Watts-Dunton, 'rustic in accent and locution.'[27] To see Borrow in a rural context helps us to realize that, for all his recalcitrance and flamboyant showmanship, he is thoroughly sincere in his basic position. Above all, it avoids the pitfalls of autobiographical speculation – whether Borrow really lived with Isopel Berners, for instance – and enables us to concentrate upon artistic matters. For *Lavengro* and *The Romany Rye* constitute the most creative and elaborate presentation of a countryside and a way of life observed and controlled by a single personality. And that personality is Borrow, not Lavengro.

A literary analysis of *Lavengro* and *The Romany Rye* ought to be able to show how Borrow employs literary means to communicate the vision of his own particular rural England. Essential to such an analysis is the rigorous distinction between author and hero mentioned at the close of the preceding section. Because Borrow's artistry has so often been ignored in the past, this all-important distinction has been similarly blurred. Nothing could be more erroneous, for example, than W.I. Knapp's contention that Borrow 'never created a character.'[28] The hero of *Lavengro* is a brilliant creation – but Knapp unfortunately confused him with his creator. So distant, in fact, is *Lavengro* from conventional autobiography that Richard Ford, who knew Borrow well, wrote: 'I frankly own that I was somewhat disappointed with the very little you told us about *yourself*.'[29] On the other hand, we know that Borrow uses the word 'autobiography' in a very special sense. 'What is autobiography?' he once asked. 'Is it the mere record of the incidents of a man's life? or is it a picture of the man himself – his character, his soul?'[30] No one would deny, of course, that Borrow has used his own experiences – indeed, his deepest experiences – as a basis for the character of his hero, but the relation between Borrow and Lavengro is, in essence, that between Lawrence and Paul Morel or Joyce and Stephen Dedalus, and it should be approached in a similar way.

This does not imply, however, that we must agree wholeheartedly with J.E. Tilford, and treat the two books as novels.[31] Such a classification may be less unsatisfactory than the 'romantic autobiography' label, but it is far from ideal. This extreme underestimates the down-to-earth aspect of Borrow's work stressed by Edward Thomas in his treatment of *The Bible in Spain*: 'It is one of Borrow's triumphs never to let us escape from the spell of actuality into a languid acquiescence in what is "only pretending." The form never becomes a fiction.'[32] The same is true, surely, of *Lavengro* and *The Romany Rye*, which Thomas characterizes elsewhere, whimsically but accurately, as 'fiction with all four legs on the ground of fact but baying at the moon.'[33] To treat them simply as novels is too constraining. We have to agree with Leslie Stephen's observation that the mixture of characters in the books is 'too quaint for fiction,'[34] and also with R.A.J. Walling's to the effect that they contain 'more essential truth than concrete fiction.'[35] The controversy is unlikely to be resolved. If *Lavengro* belongs to fiction, so does *Our Village*; so do Henry Williamson's *The Village Book* and *The Labouring Life*, in which there are similar alterations and distortions of autobiographical experience in the interests of imaginative rather than literal truth. It may be agreed, however, that these works inhabit an as yet unnamed and uncategorized midway point between fiction and non-fiction. (One thinks also of works like Jefferies' *Amaryllis at the Fair*, which, though conventionally classified as a novel, obviously has closer connections with his non-fiction writings like *Round About a Great Estate*; Edward Thomas's *The Happy-Go-Lucky Morgans* is another case in point.) We do not require such books to be true in every detail, but to separate them completely from their foundations in non-fiction would be to deprive them of a great part of their interest and significance. That the literary-critical problems of *Lavengro* and *The Romany Rye* are shared by other writings on the countryside is another good reason for treating Borrow's work within the context of the rural tradition.

'Lavengro,' to quote Jasper Petulengro, 'in the language of the gorgios [non-gypsies] meaneth Word Master' (*LAV*, I, 179); 'Romany Rye' means gypsy gentleman. Although his history bears many similarities to incidents in Borrow's own life, the figure who answers to these names is a deliberately created mask or persona. He is, perhaps, what Borrow would like to have been – which may explain his well-known description of *Lavengro*, in the preface to that book, as 'a dream' (*LAV*, I, vii). All the characters who encounter Lavengro in the course of his adventures recognize the hidden talents which so many failed to recognize in Borrow himself. Thus the Armenian insists: 'You are a singular individual' (*LAV*, II, 5); to the 'touching' man he seems 'to be acquainted with all things strange and singular' (*LAV*, II, 119). Peter Williams and his wife 'suspect that thou art not altogether what thou seemest' (*LAV*, II, 248); even the dairymaid marvels: 'Who would have thought that thou knewest so much?' (*LAV*, II, 251). Such statements – and there are many more – not only help to build up the mysterious character of the hero, but comment indirectly on the relation between author and character, on how we should read and interpret the book.

Borrow has provided us with a number of other clues within the text to facilitate a mature reading. An obvious instance occurs in the early scene when, at school in Ireland, Lavengro admits to giving his fellow-pupils 'extraordinary accounts of my own adventures' (*LAV*, I, 104). We are surely invited to extrapolate and apply the remark to the whole book. Even Lavengro's occupation as tinker, however close to Borrow's autobiographical experience, is a reminder that he may at times tinker with the truth. Other clues can readily be picked up so long as we realize that, in line with the egocentric nature of the persona, relevant remarks made about other characters are legitimately applicable to himself. Thus, when discussing Ellis Wyn's *Visions of the Sleeping Bard* with Peter Williams, Lavengro remarks: 'I do not care for wonders which occur in sleep. ... I prefer real ones; and perhaps, notwithstanding what he says, the man had no visions at all – they are probably of his own invention' (*LAV*, II, 211). Two other examples – from *The Romany Rye* – must suffice. Jasper tells Lavengro: 'We have now and then told you things about us which are not exactly true, simply to make a fool of you, brother' (*RYE*, I, 77–8). And Murtagh tells him: 'The grand thing, Shorsha, is to be able to believe oneself; if ye can do that, it matters very little whether the world believes ye or no' (*RYE*, II,168). If we still persist in taking Borrow at face value, we cannot complain that we have not been warned.

J.E. Tilford believes that Borrow began to write *Lavengro* as an autobiography, but then changed his mind. He offers as an analogy the case of Dickens's 'making notes for an autobiography that ended up as *David Copperfield*.'[36] This seems acceptable so long as we realize that Borrow – again like Dickens – must have made the change before embarking on the opening chapters of the book as we now have it.* The early chapters are, indeed, crucial for an adequate appreciation of Borrow's art. He carefully builds up his portrait of the young Lavengro by means of a series of scenes which introduce romantic-demonic images that associate him almost from birth with an aura of mystery. The first is the 'travelling Jew,' an obvious manifestation of Ahasuerus, who appears in the opening chapter to wonder at the child's unusual qualities and to recognize the lines he had been tracing on the sand as 'holy letters' of occult significance. This episode is followed in the second chapter by Lavengro's handling the viper with impunity, his eating the poisonous berries without fatal results, and his fascination with the great Danish skull in the graveyard. In the third chapter Lavengro encounters the first of a number of 'sacred' books – in this case, *Robinson Crusoe* – which are to provide the chief source of his intellectual stimulus.

These scenes perform a dual function. Structurally they anticipate the main incidents in his later life. The Jew is the first representative of a mysterious race which Lavengro encounters; he is destined to meet many others, including Jasper Petulengro the Gypsy, Murtagh the Celt, the Armenian, and the Hungarian. The holy letters, like the sacred book, associate Lavengro with the mysteries of philology and word-lore. The viper is later to become his totem – he is 'sapengro' or snake-charmer before he qualifies for the title of 'lavengro.' The berries anticipate his attempted poisoning by Mrs Herne and Leonora, while the Danish skull looks forward both to his interest in traditional Danish balladry and to his obsession with death that Jasper Petulengro counters in the well-known scene on Mousehold Heath (chap. xxv). In addition, the 'wandering Jew' is one of the romantic masks with which Borrow likes to associate himself (he was even called 'the wandering Jew of literature' in his own time[37]). And the importance of Defoe and *Robinson Crusoe* is evident throughout the two books: Borrow describes his manuscript as 'a kind of biography in the Robinson Crusoe style';[38] while Defoe's forceful egotism, his use of fictionalized biography, his particular interest in disreputables like Colonel Jacques and the apple-woman's 'Saint' Moll Flanders, his style, and, last but not least, his capacity for splendid lying, all are influences behind Borrow. But the incidents also work symbolically. They set the hero in a romantic context, and we can therefore be confident that the whole book will be told in a romantic

---

* Professor Lucille Herbert, who has worked on Borrow's papers, tells me that the manuscript evidence bears out my argument at this point.

mode. By no means the least important of its romantic features will be a hero with strange secrets and exotic tastes whose unique personality will dominate the story. Or, to take the point one step further, the story itself will be an expression of the central personality of 'Lavengro.'

Lavengro is all things to all men; they invariably see in him characteristics of themselves. To the travelling Jew the baby Lavengro 'has all the look of one of our people's children' (*LAV*, I, 12); to the Armenian he has 'something of the Armenian look' (*LAV*, II, 5). (Similarly in *Wild Wales* Borrow is very proud of being mistaken on a number of occasions for a Welshman.) But, so far as the alert reader is concerned, the resemblance works both ways. The dominance of Lavengro within the two books is even more pronounced than appears at first sight. It is not merely that every character has been 'Borrovized' – that all are forced, in Arthur Rickett's fine phrase, 'through the crucible of his temperament before we see them';[39] Borrow goes even further. As is well known, Lavengro's adventures are interrupted from time to time by stories told, in the manner of Fielding, by various strange individuals whom he meets on his travels. These include the writer cursed with the 'touching' mania, Peter Williams the preacher who believes he has committed the sin against the Holy Ghost, the postillion with his stories of Catholic 'mumbo-jumbo,' and the student of Chinese poetry. Various critics from Theodore Watts-Dunton onwards have noted the resemblance of many of these figures to Borrow himself. Biographically this is of little importance; if we examine the books as artistic documents, however, we soon realize that, in almost every case, these individuals can be seen as projections of the personality of Lavengro. Thus the writer who is perplexed by 'a doubt of the legality of [his] claim to the thoughts, expressions, and situations contained in [his] book' (*LAV*, II, 115) is offering a shrewd comment on the book in which he appears. In this case, indeed, he seems closer to Borrow than to Lavengro for he is in the process of writing his third book, and is worried about its originality and its effect upon his reputation. It is as if, in a Pirandellian fantasy, the character (Lavengro) has been seeking, and has even found, his author.

The other figures are easily interpreted in similar ways. Peter Williams seems to owe at least his name to a real character (a Bible with Williams's name in it was found among Borrow's effects), but the story of a mysterious sin in youth which overwhelms him with depression is obviously complementary to Lavengro's recurring attacks of 'the Horrors,' while his missionary activities recall those of Lavengro's creator. The postillion's story of 'mumbo-jumbo' in Rome provides what one is tempted to call a subjective correlative of Lavengro's (and Borrow's) hatred of cant and humbug, while the Chinese student's finding of peace and satisfaction after mental turmoil through the fascinations of a remote language reflects a similar pattern that Borrow transfers from himself to his hero. Even Jasper Petulengro ('a dark, mysterious personage; all connected with him is a mystery' [*LAV*, I, 451]) is a far more exotic figure than his prototype, Ambrose Smith; with his swarthy complexion, his interest in boxing, and his capacity for lying, he bears more than a superficial resemblance to the person through whose eyes we see him.

The preceding analysis of Borrow's meticulous creation of a character and mouthpiece who will both conceal and reveal, in conjunction with J.E. Tilford's structural examination in 'The Formal Artistry of *Lavengro-Romany Rye*,'[40] will help to explain, I hope, why Borrow was so long in writing these books. What little evidence we have concerning his methods of composition all suggests that he found creation an arduous process. Borrow himself writes in a letter to his publisher: 'The great difficulty ... is to blend all [his scenes and dialogue] into a symmetrical whole.'[41] He goes into greater detail in conversation with Whitwell Elwin, who recalls: 'He told me that his composition cost him a vast amount of labour, that his first draughts were diffuse and crude, and that he wrote his productions several times before he had condensed and polished them to his mind.'[42] In these instances there is no reason to doubt Borrow's word. Only those who refuse to acknowledge his artistry will be surprised at the slowness with which he worked.

One would like to think that it is no longer possible to deny Borrow his true place as a serious artist. So complex and controversial is his work, however, that one cannot be sure. After all, Tilford's articles had been available for some years before Martin Armstrong (who was, to be sure, a more than usually unsympathetic critic of Borrow) complained of Borrow's 'lack of technical equipment' and continued: 'Borrow had no literary standards and principles, no knowledge of the various methods of approach and construction which are a part of the stock-in-trade of most writers of any pretensions.'[43] One can only marvel at the extraordinary wrongheadedness of this judgment. It would be truer to say that Borrow is so dazzled by the technical possibilities of his work that he does not know where to stop. Who can tell, for example, whether the famous appendix to *The Romany Rye* is a genuine afterword or a deliberately placed segment of the total artistic design? Yet our appreciation of the two books must surely be affected, perhaps quite drastically, by the answer we give to this question. And one need not confine this kind of speculation to Borrow's literary work. As I have already suggested, his exaggeration of the hostility of the original reviewers, though partly attributable, no doubt, to his desire for enthusiastic acceptance, is also in part a careful creation of a suitably romantic myth. Even the notorious biographical problem of the so-called 'veiled period' in Borrow's life may, as Watts-Dunton has noted, be a deliberate fabrication for artistic purposes. Borrow's whole reputation for eccentricity contains suggestions of a consciously created image. Whatever the personal and psychological reasons for all this mystification, it is intimately connected with the technical aspects of his artistic gifts. We are now required, indeed, to make a distinction not only between Borrow and Lavengro, but between Borrow and what W.B. Yeats would have called his Mask. For Borrow has created, in addition to a number of remarkable works of literature, the appropriate personality from which they could originate.

In the eightieth chapter of *Lavengro* the hero reaches the border of Wales but, meeting Jasper Petulengro once again, goes no further. 'It is neither fit nor proper,' he tells Peter Williams, 'that I cross into Wales at this time, and in this manner' (*LAV*, II, 257). Lavengro never visited Wales, but thirty years afterwards – in 1854, to be exact – his creator did. Accompanied at least part of the time by his wife and step-daughter, he spent over three months travelling about the country, and the result is *Wild Wales* (1862), an account intended to be the first of a series of explorations of what might be called the extremities of the British Isles. In the first edition of *The Romany Rye* Borrow had ambitiously (and, one presumes, seriously) advertised the following titles as 'in preparation': *Bayr Jairgey and Glion Doo: Wanderings in Search of Manx Literature* and *Penquite and Pentyre; or, The Head of the Forest and the Headland: A Book on Cornwall*. These, together with descriptions of visits to Scotland and Northern Ireland, exist only in the form of rough notes,[44] *Wild Wales* being the sole example of Borrow's own idiosyncratic version of the English travel book. Although closer examination reveals some remarkable similarities to *Lavengro* and *The Romany Rye*, an initial impression of *Wild Wales* is likely to focus on the differences. The Borrow who had once discovered the oddities to be found in familiar English lanes and fields now reverses the pattern and examines the everyday life of what at that time was a little known countryside. The emphasis is no longer on 'a dream' (*LAV*, I, vii), but on a very real landscape.

Wild Wales derives its title from a phrase in a poem by Taliesin, the Welsh bard, and this offers an immediate clue to Borrow's preoccupation. He visits Wales as a literary and philological pilgrim; for him Wales, is, first and foremost, 'the land of the bard' (*WW*, I, 13). As he explains in the opening chapter, he was first attracted to Wales on account of its ancient language and literature. He is probably half-joking but at the same time half-serious when he recounts how he scraped acquaintance with a chambermaid in a Chester inn, 'not, I assure the reader, for the sake of the pretty Welsh eyes which she carried in her head, but for the sake of the pretty Welsh tongue which she carried in her mouth' (*WW*, I, 15). He is eager to study the current state of the Welsh language, to practise it himself in his conversations, and to visit the birthplaces and tombs of the ancient poets.

The result, though far removed from the conventional guide book, is by no means confined to the linguistic or the historical. Like Cobbett, he invariably has a specific purpose for any excursion – 'if one wants to take any particular walk, it is always well to have some business, however trifling, to transact at the end of it' (WW, II, 54) – but, while there must be an ultimate goal, the chief interest, as in his earlier works, lies in the adventures to be met with on the road. Like most rural writers, Borrow insists on making most of his journey on foot – 'I can't observe the country well,' he says, 'without walking through it' (WW, I, 199) – and he generally walks alone. Before embarking on his tour of south Wales, which takes up the last third of the book, he packs his wife and step-daughter off to London, and that is the last we hear of them. From this point onwards Borrow is a solitary wanderer on the open road, an older mellower Lavengro who travels light: 'I bought a small leather satchel with a lock and key, in which I placed a white linen shirt, a pair of worsted stockings, a razor and a prayer-book' (WW, II, 70). Thus prepared, he sets off to discover the real Wales.

In all his Welsh travels he eschews maps, relying on his incredible memory to follow up whatever clues he may find. He is anxious to learn the name of every village, river, or hill that he encounters, making this an excuse to question any traveller he meets on the road or to inquire at any cottage or farmhouse he may pass. He inspects every church or mine to which he can gain admittance, stops at every inn to refresh himself with beer and conversation. Every native who is prepared to answer his questions is fully cross-examined, on his religion, his work, his awareness of Welsh tradition and culture, his superstitions, his attitude to the English, his economic condition. At the same time Borrow gives a clear and often vivid description of the scenery through which he passes, saying little about the flora and fauna, but responding appreciatively to the romantic, the gloomy, and even the picturesque. All in all, Wild Wales offers as wide-ranging an account of the country in the mid-nineteenth century as any that we possess. It may be the work of an idiosyncratic artist, but it is certainly a portrait in depth.

As with Cobbett, however, the author is invariably at the centre of his canvas, and Borrow is still as intent upon portraying himself as upon communicating an impression of Wales. The mask of 'Lavengro' and 'the Romany Rye' is dropped; formally the book seems a return to the manner of The Bible in Spain, but in many respects it is surprisingly similar to its immediate predecessors. Perhaps Borrow was unable to write without a persona of some kind; at any rate we soon come to the conclusion that author and wanderer, though both answering to the name of George Borrow, are by no means identical. The technical and artistic devices of Lavengro and The Romany Rye recur. The picaresque element, the authorial mystification, the eccentric erudition, coincidences, prejudices, absurdities – the same ingredients are offered in a mixture which, if containing less wormwood than before, is still easily recognizable.

The extent to which Borrow has altered and 'improved' his material may be illustrated by noting some of the coincidences that occur in the book. Not knowing where the poet Jonathan Hughes lived, Borrow happens to call at the very house and talks with his grandson (*WW*, I, 73–4). Having read one day in a newspaper that his 'old friend Dr ———' had just died in Suffolk, Borrow gets into conversation a few hours later with a man who turns out to be the dead doctor's nephew (*WW*, II, 20–1). At the beginning of the book Borrow makes the acquaintance of a party of Irish tinkers near Chester (*WW*, I, 27–30); at the end, four months later just outside Newport, he meets one of them again. Here, one suspects, Borrow has moulded his material to provide an incidental though useful framework for his book, but there are a number of different ways in which coincidence is used. That Borrow is well aware of the humorous possibilities can be seen from the following passage. He is impressed by the beauty of a certain scene to the extent that he imagines himself in Paradise: '"I never was in such a lovely spot!" I cried to myself in a perfect rapture. "O, how glad I should be to learn the name of the bridge, standing on which I have had 'heaven open to me,' as my old friends the Spaniards used to say." Scarcely had I said these words ...' (*WW*, I, 381–2) – when two Welshmen appear out of nowhere and provide the necessary information.

This last instance is of particular interest since it raises what is perhaps the central literary-critical problem in *Wild Wales*. Where in *Lavengro* and *The Romany Rye* the relation of the narrative to autobiographical truth is a continual stumbling-block, here the questions that constantly arise are: to what extent is Borrow being humorous? is his self-presentation intended to be taken seriously or not? In this case, however, the questions are necessary and desirable in that they lead us towards, instead of away from, the central artistic issues.

The best example of Borrow's treading the razor's edge between humour and absurdity concerns his expedition to Huw Morris's chair in the twentieth chapter. Borrow is accompanied by his friend John Jones; at a neighbouring cottage they employ a girl (who is joined later by an old lady) to act as guide, and set off together in the pouring rain. 'In a little time we were wet to the skin, and covered with the dirt of birds ... ; on went the girl, sometimes creeping, and trying to keep herself from falling by holding against the young trees; once or twice she fell and we after her, for there was no path' (*WW*, I, 164). Eventually, after various wrong turnings and misadventures ('I pitied the poor girl who led the way and whose fat naked arms were both stung and torn' [*WW*, I, 166]), they arrive at their destination – 'something like a half barrel chair in a garden, a mouldering stone slab forming the seat, and a large slate stone' (*WW*, I, 167) – and the following extraordinary scene is acted out:

Taking off my hat I stood uncovered before the chair, and said in the best Welsh I could command, 'Shade of Huw Morris, supposing your shade haunts the place

which you loved so well when alive – a Saxon, one of the seed of the Coiling
Serpent, has come to this place to pay that respect to true genius, the Dawn Duw,
which he is ever ready to pay. He read the songs of the Nightingale of Ceiriog in
the most distant part of Lloegr, when he was a brown-haired boy, and now that he
is a grey-haired man he is come to say in this place that they frequently made his
eyes overflow with tears of rapture.'

I then sat down on the chair, and commenced repeating verses of Huw Morris.
All which I did in the presence of the stout old lady, the short, buxom and
bare-armed damsel, and of John Jones the Calvinist weaver of Llangollen, all of
whom listened patiently and approvingly, though the rain was pouring down
upon them, and the branches of the trees and the tops of the tall nettles, agitated
by the gusts from the mountain hollows, were beating in their faces, for enthusiasm is never scoffed at by the noble simple-minded, genuine Welsh, whatever treatment it may receive from the coarse-hearted, sensual, selfish
Saxon.   (WW, I, 167–8)

It is unusually difficult to comment on this passage. The scene is realized with
extraordinary vividness, and we could draw attention to the rhetoric and
impressionistic detail that contribute to the overall effect. But what are we to
say of our reactions to the central character? How does Borrow intend us to
regard the scene? How do we in fact regard it? These are difficult questions, but I
suggest that Borrow is aiming at a deliberately ambivalent or even ambiguous
effect, and that our proper response is to accept his joke at our expense – to enjoy
his refusal to reveal the extent of his own seriousness. We certainly cannot
accept it as an unaltered transcript from reality – even Borrow, we feel, never
made an extempore speech in such ringing, balanced periods – and we may well
doubt if the outward response of his audience is at one with their inner
sentiments; but it can hardly be denied that he has achieved an effect that is both
authentic and valuable. Set any more conventional description beside it – even
Edward Thomas's *Beautiful Wales* – and the contrast is decidedly to Borrow's
advantage. Not only do we feel that Borrow's imaginative treatment belongs
indisputably to 'literature'; we also realize that he has caught something of the
genuine Welsh 'spirit of place' which could not have been communicated in any
other way. The weather, the details of landscape, the social contrasts between
Borrow and his Welsh listeners, Huw Morris's chair itself which becomes
symbolic (also ambiguously, since it is 'mouldering' and difficult to find) of
Welsh tradition and the Welsh past – all these elements are fused into a dramatic
and unforgettable scene by the genius not only of Borrow the flamboyant and
eccentric wanderer, but of Borrow the writer who transforms the scattered
elements of experience into an ordered quintessence of art.

Borrow's effects are, of course, cumulative. It is only on a second reading of the opening chapters, for instance, that we become aware of some of the subtleties of Borrow's humour – a humour which in itself depends upon our knowledge of his earlier literary masks. It is, we need to remember, the creator of Lavengro, that proud egocentric word-master and sworn enemy of the respectable bourgeois, who describes himself modestly as 'a bit of a philologist' (WW, I, 10), characterizes his family as 'decent country people' (WW, I, 23), and asserts in the very first paragraph that he is 'anything but a selfish person' (WW, I, 2). It is the former Spanish representative of the Protestant Bible Society and caricaturist of 'the man in black' who is mistaken for the Catholic priest, Father Toban. It is 'Gypsy Borrow' who meets the Romany Captain Bosvile in the wilds of south Wales, and is told of 'a trumpery lil [book] which somebody has written' about Jasper Petulengro (WW, II, 361). If some of Borrow's jokes are at the reader's expense, many, as here, are at his own. One might even go so far as to suspect that Borrow is now able to look back at his earlier romantic mask with irony, in much the same way that the Byron of Don Juan is in a position to make fun of the Byron of Childe Harold. Ultimately we do a serious disservice to Borrow to take him at face-value. In the thirty-ninth chapter, for example, we find him asserting: 'I despise railroads ... and those who travel by them' (WW, I, 347); yet in the second chapter he has himself travelled across England into Wales by train. Are we to accuse Borrow of being inconsistent or forgetful or just incompetent? Or are we to assume that he is perfectly aware of the anomaly and is deliberately trying to amuse, puzzle, or even irritate us? The latter is surely the more sensible course. Once we grant Borrow a sense of humour, Wild Wales becomes more than an eccentric travel-guide and takes on a complexity comparable to that of Lavengro and The Romany Rye.

It may be objected that in the preceding discussion I have ranged far away from the consideration of rural writing. My defence is twofold: first, Borrow's example can teach us a great deal about the way in which a rural content can be transformed into art; second, his artistry, like that of so many rural writers, has been gravely neglected in the past, and it seems necessary to try to restore the balance. Thus I must disagree completely with Brian Vesey-Fitzgerald when he criticizes those who 'judge Borrow by literary standards, regard him as a Victorian literary gent (albeit an odd one) to be judged by the same sort of literary standards by which one would judge any other literary figure of the time.'[45] That Borrow's literary qualities are best appreciated on their own terms (which to me, and doubtless to Vesey-Fitzgerald, means against a rural rather than an urban-sophisticated background) may be readily admitted, but Borrow has now been dead for almost a century, and his reputation inevitably depends upon literary quality. Our approaches to Borrow may differ from those we use for other 'Victorian literary gents,' but our standards should (and can) remain the same.

The fact of Borrow's artistry is, I think, indisputable. Whether he was himself aware of the full implications of the artistic decisions that he made is, of course, another matter. The available evidence merely stresses the difficulty he found in writing, and one may presume that he continually elaborated and complicated his material without necessarily realizing the aesthetic effects of his alterations. Like most creative writers, once he was satisfied with a chapter, he would be unlikely to pause and analyze his reactions. More important than his attitude to his art, however, is his not unrelated attitude towards the external world, and here Theodore Watts-Dunton can be our guide. 'Borrow,' he observes acutely, 'could look at Nature without thinking of himself, a rare gift.'[46] At first this may seem a preposterous claim for the egocentric Borrow, but on further consideration it will be recognized as profoundly true. We might even say that *because* Borrow is so concerned with himself he makes no attempt to distort the natural world. He may rearrange his experiences – a thunderstorm, for example, will always appear at a dramatically opportune moment – but the storm itself will be rendered faithfully and accurately. There is always a firm distinction between observer and observed. He never tries to see nature in himself or himself in nature.

It may now be easier to understand why, as I observed earlier, Borrow takes the natural background for granted. For him, as for Cobbett, the world of nature is the starting-point for his own thoughts, not an object of thought in itself. This firmly places Borrow in the earlier and more virile period of the rural tradition. His erudite knowledge and literary experience were just sufficient to have a stimulating rather than a debilitating effect upon his essentially rural writings. His work represents, in fact, something of a climax. The maturity of the tradition is reflected in his artistry, which offers a new and fresh treatment of what was by his time a popular subject matter, but the artistic elements may often enough be unconscious, and are certainly not self-conscious. His characters frequently acquire a symbolic dimension, but are never mere allegorical tokens in an intellectual game. His England is a countryside of earth and rock, not an abstract concept in the mind.

Despite his wide travels and knowledge of foreign languages, despite his apparent cosmopolitanism that might seem to set him apart, his grass-roots 'Englishness' is one of Borrow's most striking qualities. Of this he was certainly aware. *The Romany Rye* is described as 'a book entirely devoted to England' (*RYE*, I, 293), and Mrs Borrow writes of the same volume to John Murray, almost certainly at Borrow's dictation: 'He has written a book in connection with England such as no other body could have written.'[47] Similarly Clement Shorter praises *Lavengro* as 'the most distinctively English book ... that Victorian England produced.'[48] The claim is just. Borrow's England is a genuine one, but it is to be found neither in the elegant *belle-lettrists* nor in the more conventional nature writers; it has been well characterized by René Fréchet as the England of Bunyan, Hogarth, Nelson, and Old Crome, 'un pays sain et vigoureux, formé par le Bible, qui aime le plein air, le sport et la bataille, où tout est réel, tangible et sûr.'[49] Although countless books of the sentimental-idyllic type have a more avowedly patriotic purpose, it is Borrow's writings that may be said to touch the quick of the English rural temper – blunt, obstinate, proud, suspicious of novelty, contemptuous of squeamishness, and above all, independent. Borrow feared, however, that in his own age these qualities were in the process of being lost. Lavengro claims to be 'one of the very few men in England who are independent in every sense of the word' (*RYE*, II, 209), and here, as so often, Lavengro is only a slightly exaggerated version of his creator. The stance is not, of course, without its dangers. 'Rugged individualism' so easily degenerates into crankiness; candour can soon turn into ill-tempered rudeness. Borrow did not always avoid these tendencies, and parts of his writing suffer in consequence. But it is to his eternal credit that, in an age of rapidly increasing conformity, whether in life or in literature, Borrow had the strength of character to go his own (generally rural) way.

SEVEN

Richard Jefferies

1848–87

The sweetness of the day, the fullness of earth, the beauteous earth,
how shall I say it?[1]

Although their deaths are separated by only seven years, in turning from
Borrow to Jefferies we are crossing what might be called the watershed of
nineteenth-century rural writing. There were, it seems, two distinct periods in
the century which proved especially fruitful for writers on country themes. In
very rough terms these were the first and last quarters of the century, though
one could point to the 1820s and 1880s as the decades of particular activity. Both
periods, it will be noted, were plagued with agricultural depression and social
unrest. The first, centring on the bad conditions after the Napoleonic Wars,
culminated in the machine-breaking riots and the 1832 Reform Act; the second,
heralded by the forming of the Agricultural Labourers' Union in 1872, found its
centre in the bitter years of change, contraction, and depression that hit
agricultural England in the mid-seventies and continued for the rest of the
century. No non-fiction writer dominates the second period in the way that
Cobbett dominates the first (though Hardy's contributions in both poetry and
the novel were invaluable), but of the numerous commentators on the countryside in the late nineteenth century Richard Jefferies is the most representative and the most reliable.

Jefferies is, indeed, by far the most versatile of our rural writers. He is
naturalist, angler, novelist, essayist, poet, agricultural commentator, rural
sociologist, and historian all rolled into one. It might well be argued, however,
that this distinction is achieved at the expense of absolute authority in any of the

individual areas. As a naturalist he is clearly inferior to White or Hudson, and he cannot match either Walton or Williamson as a fishing enthusiast; Mary Mitford (not to mention Hardy) is a more accomplished story-teller, Edward Thomas by far the more gifted poet; Cobbett is, of course, a more compelling representative of the rural interest, while George Sturt probes more deeply into the day-to-day life of the craftsman and labourer. As essayist, perhaps, Jefferies need yield precedence to no one, but there can be little doubt that the range of his interests results, from one point of view, in a dissipation of his talents.

On the other hand, this versatility can be seen as representing his particular merit and strength. From the informed agricultural article, through natural description, to the ecstatic but controlled prose-poetry of the later essays, he is remarkable for the breadth of his vision and the overall competence of his work. As Edward Thomas notes, 'no one English writer before had had such a wide knowledge of labourers, farmers, gamekeepers, poachers, of the fields, and woods, and waters, and the sky above, by day and night, of their inhabitants that run and fly and creep, that are still and fragrant and many-coloured.'[2] Certainly no rural writer before Hudson was so ready and able to present what E.W. Martin has called 'the natural history of minds as well as that of animals.'[3] For Jefferies a natural environment that excludes man is inevitably incomplete ('when man goes nature ends'[4]), while a human society that excludes nature is unthinkable. His ideal is a fusion of both worlds: 'My heart is fixed firm and stable in the belief that ultimately the sunshine and the summer, the flowers and the azure sky, shall become, as it were, interwoven into man's existence.'[5] And again: 'It is perhaps a fancy only, yet I think that where man and nature have dwelt side by side time out of mind there is a sense of a presence, a genius of the spot, a haunting sweetness and loveliness not elsewhere to be found.'[6]

According to E.M. Forster, 'the fibres of England unite in Wiltshire';[7] Jefferies' birth and upbringing in the Wiltshire village of Coate may therefore be considered auspicious. The immediate area was a curious mixture of the old and the new. A dairy country, not far from Avebury in the west and the ancient White Horse of Uffington on the east, flanked by the barrow-covered, encampment-topped downs, it is, in Edward Thomas's words, 'a most venerable and ancient land,'[8] yet at the same time the neighbouring town of Swindon was developing during Jefferies' early years into one of the great railway centres of southern England. A similar blending of opposites may be discerned in Jefferies' own ancestry. While he was descended on his father's side from a long line of farmers and countrymen, his mother's family, though originally agricultural, were most immediately associated with the printing industry in London. In consequence, Jefferies came in his early years under various contrasting influences which had, for the most part, a favourable effect upon his work. He developed an acute and informed sense of the past, yet he could temper the countryman's conservatism with a probing but basically optimistic vision of the future. While sympathizing with the traditional ways, he could also welcome the newer agricultural methods and inventions. A champion of the country, he was at the same time an appreciator of the city – Samuel J. Looker was able to compile a whole anthology entitled *Richard Jefferies' London*. Thus he was ideally fitted for the role of country commentator in the urbanized, industrialized world of the 1880s.

Jefferies might well be called the Janus of English rural writing; one side of him looks backward to the world of the early nineteenth century, while the other probes forward, haltingly but unmistakably, towards that of our own time. This is one reason, irrespective of its intrinsic merit, why his work is so significant – its centrality gives it an added force. We might say, indeed, that Jefferies' work, seen as a whole, *is* the watershed to which I have already alluded. His earlier writings up to (but not including) *The Story of My Heart* are traditional in theme and impersonal in approach; the later essays, questioning and introspective, anticipate the troubled individualism of such writers as Sturt, Thomas, and Williamson. The change can be observed in his subject matter, his attitude, and especially his style, but (and this is indicative of Jefferies' quality as a writer) it is virtually impossible to separate these for the purposes of literary analysis. I shall be content in this chapter to indicate the main lines of his general development.

His first piece of writing to attract anything more than local attention was a series of letters to *The Times* in 1872 on the nature and condition of the Wiltshire labourer. A few months before, Joseph Arch had been instrumental in forming the first Agricultural Labourers' Union, and Jefferies' letters were both timely and informative. The opening sentences are worth quoting since they represent, despite the apparently commonplace nature of the subject matter, a distinctive new voice in rural writing:

> The Wiltshire labourer is not so highly paid as those of Northumberland nor so low as those of Dorset; but in the amount of his wages, as in intelligence and general position, he may fairly be taken as an average specimen of his class throughout the whole portion of the kingdom.
>
> As a man, he is usually strongly built, broad-shouldered, and massive in frame, but his appearance is spoilt by the clumsiness of his walk and the want of grace in his movements. Though quite as large in muscle, it is very doubtful if he possesses the strength of the seamen who may be seen lounging about the ports. There is a want of firmness, a certain disjointed style, about his limbs, and the muscles themselves have not the hardness and tension of the sailor's. The labourer's muscle is that of a cart-horse, his motions lumbering and slow.[9]

Jefferies has been criticized for his hostile attitude to the labourers in these letters, but his description is unusually detached and neutral. There could hardly be a greater contrast with the egocentric writing of Cobbett and Borrow or the warm subjectivity of Miss Mitford. Jefferies makes no attempt to intrude his own personality, and deliberately offers a naturalistic, almost clinical account of what he has seen. He achieves what Richard Haymaker, in writing of Hudson, calls 'the baldness of actuality.'[10] In this early phase he is the most objective of our rural writers with the possible exception of Gilbert White, and his originality lies in his application of White's method (unwittingly, for he was not, it seems, acquainted with the work of the Selborne naturalist at this period) to a new subject. Here the labourers, and in subsequent papers the farmers, are exposed to the same cold, dispassionate scrutiny that is generally reserved for the natural denizens of the fields and woods. Once we have accustomed ourselves to the method, Jefferies' early 'reporter' essays come as a welcome relief after, say, the sheltered cosiness of most of *Our Village*. It should be stressed, however, that his is not the objectivity of the uninvolved outsider but that of the knowledgeable expert. The analytic, sociological mode of inquiry may seem unremarkable to us, but Jefferies is the first to apply it with any insight to a rural society.

This is not, of course, an approach that can be maintained for any length of time. Even in *The Times* letters themselves, Jefferies goes on to offer arguments and interpretations derived from the initial description. But it is clear that the early, 'naturalistic' Jefferies is anxious to correct any illusions that readers might have concerning the pastoral or idyllic aspects of the countryside. 'In the life of the English agricultural labourer,' he writes two years later, 'there is absolutely no poetry, no colour' (*TF*, 97), and his description of a bleak day in the life of a 'fogger' or fodderer provides a good example not only of his unqualified realism but also of the obvious sympathy that accompanies it:

The 'fogger' on a snowy morning in the winter has to encounter about the most unpleasant circumstances imaginable. Icicles hang from the eaves of the rick and its thatch is covered with snow. Up the slippery ladder in the dark morning, one knee out upon the snow-covered thatch, he plunges the broad hay-knife in and cuts away an enormous truss – then a great prong is stuck into this, a prong made on purpose, with extra thick and powerful handle, and the truss, well bound round with a horse-hair rope, is hoisted on the head and shoulders. This heavy weight the fogger has to carry perhaps half-a-mile through the snow; the furrows in the field are frozen over, but his weight crashes through the ice, slush into the chilly water. Rain, snow, or bitter frost, or still more bitter wind – 'harsh winds,' as he most truly calls them – the fogger must take no heed of either, for the cows must be fed.

A quart of threepenny ale for breakfast, with a hunk of bread and cheese, then out to work again in the weather, let it be what it may. The cowyards have to be cleaned out – if not done before breakfast – the manure thrown into heaps, and the heaps wheeled outside. Or, perhaps, the master has given a job of piecework to fill up the middle of the day with – a hedge to cut and ditch. This means more slush, wet, cold and discomfort. About six or half-past he reaches home, thoroughly saturated, worn-out, cross, and 'dummel.'   (TF, 94–5)

It is a harsh, unadorned, sometimes clumsy, but appropriate prose style. There is no comment, no direct message – above all, no sentimentality. Its honest clarity represents the first fruits of Jefferies' minute and faithful observation.

Jefferies had begun as a provincial journalist, and these solid, cogent essays, many of which appeared in the national magazines, were little more than extensions of his work as rural reporter. But Jefferies was soon to transcend journalism in his 'country books'; these, though beginning as newspaper articles gathered around a particular theme, became in their completed form studies of rural life and society which in their breadth and depth are unrivalled in the earlier literature of the countryside. White's emphasis on natural history and Cobbett's concern for husbandry are here combined, but Jefferies' own objective approach is maintained. His subject matter reflects the transitional rural world into which he was born. Once again he can be seen as Janus looking in two directions. In *Wild Life in a Southern County* and especially in *Round About a Great Estate*, which Mrs Q.D. Leavis calls 'one of the most delightful books in the English language,'[11] we find a rich, evocative, but balanced record of the traditional ways, sympathetic but never sentimental, while *The Gamekeeper at Home* and *The Amateur Poacher* keep their major focus on the mid-Victorian countryside of pheasant preserves and Game Laws. Even more appropriately, in *Hodge and His Masters*, a comprehensive and expert survey of contemporary farming, the old-fashioned and the new-fangled exist side by side.

These might be called seminal works on the English countryside not only because they are packed tight with information and anecdote but because they succeed in communicating the essence of country life in Jefferies' time. Judged by the rigid standards of an alien art, they are rough-edged and imperfect. The sections are often combined rather clumsily, and there are many dull pages when one cannot counter W.E. Henley's charge about Jefferies 'emptying his notebook in decent English,'[12] but the very lack of polish and sophistication serves to accentuate the homespun integrity of these books. Jefferies' contribution is to bring back to the reading public a sense of nature, as opposed to isolated natural objects. He gives us not merely aspects of the countryside, but the countryside itself in all its variety of detail. Here naturalist, observer, and sportsman are all united in the countryman; for critical purposes, however, these individual strands must be examined separately.

As a naturalist Jefferies may be described as a knowledgeable and dedicated amateur. From the references in his essays and the evidence of his notebooks we know that he had a firm grasp of the subject derived almost wholly from his own observations in the fields. Like most of the naturalists who have claims to be considered as writers, he is 'no cabinet theorist,'[13] and he even goes so far as to state:

> I dislike the term 'natural history': lists, and classifications, and Latin names, have no meaning to me. They have their use, but quite beside my purpose.
>   There is more botany in one garden buttercup than in all the shrivelled herbariums of the whole world.[14]

He takes care to insist in *Nature Near London* that his remarks 'are written entirely from a non-scientific point of view,'[15] and, so long as this is not seen as detracting from his accuracy and reliability as a field observer, the statement may be considered applicable to all his writings. Although in his early days he would shoot or trap specimens to examine or identify, this practice is ultimately abandoned. His interest lies in other directions:

> It is difficult to scientifically identify small insects hastily flitting without capturing them, which I object to doing, for I dislike to interfere with their harmless liberty. They have all been named and classified, and I consider it a great cruelty to destroy them again without special purpose. The pleasure is to see them alive and busy with their works, and not to keep them in a cabinet.   (*FH*, 234)

The best word to describe Jefferies is not 'naturalist' but 'observer.' Indeed there is no better guide to the art of observation in the fields. He talks of his 'book and pencil and observing eye' (*FH*, 21), and offers as the secret of observation 'stillness, silence, and apparent indifference.'[16] He insists, too, on the necessity to get off the beaten track. '"Always get over a stile,"' he declares, 'is the one rule that should ever be borne in mind by those who wish to see the land as it really is' (*NNL*, 14). Above all, it is a year-round activity; there can be no question of confining one's walks to sunny days or congenial seasons: 'To traverse the paths day by day, and week by week; to keep an eye ever on the fields from year's end to year's end, is the one only method of knowing what really is in them, or comes to them' (*NNL*, v). It is clear that Jefferies followed his own advice whenever he was physically able to do so. His books are an eloquent testimony to the soundness of his precepts.

The great benefit that Jefferies derived from his habits of close observation was an extension of subject matter into areas as yet virtually untapped. This was extremely important, since rural themes were becoming increasingly fashionable, while originality of treatment became more and more difficult to achieve. The public taste for 'romantic' nature was burgeoning just at the time when the creative energies of the romantics were spent. In *The Open Air* Jefferies relates an incident highly relevant to this situation:

> In these fields of which I was writing the other day, I found an artist at work at his easel; and a pleasant nook he had chosen. His brush did its work with a steady and sure stroke that indicated command of his materials. He could delineate whatever he selected with technical skill at all events. He had pitched his easel where two hedges formed an angle, and one of them was full of oak trees. The hedge was singularly full of 'bits' – bryony, tangles of grasses, berries, boughs half-tinted and boughs green, hung as it were with pictures like the wall of a room. Standing as near as I could without disturbing him, I found that the subject of his canvas was none of these. It was that old and stale device of a rustic bridge spanning a shallow stream crossing a lane. Some figure stood on the bridge – the old, old trick. He was filling up the hedge of the lane with trees from the hedge, and they were cleverly executed. But why drag them into this fusty scheme, which has appeared in every child's textbook for fifty years? Why not have painted the beautiful hedge at hand, purely and simply, a hedge hung with pictures for any one to copy?[17]

The world of *Our Village*, we might say, has degenerated into a sentimental cliché on the artist's canvas, but Jefferies is able to probe further, to discover what Gerard Manley Hopkins in 'God's Grandeur' calls 'the dearest freshness deep down things.' As Jefferies notes a little later, 'the beauty of English woodland and country is in its detail' (*FH*, 346), and it is this detail – which may include a meticulous description of birds in flight, a vivid account of pheasant-shooting, or a loving word-portrait of an old farm-waggon – that Jefferies so skilfully provides.

The artistic effect is not unlike that which Browning described through the mouthpiece of Fra Lippo Lippi:

> We're made so that we love
> First when we see them painted, things we have passed
> Perhaps a hundred times nor cared to see.

Jefferies states his own position in a passage not published in his lifetime:

> The red cone [of an oast-house] stands up clear against the blue September sky, as characteristic and singular a piece of architecture in its way as any in Italy or even

in the East. If it were not familiar, if we could look at it as we look at a dome or minaret, we should be pleased and interested in its history, its purpose and form. In that spirit I try to view the things of our own land and I find them beautiful and full of meaning.[18]

This accounts for much of Jefferies' effectiveness, particularly in the early books. In addition, this way of looking is often bolstered with accompanying information on rural topics which proved fascinatingly new to his readers though, as Edward Thomas remarks of *The Gamekeeper at Home*, it is really 'the first revelation of matters which hundreds of countrymen had known for centuries.'[19]

All this helps to remind us of the extent to which Jefferies wrote for the urban reader. For the first time in rural writing one is regularly conscious of an audience that is to be guided and even coaxed into the countryside. Jefferies soon became aware of the kind of reader who would be attracted to his work. Indeed in 1877 he even moved to the outskirts of London in the interests of his writing, and one suspects that the need to get a suburban's-eye view of the countryside was a significant motive. The very title of *Nature Near London* is indicative, but, as early as *Wild Life in a Southern County* (1879), he is insisting that 'not far outside [our] great centres we come quickly even now on the borderland of nature' and recommends his readers to 'go a few hours' journey only, and then stop just beyond the highway' (*WLSC*, 21). He is continually reminding us that the world of nature is close at hand. 'The idea that it is necessary to seek the wilderness or the thickest woods for nature is a total mistake; nature is at home, on the roof, close to every one' (*OA*, 72). Jefferies finds, however, that urban readers require more than occasional advice from a rural writer; he is forced to assume that the townsman, though interested, will know little or nothing about rural subjects. Consequently much of his work (particularly the early books, which were, significantly, the most popular) consists of the retailing of information; he was read in his own time, not primarily for relaxation or entertainment, but as an authority.

When Jefferies is studied within the context of the rural tradition, it becomes clear that there is one class of reader (in Jefferies' time generally an urban reader) for whom he has a particular concern – the sportsman. This is partly because he believes that 'there is ... an instinctive love of sport in every man's breast' (*GH*, 186), partly because of his shrewd eye for a literary market, partly (I believe mainly) because of his own inclinations. The first and last of these reasons are worth considering in more detail.

Although the outsider generally views hunting and shooting as essentially aristocratic pastimes, the participant frequently disagrees. Thus Jefferies follows Surtees in praising the ultimate democracy of the hunting-field. 'Even the bitterest Radical,' he claims, 'forgives the patrician who shoots or rides exceptionally well, and hunting is a pursuit which brings the peer and the commoner side by side'; [20] even in his later, more independent years he continues to insist on the point, declaring that 'one pack of hounds will cause more good feeling among men than fifty pulpits resounding' (CH, 254). Shooting is, perhaps, a different matter, and Jefferies, while writing keenly and knowledgeably on the sport (C.J. Longman wanted him to write 'a complete work on Shooting, to be what Hawker's work was forty years ago'[21]), continually protests against the growing expense and complexity involved in shooting 'since the flood-tide of commercial prosperity set in' (GH, 45). It is clear that such essays as 'The Single-Barrel Gun' (The Open Air) and 'Choosing a Gun' (The Hills and the Vale) were written, not for the rich game-preserver (whether rural or urban in origin), but for the middle-class town-dweller who liked to take an occasional shooting holiday. These, one suspects, were the chief readers of such books as The Gamekeeper at Home and Red Deer, and Jefferies obviously assumes in the majority of his rural writings that his readers will be sportsmen. This is evident, for example, in the following sentence from Wild Life in a Southern County: 'If you approach the trio the two old birds at once take flight, seeing your gun' (WLSC, 258). Even more revealing is this remark from the essay 'Nutty Autumn': 'They are never really nuts unless you gather them yourself. Put down your gun a moment or two ... '(NNL, 150). The assumed readership is clear.

All this, however, is a reflection not only of the demands of his readers but also of his own experience and early tastes. He tells us how he had 'been about at all hours with my gun as a boy' (LF, 199), and incidents in The Amateur Poacher and Bevis support this statement. To carry a gun seemed to the young Jefferies natural, even essential. Many of his insights into wild life were learned with a gun on his shoulder; one motive for associating in his early days with Keeper Haylock of Burderop, the model for The Gamekeeper at Home, was that he was 'a local authority on animal life' (GH, 15). Jefferies' hunting instinct will sometimes startle the non-sporting reader, as here: 'I recollect walking by a brook like this, and seeing the blue plumage of a kingfisher perched on a bush. I swung my gun round to shoot as soon as he should fly' (WLSC, 358). It would be foolish to deny that Jefferies was as fascinated by guns and gamekeepers as Borrow was by horses and jockeys. None the less, his interest is in the whole experience – the scenery, the exhilaration of the open air, the creatures and objects seen on the way. He has nothing but contempt for participants in a battue, or for those who are interested solely in the number of birds killed. 'Sport in its genuine sense,' he insists, 'cannot be had without labour' (OA, 137), and this labour is a major part of the enjoyment.

Indeed he judges all sport by the extent to which it 'brings one in contact with nature' (*LF*, 201). For this reason, though he is aware that it is 'hardly sport' by conventional standards, he is an enthusiast for 'potting' rabbits:

> It has an advantage to those who take a pleasure in observing the ways of bird and animal. There is just sufficient interest to induce one to remain quiet and still, which is the prime condition of seeing anything; and in my own case the rabbits so patiently stalked have at last often gone free, either from their own amusing antics, or because the noise of the explosion would disturb something else under observation ... Though shooting be not the object, yet a gun for knocking over casual vermin is a pleasant excuse for idling in a reclining position shoulder-high in fern. (*GH*, 108, 109)

The evolution of Jefferies' attitude is now almost complete. Once again we note how 'observation' is primary. Jefferies loved what he called 'the romance of sport,'[22] and wrote eloquently in its defence (see *CH*, 250–9), but its purpose and justification lay in the resultant knowledge and experience of the natural world. His ultimate position is expressed in *The Amateur Poacher*: 'The pleasure of wandering in a wood was so great that it could never be resisted, and did not totally arise from the instinct of shooting. Many expeditions were made without a gun, or any implement of destruction, simply to enjoy the trees and thickets' (*AP*, 83).

Much of the success of Jefferies' earlier writings results from creating the illusion of the outdoors, his skilful simulation of the experience of a country walk. Having accepted him as a knowledgeable guide, we are prepared to hear him discourse upon whatever flora and fauna may be discovered by the wayside, to listen as he interviews local countrymen on the roads or in the fields, to follow his lead, in fact – even when he turns aside from the obvious track. The pace is leisurely, the tone informal, the sense of companionship quietly satisfying. But Jefferies is more than observer and reporter, and in consequence his response to the countryside entails more than a mere cataloguing of individual details. An exact chronicler of the visible present, he is also a skilled interpreter of the historic past. 'The magic of the past,' he states in *The Amateur Poacher*, 'always had a charm for me' (*AP*, 69), but 'magic' is not quite the right word. It is neither a sentimental yearning for the old nor an academic preoccupation with the minutiae of ancient records. It is far removed from the spirit of Gilbert White's *Antiquities* on the one hand or Mary Mitford's response to the ruins of Silchester on the other. Jefferies is, indeed, the first of our rural writers to perceive history as a continuous process, as a binding, stabilizing force expressing itself not merely in battlefields and church monuments but in such homely details as the shapes of fields, the traditions of craftsmen, the names of villagers. He succeeds in capturing the rhythms of human change, apprehending the sense of a rural community, in a way that was to be developed later by Sturt and Massingham. Here, for example, is a passage that develops smoothly and effortlessly from the sight of ploughs working on the edges of the South Downs:

> The ploughs are at work, travelling slowly at the ox's pace up and down the hillside. The South Down plough could scarcely have been invented; it must have been put together bit by bit in the slow years – slower than the ox; it is the completed structure of long experience. It is made of many pieces, chiefly wood, fitted and shaped, and worked, as it were, together, well seasoned first, built up, like a ship, by cunning of hand.
>
> None of these were struck out – a hundred a minute – by irresistible machinery ponderously impressing its will on iron as a seal on wax – a hundred a minute, and all exactly alike. These separate pieces which compose the plough were cut, chosen, and shaped in the wheelwright's workshop, chosen by the eye, guided in its turn by long knowledge of wood, and shaped by the living though hardened hand of man ...
>
> In these curved lines and smoothness, in this perfect adaptability of means to end, there is the spirit of art slowly showing itself, not with colour or crayon, but working in tangible material substance.   (*NNL*, 226–7)

Once again we are impressed by Jefferies' unostentatious authority, showing not only his knowledge but his mature sensibility. The original observation is in process of being transformed into vision.

In his early writings, then, Jefferies studiously avoids intruding his own personality into his work. There is, however, another side to his character that is always crying to be heard. This is the Jefferies who first spoke out unequivocally in his disturbing spiritual autobiography *The Story of My Heart* (1883). So different is this voice from that of the early naturalistic articles that it is tempting to evolve a theory of two Jefferies, to divide him and his writings into opposed categories such as the realist and the romantic, or the reporter and the mystic. Henry Williamson has, indeed, usefully offered such a distinction in his novel *The Pathway*, where Mary Ogilvie comments: 'Uncle Sufford reads Jefferies – he doesn't care for the real Jefferies, what I call the green corn spirit – he likes the matter-of-fact books, like the Southern County and the Gamekeeper. He thinks the Story of My Heart isn't quite common-sense, somehow.'[23]

One could argue at length which aspect in fact represents 'the real Jefferies'; in any case the two extremes are by no means irreconcilable. Jefferies' realism can achieve an intensity which transcends and transforms the objective stance, and his 'natural mysticism' is as much of the earth as of the spirit. Whatever reservations we may have about his view of nature as presented in *The Story of My Heart*, we certainly cannot condemn it as insipid or excessively idealized. Jefferies sought for a clue to the mystery of the natural universe with all the passionate vigour of a D.H. Lawrence. In this connection a remark by Mary Webb may be helpful: 'The love of nature is a passion for those in whom it once lodges. It can never be quenched. It cannot change. It is a furious, burning, physical greed, as well as a state of mystical exaltation. It will have its own.'[24] The statement was intended to have general application, but it fits Jefferies perfectly.

The important point to stress here is that *The Story of My Heart* represents the first serious attempt on the part of a rural writer in prose to probe 'beyond nature.' I drew attention in my first chapter to the down-to-earth realism that seems in many respects characteristic of rural writing. The countryman, though frequently (perhaps generally) religious in outlook, has an inveterate suspicion of metaphysics. He sees no need to question the verities of earth and seasonal change; his religion is a tradition-hallowed way of life, not a spiritual revelation. But Jefferies is different. Although he becomes what the Victorians called a 'free-thinker,' although he does not believe in anything that can, in the conventional terms, be called a supernatural world, he never loses his instinctive faith in a mysterious 'beyond.' The precise object of his faith is by no means clear, but he is honest enough to acknowledge his bewilderment: 'I feel that I know nothing, that I have not yet begun; I have only just commenced to realise the immensity of thought which lies outside the knowledge of the senses' (*SH*, 126–7). If he has a religion, it is one of aspiration. Henry Williamson has called him 'spiritually the most piercing writer upon English country,'[25] and this is true. Of the writers whom we naturally associate with the countryside, only Wordsworth has the same passionate concern to look through nature towards an unseen (perhaps unknowable) reality.

That Jefferies' aspirations are the necessary obverse to his daily round of journalism may be seen by the emphasis he lays on getting away from 'the petty circumstances and the annoyances of existence' (*SH*, 20). He is preoccupied with the need for spiritual renewal: 'It is injurious to the mind as well as to the body to be always in one place and always surrounded by the same circumstances' (*SH*, 19). His walks up to the encampment on Liddington Hill, like Wordsworth's ascent of Snowdon at the close of *The Prelude*, represent a spiritual as well as a physical ascent. They offer new horizons which in turn stimulate new thoughts: 'I came to other trees, meadows, and fields; I began to breathe a new air and to have a fresher inspiration' (*SH*, 19). The stories current around Coate, and so eagerly snatched up by his early biographers, of his 'mooning about' alone and suspiciously confirm his own testimony that from an early age he needed and sought the condition of natural solitude.

None the less, it may be doubted if Jefferies' experiences were noticeably different in kind or even in degree from many other recorded instances of what Marghanita Laski calls 'ecstasy.'[26] Even if we confine ourselves to poetic instances, the list is impressive. When, for example, John Clare talks somewhat vaguely about 'the religion of the fields,'[27] he may well be referring to a similar feeling. Links with the Wordsworth of the 'Immortality Ode' and the early books of *The Prelude* are obvious, while Tennyson's reference to 'something half-divine / In earliest youth' and his desire for 'More life, and fuller'[28] appear particularly close to Jefferies' attitude, and even to his vocabulary. The poetry of Walt Whitman, as several critics have noted, yields numerous analogues. Above all, to turn to a prose writer in the rural tradition, W.H. Hudson's 'animism,' recorded so frankly and freely in the seventeenth chapter of *Far Away and Long Ago*, seems to be a more soberly reported account of the same basic experience. Unlike Jefferies, however, who assumes his own experience to be unique ('I feel so outside the general feeling'[29]) Hudson comments: 'We've all got mysticism in us; it's nothing to brag about.'[30]

It would seem, then, that Jefferies is mistaken in assuming that his own situation is exceptional. We should do well to remember that many another honest doubter in the Victorian era bears eloquent testimony to the sense of loneliness and alienation in a society of outward confidence and conformity. The whole 'cult of nature' that is so prominent a part of the nineteenth-century experience, whether it seeks like Wordsworth for an impulse from a vernal wood, like Borrow for the wind on the heath, or like Jefferies for 'the fullest soul-life' on Liddington Hill (*SH*, 129), is probably an obverse manifestation of the loss of faith that characterizes the period. Wordsworth is, of course, the high priest of the movement because he is one of the earliest to preach what we might call a gospel of natural piety, offering release from conventional restraints while at the same time maintaining the moral seriousness essential to orthodoxy. The natural world is important not so much in itself as in its capacity to reawaken the deadened spirit. We know from the autobiographical witness of John Stuart Mill and, more generally, from the poetic tribute of Matthew Arnold the significance of Wordsworth's contribution.[31] For a much smaller and later band of dispossessed spiritual seekers *The Story of My Heart* performs the same releasing and invigorating function.

But, despite obvious resemblances, the comparison between Jefferies and Wordsworth can easily be overstressed. Certainly both wish to penetrate 'beyond nature,' but their motives and expectations are not merely different but diametrically opposed. Wordsworth thinks that he can perceive, however imperfectly, at least the outlines of 'Nature's holy plan,' and he sums up his confident faith in the famous lines intended to occupy an important place in his never-completed philosophical epic *The Recluse*:

> How exquisitely the individual Mind
> (And the progressive powers perhaps no less
> Of the whole species) to the external World
> Is fitted: – and how exquisitely, too –
> Theme this but little heard of among men –
> The external World is fitted to the Mind.[32]

Jefferies, who denies any design in nature, makes no reference to Wordsworth in any of his writings, and we cannot be certain that he was familiar with his work; he appears, however, to be deliberately contradicting Wordsworth's position in the following sentences from *The Story of My Heart*: 'By no course of reasoning, however tortuous, can nature and the universe be fitted to the mind. Nor can the mind be fitted to the cosmos' (*SH*, 54). We must remember that between Wordsworth's time and Jefferies' had fallen the disturbing shadow of Darwin's *Origin of Species*, and, although Jefferies is highly sceptical, not to say contemptuous, of Darwin's theory, he can no longer take refuge in the comforting assumptions of the earlier period. He has observed in the lanes and on the downs of Wiltshire the same cruel facts of nature which Darwin had recorded on the voyage of the *Beagle* – the facts which, according to Aldous Huxley, Wordsworth would have been forced to acknowledge had he lived in the tropics.

As a result Jefferies' outlook seems in many respects much closer to the world of the twentieth century. Ultimately he belongs not with Wordsworth but with such men as D.H. Lawrence and Llewelyn Powys. The resemblances between these three are in fact remarkable. All were believers in 'sun-life,' and could take as their motto Lawrence's 'start with the sun.'[33] All three rejected a personal deity but at the same time maintained an intense commitment to the art of living that could legitimately be termed religious. All were consumptives whose love of nature had the feverish, ecstatic quality of those who know themselves condemned to an early death. Often they create in prose the shimmering vision offered on canvas by Van Gogh – the vision, to use Jefferies' words, of 'a life which burned around us as if every grass blade and leaf were a torch' (*SH*, 25). It is worthwhile juxtaposing extracts to indicate the striking similarity in their outlooks. Here is Jefferies:

> Burning on, the great sun stood in the sky, heating the parapet, glowing stead-
> fastly upon me as when I rested in the narrow valley grooved out in prehistoric

times. Burning on steadfast, and ever present as my thought. Lighting the broad river, the broad walks, lighting the least speck of dust; lighting the great heavens, gleaming on my finger-nail. The fixed point of day – the sun. (SH, 64)

Here, D.H. Lawrence:

When I can strip myself of the trash of personal feelings and ideas, and get down to my naked sun-self, then the sun and I can commune by the hour, the blazing interchange, and he gives me life, sun-life, and I send him a little new brightness from the world of the bright blood.[34]

And here, Llewelyn Powys:

To those who worship the sun there come moments of rapture that can never be gainsaid. This is no dream God that rises each morning into the sky. Before his steadfast affirmation all our misconceived timidities, all our morbid preoccupations, vanish. The sun shines upon the just and upon the unjust alike, and is concerned with nothing but the dance of life.[35]

Lawrence certainly knew *The Story of My Heart*, and Llewelyn Powys may well have done so, but the possibility of direct influence is unimportant. Lawrence could not have known that in his private notebooks Jefferies employs his phrase 'Sun-Life' as a heading for entries relevant to *The Story of My Heart*.[36] When in *Impassioned Clay* (a book, incidentally, that is also the spiritual confession of a philosophical layman) Llewelyn Powys recalls meditating on earth and sun 'in a cleft of the White Nose,' or when in *Love and Death* he lies down flat on the downs and gives himself up to worship,[37] he need not be following the example of Jefferies, but it is clear that they are spiritually akin. I am concerned here with a basic attitude to life that the three writers share, a passionate response to the natural world that is in no way diminished by lack of belief in a personal creator.

For the purposes of this discussion the opening chapters of *The Story of My Heart* are the most important. Once his soul-life has been awakened, Jefferies' concerns extend to the flesh, to art, and to the life of the city (indeed the passage just quoted about the sun is part of an experience in London), but the initial stimulus derives from rural nature. The downs, the trees, the streams, the sea, all contribute to his sense of exaltation, all are transformed and vivified by his enveloping self. The aim is to enter 'into the intense life of the summer days,' to extract 'from all green things and from the sunlight the inner meaning which was not known to them' (SH, 25). This last remark neatly illustrates the two directions in which Jefferies is pulled. Nature is both sufficient and insufficient.

Without it man can never rise to the summit of his powers, but in itself (and this is a strange idea to come from a leading member of the rural tradition) it is not only alien but essentially lifeless. For Jefferies, in the most literal sense of the phrase, 'thought is life' (SH, 62). Unless a human soul is present to appreciate it, 'everything is dead' (SH, 53). Whatever the merits of this line of thought as philosophy (and these are arguable), it is a surprising and somewhat ominous development for a writer on the countryside. Gradually – and here once again one thinks of Wordsworth substituting intellectual comprehension for the weakening life of the senses – the natural world is not so much appreciated for itself as employed as emblematic of soul states. In the very first paragraphs Jefferies talks of 'the rain of deep feeling' and 'the pure air of thought,' and by the end of the book such references abound; we hear of 'waves of ideas,' 'an ever-widening ocean of idea and life' (SH, 127), and 'the valley of my thought' (SH, 128). The intellectual horizons may have widened, but something has been lost on the way. Nothing quite makes up for the physical immediacy of the early chapters, where Jefferies succeeds in making us feel with him 'the embrace of the earth' (SH, 25).

But what is this 'something' that has been lost? A simple yet not necessarily insufficient answer would be the connection between God and nature. No less important than the increased emphasis on the self in The Story of My Heart is the concomitant break with Christianity. The following passage seems crucial not merely to Jefferies but to subsequent developments in rural writing: 'There being nothing human in nature or the universe and all things being ultra-human and without design, shape, or purpose, I conclude that no deity has anything to do with nature. There is no god in nature, nor in any matter anywhere, either in the clods of the earth or in the composition of the stars' (SH, 55). If we see this as just one more example of the decline of orthodoxy in late Victorian England, it may not seem a very remarkable statement; viewed in the context of the rural tradition, however, it is revolutionary. All the writers treated so far would have had no hesitation in calling themselves Christians (though Mary Mitford, the most urban-minded of them, had temporary doubts); the writers to follow – with the significant exception of Massingham – are obviously, sometimes ostentatiously, agnostics. This is not, I think, a purely accidental concomitant of my choice of writers. Exceptions could certainly be found, but I am concerned here with general trends. The old rural community depended so much on the Church that the decline of one can hardly be dissociated from the decline of the other. If Massingham is right in emphasizing 'the siting of every authentic village into church-house-fields, themselves a microcosm of God-Man-Earth,'[38] the connection is close indeed.

Jefferies insists that his opinions in no way detract from the intensity of his love for the earth, and there is every reason to believe him. All I am insisting upon is the change that comes over his work. No thinking person would argue that good country writing is possible only from within the traditional fold – allusion to Jefferies' later essays would in itself represent sufficient contradiction – but there is no denying that it will be very different from the writing of the past. An agnostic can never view the natural world with the same eyes as the believer who sees it as the art of a divine creator. Once Massingham's God-Man-Earth trinity is snapped, alienation must surely follow. One sees this not only in Jefferies' later writings but in those of his successors. Sturt's bitter helplessness and irresolution, Hudson's obsessive sense of mortality, Thomas's overbearing melancholia, Williamson's isolation (which he never quite succeeds in identifying with the loneliness of the true artist) – all these are symptomatic of a radical shift in values that cannot but have an equally momentous effect on subsequent rural literature. Thomas, it is interesting to note, comments broodingly and evasively in his biography of Jefferies on the passage quoted in the preceding paragraph, and thus reveals how deeply he is troubled by it.[39] Hudson dislikes the whole book – possibly because he sees in it an extreme expression of views he recognizes as embryonic within himself.[40] To Williamson, encountering the book immediately after the First World War, it comes with all the force of a revelation, and his confident separation of 'the real Jefferies' (see p. 137 above) parallels his own exaltation of the romantic self. Here indeed is a watershed; from this point we are descending into different country.

The writing of The Story of My Heart coincided with the breakdown in Jefferies' health. For the last five or six years of his life he was often an invalid, always a sick man. The final essays, most of which are gathered together in The Life of the Fields (1884), The Open Air (1885), and the posthumously published Field and Hedgerow (1889), are strongly affected by the ideas in his 'spiritual autobiography,' but this development is heightened by an enforced change in the pattern of his life. No longer could he walk out in all seasons and weathers; his strength precluded his venturing far afield, and for weeks at a time he was confined to his home and even to his bed. There are few more pathetic passages in literature than his description of the difference between clouds seen through a window and those seen in the open air (FH, 360) or the remarks in 'Hours of Spring' beginning: 'Through the bars of my prison I can seen the catkins thick and sallow-grey on the willows across the field' (FH, 35). It is hardly surprising that his predominant topic becomes himself rather than nature; at best, he is forced to substitute memory for observation.

Fortunately his memory was excellent. As he had written in his more active days, 'it is not only what you actually see along the path, but what you remember to have seen that gives it its beauty' (NNL, 119). In Jefferies' case this seems to have amounted to almost total recall, and he is continually returning to incidents from his earlier years, particularly the Wiltshire years, which are described with an astonishing wealth of detail. After one description from memory in 'Meadow Thoughts,' he observes: 'It is ten years since I last reclined on that grass plot, and yet I have been writing of it as if it was yesterday, and every blade of grass is as visible and as real to me now as then' (LF, 86). Moreover, as is clear from such essays as 'Hours of Spring' and 'My Old Village,' the effect of memory is to cast a warm glow of nostalgia and pathos over earlier experiences.

But if his new situation enables Jefferies to draw upon a hitherto untapped supply of personal reminiscence, his recently articulated intellectual position raises an added difficulty. Once nature is no longer seen as 'the art of God,' once he is convinced that there is no god (and therefore no conscious plan) in nature, the formal problem that is always a factor in rural literature becomes even more crucial. The final essays are, in fact, dominated by two ideas almost impossible to reconcile. On the one hand, Jefferies emphasizes his own personal feelings and responses so that we come to recognize a particular personality behind the writing; on the other, he is acutely conscious of the virtual impossibility of his adequately communicating his feelings and thoughts. This dilemma is well presented in the following extract from 'Wild Flowers':

> When the efforts to photograph began, the difficulty was to fix the scene thrown by the lens upon the plate. There the view appeared perfect to the least of details, worked out by the sun, and made as complete in miniature as that he shone upon in nature. But it faded like the shadows as the summer sun declines ... Image after image faded from the plates, no more to be fixed than the reflection in water of the trees by the shore. Memory, like the sun, paints to me bright pictures of the golden summer time ... ; I can see them, but how shall I fix them for you? By no process can that be accomplished. It is like a story that cannot be told because he who knows it is tongue-tied and dumb. (OA, 41)

By means of a radical shift of emphasis the true subject of this essay is not 'wild flowers' but the problem of the writer in communicating the beauty of the natural world. In a universe in which 'there is no word for design without plan' (OA, 42), the 'meaning' of any natural object is relative, and so cannot be fixed by words with similarly relative connotations. Precise expression is therefore impossible, and the artist falls 'tongue-tied and dumb.' So Jefferies argues in 1885, but this had not been a difficulty in the earlier country books. It is not the subject that has changed but Jefferies himself. The more subtle his thoughts about nature, the more difficult communication becomes – and this is a dilemma that he bequeaths to his successors.

Another problem confronting Jefferies in his later years was his inevitable loss of contact with the realities of rural living. Although in June 1880 he had written in his notebook, 'Of *men* now *instead* of trees and plants' (*JN*, 98), circumstances isolated him from the rural society about which he desired to write. In consequence his writings on social questions became more theoretical but at the same time more detached from their rural context. That they are, by the same token, less opposed to urban-oriented political thinking may explain why it has been customary to applaud Jefferies' later attitudes. Samuel J. Looker's comment on ' Walks in the Wheatfields' is representative: 'It is most interesting to discover in this late essay, written in the last year of his life, how far Jefferies had travelled from the tentative and conventional political sentiments in the famous letters to *The Times* of fifteen years before. Now he writes as an enlightened and progressive reformer' (*FH*, 379). But I have already argued that the objectivity of *The Times* letters is a matter of literary technique rather than political theory, and it is worth while asking the question: are Jefferies' insights into village life and culture more profound in his last years than they had been in, say, *Round About a Great Estate*? As he becomes increasingly introspective, his ideas certainly grow more challenging, but I suggest that too often they lack the bedrock of up-to-date rural experience.

In her *Scrutiny* review article, which smacks strongly of the social thinking of the 1930s, Mrs Q.D. Leavis feels herself bound to plead for a Jefferies congenial to the political left, but she makes the essential point when she remarks: 'Jefferies was one of those comprehensive geniuses from whose work you can take what you are inclined to find.'[41] The fact is that for every 'progressive' quotation a reader of such inclination can quote, a backward-looking passage can be produced as a counterbalance. Here, for example, is a passage from *The Open Air*: 'Dearly as I love the open air, I cannot regret the mediaeval days. I do not wish them back again; I would sooner fight in the foremost ranks of Time' (*OA*, 183). Progressive indeed, but the following sentiments can be found in the same volume: 'I do not want change: I want the same old and loved things, the same wild-flowers, the same trees and soft ash-green; ... and I want them in the same place. Let me find them morning after morning, the starry-white petals radiating, striving upwards to their ideal' (*OA*, 45). The passages are not contradictory, but it can hardly be denied that a general response to one is inevitably qualified by a reading of the other. Similarly in his most forthright political essays, 'Primrose Gold in our Village' and 'Thoughts on the Labour Question,' collected in the volume *Field and Farm* and frequently praised for their 'enlightened' radicalism, a neutral reader will find as much reactionary as progressive sentiment. If he is familar with Cobbett, he will not, of course, be unduly surprised. Jefferies' brand of radical thinking has the usual admixture of rural conservatism.

Yet, despite the difficulties that they raise, these later essays represent a remarkable artistic accomplishment. Their eloquence and immediacy are unrivalled, and I do not wish the last few paragraphs to be interpreted as in any way a critical detraction. Indeed, in an earlier treatment of the subject, I praised them as the summit of Jefferies' achievement, and I stand by that evaluation.[42] All I intend here is a demonstration that Jefferies' art consists of a perilous balance of opposing trends; the best of the later work represents a new departure for rural prose writing in which the focus is not so much upon external objects as upon that inward eye which is the bliss – and also, perhaps, the curse – of solitude. This development is, of course, analogous to contemporary trends in literature – one thinks particularly of the way the novel moves from the world of external action in Fielding and Scott to the internal analysis characteristic of the writings of Jane Austen, George Eliot, and Henry James. In a specifically rural literature, however, the external is an essential part of the total effect. If the urban emphasis is on mental isolation, the rural equivalent demands a practical world of community. Once the action lies solely in the mind, the distinctions of rural and urban are no longer relevant. This is a trend in rural writing that may have been inevitable in the same way that (so we are told) enclosure and the industrialization of the countryside were inevitable, but the effects are equally dismal.

In Jefferies' case the new approach is stimulating rather than inhibiting. It opens up a whole new area of interest, and helps to give his work a moving, personal directness that it had previously lacked. In so far as the self rarely lapses into the self-conscious, the 'I' behind his later writing may appear closely related to the unifying personalities with which we are now familiar in the work of Walton or Cobbett or Borrow, and indeed the backward-looking aspect of Jefferies belongs with the earlier writers. But in cultivating the introspective Jefferies looks forward as well as backward, and in so doing – in accepting, as it were, the role of Janus – he occupies a unique position in our rural prose literature, acting as both connector and divider.

In an essay on 'Country Literature' Jefferies remarks that the villager has not yet reached 'the stage when the mind turns inwards to analyse itself' (LF, 245). When, a few months before his death, he claims (with more ambition than accuracy), 'I am nothing unless I am a metaphysician' (JN, 282), he is obviously aware that he has himself reached the stage that separates him from those about whom he writes. As one determined to think through the old assumptions in the light of modern discoveries and challenges, he is very much a man of his age, though it may not have been clear to him that this is a feature of the Victorian period essentially alien to the rural way of life, and particularly to rural writing. For just as village society had been communal and co-operative, so rural writing up to this period had been a shared experience. In the earlier writers one is always aware of human interchange. The dialogue form of Walton and the epistolary form of White are obvious examples. Cobbett's blustering conversational style implies an audience, and the constant interviews with farmers and countrymen in *Rural Rides* emphasize the same point. Mary Mitford's village gossip and Borrow's gypsies and companions of the road similarly imply community (though Borrow's comment in *Wild Wales*, 'I am never happier than when keeping my own company' [*WW*, II, 296] can now be interpreted as ominous). Viewed from this angle, the pattern of Jefferies' work is of unusual interest. The communal suggestiveness of the early country books contrasts dramatically with the very title of *The Story of My Heart*, while the later essays continue the shift towards introspection. Those who come after Jefferies generally follow him rather than his predecessors. The solitary wanderings recorded by Hudson and Thomas and the hermitlike isolation that haunts Williamson are all parts of the Jefferies heritage. But it is in the work of George Sturt that the split becomes most conspicuous. Here solitary theorizing and intellectual analysis form the main staple of the work. An almost obsessive introspection becomes the norm.

EIGHT

George Sturt / 'George Bourne'

1863–1927

The heart-ache one feels at the sight of innovation removing the older features of English country life is an emotion worth explaining to oneself.[1]

In June 1810, the month in which Cobbett was found guilty of sedition, a young man named George Sturt bought the wheelwright's shop in Cobbett's native Farnham. So began a family business that flourished for a little more than a hundred years; it was eventually sold in 1920 by his grandson, the George Sturt of this chapter, who was to preserve a record of the detailed arts and customs of this rural industry in his best-known book, *The Wheelwright's Shop*.

Sturt had taken over management of the business just before the death of his father in 1884. Almost from the start, however, his interests were split between the shop and the world of letters. While the craftsman's life, viewed with all the warmth of retrospect in his book, might appear highly congenial and satisfying, at the time he found it irksome, and admitted in the privacy of his journal: 'My business is a thorough nuisance to me.'[2] Behind the shop he had an office or study, ostensibly as a place for working on accounts, but here, whenever he could spare time from business affairs, he would retire – sometimes to read, sometimes to meditate, sometimes to set down his thoughts on paper. As early as 1891 he employed a foreman-manager in order to give himself greater leisure for literary pursuits – or 'playing at authorship,' to use his own characteristic, self-critical phrase.[3] In the same year the Sturts moved out of Farnham itself to Vine Cottage in the neighbouring village of the Lower Bourne. Much later Sturt would come to realize the full significance of this separation of his residence from his place of work. Here, however, he was to spend the rest of his life, working slowly and laboriously on his books, attended for the most part by his two sisters, Mary and Susan, who, like himself, remained unmarried.

Sturt's literary apprenticeship was necessarily slow and arduous, his progress being hampered by unusual difficulties. In the first place Farnham offered him little intellectual society – he reported that in the days of his childhood there were probably not a dozen men besides his father who cared for reading[4] – and this increased Sturt's seemingly innate sense of isolation. Even when his first writings appeared in print, he was forced to employ a pseudonym for fear that his rustic customers might doubt his capacity as a wheelwright if they knew that he was also a man of letters. (The pen-name he chose, 'George Bourne,' was derived with a probably deliberate irony from the dry watercourse that gave his village its name.) This incident is of more than biographical interest since it bears witness to a significant break between the sophisticated 'book-culture' of the town and the rural folk-culture that Sturt spent a lifetime in attempting to define and describe.

Furthermore Sturt took a long time to discover precisely where his literary talents lay. His first full-length published work was a novel, *A Year's Exile* (1898), though by temperament and attitude, as we shall see, he was clearly ill-equipped for the writing of fiction. An astute reviewer of this initial effort recommended that he 'should treat of country life next time' – and, ironically enough, Sturt had already completed the manuscript of *The Bettesworth Book*.[5] Yet he continued to dabble with little success in both fiction and artistic theorizing before settling down at last to his true vocation as a commentator on rural life and crafts. None the less, despite this uncertain start the modern reader faced with the whole corpus of Sturt's rural writing is likely to be struck by the remarkable homogeneity of his work. In fact, his books develop in a logical, ordered progression that I hope to trace out in the course of this chapter.

Though he was born only fifteen years after Jefferies, the two seem to belong to different worlds. Sturt is perhaps the first country writer who finds it necessary to assume from the start that the rural viewpoint (as distinct from rural facts) is likely to be either unfamiliar or misunderstood. When Jefferies wrote *Hodge and His Masters*, for instance, he was aware of the lack of information about rural matters on the part of his readers, of the need to spell out (and so to defend) the farmer's position, but he had no doubt that the situation could be remedied. The difference between country and town presented itself as a challenge, not as a well-nigh insuperable barrier. With Sturt, however, rural life has to be seen as essentially remote and mysterious – even, perhaps, alien – to the average reading public. It is an area to be studied – a sociological and even anthropological 'field.' Indeed one might well see Sturt's work as documenting the occurrence, sometime in the 1880s, of an urban-rural dissociation of sensibility.

For our purposes this manifests itself most clearly in the attitude of the writer towards his material. The early Jefferies showed little evidence of having thought about the problem – and there was no reason why he should. He wrote plainly and straightforwardly about what he knew. His descriptive writing may often seem detached and clinical, as in *The Times* letters on the Wiltshire labourer, but this, though a deliberate stance, in no way implied an impassable gap between writer and subject. And Jefferies' later problems concerned the relation between man and nature, not between man and man. It never occurred to him that he might be unable to comprehend – let alone communicate – the outlooks and attitudes of the labouring class. To suggest that his view of rural life and the countryside might in any way be *limited* by his upbringing and assumptions would have seemed to him nothing less than absurd. Yet this is precisely the problem that plagues Sturt. Does he understand? Is he prejudiced? Is he capable of telling the whole truth? Does his position as employer cut him off from the community life that he is struggling to describe? Such questions recur continually in his journals, and are by no means uncommon in the books themselves. Sturt is no less a countryman than Jefferies – indeed one suspects that he inherited a stronger, more deeply rooted rustic tradition – yet he is embarrassingly conscious (almost, indeed, guilt-ridden) concerning his own shortcomings in his chosen task. There is so obviously a gulf between himself and his subjects, whether the Bettesworths or the craftsmen in the wheelwright's shop, a gulf that he fears is becoming increasingly difficult – perhaps impossible – to bridge. Moreover he comes to suspect that his education, an essentially urban education, is more of a liability than an asset. The obvious and acknowledged influences upon his thought and often upon his style are those of Arnold, Ruskin, and Pater. In the early days as manager of the wheelwright's shop we find him using his spare time in writing 'literary exercises – imitations of Thoreau or Emerson or Carlyle' (WS, 14). The relevance of Thoreau is easily understood, but what he learns from these other thinkers clashes awkwardly with the rustic 'culture' of which he is so sensitive, and often oversensitive, a recorder.

Sturt is almost obsessively on guard against himself, and is especially fearful of the charge of sentimentalizing the past. 'I suspect myself, not for the first time, of sentimentality,' he writes in *Change in the Village* ;[6] 'one must beware of idyllicizing' (LB, 9), he notes in *Lucy Bettesworth.* Later we find him pondering the thought 'that the old village life was not so nice in reality as I have made out, in "Change in the Village"' (J(M), 669). One journal entry is particularly revealing: 'It isn't much good to look on – to be an enraptured appreciator, or a "George Bourne"' (J(M), 696). Similar self-doubts are to be found in his frequent questionings of his accuracy and fairness in his presentation of the labouring class in *The Bettesworth Book.* Once again the uncertainties reveal themselves in the privacy of his journal: 'I am realising now that my reports of these talks of Grover's [i.e., Bettesworth's] are and always have been all but a failure ... It's a dry dead thing I get – the substance there, but the life gone out of it. It has neither flexibility nor progression' (*J(M)*, 444). He is continually worried that, as Bettesworth's employer, he can never be in a position to hear the old man speak freely and openly. He is invariably conscious of the all-important detail he has probably missed. While being extremely suspicious of 'the literary kind and those that live in studies, and test all things by their own over-strung nerves' (*J(M)*, 338), he is obviously aware that there but for the grace of God goes George Sturt.

Like Matthew Arnold Sturt is continually 'Wandering between two worlds, one dead, / The other powerless to be born.' The point can be documented in a number of ways, but nowhere is it more conspicuous than in the rival claims of a life of action and a life of thought. Sturt resembles Jefferies in yearning for a vigorous kind of life for which he was physically unfitted. One comes to suspect that he never quite reconciled himself to abandoning the wheelwright's shop for a life of leisure and literature. The distinction recurs again and again, like a bad conscience. 'While I had sat at the window,' he writes, 'looking out upon existence as at a lion in the street, Bettesworth had met it face to face every day;'[7] the farmer John Smith 'was a partaker of that English life of which it had to suffice me to be a spectator';[8] and in *The Wheelwright's Shop*, in a queer combination of whimsicality and bitterness, 'authorship' is contrasted with 'genuine work' (*WS*, vi).

A similar split can be noted in the matter of political allegiances. Sturt considered himself in the vanguard of progress. He was on the left wing of the liberals, dabbled in Fabianism, wrote articles on socialism, and rejoiced in the early successes of Labour party candidates. He was, then, on the side of 'the people,' but ironically, when he records the views of the rustic section of 'the people' in his books, he finds that their attitudes are very different from his own. Thus Bettesworth considered that the higher wages paid at the time of the Boer War were 'having an injurious effect upon young men giving them an exaggerated opinion of their true worth as labourers.'[9] Half the carters of the day, he asserts, were 'unfit for employment' (*LB*, 98). A peasant woman is recorded as objecting to the Board School on the grounds that it 'was doing nothing else than sap the vigour of the working classes' (*LB*, 66). Sturt's intellect was shocked by these opinions, but he was too honest – too much a countryman, perhaps – to ignore or ridicule them. Once again he began to suspect his own 'superiority,' and he came to realize that his own reactions were less clearcut than he thought. He was thus saved from an uncritical acceptance of the 'progressive' political movements of his time. Like so many rural writers, including Cobbett, Mary Mitford and Jefferies, his democratic head was at odds with his reactionary heart – or, to use his own words, 'if my theories are "liberal" my tastes are often conservative' (*J(M)*, 483).

As might be expected from what has already been said, a detailed reading of Sturt's work, while immensely rewarding, can also be an infuriating experience. One cannot help being impressed by the honesty and sincerity of his intentions and the fastidious clarity of his prose. At the same time it is easy to be irritated, particularly while reading the *Journals*, by his hypochondria and – what is perhaps its intellectual equivalent – his Hamlet-like vacillation. 'I always dislike to make a *final* choice,'[10] he admits, and this can be both a strength and a weakness. Moreover it is very easy to convict him of inconsistency. He can describe his overall theme as 'the education of one's soul to a greater sensitiveness' (*J(M)*, 80), while at the same time he is praising the non-individualized peasant qualities that are 'unimpaired as yet by culture' (*BB*, 9). He professes to hate 'superior persons' in the village, 'people who cannot exist without servants' (*LB*, 229), yet blandly presents himself relaxing in a hammock watching the aged Bettesworth mowing his lawn for him in the hot sun (see *BB*, 61). He carries mental theorizing to an extreme, yet is continually lashing out at 'intellectuals.' Above all, against his scrupulous and apparently humble self-questioning must be set the tone of arrogant confidence (smoother even than Matthew Arnold's) that so often manifests itself in his style. Yet, when all the criticisms have been offered and sustained, his stature seems unaffected. Like Walt Whitman he can contain multitudes, and like his own Bettesworth his significance is by no means diminished by being offered up in a series of not always reconcilable fragments. Indeed his chief strength lies in his reluctance to select or impose an artificial pattern upon his observations. As W.A. Ward has noted in a challenging review, in the chaos of the *Journals* lie their appeal and their true import.[11] By recording his impressions of the rural scene so faithfully and comprehensively, he becomes less a spokesman than an embodiment of its insoluble complexity.

Sturt's early experiments in fiction and art theory need not be discussed here, but, before proceeding to a consideration of *The Bettesworth Book* and *Memoirs of a Surrey Labourer*, it is worth while reproducing some of his comments on novels and novel-writing, since they provide some interesting sidelights on his rural works. The unlikelihood of his ever achieving success in fiction is clearly indicated in a journal entry recording an attempted reading of Hardy's *Far From the Madding Crowd*: 'But – the "plot" is beginning, and my pleasure in the book is already on the wane (*J(M)*, 363). Elsewhere he makes the following revealing statement: 'Besides the vividness of reality, anything I could imagine (i.e. my fiction) seems flimsy dull stuff, remote from life' (J(M), 15–16). In short, he finds the world far more interesting than any book (see J(M), 289).

His dissatisfaction with fiction involves the suspicion, seemingly deep-ingrained in rural attitudes, that novels are false because they are not literally true. With Sturt, of course, the argument is much more sophisticated, but ultimately it always returns to the possibility of distortion. We can detect the same preoccupation in his discussion of rustic speech. He admits it to be 'monotonous,' 'like the twittering of sparrows' (LB, 152), but he finds 'the well-worn platitudes of rustic folk' more real – and therefore more interesting – than the 'original' phrases of the novelists (LB, 155). In much the same way his artistic theorizing applies these ideas to the art of painting. For Sturt, arrangement or 'form' in a picture is alien: 'There are certain landscapes – almost any pleasant bit indeed – which I like so well that there is a charm in thinking of them and remembering them *as they are*. I do not want them better. Pictures of them were good enough (and better than any pictures known to me) if they could record for me the beauty that the reality presents, without altering' (J(M), 363). We may note in passing that this is in direct opposition to the painting analogy made by Mary Mitford when discussing *Our Village* (see p. 91 above). The difference is crucial.

More is involved, however, than the vexed question of actuality versus the literary presentation of actuality. Sturt believed, rightly or wrongly, that the novel portrays the exceptional, whereas he had an instinctive preference for the commonplace. His democratic political convictions (plus the influence of Arnold Bennett) convinced him, moreover, that his own views represented the wave of the future. 'The time has come,' he writes in his journal, 'when artists in fiction ... will set themselves the task of rendering not imaginative scenes and incidents and characters, but the beauties – really so much more satisfying – of ordinary life as it goes on around us ... Sometimes, even, I think that a new art must be invented, proper to [the] unrecorded and intangible beauties of the common-place' (J(M), 335). A little later he sums up his position with the simple statement: 'The ordinary suffices me' (J(M), 409).

With George Sturt the practical application of a principle frequently precedes its clear verbal expression. It is not until July 1899 that he successfully sums up his literary aims and beliefs: 'What is it that I like to watch? That should be the writer's first question: and his second would be, How am I going to show it to the public? How hold it under the reader's nose, so that he cannot fail to get the whiff of life?' (J(M), 289–90). But Sturt had silently asked himself these questions some years earlier, probably about the time of his moving out from Farnham to the Lower Bourne in 1891. There he had begun to employ Frederick Grover (i.e., Bettesworth) as gardener and general handyman, and gradually the old man's conversation fascinated him, and made him realize that here at last was a subject uniquely suited to his talents.

Thomas Hardy had complained in his essay 'The Dorsetshire Labourer' (1883) that in the public mind the peasant community was 'seriously personified by the pitiable picture known as Hodge.'[12] What was the agricultural labourer really like? Sturt became convinced that Bettesworth was 'a type of his class' (BB, 7) and that as accurate a portrait of him as possible should be perpetuated in words. This was all the more imperative, he believed, because of the extraordinary barriers to understanding that had arisen with the development of an industrialized, acquisitive society. Sturt freely admits that at first Bettesworth had been 'something of a comic character in [his] eyes' (BB, 3). In other words Sturt saw what his conventional preconceptions had prepared him to find – the traditional quaint 'yokel.' As he gets to know Bettesworth better, however, the labourer begins to take on an unexpected dignity. 'In his quiet voice,' Sturt writes, 'I am privileged to hear the natural, fluent, unconscious talk, as it goes on over the face of the country, of the English Race, rugged unresting, irresistible' (BB, 8). By 'irresistible,' however, Sturt does not mean 'immortal.' On the contrary, he feels certain that Bettesworth is among the last of his kind: 'In gossiping about his own life Bettesworth is unawares telling of the similar lives, as lived for ages, of a type of Englishmen that may perhaps be hard to meet with in time to come. For it seems as though destiny had decreed that this class of men, by centuries of incalculable struggle and valiant endurance, should prepare England's soil not for themselves, but for the reaping-machine and the jerry-builder' (BB, 10–11). Bettesworth belongs to the past; Sturt's portrait is therefore valuable not only as a contemporary record but as a historical reconstruction.

The more Sturt listens to Bettesworth's talk, the more he is impressed by the value of what he hears. Yet as a writer he is at first disturbed by the fragmented quality of the old man's observations. A journal entry for May 1896 (while the book was being written) draws attention to Sturt's formal problem in arranging the material: The man's brain is a miracle. Nothing is without interest for him. His mind is crowded with facts – local knowledge mostly – all loose and disconnected, yet all ready, so that he can refer to them as instances whenever he wants' (J(M), 245). Sturt's problem is to find a way of presenting the old man, without distortion, so that the reader can indeed 'get the whiff of life.' But how does one attain to what Crabbe a century earlier had called 'the real picture of the poor'? In 1907 (just after proofreading Memoirs of a Surrey Labourer) Sturt distinguishes two modes of studying the peasant class:

One – an 'objective' method – views them with biologist eyes, as though they were animals whose ways were to be observed wholly from the outside; and this method seeks all explanation of their condition and behavior in the formative influences of environment ...

The 'subjective' method on the other hand would seek in the labourer himself and his emotional life the chief formative influence.   (J(M), 540)

Jefferies' style in *The Times* letters would be an obvious example of the first, though Sturt was probably thinking in terms of French naturalism. The second (which Sturt admits 'is hardly ever done, and perhaps hardly ever can be done' [J(M), 541]) is attempted in *The Bettesworth Book*. And, as so often, the secret consists in avoiding the usual temptations. Sturt makes no attempt to describe Bettesworth physically, for this would catch 'merely the accidentals, the man's superficial differences from his neighbours: it would leave out of account the essentials, the typical race-characteristics which he shares with other men' (*BB*, 9). Instead he allows Bettesworth to tell his own story, and it is the reproduction of the old man's speech rhythms, his digressions, and at least a fair sample of what might seem unnecessary details and qualifications (directions, relationships, and the like) that gives an authentic reality to Bettesworth. Sturt has, of course, been a quiet and scrupulous editor, but he keeps as much in the background as possible. He is merely the person to whom Bettesworth talks; he puts in a question here, an observation there – but his role is essentially that of a foil.

Sturt is successful in presenting Bettesworth because he does not stand between subject and reader, but lets us discover Bettesworth for ourselves. He realizes that 'whoever would hear Bettesworth must let him have his own way in talk' (*BB*, 290). There is no 'preparation' in the introductory chapter – merely a straightforward account of the circumstances under which the conversations took place. Sturt has been content to arrange and select as inconspicuously as possible. He is careful not to insist too much on arrangement – chronological or otherwise – since one of the essential features of the old man's recollections is that they arise in random fashion. Or are they random? Gradually we come to realize that they arise out of the work done or the accidental but no less comprehensible associations of the moment. A tool, a sudden storm, news of the death of a villager, any of these can set reminiscences going. And we learn that an appreciation of these associations is one of the keys to Bettesworth himself. We have presented before us an example of the workings of the folk mind.

This is important, not merely as a sociological insight, but as a clue to the labourer's interest and satisfactions. Sturt insists that to see Bettesworth's life as dull, degraded, or unprofitable is to look with cultured, 'educated' eyes that do not see as Bettesworth sees. 'His true interest,' Sturt tells us, 'is that which he shares with all the other villagers – interest in their work, and especially in the management of their gardens' (BB, 257). And this is how Sturt presents Bettesworth, clearing a patch of rough ground, laying turf, hoeing, resting in the evening over his beer. Indeed Sturt's artistry consists less in presenting Bettesworth's life than in recreating the circumstances under which he begins to talk.

Sturt's method, then, is essentially empiric. Once he has realized the possibilities of Bettesworth's conversation and begins to take more detailed and systematic notes, he is content to follow Bettesworth's lead. This may seem elementary, but it is in fact a significant 'break-through.' As he notes in the introductory chapter, 'it is not so much in the narratives themselves that there is anything unusual, as in the circumstance that I have been permitted to hear them' (BB, 5). Sturt came to understand and appreciate Bettesworth – and the book itself is made possible – because the normal barriers of the employer-employee relationship were, at least to some extent, set aside. 'I felt, as I gardened occasionally side by side with him, not like his employer, but rather as if I were an apprentice learning my trade from him' (BB, 6). More significantly the reader has the sense of learning the trade in the same way. What distinguishes The Bettesworth Book from other attempts to portray the rural labourer is that here we are not just told about Bettesworth, but actually get to know him.

What we learn is considerable. Many of the time-honoured generalizations about the labourer – even those made by earlier and skilled writers in the rural tradition – now need to be qualified. We discover, for instance, that Hardy was only aware of part of the truth when he stressed the immobility of the old peasant population. Bettesworth's experience cannot be squared with this. He claims to have 'done it all. Bin up to C'rlisle, Newcastle, Tinmouth, an' worked my way right 'long as fur's Liverpool' (BB, 47). As haymaker he had made regular journeys into Sussex and as far as the Isle of Wight. Subsequently, in Memoirs of a Surrey Labourer, we learn that he had even served in the Crimea. He admits that 'there's some, you'll see, never gits two mile away from 'ome; or if they do they be lost' (BB, 50), but we are left with the distinct impression that 'wanderings' were commoner than we might expect.

Another fact that Bettesworth's record drives home for us is the extraordinary variety of skill and 'know-how' of which the rural labourer was master. Jefferies had stressed that 'nothing is so contrary to fact as the common opinion that the agricultural labourer and his family are stupid and unintelligent' (LF, 235), but Sturt documents the truth of this in the person of Bettesworth. The old man had worked as carter, as builder, as road-mender, as well-sinker, as harvester, as 'pole-puller' in the hop-grounds, and in many other occupations. He eloquently embodies the simple but all-important truth expressed by Francis

Brett Young that there is no such thing as an unskilled agricultural labourer.[13] It is the manifold nature of Bettesworth's ability that sets Sturt thinking about the obvious limitations of our middle-class definitions of knowledge, education, and skill. One might say that this is the germ from which the rest of Sturt's work grows.

Memoirs of a Surrey Labourer, the sequel to *The Bettesworth Book*, fills in a number of details without adding much to the general picture. Here Sturt has pared down his own role still further, as he explains in the introduction: 'I might not aim to make another book after the pattern of the first, grouping the materials as it pleased me for an artistic end; but by reproducing the notes in their proper order, and leaving them to tell their own tale, it should be possible to engage as it were the co-operation of Nature herself, my own part being merely that of a scribe, recording at the dictation of events the process of Bettesworth's decay' (*MSL*, viii). The effect of this diary method (which proves, like Gilbert White's letters, to be at least partly a literary device rather than a straight transcription) is to recreate the village situation in which one individual's life is built up from the irregular, almost random glimpses of another. This is hardly the 'new art' that Sturt had envisaged, but it proves an admirable vehicle for expressing the 'intangible beauties of the commonplace.' The method has its disadvantages, as Sturt himself admits – 'Much explanatory comment, ... which I should have preferred to omit, has been introduced in order to give continuity to the narrative' (*MSL*, ix) – but it works especially well in the closing sections in which Bettesworth's decline is relentlessly chronicled, and the end is deeply moving, justifying John Fraser's praise of it as the most distinguished of the 'Bettesworth' books.[14] Sturt achieves a perfect balance in which Bettesworth is seen at one and the same time as dirty yet dignified, as a slovenly old man yet one who deserves, in his champion's own words, to be 'remembered with honour' (*MSL*, 273).

'Should "Bettesworth" succeed,' Sturt writes, 'there are various little ideas that it seems almost a moral duty to set afloat, respecting the labouring classes' (*J(M)*, 20). The success, though modest, was sufficient, and Sturt, encouraged no doubt by a sense of mission, proceeded to extend his rural inquiries. The next step, clearly, was to enlarge his perspective to take in, not just the experiences of a single labourer, but the communal life of the whole village. Yet there was more than the obvious logic behind this step: it coincided with Sturt's developing views concerning the unindividualized, tribal quality of folk life. The immediate result was *Change in the Village* (1912).

In this book Sturt attempts to analyze the historical factors leading, in his own time, to the virtual disappearance of the traditional rural way of living that had held sway for centuries. It offers neither a lament for the past nor a vindication of the present; it is, rather, a plain statement of the situation as Sturt sees it. He tries to avoid the Scylla of sentimentality on the one side and the Charybdis of impersonality on the other. Just as in the 'Bettesworth' books a balance is achieved between a naively romantic and a rigidly objective presentation of the labourer's life, so here a sympathetic picture of the organic community is tempered with a harsh sense of realism. Sturt, one might say, has no axe to grind save that of truth; he extenuates nothing and sets down naught in malice.

No summary can hope to suggest the close-packed and persuasive arguments of the original, but Sturt's position needs to be indicated here, and it will be as well to begin with what he has to say in favour of the traditional life pattern. He is clearly convinced of its very real strengths in its own day: 'It was of the essence of the old system that those living under it subsisted in the main upon what their own industry could provide out of the soil and materials of their own countryside, ... and their well-being depended on their knowledge of its resources' (CV, 117). This last point, we may note in passing, becomes increasingly important for Sturt. Next the peasant tradition 'permitted a man to hope for well-being without seeking to escape from his own class into some other' (CV, 118). Above all, unlike the existence of the modern urbanized wage-earner, 'this life of manifold industry was interesting to live. It is impossible to doubt it' (CV, 119). Whatever the peasant lacked, what he certainly possessed was, in a word, 'roots.' He was a part of something larger than himself, and his place, even if humble, was both significant and secure. In the most literal sense of the phrase he knew where he stood. Sturt underlines the extreme importance of this fact:

> The succession of recurring tasks ... kept constantly alive a feeling that satisfied him and a usage that helped him. The feeling was that he belonged to a set of people ... necessarily different from others in their manners, and perhaps poorer and ruder than most, but yet fully entitled to respect and consideration. The usage was ... the accepted idea in the village of what ought to be done in any contingency, and of the proper way to do it. In short, it was an unwritten code ... – a sort of *savoir vivre* – which became part of the rural labourer's outlook, and instructed him through his days and years. It was hardly reduced to thoughts in his consciousness, but it always swayed him. (CV, 123)

Like D.H. Lawrence, Sturt believes that the restlessness and dissatisfaction so characteristic of the modern temper is a direct result of our separation from the natural rhythms of the earth.

As we might expect, Sturt is only too well aware of the way in which these arguments can be distorted into excuses for either emotional debauch or political reaction. He is continually offering warnings against the first temptation:

'Of the namby-pamby or soft-headed sentiment which many writers have persuaded us to attribute to old-English cottage life I think I have not in twenty years met with a single instance ... There is no room for sentimentality about the village life. Could its annals be written they would make no idyll; they would be too much stained by tragedy and vice and misery' (CV, 12, 14). He is suspicious of 'that almost festive temper, that glad relish of life, which, if we may believe the poets, used to characterize the English village of old times' (CV, 97), and he has no use whatever for 'those self-conscious revivals of peasant arts which are now being recommended to the poor by a certain type of philan-thropists' (CV, 111). As for the second temptation, that of political reaction, Sturt devotes the important last lines of the book to an unambiguous statement of his own position: 'I would not go back. I would not lift a finger, or say a word, to restore the past time, for fear lest in doing so I might be retarding a movement which, when I can put these sentiments aside, looks like the prelude to a renaissance of the English country-folk' (CV, 309). As Jefferies wrote a quarter of a century before, his 'sympathies and hopes are with the light of the future' (RGE, xvi).

The Lower Bourne was not the ideal spot in which to carry out observations requisite for such a study, since it had only been settled for a little more than a century and lacked the 'corporate history of its own' which, Sturt knew, a true village ought to have (CV, 3). Sturt himself was, however, the ideal commen-tator. Here, for once, his 'double life' stood him in good stead. He was a countryman whose experience as wheelwright enabled him to appreciate the finer points of the folk skills which would escape an outsider; at the same time his education had given him the wider perspective that the true villager lacked. Thus his 'point of view' (I am using the phrase in the sense that refers to a creative artist rather than to a committed student of politics) is admirably central. On the one hand, he is detached from the life he describes and is therefore able to weigh the pros and cons with reasonable objectivity; on the other, he is himself a resident, and is aware of the immediate background in a way that no visiting expert could hope to rival.

This accounts, I think, for much of the unique quality of the book. It does not, like Flora Thompson's Lark Rise to Candleford, tell its story from the inside, and thus, while missing the intimate details, it can build up a logical and sustained argument that is beyond the scope of Mrs Thompson's impressive study; yet it contains the personal experience and understanding denied to an official 'Blue Book' or a sociological monograph. Again its clear focus upon an actual village sets it apart from more generalized reports on village life such as J.W. Robertson Scott's England's Green and Pleasant Land. It partakes, in fact, of the same vivid sense of locality which it chronicles. But above all, the dignified and precise prose, evident, I hope, even from the extracts I have quoted, while never employing the persuasive techniques of a dishonest rhetoric, is an admirable vehicle for upholding and strengthening the argument. Its quiet eloquence acts as a guarantee of the author's sincerity of purpose. Even if the book's social and historical approach separates it from the field of literature, it is clear that only an accomplished literary artist could have written it.

Sturt's next book, *Lucy Bettesworth* (1913), need not be discussed at any length. Though in one respect his most representative work, since some of the essays, including that which gives its name to the volume, look back to his earlier writings, while others, including 'Rural Techniques' and 'Our Primitive Knowledge,' anticipate parts of the *The Wheelwright's Shop*, it is a collection of fugitive articles (many of them written as early as 1902–5) which, interesting in themselves, indicate no particular development in his work. It marks, however, the end of a phase, since it is the last of his books to be published before paralysis struck him down in 1916. After that time Sturt was dependent more than ever upon his private journals to provide him with material for new books. His active life was over, and this doubtless increased the nostalgic mood that was always strong in Sturt. He turned now to the records he kept of the stories and memories of his own relatives, particularly those on his mother's side. This interest resulted in two books in which he becomes a sturdy defender of the long-abused 'provincialism': *William Smith: Potter and Farmer*, published in 1919, and *A Farmer's Life* which followed three years later.

Both books originated in the memories of John Smith (the subject of *A Farmer's Life*) and his sister Ann, memories which Sturt had religiously copied into his journals in earlier days. Although he is turning, like Jefferies before him, from a consideration of Hodge to that of his masters, in many respects his method – and certainly his motive – remains the same. Like Bettesworth, these men were not isolated individuals, unique in their attitudes and abilities; rather they were characteristic of their class and of the environment from which they had sprung. Thus John Smith was, for Sturt, 'truly representative of a type once very important in England's life: the type that kept the country steady during all the upheavals of the last hundred and fifty years' (*FL*, xii). In *A Farmer's Life*, indeed, Sturt does for John Smith what he had previously done for Bettesworth – he preserves, often in Smith's own words, the memories of village customs and characters recalled by the fields and roads that he had known since he was a boy. In *William Smith: Potter and Farmer*, however, he attempts something rather different, for William Smith had died five years before Sturt's own birth, and in this case Sturt is trying to build up the record of a life which was as unknown to him as it was to his readers.

Through both books runs a strong and often rather sad yearning for the English past. There are many reasons why Sturt should have been looking backward at this time. One, I suspect, was connected with the patriotism generated by the First World War – a patriotism which clearly affected Sturt without ever, in his case, degenerating into chauvinistic jingoism. Another was his age and circumstances – crippled and ailing as he was, he had little cause to look to the future. Most important, though, was the logical outcome of the investigations in *Change in the Village*; Sturt is here seeking the old England out of which the organic community, which he observed in a decayed and degraded state in the Lower Bourne, had evolved. He is searching, in other words, for the tradition from which Bettesworth had been disinherited. At any rate references to earlier historical periods abound in these two books, and in almost every case the subject – and therefore, by implication, Sturt himself – is associated with this rougher but more invigorating life. We are told, for instance, that William Smith (1790–1858) 'was old-fashioned even in his own day,'[15] and consequently Sturt feels that the picture is really one of an eighteenth-century farmer. He sees himself as recreating a specimen of 'the England Cowper had known, Nelson had fought for' (*PF*, 2). Similarly he writes of John Smith: 'To know him was to know the sort of man Shakespeare knew, "whose thews were made in England"' (*FL*, xiii).

But the balance between nostalgia and realism, so admirably maintained in *Change in the Village*, is less certain here. There are passages where we feel that Sturt is producing an effect which he would distrust if he encountered it in others. In recalling William Smith's home, which he had known as a child, Sturt writes: 'The whole inside of the farmhouse seems, to my memory, packed with details exciting to the sentiment of ancient English peace, order, industry, simplicity, rustic plenty' (*PF*, 6); and there is a later reference to the 'serenity and stillness' that the older farmers and peasants knew (*PF*, 104). In *A Farmer's Life*, too, he concentrates on the tranquillity of the farm: 'Peace lived here; peace and quiet, with the acorns, the steady-rustling rains' (*FL*, 51–2). Admittedly the darker side of the picture is not omitted – we are told of open ditches at the sides of roads, gory pig-killings, the not-yet-disused stocks, and even such unsavoury details as 'the collecting of urine for steeping the seed-wheat' (*PF*, 96) – but the extremes are difficult to reconcile.

Yet this should not detract unduly from the impressiveness of these quiet, moving eloquent books. It is probably inappropriate to demand the hard logic and controlled arguments that we have encountered in his earlier work. These are, after all, memoirs; they address themselves to the emotions rather than to the reason. Sturt is quite explicit about this. Listening to his uncle's recollections, he tells us, 'I began to feel (and that was better than knowing intellectually) the meaning of the lanes and hedges, the crops and hamlets' (*FL*, xiii). The books aim, then, to be evocative rather than persuasive, and they certainly recreate the pace and tone of a vanished age. Who is to say, moreover, that the inconsistencies we have noted are not inherent in the life presented rather than in the author who presents them?

More important, in any case, is the almost Keatsian richness which glows through these books, particularly *A Farmer's Life*. It is present in his description of the local farmers – 'In their sun-burnt faces, and through their nutty vernacular, the gorgeous English countryside seemed to live and speak, and they were worthy of it' (*FL*, xv) – and in the portrait of John Smith himself – 'With the apple-trees, and the birds, and the May-time, the old farmer's mind seemed much in tune' (*FL*, 137). This effect is like that of a scent wafting us back to memories of *temps perdu*; indeed Sturt employs this very image: 'Mr Smith's teeming tales ... had the air of old times hanging about them, like the reek of his father's pot-kilns – a scent as of Farnborough village long ago' (*FL*, 63). As often as not the emphasis is not so much on the memories themselves as upon the other reactions they evoke or the situations – always leisurely – in which John or Ann Smith recounted them. Consequently the tone is more nostalgic – more sentimental, even – than in the earlier books. But this is no unconscious weakness on Sturt's part. It is something he admits, a risk he is prepared to take: 'Sentiment has a way of picking out the otherwise-unnoticed values and thus finding the deepest truths' (*PF*, 103).

In *The Wheelwright's Shop* (1923) many of the subjects and themes that have preoccupied Sturt in earlier books are brought together and united. Like the two books immediately preceding, it is a memoir, but here Sturt is focusing on his own generation and his own experience; like *Change in the Village*, it provides a glimpse of the old peasant life and peasant methods, while in the chapters that concentrate on Sturt's chief workmen, George Cook and Will Hammond, the intimate and satisfying relation between the traditional worker and his work is presented with vivid, personal details that recall the 'Bettesworth' books.

Although Sturt describes the book as 'an autobiography for the years 1884 to 1891' (*WS*, v), this is in fact an unduly limiting time-span, for his retrospective comments from the time of writing in the early 1920s really bring the story down to the end of the First World War. And it was this whole period that was so crucial – and fatal – for the ancient craft of the wheelwright. When Sturt first took over the management of the shop, it was still 'a "folk" industry, carried on in a "folk" method' (*WS*, 17). Catering for the particular needs of the Farnham area, it took into account not only factors determined by geographical situation, but also the individual requirements – or even quirks – of the local inhabitants:

> We got curiously intimate with the peculiar needs of the neighbourhood. In farm-waggon or dung-cart, barley-roller, plough, water-barrel, or what not, the dimensions we chose, the curves we followed, ... were imposed by the nature of

the soil in this or that farm, the gradient of this or that hill, the temper of this or that customer or his choice perhaps in horseflesh. The carters told us their needs. To satisfy the carter, we gave another half-inch of curve to the waggon-bottom, altered the hooks for harness on the shafts, hung the water-barrel an inch nearer to the horse or an inch farther away, according to requirements.   (WS, 17–18)

At the same time the basic methods and principles were hallowed by centuries of custom and experience: 'What we had to do was to live up to the local wisdom of our kind; to follow the customs, and work to the measurements, which had been tested and corrected long before our time in every village shop all across the country' (WS, 19). In addition, prices were also fixed by tradition, and the standard of workmanship was maintained by the pride and integrity of the workers themselves. Sturt remarks of his craftsmen that they 'would sooner have been discharged than work badly, against their own conscience' (WS, 100).

Ironically it was Sturt himself who, having entered the profession with Ruskinian ideals concerning craftsmanship and a temperament in sympathy with the old methods, eventually brought the Trojan horse of industrial organization into the citadel of the wheelwright's shop. It was 'probably in 1889' that he 'set up machinery: a gas-engine, with saws, lathe, drill and grind-stone. And this device, if it saved the [immediate] situation, was (as was long afterwards made plain) the beginning of the end of the old style of business' (WS, 200). Moreover we learn from the *Journals* that within two years 'time-sheets' were installed (*J(M)*, 143). The result was the dehumanization of what had been a co-operative folk enterprise. The shop was transformed into a factory, and, even worse, ' "the men," though still my friends, as I fancied, became machine "hands" ' (WS, 201). It was not long, Sturt records bluntly but sadly, before 'machinery made drudges of them' (WS, 202).

The Wheelwright's Shop is the book for which Sturt is best known, though it is not immediately clear why this should be so. On the surface it is a technical account of the complexities of wheelwrighting, and the textbook-like drawings, though impressive, might well deter the non-specialist. This technicality is, however, no more than the central hub from which the book's other themes and interests spread out in all directions. The previous paragraphs may have given an impression of a historical document with a sociological message. But this too is inadequate, for what becomes clear in the opening pages (even to a reader unfamiliar with Sturt's other work) is that *The Wheelwright's Shop* is written by an artist. The account of rural decline, for example, is told not only through close argument and carefully gathered evidence but also through the more purely creative effects of allusion and symbol. It is as if the evocative method of

A Farmer's Life had been grafted on to the more abstract thesis of *Change in the Village*.

The replacement of the old by the new, for instance, is presented in a deeply personal reminiscence wedged in between two technical chapters, entitled 'Bottom-Timbers' and 'Waggon-Locking' respectively. Sturt tells of his reactions on seeing an old farm-waggon, converted into a brick-cart, its shafts removed 'as when Samson was mutilated to serve the ends of his masters,' being pulled by a tractor to assist, as it were, in the destruction of the way of life that had produced it. The account is vivid, detailed, precise, but these are qualities which many a talented writer can learn to reproduce. What makes Sturt's treatment unique is the feeling of human torture and degradation that pervades the whole scene. The waggon is humanized as 'the victim of an implacable conqueror'; he imagines the timbers 'trembling' and axles 'fretting' under the humiliating labour, and finally remarks: 'I felt as if pain was being inflicted; as if some quiet old cottager had been captured by savages and was being driven to work on the public road' (*WS*, 66). This is no mere detachable interlude, still less an indulgence in 'literary' sentiment. The passage is at once an example of the close identification of the traditional workman with the objects of his work (comparable to Bettesworth's affectionate banter with his spade and turfs [see *BB*, 182]) and an embodiment of the concept of organism that is so central a feature of the book.

Similarly the chapters on George Cook and Will Hammond are striking character sketches, almost complete in themselves, that do not extend the argument so much as reinforce it in another, more personal mode. They too are interspersed between chapters of technical detail. One realizes at last that the book itself is an example of the method that it describes. In the separate chapter concerning the old waggon this is reasonably obvious. It is evident, too, in certain other sections, particularly the series of chapters with the overall title 'Tyring.' Here the co-operation between individual workmen displays the habits of the village society in miniature. And so it is, ultimately, with the book as a whole. At first sight it may appear a rather clumsy conglomeration of essays in differing modes and involving differing interests and approaches, Gradually, however, one perceives the lumbering but appropriate form of one of the old waggons themselves. Some parts may appear unnecessary, but detach them, as the shafts were removed in the interests of carting bricks, and the whole organism is damaged. Once it becomes clear that the personal reminiscences are inseparable from the technical detail, that the tools cannot be dissociated from the craftsmen who use them, nor the craftsmen from the object they have made, then the form of the book justifies itself: rough in texture, often unwieldy, but solid, sturdy, and built to last.

As he forecast himself, the core of Sturt's writings is to be found in his private journal. 'It will be,' he writes to his fellow journal-keeper Arnold Bennett, 'the most vividly interesting work I shall ever write, but it will not be published, probably, until I'm dead – except in bits which will be incorporated into schemed-out books' (SBS, ix). This proved correct; the journals have only recently been published in anything approaching representative bulk, and, as Bennett knew, they were 'directly or indirectly, the basis of nearly all that George [Sturt] wrote' (SBS, ix). With the exception of the autobiographical memoir of his Farnham childhood A Small Boy in the Sixties (which is, in any case, derived from memories rather than journal entries), The Wheelwright's Shop is the last of Sturt's 'schemed-out books' and has come to be regarded as the culmination of his work. But one cannot read the Journals with any care without suspecting that the volume that would have become the real culmination was never written. The later entries in particular suggest that, had he lived, Sturt would have attempted not only a definition of 'the folk' but an extended examination of folk art and folk culture. This is surely the undiscovered centre to which all Sturt's writings point. As it is, we are left with a number of intriguing entries, plus the relevant passages in earlier books, that often seem to be crying out for more detailed treatment, and, however reluctant we may be to tamper with the chaotic richness of the Journals, it is surely legitimate to speculate on what such a book might have contained. At least it will help to round off our study of Sturt's unique contribution to rural writing.

The more Sturt pondered the break-up of the old peasant community and saw 'villa-people' displacing the native inhabitants of the Lower Bourne, the more he came to question the values of the 'new' way of life. Soon key concepts were being challenged. What, for instance, do words like culture, art, and civilization really imply? Are their definitions fixed and absolute, or are these determined by the dominant society or class of the time? Sturt became increasingly suspicious of such high-flown terms. He suspects that his own culture is 'something of a hot-house thing, that requires forcing' (J(M), 153), and this is not just modesty; he has the uneasy feeling that much of what is called culture is similarly artificial and unnatural. It can, he believes, impair 'the native orderliness, the self-reliance, the indomitable vigour of our English breed' (BB, 9). In addition he finds that art in any elevated sense is alien to the true countryman: 'For modern people, art supplies the place that was filled by tradition in the case of the Folk' (J(M), 596). Even civilization can become a mere facade for dilettantism. At the close of The Wheelwright's Shop he puts his finger on a basic anomaly of his age: 'That civilisation may flourish a less-civilised working-class must work' (WS, 202). Sturt doubts, of course, if the working-class is less civilized. This is an underlying theme of Change in the Village, as John Fraser has recently emphasized. Sturt, he reminds us, shows that 'the concept of society in spatial terms of higher and lower was untenable. There was not one "culture" that trickled downwards and "civilized" people along the way. Rather there were a number of different cultures and patterns of civilization, overlapping horizontally and each with its own kinds of strengths.'[16]

In short, all these words are limiting, inadequate. We generally assume that they are all dependent upon education, but Sturt doubts even this. As he writes in *Change in the Village*, 'the "peasant" tradition in its vigour amounted to nothing less than a type of civilization – the home-made civilization of the rural English' (*CV*, 116). The traditional countrymen may have lacked education in the formal (urban) sense – one of Sturt's best and most intelligent workmen in the shop was illiterate (see *WS*, 132n) – but they possessed their own knowledge and skill, and these two are the peasant equivalents of culture and art. The knowledge, the hoard of local tradition and lore which had grown up over the centuries and was handed down from generation to generation, is documented throughout Sturt's work. That this knowledge went unrecognized by the 1870 Education Act is no reflection on its quality or its importance. The ignorance, as Sturt knew, was not on the side of the countryman: 'To the labouring people we offer an education, assuming that they are utterly ignorant. Impertinent proffer! These have their "science" as Turner [a carpenter] calls it, dear-bought, intricate, mysterious, and of incalculable value' (*J(M)*, 473).

Similarly the artistic impulse, which to a leisured class manifests itself in painting and *belles-lettres*, is here subsumed into the active rural tasks – ploughing a straight furrow, thatching a roof, constructing a farm-cart. Like H.J. Massingham and numerous other rural commentators, Sturt recognizes no qualitative difference between arts and crafts; country tools are works of art in themselves, as well as implements by which other arts are practised. Sturt suggests, for example, that 'a scythe is a book – a book composed entirely out of doors by the English peasantry' (*LB*, 131). Later he describes 'the gracefulness of a ploughshare' as 'pliant ... as a line of English blank verse,' and this, he explains, is because the ploughman's technique requires it – 'it is the accomplished artist who is fastidious as to his tools' (*LB*, 178–9). He continually sees countrymen in this light. George Cook is 'an artist in spokes' (*WS*, 98), and the charm of listening to Bettesworth is likened to the 'rare pleasure of hearing an artist upon his art' (*J(M)*, 247). Thus even the agricultural labourer, officially unskilled, can legitimately be considered an artist.

It would be inaccurate, however, to claim that Sturt *equates* arts and crafts. In one sense he makes a radical distinction between them, since he maintains that 'the true antithesis to Folk is Individual' (*J(M)*, 551). What he rejects is the mystique surrounding the so-called fine arts – the idea that the originality behind a decorative carving puts it on a higher plane than one of Cook's wheels which is the result of the gradually developed wisdom and experience of centuries. Folk culture, which includes folk art, is nothing more nor less than the collective, unformulated sum of the total resources of the community. It can be experienced (tribally, not individually), but it can never be articulated, since any description or definition involves a conscious process of thought and analysis which does not exist in the folk state. Folk art, which for Sturt is barely distinguishable from the art of living, is devoid of self-conscious principles, and is to this extent diametrically opposed (though not inferior) to art as we know it – 'it does not start with an idea, but works up to it' (*J(M)*, 555). Folk art, he notes elsewhere, is 'that which people make for themselves when there is no specialist to help them' (*J(M)*, 522). By the same token Education is something essentially 'artificial' and post-folk (see *J(M)*, 684).

If Sturt never came formally to examine all the ramifications of this line of thought, it is an idea – one might almost say an instinct – implicit in almost all his work. Once this becomes apparent, many of the otherwise disparate aspects of his thinking fit neatly into place. His insistence on seeing the apparently individualized Bettesworth and John Smith as types; his reluctance (that might at first seem contradictory rather than complementary) to make statements about 'the peasant' ('these things should rather be said of the tribe – the little group of folk – of which he was a member' [*CV*, 122]); his treatment of the villagers as 'human fauna' (*CV*, 122), linking up with the frequent animal imagery applied, in no way disrespectfully, to Bettesworth and his wife; his patriotic concern for England which ultimately proves to be not national but tribal: all these are readily explicable in the light of Sturt's beliefs concerning folk culture. His dissatisfaction with the novel as an art form also fits here. The point is made magnificently in a journal entry for 1899 which by itself could assure Sturt a high place in the ranks of English prose writers:

I suspect that my way of viewing the world doesn't lend itself easily to the methods of fiction. In connection with the great storm the other Wednesday night, when houses were being flooded, roads torn up, crops washed out of the ground, none of the incidental details struck me so much as did the subsequent imagination of the whole South-Saxon tribe of us from here to the sea, in our long sheltered valleys, hurrying when the great rain was over to put our houses in order, like ants that have been disturbed in their nest. I could fancy them in the haggard dusk, innumerable specks on the hill-sides and by the swollen streams, hard-working, shrill-talking, laughing the grim laugh of those who 'grin and bear it.' That was the aspect of the subject that most appealed to me. And so in other things of man's life. I don't want heroics: but most details have a trick of looking petty, until they can be seen as parts of an immense lump which dignifies them.   (*J(M)*, 290)

Sturt is fully aware of the paradox that an appreciation of folk life is only possible through a repudiation of the old folk habits. His own thoughtful, analytical prose is itself an example. Though the peasant community was essentially inarticulate, we shall only understand it by using all the resources of the literate culture that has absorbed and destroyed it. If, in reading the last quotation, we are granted an insight into the old life, this is as much a tribute to Sturt's stylistic powers in evoking it as to his intellectual ability in comprehending it. His importance within the rural tradition is dependent, ultimately, on the literary equipment by means of which he expresses his purpose. In other words, Sturt's use of prose is comparable to George Cook's use of the wheelwright's tools, and deserves equal attention.

Sturt's effort to find the proper style for his needs was as slow and arduous as the struggle to find his true subject. Once more we detect a split in Sturt's early attitude, a temptation towards 'fine prose' on the one hand, and a countryman's suspicion of the sophisticated on the other. In 1891 he expresses the desire to do 'some careful literary work, turning the sentences' (J(M), 136), but when a few years later he comes to record Bettesworth's conversation, he is aware of naturalness beyond the grasp of his recording pen. His ultimate realization involves, of course, a compromise between the two extremes. His prose demands care, the sentences must be 'turned,' but not in the direction of 'literary effects.' On the contrary, anything unnecessary or high-flown is ruthlessly expunged in the interest of the integrity of his subject. It is only at the close of his life that he can offer, still haltingly and uncertainly, a statement of his own practice: 'I do not know what "style" is. Critics have praised my own "style": but all I am conscious of is the effort to get very close home to a subject, to be very truthful in dealing with it, even to the faintest cadence' (J(M), 868). Verbal expression and moral attitude are thus, for Sturt, inseparable.

The importance of this coupling of method and outlook can hardly be exaggerated. Sturt could never be satisfied, as Jefferies sometimes was, with unalloyed description; there must always be a motive – an argument or an idea to be communicated. The direct converse to the folk whose group life he reconstructed, he was preoccupied with things of the mind. Even his country walks were devoted rather to thinking than to observation: 'I like to put my hands in my trouser pockets and wander easily, nursing the ideas. I would lie in wait for them to entrap them, not scare them by unseemly hurry' (J(M), 79). He admits in the same passage to being 'a hunter of impressions'; and, when caught, these would be carefully preserved in his journals like specimens in a butterfly collection, the value depending on the variety of kinds and the beauty of the individual examples. This is not, I hope, an idle comparison; it explains why the Journals, for all their inevitable fragmentation, prove the most satisfying of Sturt's writings. Here, above all, the virtues of exact and economical expression combine with sincerity of emotion to reveal an otherwise elusive intellectual truth.

No one in the English tradition has better claims to the title of rural philosopher than George Sturt. Certainly he carried to an extreme the brooding introspective tendency characteristic of the later writers considered in this book. It is a role beset with difficulties, and Sturt's particular dilemma is brilliantly summed up in the following journal entry, written at the end of an autumn day when the claims of the physical and mental lives seemed more than usually opposed: 'The choice was before me: should it be plums, or my ideas, that should be left to fall and spoil? I chose to save the plums; and am not quite sure whether the other is still to be had for the picking' (*J(G)*, 92). One of Sturt's chief strengths is the ability to acknowledge his difficulties with such frankness and grace. In other respects he may well be considered deficient; his lack of formal philosophical training renders him vulnerable when the admitted anomalies and inconsistencies in his work are pointed out, even if these can be explained, at least in part, by the paradoxes inherent in rural life. The fragmentary nature of his observations may also be held against him, though this is by no means inappropriate in view of the break-up of the way of life with which he was concerned; besides he would not be the first thinker to have expressed himself in detached axioms. But whatever the verdict on his philosophical abilities, Sturt's capacity for speculation, his independence of outlook, his dogged pursuit of a line of argument both unfashionable and (if accepted) highly disturbing, all these qualities distinguish his contributions to rural literature and make him appear a far more important figure than his literary output might at first suggest. Moreover his devotion to 'England's inner life' (*J(M)*, 783) provides a basic vision (the word is not, I think, inappropriate) which serves as a common ground for all his writings. Here, despite the fragmentation and the inconsistencies, we can detect a positive and unifying purpose. His work may be said to hang upon an unseen, undemonstrable, but secure thread – the common humanity that links Bettesworth, John Smith, and George Sturt himself, the same urge that unites the village craftsman and the artist. Characteristically Sturt sums this up in one of his dazzlingly simple journal entries: 'I think life lies very deep' (*J(M)*, 64).

NINE

W.H. Hudson

1841–1922

My chief interest and delight is in life – life in all its forms, from man
who 'walks erect and smiling looks on heaven' to the minutest organic atoms –
the invisible life.[1]

Hudson is unique among our rural writers by reason of his foreign birth, yet,
although he did not set foot on English soil until he was in his thirty-third year,
he never considered himself an alien. His ancestors had lived for generations in
Devonshire, but his grandfather emigrated to the United States, and his parents
moved from there to Argentina to engage in sheep-farming. As a consequence
Hudson was born, in 1841, on the pampas, and might reasonably have been
expected to remain there all his life. Although his father was by no means
prosperous, the Hudsons established themselves firmly in the new land. As
H.F. West has remarked, 'all of Hudson's family were and are Spanish speaking
Argentinians,'[2] and since his time, apparently, no member of the family has
visited either England or the United States. But the attraction of England, so
weak in the others, was in Hudson's case felt in the blood and felt along the
heart. He looked upon England, he tells us, as 'my spiritual country which so far
as I knew I was never destined to see,' but it was, none the less, 'the land of my
desire' (AIE, 275, 278). Throughout his youth and early manhood in Argentina
he always insisted on referring to England as 'home' (FAR, 328), and in his later
years he was fond of speculating upon the influence of ancestral memories in
drawing him to its shores. At all events once he arrived in England he settled
down permanently. A quarter of a century later he went through the formal
procedures and became a British subject.

When he walked down the gangplank at Southampton in 1874 Hudson saw himself as a returned exile rather than as a visiting stranger, but he seems to have been more of a South American than he was prepared to admit. His friend R.B. Cunninghame Graham described him later as 'an old Gaucho, born on the plains, with the slow speech, and silent ways of the plainsman,'[3] and most contemporary references stressed his apartness. His preoccupation with wild life caused many to liken him to an unfamiliar bird blown accidentally into strange country – in ornithological terms, a vagrant on the British list. While he was acquainted with many of the writers of his time, he never belonged to any literary society or clique; wherever he went, he maintained a sense of isolation. That he should emerge as a leading figure in the literature of the English countryside is, in one sense, no less remarkable than the rise of Joseph Conrad (whom Hudson knew well) as a major English novelist. In another sense, however, it is not so strange. The newcomer brings a fresh approach to his subject; he supplies, as Edward Garnett put it, 'a new lens to our faculties' (*TLT*, xii). New eyes notice what others miss – and at this time rural writing needed the stimulus of an original point of view. But we shall never appreciate the significance of Hudson's attitude unless we are aware of the circumstances of his earlier life.

He has left us a vivid if impressionistic account of his Argentinian upbringing in *Far Away and Long Ago*, and the frequent references to his early life in Argentina, scattered through his English books, show that he was constantly aware of its possibilities as a yardstick. The pampas were always available for purposes of comparison or contrast, and the key words which derive from them are 'open,' 'wild,' and 'free.' His early memories reveal a childhood of truly remarkable freedom – freer by far than Jefferies' English ideal as portrayed in *Bevis* – and the effect of these early years upon his interests and tastes is soon apparent. 'Most of the daylight hours were spent out of doors,' he recalls (*FAR*, 273), and he claims that at the age of six he was 'well able to ride bare-backed at a fast gallop without falling off' (*FAR*, 65). He had his own pony and was allowed to ride it as long and as far as he liked. As a result he could fairly regard himself as 'a field naturalist of six with a considerable experience of wild birds' (*FAR*, 82).

What Hudson learnt was not confined to ornithological facts, however; he obtained a lasting insight into the nature of wildness itself, and its relation to the concepts of freedom and solitude. The gaucho to whom Cunninghame Graham compared him is described by Hudson as one 'who lives half his day on his horse and loves his freedom as much a wild bird' (*FAR*, 70). According to Hudson's own testimony he would seem to have out-gauchoed the gauchos, since he records that 'during the first half of my life, I was constantly riding and sometimes passed weeks at a stretch on a horse every day from morning to night' (HRP, 36). Above all he learnt while still a child how to amuse himself on his own. For Hudson solitude never presupposed loneliness, and this is one reason, as we shall see, why his work escapes the oppressive melancholy of so much rural writing in his time.

Hudson's early life, then, was decidedly one of action, and he often looked back to it with nostalgic regret. To quote once more from Far Away and Long Ago, which Basil Willey has justly called 'Hudson's Prelude':[4] 'I had lived till [the age of fifteen] in a paradise of vivid sense-impressions in which all thoughts came to me saturated with emotion, and in that mental state reflection is well-nigh impossible' (FAR, 306). But Hudson's soul, like Wordsworth's, had enjoyed a fair seed-time which was to result in a rich literary harvest in later years. For Hudson's subsequent career, 'the life ... of the mind and spirit' as he calls it (FAR, 314), was in no way abstract, or detached from the earlier, active life on the pampas. Indeed he shows clearly how the one arose from the other. His love of nature led him, again like Wordsworth, to an interest in books. As he recalls in Afoot in England, 'in the distant days of my boyhood and early youth my chief delight was in nature, and when I opened a book it was to find something about nature in it, especially some impression of the feeling pro-duced in us by nature, which was, in my case, inseparable from seeing and hearing, and was, to me, the most important thing in life' (AIE, 272). Moreover the experience of wild and open places, of 'a vast solitude, where man has perhaps never been, and has, at any rate, left no trace of his existence' (IDP, 7) could raise him to feelings of sublimity and encourage the animistic feelings which ultimately had a profound effect on his world-view. In addition, as Richard Haymaker has noted, his wanderings across the plain in search of bird life led to an extension of his interest from birds to people and a consequent enlargement of his sphere from that of ornithologist or field naturalist to his higher, more demanding role as student of all life.[5]

Even if Hudson had made the move from Argentina to England under the most favourable circumstances, the change would have been momentous; as it was, however, it must have seemed little short of catastrophic. The years im-mediately following his arrival have with reason been described as the 'dark period' in his life. In Far Away and Long Ago he describes himself as one 'who feel[s], when I am out of sight of living, growing grass, and out of sound of birds' voices and all rural sounds, that I am not properly alive' (FAR, 3). Yet he discovered in 1874 that he could not earn even a meagre livelihood in England without residing in London. This was all the more tragically ironic since he possessed an uncompromising hatred for towns and cities. Even Buenos Aires, which fascinated him as a child, is remembered in *Far Away and Long Ago* chiefly as a city of smells and pestilence. London was less unhealthy, but also less colourful and invigorating.

Furthermore his marriage in 1876 to Emily Wingrave, who combined the roles of singer and landlady (with a singular lack of financial success in both enterprises), resulted in an additional limitation on his freedom. He seemed confined to London as to a prison. Twenty years later we find him describing his London house as situated in 'a treeless district, most desolate' (*BL*, 86), and his hatred of the capital is evident throughout his work. It is 'London the Monotonous' (*BL*, 195), 'that mighty, monstrous London' (*SL*, 22), and he complains to Morley Roberts of 'the pestilent atmosphere of London and its smart Society.'[6] The difficulty of escape is expressed in a moving, pathetic passage of rare personal confession in *Afoot in England*:

> The 'walks' already spoken of, at a time when life had little or no pleasure for us on account of poverty and ill-health, were taken at pretty regular intervals two or three times a year. It all depended on our means; in very lean years there was but one outing. It was impossible to escape altogether from the immense unfriendly wilderness of London simply because, albeit 'unfriendly,' it yet appeared to be the only place in the wide world where our poor little talents could earn us a few shillings a week to live on.   (*AIE*, 33)

Almost all the people who knew him comment on the inappropriateness of his London homes, of the shabby lodgings, and of his resemblance there to an imprisoned bird. Indeed the idea of Hudson confined like a caged eagle in Cobbett's 'Wen' readily explains his unending crusade against the keeping of wild animals as pets; Hudson had suffered with those whom he saw suffer.

Above all he needed liberty, freedom of movement, the freedom of an animal in the wild. His boyhood on the pampas had developed in Hudson a wanderlust comparable to Borrow's, and consequently, when the opportunity at last presented itself, Hudson made up for lost time. One has only to note the numerous addresses from which his later letters were written to realize the extent of his wanderings. He admits at one point to 'being rather of the Gipsy mind who loves the open heath better than the house' (*MBB*, 23), and it is scarcely surprising that on at least one occasion he was mistaken for 'nothing but a common tramp' (*TLT*, 120). Ruth Tomalin has commented on the preoccupation with the theme of imprisonment in *Nature in Downland*, most often manifesting itself in image and metaphor, but once directly in his acccount of meeting the released convict near Lewes.[7] But it was not just a matter of personal freedom. Hudson's genius for rural writing could not blossom in the claustrophobic presence of bricks and mortar. On one occasion he writes to

Morley Roberts: 'There is no prospect of a country book at present. I have had to be too much in town (where I can't do it)' (*MBB*, 57). He needed the release which only the freedom of the countryside could provide.

Ultimately, of course, Hudson became a great traveller, to the extent that Edward Thomas could justly write of him: 'He has seen England as few writers have since Cobbett.'[8] But whether he went on foot or by bicycle – or even, in the weakness of old age, in 'loathsome motor-cars'[9] – travelling for Hudson was always an end rather than a means, and the destination was rarely worked out in advance. He disliked a set scheme as much in his wanderings as in his books. 'My plan,' he writes in a letter to Roberts, 'is not to appear to have a plan' (*MBB*, 269); the subject is *A Hind in Richmond Park*, but it might as well have referred to a holiday in Hampshire or Wiltshire. He avoided any preconceived plan because it threatened to rob him of the exquisite sensation of freedom. For the same reason he eschewed maps – and particularly guide-books. His general policy was 'not to look at a guide-book until the place it treats of has been explored and left behind' (*AIE*, 4) because his desire, in the words Jefferies used of Gilbert White, was to keep his mind free and his eye open. His favourite days were those in which, as he says, 'I wandered miles in some new direction, never knowing whither the devious path would lead me' (*AIE*, 179). To this habit, he claims, he owed his most valuable experiences: 'In recalling those scenes which have given me the greatest happiness, the images of which are most vivid and lasting, I find that most of them are of scenes or objects which were discovered, as it were, by chance, which I had not heard of, or else had heard of and forgotten, or which I had not expected to see' (*AIE*, 5).

In *Hampshire Days* Hudson describes himself as 'a rambler about the country who seldom stays many days in one village or spot' (*HD*, 238). This is characteristic of him, and separates him from such writers as White or Mary Mitford or Jefferies who generally concentrate on giving a detailed picture of a deliberately limited area. The majority of Hudson's English books could have been called *Afoot in England*. Wherever he goes, he is the interested outsider who wanders accidentally into a particular situation, observes it, and passes on. This is most evident in *The Land's End*. Hudson had not visited Cornwall until 1905 and the book appeared in 1908. Throughout it he presents Cornish scenes and Cornish people as interesting but alien. The objective description of the naturalist is especially noticeable. He is essentially a wanderer among the rocks and in the villages, building up gradually but surely a panoramic picture of the land and its inhabitants. We get the distinct impression that Hudson is in a hurry, that he cannot afford to linger where he is for fear of missing something new around the next corner. He makes the point for himself in *Afoot in England*: 'It came into my mind that I could not very well settle there for the rest of my life; I could not, in fact, tie myself to any place without sacrificing certain other advantages I possessed; and the main thing was that by taking root I should deprive myself of the chance of looking on still other beautiful scenes and experiencing other sweet surprises' (*AIE*, 17). It is not by chance that Hudson's favourite natural object is not the tree, 'rooted in one dear perpetual place' in Yeats's words, but the bird with wings unclipped who is free at any moment to fly off in any direction as the mood takes him.

None the less, much as Hudson loved England, it could never offer him the wildness and liberty of the open Argentinian plains. In his more disillusioned moments it could become 'this tame England – this land of glorified poultry-farms' (*AAB*, 265), and his preferences in landscape and terrain often reveal the influence of the South American pampas. Of one sheltered village, a place that would have delighted Gilbert White or Jefferies or Edward Thomas, he writes: 'It did not suit me to stay in that village. Its charm consisted mainly in its seclusion, in its being hidden from the world in a hollow among woods and hills, and I love open spaces best, wide prospects from doors and windows, and the winds free to blow on me from all quarters' (*AAB*, 160). It is no accident that his first English book fully to demonstrate his particular gifts was *Nature in Downland*, which begins with a consideration of the exhilaration that he feels on the wind-swept hills. And, according to Richard Haymaker, even his attraction to 'Winterbourne Bishop,' the setting for *A Shepherd's Life*, lay in the fact that 'its very barrenness, when compared with many arcadian ones, was more like the home of his earliest years ... than any other place known to him in England.'[10] He is often to be found yearning for 'that solitariness and absence of human interest now so rare in England' (*BM*, 68), and more than anything he misses the truly wild animal, the creature of an unspoilt, non-human wilderness. Thus he loves the stag because it is 'an undoubted survivor, one which, encountered in some incult place where it is absolutely free and wild, moves us to a strange joy – an inherited memory and a vision of a savage, prehistoric land of which we are truer natives than we can ever be of this smooth sophisticated England' (*BN*, 32). Although he becomes 'a traveller in little things,' this Argentinian gaucho never quite reconciles himself to a small, overcrowded country. Fortunately, however, its size is offset by the abundance of its wild life, which fascinated the man who had qualified as a naturalist at the age of six. And it is to Hudson the naturalist that we must now turn.

Hudson is the only important rural writer since White to gain a considerable reputation as an expert naturalist. Three of his books, *The Naturalist in La Plata*, *Birds of La Plata*, and *British Birds*, clearly belong to natural history first and literature second, and it is obvious from most of his other works that his knowledge, particularly of ornithology, was more exact and more disciplined than that of the average observer. It is therefore important that we establish at the outset precisely the kind of naturalist that Hudson was or claimed to be.

In his introduction to *Men, Books and Birds* Morley Roberts, who combines the roles of scientist and imaginative writer while at the same time claiming to play Boswell to Hudson's Johnson, sums up Hudson's qualifications as follows:

> It is impossible to regard Hudson as a man of science. He was at once more and less ... The science under which the rank of a naturalist falls is obviously biology, and Hudson was certainly no biologist. He had not even the more or less complete text-book knowledge of the student and it takes far more than that to be a leader in biology ... He often reasoned and invented hypotheses without being aware of what had been said by his predecessors. This is shown plainly in ... his views on avian migration ... But he had a great grasp of facts and never pretended to be more than a field-naturalist.   (*MBB*, 12)

All this is clearly true, though it represents the attitude of the reigning scientific establishment, whose views Hudson himself was by no means prepared to accept as gospel.

For Hudson, like White and Jefferies before him, the field naturalists are the opposite of the closet naturalists, and he has little respect for the latter group, for men like Herbert Spencer, 'who was obliged to study animal habits in books' (*BN*, 163). He is continually irritated by the tendency of bird books to copy from each other instead of checking the previous findings by personal observation. Hudson's own book on British birds is refreshingly original because he makes maximum use of his own field experiences. The difference is well illustrated by an anecdote which Hudson later includes in *Birds and Man*:

> When I stated in a small work on *British Birds* a few years ago that jays had the custom of congregating in spring, a distinguished naturalist, who reviewed the book in one of the papers, rebuked me for so absurd a statement, and informed me that the jay is a solitary bird except at the end of summer and in the early autumn, when they are sometimes seen in families. If I had not made it a rule never to reply to a critic, I could have informed this one that I knew exactly where his information on the habits of the jay was derived from – that it dated back to a book published ninety-nine years ago. It was a very good book, and all it contains, some errors included, have been incorporated in most of the important ornithological works which have appeared during the nineteenth century. But though my critic thus 'wrote it all by rote,' according to the books, 'he did not write it right.' (*BM*, 79–80)

Throughout his life Hudson rebelled against the traditional knowledge that was hallowed by print but did not stand the test of verification in the field. The information contained in his own books is independent of the dust of the study.

His particular dislike is the scientific monograph which isolates a particular species and refuses to see it in relation to its neighbours, its environment, and the whole interrelating web of the world to which it belongs. He dislikes the scientific naturalist's 'anxiety to classify everything, ... his little busy brain, which loves neatness and symmetry' (LE, 167). Hudson himself, following Jefferies, is far too aware of the rich variousness of nature to see such narrowness as anything but a distortion. Not that he underrates the legitimacy, and indeed the importance, of such classification – this was one of Gilbert White's great strengths, and Hudson is highly appreciative of White's contribution. But Hudson knew that for White this was a means, not an end; he also knew that the state of natural history studies at the close of the eighteenth century demanded the kind of emphasis that White provided. He is conscious, however, of the new interests and demands of his own time. In his chapter on Selborne in *Birds and Man* he discusses at some length 'the marked difference in manner, perhaps in feeling, between the old [like White] and the new writers on animal life and nature.' This difference, he decides, centres upon their respective attitudes to facts: 'We are bound as much as ever to facts; we seek for them more and more diligently, knowing that to break from them is to be carried away by vain imaginings. All the same, facts in themselves are nothing to us: they are important only in their relations to other facts and things – to all things, and the essence of things, material and spiritual' (BM, 243, 244).

When Hudson landed in England in 1874 he had already won recognition as a field naturalist. He had been employed as a collector of specimens by the Smithsonian Institution in Washington, and had contributed various field reports concerning the bird life of Argentina and Patagonia to the *Proceedings* of the London Zoological Society. He had even criticized, and corrected, some of Darwin's South American observations. Once in England, however, Hudson abandoned such pursuits and turned his attention to the cause of bird protection. If this seems like a narrowing rather than a broadening of interests, the reason for the change is not far to seek. On the pampas, as Ruth Tomalin has demonstrated, Hudson followed the example of White, and this was only proper since the state of South American natural history demanded methods and approaches that were a century out of date elsewhere.[11] But Hudson was quick to realize that, in the rapidly developing world of the late nineteenth century, the old practices were no longer sufficient. The species which White had been content to observe and classify were now threatened by the commercial and destructive impulses of mankind, and needed to be preserved for future generations.

Once again Hudson's knowledge of the natural history of two continents proved invaluable. The dangers threatening wild life in England may have seemed obvious, but his experiences in South America were even more compelling. In the eleventh chapter of *A Hind in Richmond Park*, one finds dramatic – indeed, unforgettable – descriptions of the flocks of migratory birds on the pampas. 'It was not only the number of species known to me,' he writes, 'but rather the incalculable, the incredible numbers in which some of the commonest kinds appeared, especially when migrating' (*HRP*, 165). He describes the golden plover in immense multitudes 'covering an area of two or three acres, looking less like a vast flock than a *floor* of birds' (*HRP*, 166), and provides other accounts of the migrations of glossy ibis, doves, cowbirds, rock swallows, and upland plover. But, having built up his apparent climax, Hudson springs the trap by telling us that all this is a thing of the past, that in many instances the species have been brought to the verge of extinction:

> All this incalculable destruction of bird life has come about since the seventies of the last [i.e., nineteenth] century, and is going on now despite the efforts of those who are striving, by promoting legislation and by all other possible means, to save 'the remnant.' But, alas! the forces of brutality, the Caliban in man, are proving too powerful; the lost species are lost for all time, and a thousand years of the strictest protection – a protection it would be impossible to impose on a free people, Calibans or not – would not restore the still existing bird life to the abundance of half a century ago.
>
> The beautiful has vanished and returns not.   (*HRP*, 173–4)

Hudson's work on bird protection, then, was no abstract theory; it arose, like his overall interest in natural history, directly out of his experience 'in the field.' And he used, and appealed to, the experience of others. 'Probably there is not a local ornithologist in all the land,' he writes (and the land is now England), 'who could not say of some species that bred annually, within the limits of his own country, that it has not been extirpated within the last fifteen years' (*BM*, 190). In taking up this cause Hudson was challenging and condemning all sorts and conditions of men and women – egg-collectors, gamekeepers and their employers, specimen hunters for private collections, those who catch birds for their ornamental feathers, 'the regiment of horrible women who persist in decorating their heads with aigrettes and carcasses of slaughtered birds' (*AAB*, 39), and especially 'the cockney sportsman – the man who shoots birds that are unfit for food, merely for the pleasure of the thing.'[12] He can be witheringly contemptuous of those whose position and precepts ought to make them his associates rather than his enemies. Examples include certain naturalists and scientists whom Hudson saw as in league with the 'Plumage Merchants' (*MBB*, 344) – including the British Ornithologists' Union from which he resigned in protest against its failure to condemn collectors; most memorable of all, perhaps, is an acid portrait of 'a clergyman who was a zealous collector not of men's souls, but of birds' skins' (*BM*, 207). Hudson was a tolerant and magnanimous man, but the crimes committed against natural life roused him to a pitch of detestation: 'The only creatures on earth I loathe and hate are the gourmets, the carrion-crows and foxes of the human kind who devour wheatears and skylarks at their tables' (*AIE*, 153). As for game-preserving, the pheasant was the one bird in England that Hudson wished to see exterminated because its artificial protection was used as an excuse for the indiscriminate destruction of the native fauna (see *AAB*, 91).

Bird protection was the one matter of public concern in which Hudson actively participated in his English years. When we turn to his more general books, however, we find that, although the subjects upon which he writes are remarkably broad in range, this is a topic which recurs as a continuing and disturbing theme. Nor should this surprise us, for once again it sets him firmly in the camp of the field naturalists against the scientific theorists. The latter, in Hudson's view, were preoccupied with dissection and analysis – and he would have relished D.H. Lawrence's remark (adapted from D'Annunzio), 'Analysis presupposes a corpse.'[13] His own effort to keep wild animals and birds alive in the field was far more than a personal fanaticism; it was a basic principle that lay at the root of his attitude to the natural world. Nature was for him essentially living, and he had nothing but contempt for those who automatically associate natural history with dead, mounted specimens arranged according to scientific orderliness. The point is clearly made in *The Book of a Naturalist*, where the subject in question is snakes:

> That which we seek is not the viper, the subject of Fontana's monumental work, the little rope of clay or dead flesh in the British Museum, coiled in its bottle of spirits, and labelled '*Vipera berus*, Linn.'
> *We* seek the adder or nadder, that being venerated of old and generator of the sacred adder-stone of the Druids, and he dwells not in a jar of alcohol in the still shade and equable temperature of a museum.   (*BN*, 14–15)

By the same token Hudson's own writings are concerned not to describe with deadly statistical accuracy the precise length, weight, and other measurable facts to be discovered on the dissecting table. Instead he attempts to succeed where, he insists, the scientific naturalist invariably fails – in gaining 'the power to convey to the reader's mind a vivid image of the thing described' (*BN*, 210). He always writes for the amateur in the most literal sense of that much abused word, for the keen though not necessarily well-informed lover of nature, not for the professional specialist. Even the most 'scientific' of his English books, *British Birds*, is offered as 'a book intended for the general reader, more especially for the young' (*HBB*, vii). Consequently he is refreshingly unorthodox in his descriptions, even calling the poets to his aid and recommending Shelley on the skylark: 'Some ornithologist (I blush to say it) has pointed out that the poet's description is unscientific and of no value; nevertheless, it embodies what we all feel at times' (*HBB*, 247).

Hudson is convinced that the naturalist needs to be complemented by the poet if a complete picture of the natural world is to be communicated. He is well aware that the poet is often inaccurate and untrustworthy. At one point he calls William Cowper 'as bad a naturalist as any singer before or after him, and as any true poet has a perfect right to be.' He is 'as bad, let us say, as Shakespeare and Wordsworth and Tennyson' (*BM*, 65). It is typical of Hudson that he is sufficiently a naturalist to notice the poets' errors, but at the same time sufficiently an artist not to be disturbed by them. He is confident that 'poets and naturalists inhabit and cultivate separate but adjoining plots, and should be neighbourly' (*DMP*, 302). But if he is forced to make a decision, the artist in him requires him to honour the poet. As he admits in *The Book of a Naturalist*, the very title of which implies modestly but not altogether fairly that he himself belongs to the lesser group, 'the poet has the secret, not the naturalist.' And the reason he gives is one that we might expect: 'It is because the poet does not see his subject apart from its surroundings, deprived of its atmosphere, ... that we, through him, are able to see it too' (*BN*, 182, 183).

Hudson may be said, then, to occupy a place approximately half way between the 'naturalist' and the 'poet.' His distinction depends not so much on the facts he knows as on the events he observes, the open mind with which he ponders the consequences of his observations, and the essential imaginative faculty that enables him both to draw legitimate conclusions and to express clearly and vividly the complete experience he has known. The ideal naturalist, he would insist, is never merely passive, never just an observer. His true function is to create valid rules and principles out of the scattered facts that he has acquired, and in this creative challenge lies an aesthetic gratification. Far from qualifying his reputation as a scientist, this is, in Hudson's own opinion, a fundamental requirement for all scientific work of permanent value. As he writes to Morley Roberts, 'I believe, with Tyndall, that [imagination] is essential in science – that observing, experimenting, accumulating facts would lead to little or nothing without the faculty that is like intuition, or prophetic, which leaps forward to great generalization' (*MBB*, 259). Hudson differs from the orthodox scientist in the emphasis he puts on the generalization itself rather than on its validity. In *The Book of a Naturalist*, for example, he builds up a theory concerning the serpent's tongue, but its value for him does not reside solely in its relation to truth. 'Who cares,' he asks, 'if the structure [i.e., of his hypothesis] is all to tumble down again? Not I. Nevertheless the mere building is a pleasure, and the completion of the structure a satisfaction in that it puts something where before there was nothing' (*BN*, 142). His interest in nature is an essential part of his creative make-up, and vice versa. He is not content merely to share in the advance of knowledge; his own aesthetic satisfaction is central.

If the preceding discussion has suggested that Hudson's interests focus on a natural world from which man is excluded, such an implication should be qualified, though not altogether denied. When writing of his childhood in *Far Away and Long Ago*, he admits that 'my feathered friends were so much to me that I am constantly tempted to make this sketch of my first years a book about birds and little else' (*FAR*, 63–4). His title *Birds and Man* is clearly ordered according to Hudson's hierarchy of interest, and he is probably at least half-serious in the following declaration to Edward Garnett: 'You are, I am afraid, more interested in humans than in birds. 'Tis the other way about with me' (*HL*, 82). In *Adventures Among Birds* the prejudice is equally clear: 'I go not to Wells [-Next-the-Sea] in "the season" ... The wild geese are not there then ... Autumn and winter is my time' (*AAB*, 27). One detects here traces of a rather prickly humour that may well have been misinterpreted on occasion as acute misanthropy; Joseph Conrad, for instance, once complained that Hudson would have thought more of him if he had been a bird.[14]

But, as Edward Thomas remarks, Hudson is 'never a mere bird-man,'[15] and his own definition of a true naturalist emphatically denies the exclusion of the human species. 'A field naturalist,' he writes, 'is an observer of everything he sees – from a man to an ant or a plant' (*HRP*, 332). Moreover it is essential that mankind is considered in the same frank and impartial spirit. This habit of objective scrutiny, when applied to man, doubtless played its part in the creation of the myth of Hudson the misanthropist, but a more important factor was Hudson's avowed dislike of the urban population. The townsman, he declares, is 'the one living creature on the earth who does not greatly interest me' [*SL*, 150], but this statement should be read more positively to indicate his extreme interest in those who live in the country. His admiration is reserved for those 'simple people who live and for long generations have lived the simple life, who are on the soil with some of the soil on them' (*AAB*, 176–7).

In other words, Hudson is most interested in man when he is closest to being a creature of nature – when he can be considered as merely one of many species inhabiting the earth. He tells us in *A Shepherd's Life* that his liking for 'Winterbourne Bishop' derived from the fact that there the intimate association of man and nature is most evident. 'The final effect,' he writes, 'of this wide, green space with signs of human life and labour on it, and sights of animals – sheep and cattle – at various distances, is that we are not aliens here, intruders or invaders on the earth, living in it but apart, perhaps hating and spoiling it, but with the other animals are children of Nature, like them living and seeking our subsistence under her sky, familiar with her sun and wind and rain' (SL, 40). He is confident that the agricultural labourer is 'the healthiest and sanest man in the land, if not also the happiest' (SL, 55), and believes that this can be explained by the fact that his life, in its natural regularity, is closest to that of the animals: 'The labourer on the land goes on from boyhood to the end of life in the same everlasting round, the changes from task to task, according to the seasons, being no greater than in the case of the animals that alter their actions and habits to suit the varying conditions of the year' (SL, 54). But because this is so unusual a human condition, Hudson's preference is for other creatures. He admits at the close of A Shepherd's Life that Caleb Bawcombe's 'anecdotes of wild creatures interested me more than anything else he had to tell' (SL, 319).

In consequence human affairs, being only a part of the life of nature, must often take a backward place. Only occasionally (A Shepherd's Life is the best example) do we encounter in Hudson that loving awareness of the human past which is so characteristic a feature of the work of his disciple, H.J. Massingham. While writing of a visit to Ditchling, in Nature in Downland, Hudson observes that 'the extraordinary abundance of swallow and swift life interested me more than the ancient traditional yarns about Alfred the Great's connection with the village' (ND, 174). Though such remarks may also be explained by a pugnaciously provocative sense of humour, it would not be surprising to find an anti-historical streak in Hudson.

But it is not only the records of history that Hudson subordinates to the larger context. Even the beauties of landscape are not exempt. Those who begin to read The Land's End in the hope of finding memorable descriptions of scenery are doomed to disappointment. He tells his readers at the outset that 'the observables which chiefly draw me are the living creatures – the wild life – and not hills and villages and granite and serpentine cliffs and seas of Mediterranean blue. These are but the setting of the shining living gems' (LE, 2). The difference can be seen by comparing The Land's End with a book like Jefferies' Red Deer. The comparison is perfectly fair since Red Deer, the product of a brief but concentrated acquaintance with Exmoor where Jefferies was obviously an outsider, is of all Jefferies' books the closest in its essentials to the work of Hudson. But the first two chapters are significantly 'Red Deer Land' and 'Wild Exmoor.' The most vivid and memorable sections describe the country rather than the deer, and, even when the deer are the centre of interest, they are inseparable from the background against which they move. In The Land's End, by contrast, we remember the gulls, the jackdaws, the flowers, the surly Cornish people who fascinated but puzzled Hudson, yet we find remarkably little about the scenery. Background always remains background. Even in the chapter on Land's End itself the focus is less on the rocks and sea than on Hudson's viewing the tourists and trying to find an explanation for the area's popularity as a sight-seeing attraction.

It is with some shock that we become aware of the lack, at least in his English books, of landscape for its own sake. The virtues of a landscape are generally negative – it is not London and it is deserted by human beings, or, if a village, by the urban human beings whom Hudson detests. It may be of interest for what it contains – the birds, flowers, and insects, or even, if a village, its congenial inhabitants – but it is seldom of interest for what it is. Absent are the long passages of pure description that can be the high points of an essay by Jefferies, and are frequently the weak points in the prose of Edward Thomas. With Jefferies, however, the success depends upon his ability to record what he sees with brilliant objectivity. Thomas is less successful because he is continually striving to impress himself upon the landscape, to transform it into his own image. But Hudson, whose objectivity is supreme when he is recording the habits of wild creatures, spends all his time between such observations in meditating upon the significance of what he has seen. The landscape is 'good' if it contains no one to interrupt him. As a consequence, despite the objectivity, we are constantly aware of Hudson's own unifying presence. In his early *Birds in a Village* he is clearly conscious of the paradox: 'I might say, borrowing the pet notion of Anatole France, that in this small volume I have only been writing of myself *à propos* of British birds' (*BV*, 188). The countryside may provide 'the setting of the shining living gems' but (though Hudson is far too modest to say or even think it) the brightest and most central of the gems is himself.

In the latter part of his life Hudson's works enjoyed a considerable vogue. Unfortunately this was more on account of his style than his subject matter, and the separation of the two has had an unfortunate effect on his subsequent reputation. Joseph Conrad and Ford Madox Ford were particular enthusiasts. Two years after Conrad's death Ford wrote: 'Our greatest admiration for a stylist in any language was given to W.H. Hudson of whom Conrad said that his writing was like the grass that the good God made to grow and when it was there you could not tell how it came.'[16] This excessive and curiously naive adulation was bound to provoke an opposite reaction – especially since much of Hudson's writing is stylistically fastidious – and it is scarcely surprising to find Mrs Q.D. Leavis protesting a decade later against 'the Bloomsbury cult of W.H. Hudson' and 'the precious style that Hudson affected.'[17] But this, too, is extreme and has led to an unfortunate and undeserved neglect of Hudson's contribution to literature.

It is strange that Conrad, of all people, should have mistaken the illusion of effortlessness for actual facility. Morley Roberts assures us that Hudson 'wrote his books slowly and with infinite labour. During many of his later years he often set down no more than a hundred words or so in a day' (*MBB*, 7). This is understandable, though the statement that 'his preference was for the simplest style' (*MBB*, 8) is more difficult to accept, since it is so much more evident in his theory than in his practice. Perhaps the best way of illustrating the problem involved here is to quote Hudson's own stylistic analysis of Cobbett:

> He talked ... just as he wrote and as he spoke in public, his style, if style it can be called, being the most simple, direct and colloquial ever written. And for this reason, when we are aweary of the style of the stylist, where the living breathing body becomes of less consequence than its beautiful clothing, it is a relief, and refreshment, to turn from the precious and delicate expression, the implicit word, sought for high and low and at last found, the balance of every sentence and perfect harmony of the whole work – to go from it to the simple vigorous unadorned talk of *Rural Rides*. (*AIE*, 111–12)

While comparing Cobbett favourably with the elegant stylist, Hudson is seemingly unaware that he belongs himself to the latter category. This passage is, indeed, an excellent example of Hudson's almost exquisite concern for the right word and the harmonious rhythm. 'When we are aweary of the style of the stylist ...' The clause might legitimately be described as 'pure Hudson,' yet it is 'the style of the stylist' itself.

Here it may not be irrelevant to note that much of Hudson's early work appeared in the 1890s. True, one finds nothing in his writing that could be labelled decadent, but a love for the delicately convoluted sentence, the occasional attempt at 'fine writing,' and especially the straining towards a sophisticated whimsicality – all these may be seen as *fin de siècle* traits occurring incongruously in the work of one whose interests and attitudes seem so refreshingly opposed to the artistic fashions of the period. Hudson ultimately came into his own, of course, in the early years of this century when the cult of the open road developed as a necessary reaction against the hothouse aestheticism of the nineties. He succeeded in acclimatizing himself with little difficulty – we find none of the opposition between rural subject matter and Paterian treatment that detracts from the earlier work of Thomas – but traces of the earlier decade remain in his prose. There is, for example, his unfortunate fondness for baby language and patronizing diminutives. Even if we confine ourselves to a single volume, *Nature in Downland* (1900), we soon find references to 'little birds' nesties,' 'the little winged men and women called birds,' 'the wee fairy yellow trefoil,' and even 'bunny' (*ND*, 10, 49, 69). Likewise his use of pathetic fallacy often jars, and the comparatively numerous scenes in which he imagines birds talking are rarely successful. The embarrassingly cute sketches from *A Travel-*

ler in Little Things in which Hudson plays Ruskin or Lewis Carroll to a succession of young girls whom he insists on describing as 'maidies' (*TLT*, 109, 117) are only extreme instances of a sentimentalizing tendency that can frequently be detected not far below the surface of even his best work. All this is surprising since it seems so clearly at odds with the impression of Hudson we receive from the memoirs of those who knew him.

Fortunately it is also at odds with the personality most often visible in his writings. Perhaps the predominant effect of Hudson's work is a conversational casualness in which apparent effortlessness is achieved not only by the colloquial rhythms of much of the prose, but by the way in which he takes the reader into his confidence. In *A Shepherd's Life*, for example, he explains openly and frankly how he came to gather the information out of which the book was created. He is, moreover, disarmingly honest about his digressions ; the following paragraph-opening from *Afoot in England* is typical: 'Here is a true and pretty little story, which may or may not exactly fit the theme, but is very well worth telling' (*AIE*, 162). Hudson carries this sort of effect to an extreme in *Birds and Man* where the technically irrelevant chapter on 'The Secret of the Charm of Flowers' is deliberately introduced because 'it must strike most readers that a great fault of books on birds is, that there is too much about birds in them' (*BM*, 112). This casualness (which an unsympathetic reader might describe as excessively whimsical or blatantly slapdash) may in fact be just as calculated as his more rhetorical stylistic effects, but at least it has the merit of breaking down the barrier between writer and reader. He does not try to deceive us with false connections or to foster the illusion that he is more organized than he is ; we know where we are with Hudson.

Once again we find ourselves explaining a rural writer's success by his ability to present himself as much as the world of nature; but the ways in which this can be achieved are, of course, numberless. A writer like Borrow will mould his personality until he has created a new character, but we do not feel this about Hudson. He is more like White, demonstrating his approach to wild life while at the same time presenting information. His style is by no means artless or uniform, but at any given moment it is appropriate to Hudson's mood. His praise of Gerarde's style may be applied to his own: 'He is for ever fresh and full of variety and agreeable surprises, like Nature herself' (*ND*, 52). Just as Hudson is anxious to present the whole of nature, so he is prepared to reveal the whole of himself – and when he is at his best the two work in unison. For the shrewdest and most balanced account of Hudson as a stylist we must turn (as so often for writers in the rural tradition) to the assessment of Thomas:

> At first sight, at least to the novice who is beginning to distinguish styles without discriminating, Mr. Hudson's is merely a rather exceptionally unstudied English,

perhaps a little old-fashioned. Nothing could be farther from the truth. It is, in fact, a combination as curious as it is ripe and profound, of the eloquent and the colloquial, now the one, now the other, predominating in a variety of shades which make it wonderfully expressive for purposes of narrative and of every species of description – precise, humorous, rapturous and sublime. And not the least reason of its power is that it never paints a bird without showing the hand and the heart that paints it. It reveals the author in the presence of birds just as much as birds in the presence, visible or invisible, of the author.[18]

The last point is essential.

'Everything in nature interests me,' Hudson once remarked (*MBB*, 212), and although he understandably gives rein to his own preferences, he never loses sight of the whole. This, indeed, is his great contribution to the rural tradition – a vision of nature that is capable of uniting what we too often keep separate in isolated compartments. Thus the mind that created Rima, the nature spirit of the tropical forest in *Green Mansions*, or the post-Ovidian fantasy of the boy metamorphosed into a wryneck in *Birds in Town and Village*, can also speculate about avian migration and develop theories of sense perception in *A Hind in Richmond Park*. This is not merely a matter of versatility, nor is the connection achieved through style alone. The fact is that Hudson's animistic sense of the unity of all life provides him with an *a priori* unity that survives the crumbling of his orthodox faith. His subsequent description of himself as a 'religious atheist' (*MBB*, 153) shows that, although, like Jefferies, he was no longer able to believe in a personal and benevolent creator, he could never accept the claims of scientific materialism to explain (or, rather, explain away) the mystery of life. To him, in the words Wordsworth used of Coleridge, 'the unity of all hath been revealed.'[19] As parts of the whole, we are incapable of fully comprehending the overall unity, but this no more absolves us from speculating on the mystery than it justifies us in pretending that no mystery exists. His unshaken and unshakeable faith in the beauty and coherence of the universe provides the poetic spark which unifies his creative work. It is, indeed, a correlative to the unifying force behind all life.

I have described Hudson as a field observer, and I have also spoken of his vision of nature. If we are incapable of connecting observation and vision, if 'seeing' is no more to us than an automatic reflex action of the eye, then we shall never succeed in understanding Hudson. His elevation of the poet above the naturalist has already been referred to [see p. 181 above], and the distinction is ultimately the same as Blake's – between those who see with and those who see through the eye. The 'single vision' of the microscope-peering, data-recording scientist is, for Hudson as for Blake, no more than 'Newton's sleep.'[20] If the object seen does not produce an emotional effect upon the seer, it lacks significance. In *A Shepherd's Life* Hudson contrasts Caleb Bawcombe's vivid and retentive memory with those of naturalists who have to set down all that they see in a notebook before they forget it. Caleb had no need for a notebook, and Hudson comments: 'It was, I take it, because he had sympathy for the creatures he observed, that their actions had stamped themselves on his memory, because he had seen them emotionally' (*SL*, 287). This last clause is crucial. The same thought turns up again and again. In *The Book of the Naturalist* he observes: 'Unless the soul goes out to meet what we see we do not see it; nothing do we see, not a beetle, not a blade of grass'' (*BN*, 211). And as early as *Nature in Downland* he sums up the matter in five italicized words – '*what we see we feel*' (*ND*, 24).

But Hudson's responsibility as a writer is to make *us* feel – to communicate the vision, or at least the result of the vision, that he has known. What he has called the 'sense of the supernatural in natural things' (*FAR*, 237) requires the poet or artist not only to feel it but also to recreate it. This, indeed, is man's privilege and function within the whole. Hudson is less emphatic on the point than Jefferies, but would ultimately agree that man's capacity for vision, his gift for creating out of the varied elements of the natural world a consistent and satisfying landscape of true reality in the mind, earns him a central place. Hudson's success as a writer depends upon his ability to present as clearly as possible the all-important relationship between his own temperament and the world as he interprets it.

Hudson's attitude to the natural world which he loved so well was a mixture of despair and hope. While he was by no means exempt from the rural equivalent of *fin de siècle* melancholy so characteristic of even the outdoor writing of his day, his interests and temperament saved him from the extremes of self-conscious intellectualism. In the early 1920s H.J. Massingham found his work full of 'the profound melancholy that must be the lot of all true naturalists and lovers of life to-day who see the heritage of evolution vanishing,'[21] and his accounts of the contemporary destruction of wild life, symbolized most painfully by the fate of Rima in *Green Mansions*, certainly make depressing reading. But, although in his more pessimistic moments (when, for example, he refers in *A Shepherd's Life* to 'the beautiful, which cannot be preserved in our age' [*SL*, 20]) he seems close to despair, this is offset by what Edward Garnett calls 'his intense zest for the living fact' (*HL*, 5).

The energetic enthusiasm, legacy of his pampas childhood, which so impressed all who met him may not be immediately discernible in his English books, but it is indirectly responsible for much of their quality. Thus his strenuous efforts on behalf of bird protection were (though he was doubtless unaware of this) even more beneficial to himself than they were to the birds themselves. If Hudson is the most natural and well rounded and, on balance, the happiest of our latter-day rural writers, one of the chief reasons lies in this purposeful activity. While Sturt was forced back upon the detailed reconstruction of a vanished society, while Thomas continually analyzed the workings of his own mind and Williamson was haunted and obsessed by the horrors of war, Hudson succeeded in balancing action against thought, hope against despair – even, perhaps, nature against art. Jefferies had separated man from nature, with the result that, although he longed for the healing power of nature, his feverish search prevented him from achieving his goal. Hudson was more circumspect; in exploring nature for its sake, rather than his own, he was able to find personal peace.

Hudson was only too aware of 'the oppression, the curse of books, the delusion that they contain all knowledge' (*HRP*, 85). When he went into the countryside, he left books and the worries of intellect behind. This does not mean, of course, that he ceased to think – merely that thinking was focused upon the actualities confronting him, not upon intellectual abstractions. He could, therefore, write knowingly of a wilderness 'to which a man might come to divest himself of himself – that second self which he has unconsciously acquired – to be like the trees and animals, out of the sad atmosphere of human life and its eternal tragedy' (*TLT*, 201). Consequently the state of nature did not depress or repel him, as it did Jefferies, when he saw it in its inhuman and antihuman forms. Hudson's attitude – unintellectual, perhaps, but obviously healthy – is best indicated by his reaction on seeing a spider consume a grasshopper: 'He who walks out of doors with Nature, who sees life and death as sunlight and shadow, on witnessing such an incident wishes the captor a good appetite, and, passing, thinks no more about it' (*HD*, 45). Only a sentimentalist could condemn this as callous; it is, rather, a sign of maturity. Hudson, the 'religious atheist,' was above all else a worshipper of life, and he knew that death was an inevitable part of the life process. To an over-conscious humanity death is fearful because it is continually anticipated. Hudson himself, all too human, possessed this fear unusually strongly. As he remarks to Morley Roberts in words that are far more profound than their apparent conventionality suggests, 'death is too horrible to think about.'[22] But, as the Keats of 'Ode to a Nightingale' knew, there is no such fear in unthinking nature, because wild creatures are incapable of comprehending the idea of death. 'They are always happy in their way,' Hudson writes,' and when they die, die quickly ... The lower animals are only unhappy when made so by man' (*BV*, 193). 'Nature red in tooth and claw' was, he believed, an incomplete picture, but its main inadequacy lay in the false emphasis created by the observer. Hudson's own angle of vision is clearly preferable: 'The main thing was the wonderfulness and eternal mystery of life' (*BN*, 22).

TEN

Edward Thomas

Who shall measure the sorrow of him that hath set his heart upon that which
the world hath power to destroy, and hath destroyed?[1]

The last work of W.H. Hudson, found unfinished among his papers at the time
of his death, was a foreword to the posthumous collection of essays by Edward
Thomas entitled *Cloud Castle*. There Hudson, an unusually reserved man, pays
tribute to Thomas as 'my friend and one of the most lovable beings I have ever
known.' At the same time, however, he stresses the fundamental difference in
their situations: 'We were poles apart in the circumstances of our lives. He, an
Oxford graduate, and a literary man by profession; I, unschooled and unclassed, born and bred in a semi-barbarous district among the horsemen of the
pampas.'[2] This unrevised statement is not as clear as it might be – Hudson too
was 'a literary man by profession' (though this was the result of accident rather
than of intention), and Thomas's progress from the lower-middle-class world of
Wimbledon through Oxford to an uncertain and precarious livelihood as, for
the most part, reviewer and publisher's hack left him, if not unclassed, at least
declassed. None the less, the observation draws attention to features of
Thomas's life which separate him not only from Hudson but from almost all
earlier writers in the rural tradition.

One major difference is even more extreme than Hudson suggested. While
Hudson lived out his early years on the pampas, Thomas was the first of the
writers we are considering to have been born and bred in London, and he is
obviously sensitive to what he once called his 'accidentally cockney nativity.'[3]
Some writers might have turned this circumstance into a source of strength. It is

characteristic of Thomas, however, that instead of making the best of both worlds he should see the fact as a liability. In *The South Country* he describes himself as 'neither townsman nor countryman,'[4] and numerous references throughout his work suggest that this was a sensitive subject. It is clear that, to quote Herbert G. Wright, 'he brought with him an equipment of mind and sense very different from that of the rustic.'[5] Moreover he was painfully aware of his lack of rural roots, an awareness that had a palpable effect upon his writing.

In Thomas's life the pull between town and country manifested itself early. His first memory, significantly enough, was of being 'alone and happy to be so … in the tall grass and buttercups of a narrow field at the end of London.'[6] This must have been the earliest revelation of a new and exciting world beyond the bricks and mortar of the south London suburbs in which he grew up. When he was a little older, he was fortunate enough to spend many of his school holidays away from home, with relatives in Wales and, more often, in Wiltshire where, according to his own testimony, he 'became a Wiltshire boy in accent' (*CET*, 63). The chance of having a grandmother living in Swindon played a crucial part in the growth of the future writer, since it caused him to explore and fall in love with the Jefferies country at an early and impressionable age. Here his interest in natural history, stimulated by his friendship with David Uzzell, the peasant and ex-poacher who, as John Moore has noted, 'might have walked clean out of the pages of his beloved Jefferies,'[7] blossomed into a lifelong enthusiasm. He went on fishing expeditions, of course, and indulged in the boyish pursuits of butterfly- and egg-collecting; it is noteworthy, however, that 'the moving to and fro among quiet places in the warm weather was the substantial part of the pleasure' (*CET*, 118). By the time he was fourteen or fifteen he kept 'a more or less daily record of notable events, the finding of birds' nests, the catching of moles or fish, the skinning of a stoat, the reading of Richard Jefferies and the naturalists.'[8] The emergence of the observer and writer can therefore be seen as a clear and straightforward development from his Wiltshire visits. As his wife Helen has rightly emphasized, 'the years which he had spent in the Jefferies country in Wiltshire were the most treasured memories of his boyhood … The downs country about Swindon he knew and loved as no other part of England.'[9]

But if Wiltshire brought sunshine and happiness into Thomas's early life, the outskirts of London provided the accompanying shadows and hints of melancholy that figured equally in his personality and are invariably present in his writings, whether in prose or in verse. Although the Balham of his boyhood is evoked with nostalgic affection in Thomas's single attempt at extended fiction, *The Happy-Go-Lucky Morgans*, his more frequent reaction is to be found in a reference, from one of his letters to Gordon Bottomley, to 'my chiefly pathetic memories of the Suburbs.'[10] These recollections, significant documents for assessing the psychological effects of urban sprawl, usually involve sad stories of loss and deprivation. Thus he begins one essay, 'Broken Memories,' with an apparently genuine extract from a local London newspaper: 'Mr.— the well-known merchant, is building a fine house, half a mile from the — Road. Close upon two acres of woodland have been felled, where, by the way, the largest and juiciest blackberries I know used to be found.' This, for Thomas, is typical. He comments: 'And in this way many suburbans have seen the paradise of their boyhood effaced' (HS, 103). Such was the world into which Thomas was born, and from which he was constantly trying to escape. While Jefferies, born in the country, had been impressed when living in the suburbs by the amount of countryside within easy reach of the metropolis, a subject which he treats in Nature Near London, Thomas, in the reverse situation, has a very different viewpoint. Writing a quarter of a century after Jefferies, he concentrates rather on the domination and destruction of Nature by London. The (urban) shadows were lengthening rapidly.

The chapter 'London to Guildford' from In Pursuit of Spring is important here. Thomas clearly sees this no-man's-land between city and country as his physical home, and he hates the insult that it offers to his spirit. Its ugliness and the ease with which it can be exploited are central issues:

It is so easy to make this flat land sordid. The roads, hedges, and fences on it have hardly a reason for being anything but straight. More and more the kind of estate disappears that might preserve trees and various wasteful and pretty things: it is replaced by small villas and market gardens. If any waste be left under the new order, it will be used for conspicuously depositing rubbish.[11]

Thomas is less conscious of the plants growing up between the paving-stones than of the rash of 'hotels, inns, tea-shops, and cottages with ginger-beer for the townsman who is looking for country of a more easy-going nature' (IPS, 45). He finds it more and more difficult to reach a haven 'far enough from London for feelings of security' (HS, 108). Even in The Happy-Go-Lucky Morgans he refers to 'an angry murmur broken by frantic metallic clashings' which turns out to be the 'devilish babble' of London. Thomas insists that it is 'inhuman,' and continues: 'As I listened it seemed rather to be a brutish yell of agony during the infliction of some unspeakable pain, and though pain of that degree would kill or stupefy in a few minutes, this did not.'[12]

The opposition between city and countryside was exacerbated in Thomas's case by the clash of attitudes and ambitions between himself and his father. A civil servant committed to the cult of progress, full of exalted, urban ambitions for his eldest son, the father was wholly unsympathetic to Thomas's love for useless and unprofitable rambling in the outdoors. Though himself a writer, the father's interests were limited to positivism and the 'religion of humanity,' and it is clear that Edward, though he writes diplomatically of 'the radical and the free-thinking influence of home' (*LS*, 19), found this insipid and complacent rationalism highly oppressive. Helen Thomas noticed 'a strange feeling of disharmony in that house' and remarked that Edward 'was the only one who had a love of nature and literature.'[13] For his own part, Thomas complained to Bottomley: 'All my life I have been in the hands of those who care for other and even opposite things' (*LGB*, 52). More relevant to our purpose, however, is the fact that, in his autobiographical fragment posthumously published as *The Childhood of Edward Thomas*, he explains his immediate attraction to Jefferies' work by its dramatic contrast to his own upbringing. He was fascinated by Jefferies' accounts of 'the free open-air life, the spice of illegality and daring, roguish characters – the opportunities so far exceeding my own, the gun, the great pond, the country home, the apparently endless leisure ... Obviously Jefferies had lived a very different boyhood from ours' (*CET*, 134–5). At this point Thomas doubtless underestimated the degree of idealization in Jefferies' memoirs. Throughout his life, however, he was searching for the world about which Jefferies wrote – a world preserved, he hoped, somewhere in the elusive 'heart of England.'

We have already noted the extent to which the rural tradition in literature was stimulated by the effects of the Industrial Revolution, that it was a literature created in the main for urban consumption. As Thomas writes somewhat sardonically, 'for the villa residents and the more numerous others living "in London or on London" who would be or will be villa residents, all our country literature is written.'[14] In Thomas's case the townsman has himself created the product, yet, as the tone of the quoted passage indicates, his attitude is ambivalent. He is at one and the same time personally aware of the need for such a literature, yet scornful of the attitudes that so often accompany it. This leads to a pronounced self-consciousness in his writing, an impassioned straining towards the experience so greatly to be desired, balanced by a lack of confidence frequently manifested in studied flippancy or cynical bitterness. Subject (Thomas) and object (the natural world) are separated as if by an unbridgeable ravine; the very words themselves seem barriers between man and nature. In 'Cloud Castle' he puts into the mouth of an artist sentiments that clearly reflect a consciousness of his own upbringing and attitudes: 'This Nature poetry-stuff,' the artist maintains, 'is the jejune enthusiasm of townsmen who are ashamed to confess that they are such. It dates from the turning of England into a town with a green backyard. When men lived in the fields and rose early, they cared too much for these things to please each other by writing impressively upon them' (*CC*, 35). When Thomas seeks 'as complete a remoteness as possible from towns, whether of manufactures, or markets or of cathedrals' (SC, 3), he knows perfectly well that his writing suffers by contrast with that of earlier ages in being primarily escapist and therapeutic.

The Heart of England, whose first chapter is entitled 'Leaving Town,' and In Pursuit of Spring both present his own individual version of the Londoner's escape into the countryside, but the chapter called 'A Return to Nature' in The South Country contains his most moving and eloquent expression of this theme. In this sketch a man whom Thomas meets by chance at an inn invites him to 'come and share his place' (SC, 73), which turns out to be beneath an oak tree in a field. There in the gathering darkness he tells the story of his life: how his father, whose favourite books were 'The Compleat Angler and Lavengro, the poems of Wordsworth, the diaries of Thoreau and the Natural History of Selborne' (SC, 76), was driven to a consumptive's death by mean, soul-destroying labour in London, but bequeathed to himself a passionate desire for the rural life; how, for the past ten years, he has lived a schizophrenic existence working as a clerk in London during the winter and as a wandering agricultural labourer in the summer. This is not, however, an ideal solution, and every year the change becomes more difficult. He goes on to describe with deep pathos the irony of the situation which, we cannot help thinking, is Thomas's also: 'I realize that I belong to the suburbs still. I belong to no class or race, and have no traditions. We of the suburbs are a muddy, confused, hesitating mass, of small courage though much endurance' (SC, 85). They part next morning, but a few years later Thomas (or, rather, the 'I' of the story) catches a last glimpse of him in London in a pathetic, helpless procession of the unemployed. It is a characteristic Thomas sketch, midway between fact and fiction, between a personal experience and a deliberate short story, reminiscent of Borrow's encounters with figures who embody some of his own traits. Much of its force is derived from its being a possible allegory both of Thomas himself and of all those (E.M. Forster's Leonard Bast in Howards End immediately springs to mind) who feel alienated from modern city life but are unable to escape it. In a number of ways, including the Welsh ancestry of the suburbanite and the explicit comparison between his situation and that of the hack-writer, Thomas conveys the personal relevance of the narrative.

As his wife reminds us, however, Edward Thomas's was a 'strange complex temperament,'[15] and much of the complexity stems from the fact that he was not only a suburbanite with a yearning for the country but also, as Hudson stressed, an Oxford graduate. At this point we may realize with some surprise that, Gilbert White excepted, he is the first writer under consideration in this book to have attended a university. In White's time, of course, the distinction between town and country was by no means rigid. England was still predominantly agricultural, and her colleges were filled with the sons of rural squires and rural clergy. But even by the close of the eighteenth century the change from the countryside to a university town was found by Wordsworth to be 'Migration strange for a stripling of the hills, / A northern villager.'[16] The same difficulty of adjustment was experienced in the nineteenth century by Tennyson and numerous others, but for Thomas, the middle-class suburbanite whose first book, *The Woodland Life*, had already been published, the contrasts must have been particularly strong. The friend of a Wiltshire poacher, the authority on both moles and mole-catchers, now found himself in the company of sophisticated young undergraduates who, though less well read and far less mature than himself, were confident in their manners and judgments (in a way that Thomas most decidedly was not) and failed to share his enthusiasm for Borrow and Jefferies. The surviving biographical evidence suggests that he found adaptation a considerable strain.

More important for our purposes, however, is the effect of this period upon his writing. I shall be discussing later the unfortunate, because unsuitable, stylistic influence of Walter Pater that is clearly strengthened by, if not wholly attributable to, his Oxford years. But this stylistic influence is itself the reflection of a more general attitude, an awareness of an intellectual position that is brought to, instead of derived from, the rural subject matter. Thomas now realizes that this 'sad passion for Nature,' as he calls it on at least two occasions,[17] is a predominant feature of contemporary rural writing for which there are historical and sociological explanations. 'There are passages in Fielding,' he claims, 'which have a country sentiment not to be challenged in our more elaborate style: they are of a genuine rusticity, while in the finest things of a later day the landscape is pensive with a by no means rustic colouring' (*TC*, 20). This is not just a matter of following out a new line of thought or exploiting a prevailing fashion; Thomas is particularly conscious of this languid, introverted streak in himself. Thus at one point he goes so far as to state, 'I rarely see much in the country,' an astonishing remark from one so often praised for the minuteness of his natural observation, but he goes on to explain the paradox by admitting: 'I always carry out into the fields a vast baggage of prejudices from books and strong characters that I have met' (*HE*, 138). While lamenting the Londoner's physical spoliation of the countryside, Thomas may be found guilty of a kind of mental spoliation. He brings, one might say, not waste paper and empty bottles, but urban restlessness and melancholy. There is a brooding, introspective, academic quality about so much of Thomas's prose writing that is foreign to his material; what he calls in one place 'a compulsion to meditation' (*HE*, 36) too often emanates not from the land but from himself. That the influence of his Oxford years is responsible for much of this can be seen, I think, from the following sentence: 'I have found only two satisfying places in the world in August – the Bodleian library and a little, reedy, willowy pond' (*HE*,

73). The thought is perhaps less significant than the stance which Thomas takes up in order to express it. This is a new but not altogether reassuring note in rural writing.

Thomas once commented in a letter that 'a man in the country must be a naturalist, an historian, an agriculturist, or a philosopher, and I am none of them' (*LGB*, 139). He meant, of course, that he was not a trained expert in any of these areas. But he more than made up for this deficiency, not only (like Jefferies) by his wide if 'amateur' knowledge of most aspects of the countryside, but by his intimate acquaintance with earlier writers in the rural tradition. It is not surprising that, forced to spend most of his boyhood in a south London suburb, he should be attracted by those writers who could recreate for him the experience of being in the country. Thus he reports reading a number of books on natural history as a child and receiving *The Compleat Angler* as a birthday or Christmas present, and a little later, in his own words, 'I read books of travel, sport and natural history. I remember those of Waterton, Thomas Edward, Buckland, Wallace, Charles Kingsley, but above all Richard Jefferies' (*CET*, 56, 134). Of all the authors considered in this study, Thomas is the most knowledgeable on rural writing. This knowledge results in some sensitive and abiding literary criticism. His studies of Borrow and Jefferies remain valuable after well over half a century, and it is to be regretted that he never wrote the projected volumes on Gilbert White and Hudson. Although he disliked *A Literary Pilgrim in England* 'more than anything he had ever had to write for bread-and-butter,'[18] both the detail involved and the speed at which it was written demonstrate the extent to which such literary associations had penetrated into his being.

There was, however, a less fortunate aspect of his wide reading in the rural writers. W.H. Hudson shrewdly argued that Thomas's literary awareness had an inhibiting effect on his noncritical books: 'His appreciation of other men's work has been too keen – too ineradicable, and only allows him at rare moments to be unadulterated Edward Thomas' (*HL*, 239). A good deal of Thomas's self-consciousness stems, I suspect, from his knowledge that his subject matter had been treated often enough in the past. And not only in the past. 'A great many,' he observes bitterly, 'must be walking over England nowadays for the primary object of writing books,'[19] and one often gets the impression that he is desperately searching for a new approach. On at least one occasion he is explicit on this point. In *Beautiful Wales* he writes: 'I find it impossible to visit the famous places (and if I visit them, my predecessors fetter my capacity and actually put in abeyance the power of the places).'[20]

Thomas comments indirectly on his own approach to the countryside in a section of *The South Country* concerning an artist who serves, like the suburbanite and so many of Thomas's inventions, as an *alter ego*. He lives in a village which provides the perfect context for his work, and Thomas describes it in characteristic terms: 'Like all beautiful things in their great moments the whole scene was symbolic, not only in the larger sense of expressing in an outward and visible way an inward grace, but in the sense that it gathered up into itself the meanings which many other scenes only partly and in a scattered way expressed.' Thomas approves of the artist because, unlike many landscape painters, he does not enter into competition with the nature in which he lives and works:

> He was a great lover of [natural objects] ... But he loved them too well to draw and paint them ... He painted the images which they implanted – such was their love of him and his of them – in his brain ... Such is the personality of the artist that all this refinement only made more powerful than ever the spirit of the motionless things, the trees, the pools, the hills, the clouds.   (SC, 205–6)

Thomas's ideal is similar, but unfortunately his own personality is less positive and assured than that of his creation. Besides, Thomas uses words rather than pigments, and the artistic problems involved are somewhat different: Thomas's need is to move closer to, not farther from, his natural subject matter. The importance of the whole sketch lies in its applicability to Thomas's own situation, here interpreted, unambiguously, as an *artistic* problem. It both describes and embodies Thomas's hard and intensive search for an appropriate form and style.

'Dark furrowed boughs of elm-trees in line dip like a bank of galley-oars towards the meadow.' This is the opening sentence of 'The Sweet o' the Year,' the first essay in Thomas's first book, *The Woodland Life*, and it is worth examining in some detail since it contains elements which are to loom large in his later writings. We notice at once that it is the work of one who combines original observation with imaginative sensitivity. The picture is vividly conveyed to us, but it is clear that the writer is concerned not only with a visual image but also with a personal mood communicated through the rhythms and associations of the words selected. At the same time the simile, though original and striking, is one that directs us from rather than towards the objects described. This is a far cry from Cobbett's natural images that enforce and embody the rural point of view. Although Thomas claims at one point that he 'had begun to write accounts of [his] walks in an approach as near as possible to the style of Jefferies,' he also admits that he 'had begun to euphemize' early (CET, 136, 145), ravishing the language, as he writes elsewhere, 'at least as much for ostentation as for use' (LS, 19). It is clear from *The Woodland Life* that, even if he was not fully aware of the fact at the time, the 'literary,' even academic attitude to the natural world was dominant from the start. His later weakness for 'style' and fine writing, encouraged by Pater and Oxford, was only a conscious development of a strain that had always been latent. The self-conscious sensitivity, which was to become a conspicuous and inhibiting feature of his work, was never far below the surface.

The Woodland Life, while obviously of only minor importance, is a promising first book. The influence of Jefferies is strong. This can be seen in 'The Spring o' the Year,' whose title (but not the archaism within it) seems to have been borrowed from a posthumously published essay of Jefferies which, ironically enough, Thomas himself was later to collect for publication in *The Hills and the Vale*. The scene is set in 'Wiltshire meadows'[21] and evidently deals, like the second essay, 'Lydiard Tregose,' with the Jefferies country around Swindon, while the nature diary reproduced at the end records for the most part observations at Swindon, Burderop, and Coate. When he changes his locale to 'quite close to London' (*WL*, 75) for 'Wild Fruits,' 'A Pine-wood Near London,' and 'A Surrey Woodland,' he is in another Jefferies country – what Thomas himself was later to call 'Jefferies' second country' (*IPS*, 29). But these resemblances are superficial, resulting as much from the geographical limitations of Thomas's early life as from a conscious imitation of his predecessor. More significant are the similarities of tone and attitude which are found most clearly in 'A Wiltshire Mole-catcher.' 'On these wide open hills,' Thomas writes, 'there is hardly a man without woodcraft enough to know the ways of his fellow-denizens of the waste, and, if need be, the way to set up a wire' (*WL*, 48). This is clearly the world of *The Amateur Poacher*, and the resemblance extends to the style which here loses its concern for literary effect and becomes more natural and smooth-flowing. Of course Thomas is not yet a serious rival of Jefferies, as his presentation of the mole-catcher shows. It is clear that Thomas has interviewed him and gathered all sorts of useful information about him. This provides material for an interesting essay, but we never feel close to the mole-catcher himself. He does not spring out of the page, like Oby the poacher in Jefferies' book. He is described, and we acknowledge the facts, but he never comes to life – partly, perhaps, because Thomas never lets him talk. Moreover one gets the impression that Thomas is more interested in the moles than in the catcher.

Thomas himself, it is worth noting, is inconspicuous here. With the exception of the nature diary at the end, there is no 'I' in the book, but this is less important than the more general fact that the personality of the writer hardly ever intrudes itself. Though the style may sometimes tend towards the elaborate, the description is generally objective, and this too may reflect the influence of the early Jefferies. When we turn to *Horae Solitariae*, however, we find ourselves in a more rarified atmosphere. Both the title and the epigraph –

'Dreams have their truth for dreamers,' a quotation from Thomas's friend E.S.P. Haynes – suggest a new emphasis upon the self rather than the environment, and we soon discover that both the style and the references have undergone a surprising transformation. The name essay, the first in the collection, begins: 'Among a thousand books, I find hardly one title so opulent as *Horae Solitariae*. It has for the inward ear a melody that sings apart.' We have moved from nature to books, from an invigorating landscape to an aesthete's study, and the use of such a word as 'opulent' and the languid, pseudo-poetic rhythm of the second sentence easily place the writing in the bejewelled, decadent tradition of the nineties. A later reference to Oxford (*HS*, 3) clearly reveals the origin of the change. Thomas was, of course, a voracious reader before he became an undergraduate, but it seems evident that his new situation introduced him to new fashions and trends that encouraged a fondness to which he had always been susceptible.

It would be foolish to argue that such a style is wrong in itself. In Thomas's case, however, it seems woefully inappropriate to his characteristic subject matter. As John Moore has written, 'it was too "literary," too consciously it was *belles-lettres*,'[22] and Thomas fails to offset the conviction that *belles-lettres* and an honest presentation of the rural just do not mix. When he abandons his own subject matter and writes familiar essays on books and personal states in a style derived from Sir Thomas Browne via Charles Lamb, the effect is of pleasant minor pastiche, but, when applied to the rural, such a treatment brings less charm than distortion. What are we to make, for example, of the servant in the south of England and the cottager in Wales who quote, in the originals, from Quintilian and Virgil respectively (*HS*, 17–20)? We cannot believe in them as fact, they are equally incredible as fiction, and as pastoral fantasy they seem pointless. Borrow might have made intriguing stories out of them, but this would require a style and personality that were Borrovian, not Paterian. Thomas himself became aware of these limitations. His verdict on the book is as follows: 'Sentence by sentence it is good, essay by essay it is bad.'[23] The reduction of interest from the whole to the part is a well known phenomenon in the writing of this period, but the significant weakness for Thomas is that it is an emphasis on the word instead of the object. He seems to have lost control of the actual; he is continually retreating into the world of dreams and waking visions that are employed clumsily and perfunctorily, as in 'The Passing of Pan' and 'On the Evenlode.' The countryside wavers and collapses before our eyes, and we are forced back to Thomas's less interesting inner landscape.

The trend continues in *Rose Acre Papers* and even *Beautiful Wales*. The latter, whose very title suggests Borrow's *Wild Wales* while at the same time guaranteeing a more picturesque and less virile approach, was one of his earlier commissioned books, and its subsidiary status as accompaniment to some rather old-fashioned water-colour reproductions doubtless encouraged Thomas to produce another collection of dreamy, aesthetic sketches. The following passage conveniently illustrates both the strengths and weaknesses of his writing at this period:

> The last village was far behind. The last happy chapel-goer had passed me long ago. A cock crowed once and said the last word on repose. The rain fell gently; the stems of the hazels in the thickets gleamed; and the acorns in the grassy roads, and under the groups of oaks, showed all their colours, and especially the rosy hues where they had but just been covered by the cup. ... Doves cooed in the oaks, pheasants gleamed below. The air was full of the sweetness of the taste of blackberries, and the scent of mushrooms and of crumbling, wild carrot-seeds, and the colour of yellow, evening grass. The birches up on the hills above the road were golden, and like flowers. Between me and them a smouldering fire once or twice sent up dancing crimson flames, and the colour and perfumes of the fire added themselves to the power of the calm, vast, and windless evening, of which the things I saw were as a few shells and anemones at the edge of a great sea. The valley waited and waited.
>
> Then by the roadside I saw a woman of past middle age sitting silently. Her small head was poised a little haughtily on a blithe neck; her fine, grey, careful hair spared gloomy white forehead and round ears, which shone; her full, closed lips spoke clearly of both the sadness of today and the voluptuousness of yesterday. She was beautiful, and not merely because she had once been a beautiful girl. She had become mortal through grief, and though I could not see her crowned, yet crowned she was.
>
> Will you always, O sad and tranquil Demeter, sit by the wayside and expect Persephone?   (BW, 184–6)

This passage might almost be called an anthology of Thomas's characteristic effects. It contains some delicate natural description, it is a rain scene, and it ends with a somewhat artificially contrived 'epiphany' (the Joycean phrase springs naturally to mind) of a female figure in statuesque and meaningful stillness. The description is effective without being vivid. 'A cock crowed and said the last word on repose' is unusual in thought, but in itself reposeful. It lulls the reader into acceptance, discouraging him from creating too specific a mental picture. It builds up what Thomas was later to call 'my special brand of vagueness.'[24] Although an attempt is made to communicate a Keatsian multiplicity of sense impressions ('the taste of blackberries,' 'the scent of mushrooms'), the reader is aware not so much of a particular landscape as of a particular reaction to it on the part of the writer. This melancholy dreaminess is enhanced by the romantically evocative simile – 'as a few shells and anemones at the edge of a great sea' – which once again directs attention outwards, away from the scene that is being described. The woman, too, is veiled by the shimmery vagueness of her description, by the carefully chosen but deliberately inapposite adjective in the phrase 'a blithe neck' and the internal rhyme of 'hair spared' (not, I am convinced, accidental, since it often occurs in his poetry and may be a reflection of his interest in Welsh). Finally the distancing of the whole effect by the classical reference to Demeter and Persephone is typical of Thomas's work at this period.

A rather surprising feature of *Beautiful Wales* – and one which carries over into *The Heart of England* and *The South Country* – is the lack of a sense of locality. There is a noticeable scarcity of proper names, and the descriptions are of the most general. A defence and explanation of his method has been made by Herbert G. Wright. Commenting specifically on *The South Country*, he argues: 'The picture he gives is ... a composite one. It does not contain name after name in regular local order nor does he attempt to distinguish between one county and another. His landscape has, nevertheless, all the texture of reality combined with the charm of "an ideal country, belonging to itself and beyond the power of the world to destroy."'[25] This is well said, and Wright goes on to claim it as the great secret of Thomas's charm as a rural writer. It enables us to see a link between the rural and the Paterian that is otherwise lacking. However the question is: does Thomas succeed in combining the two in practice – for it is Thomas who must do this by his style and the associations conjured up by his words? It seems clear from *The Heart of England* that he does not. The chapters seem to divide themselves off uncomfortably. In some, like 'Faunus' where, despite the unfortunate title, he succeeds in conveying to us something of the essence of ploughing, we are left with an experience that lacks specific details but none the less – perhaps because of this – 'stands for' all that we can imagine of such a scene. But this is immediately followed by 'Not Here, O Apollo!' in which we find all the stock properties of a conventional pastoral – Apollo, Pan, nymphs, etc. – without any originality or grace. What relevance has this, we may ask, to the heart of *England*? The two elements remain separate; there is no hint of fusion. Thomas may insist on turning the countryfolk whom he sees 'into creatures of dream' (*HE*, 58), an old farmer may suggest to him 'the thought of a Centaur' (*HE*, 66), but for the reader the connections are forced and smack of the artificial – even of the pretentious.

Much the same can be said of *The South Country*, though on opening this book after the earlier volumes one is immediately struck by a dramatic change of style. The first chapter is direct, forthright, terse – even confident. Thomas is writing as if at ease, allowing himself to employ a delicate humorous irony which is sometimes present but almost always stifled in the earlier work. Here, at least temporarily, the style is remarkably effective because we are not conscious of it as style. But this is not maintained for long, and, although the book never returns to what Edward Garnett has called 'the stage of scholarly aestheticism' of *Horae Solitariae*,[26] it fluctuates oddly between the simple and the high-flown. The book is divided into chapters, but there is little continuity, and the effect is that of a collection of essays. Like *The Heart of England* and other books in the rural tradition which we have already encountered, *The South Country* could be described as a hodge-podge – or, to be kinder, an anthology. We are offered sometimes a story, sometimes a description almost like a water-colour, sometimes a true anecdote, sometimes a mythical fantasy, sometimes a painful meditation on 'the tears of things.' But whereas other books of this kind – *Our Village, Lavengro*, or even *The Amateur Poacher* and *Round About a Great Estate* – are unified by a recognizable and consistent attitude, Thomas's tend to fall apart for want of this. *The South Country* contains much of his best writing, but it lacks a focal point of reference. Thomas is perhaps too uncertain within himself, too self-questioning, too various in his moods and reactions to provide the personal centre so necessary for books of this kind. The result is that, though we find much to admire, the book does not remain in the memory as an achieved whole.

Rest and Unrest (1910) and Light and Twilight (1911) are remarkable less for any stylistic development as for Thomas's increased use of symbolic scenes and characters. Conscious, perhaps, of his lack of roots, he now avoids the direct though rich presentation of the natural world to be found in Cobbett and Jefferies, preferring instead to evoke an intellectual landscape – 'the world in the brain,' as he calls it (SC, 15). This tendency is particularly conspicuous in *Rest and Unrest*. 'The Maiden's Wood,' for example, takes place in 'a kingdom of the spirit rather than of the earth,'[27] and in the fantasy 'Snow and Sand' a robin that suddenly appears is 'more like a thought than a bird' (RU, 170). For a speaker in 'The Queen of the Waste Lands,' 'the land where I now am is an imagination of my heart' (RU, 189), and this, one feels, is often true of Thomas himself. The absence of precise locality that we have already noted in Thomas's books is more understandable in this context. As he writes in *The South Country*, 'in a sense this country is "all carved out of the carver's brain" and has not a name' (SC, 11). Even the Icknield Way, in the book of that title, for all the precision of geographical reference, is seen as 'a symbol of mortal things with their beginnings and ends always in immortal darkness' (IW, vii).

This symbolic interest is not in itself unpromising; indeed it can be seen as reaching its culmination in Thomas's poetry, where, as H. Coombes has pointed out, forests, roads, and inns, while losing nothing of their immediacy, take on profound and compelling significances in a complex symbolic geography.[28] But this development was several years ahead, and meanwhile Thomas was in danger of losing his way in a world of dreams and unrealities. It was doubtless salutary that his commissioned work had the effect of keeping his attention fixed on the here and now and discouraging at this time an unlimited exploration of his imaginative never-never-land. The biographies of Jefferies (1909) and Borrow (1912) united his considerable powers of literary criticism, evident in his numerous reviews, with congenial subjects, and the necessary researches, whether 'in the field' or in libraries, probably assisted him in understanding himself as much as the writers in question. In addition, the two main rural books of this time, *The Icknield Way* (1913) and *In Pursuit of Spring* (1914), both confined him to particular stretches of country and enforced a greater emphasis on the actual. None the less, a mood of boredom and bitterness hangs over much of this later writing. It represents the last working of an old vein, and there are few hints of fresh discovery. Yet the crucial development in Thomas's career as a writer was imminent; the long and painful apprenticeship was soon to bear fruit. Thomas at last found his true vocation not as prose writer but as poet. Unfortunately the discovery was made at the most inopportune time imaginable – summer 1914.

Although this study is primarily concerned with rural prose, an exception must be made in the case of Edward Thomas, since his poetry is essentially a distillation and, indeed, a culmination (his own word [see *LGB*, 251]) of his prose work. Most of the writers considered here, notably Gilbert White and Mary Mitford, attempted verse at one time or another, but the result was usually mediocre. They needed a more extended, less formal medium for their best effects, and Thomas's verdict on Jefferies' poetic attempts – 'he gives away all that he has for the mere form of verse'[29] – might be generally applied. But Thomas's own gifts were different; unlike his rural predecessors, he required the concentrating discipline which poetry demands. It was in verse that Thomas achieved the artistic maturity that had eluded him for so long.

As early as 1908 Edward Garnett had insisted that Thomas was a poet (*LGB*, 156), and Thomas was himself aware of the poetic tendency of much of his work. While preparing *The Heart of England*, he uses the phrase 'spurred lyric' to describe much of the contents (*LGB*, 107), and often enough in the earlier books we feel that he is on the brink of verse. In December 1913, in a letter to Garnett, Hudson made the same discovery: 'I believe he has taken the wrong path and is wandering lost in the vast wilderness ... He is essentially a poet ... In his nature books and fiction he leaves all there's best and greatest in him unexpressed' (*HL*, 185). These were remarkably astute observations, but it is Robert Frost who must take the credit for actually supervising the transformation, though there is evidence to suggest that Thomas was already considering the possibility of writing in verse.[30] Frost pointed out passages in the recently published *In Pursuit of Spring* that could be seen as providing the prose superstructure for possible poems. Thomas took the hint, and was soon writing freely if we may judge by the number of poems he actually wrote – a hundred and forty-one produced, along with prose writing and intensive military duties, during the last two and a half years of his life.

We know from biographical evidence that the two writers learnt much from each other during their close association and friendship during 1914, but Frost's influence on Thomas's verse is clear enough from the poems themselves. 'Up in the Wind,' for example, the first poem that Thomas wrote,[31] bears more than a superficial resemblance to the dramatic dialogues in *North of Boston* which Thomas had reviewed thoughtfully and sympathetically earlier in the same year. It seems worthwhile, then, to approach Thomas's poems through the critical approaches that have proved valuable in Frost's case. In one of the best and most stimulating studies of Frost's poetry John F. Lynen has laid stress on what he calls Frost's 'pastoral art.' For Lynen pastoralism is a kind of poetic structure: 'Pastoral comes to life whenever the poet is able to adopt its special point of view – whenever he casts himself in the role of the country dweller and writes about life in terms of the contrast between the rural world, with its rustic scenery and naive, humble folk, and the great outer world of the powerful, the wealthy, and the sophisticated.'[32] To what extent, we may ask, can this scheme, which fits Frost's poetry admirably, be applied to that of Thomas? An answer can best be made through an examination of one of Thomas's poems which is characteristic, yet decidedly Frost-like, 'As the Team's Headbrass.'[33]

The speaker of the poem is sitting on a fallen elm by the side of a wood into which two lovers have just disappeared. He is watching a plough-team 'narrowing a yellow square / of charlock,' and each time the horses turn at the end of a furrow, the plough-man pauses 'to say or ask a word / About the weather, next about the war.' For Thomas the 'great outer world' which contrasts with the rustic setting is a world at war. References, sometimes direct, sometimes indirect, recur throughout his verse, and, as here, more is involved than a mere contemporary reference. Idyllic as the agricultural scene may appear, it is by no means unrelated to the fighting in the trenches. The elm on which the speaker sits will only be taken away 'when the war's over.' One of the ploughman's mates was killed in battle ('the second day / In France they killed him') on the very day on which the blizzard felled it, and the ploughman remarks: 'Now if / He had stayed we should have moved the tree.' It becomes clear that the fallen elm serves as an emblem for the fallen comrade. Moreover in its fallen position it is, like the charlock (traditional sign of neglected husbandry), indicative of a world that has lost touch with its rural roots. The very solitariness of the ploughman ('Only two teams work on the farm this year') is explained by the demands of war.

So far I have concentrated on the negative elements in the poem. These are, however, balanced by positives, and it is noteworthy that these positives reflect the rural (Lynen's 'pastoral') way of life. At the close 'the lovers came out of the wood again,' and one is reminded of the 'maid and her wight' who provide a similar sense of continuity in Hardy's poem 'In Time of "The Breaking of Nations."'' The shining of the headbrass as the horses turn in the sun represents another positive, while the regularity of the snatched bits of conversation at the turn of the furrows ('One minute and an interval of ten, / A minute more and the same interval'), far from suggesting a dull monotony, is indicative of a regular pattern and rhythm which the unnatural state of war can interrupt but can never finally destroy. None the less, an artificial balance between the forces of life and despair would be hardly appropriate to the state of the times or the mood of the poem, and the last lines, after the talk has ended, are suitably ominous:

> The horses started and for the last time
> I watched the clods crumble and topple over
> After the ploughshare and the stumbling team.

In a world that is itself crumbling and toppling a stumbling plough-team becomes an image of imminent disaster, and our response to the deliberate ambiguity of 'for the last time' is only heightened, not created, by our awareness of Thomas's fate at the Battle of Arras (he once contemplated stressing the point by calling the poem 'The Last Team'[34]).

The way in which he comments on the great world by reference to a scene of pastoral tranquillity is clear enough, and the point could be demonstrated equally well from other poems. Where Thomas differs from Frost is in his choice of mouthpiece. The unidentified speaker is apparently a soldier and certainly an outsider. Indeed he provides a point of contrast between the country and the town, as the following exchange makes clear:

> 'Have you been out?' 'No.' 'And don't want to, perhaps?'
> 'If I could only come back again, I should.
> I could spare an arm. I shouldn't want to lose
> A leg. If I should lose my head, why, so,
> I should want nothing more.'

The sardonic ambivalence of the final remark indicates to those aware of the character of the poet that this is Thomas himself speaking, but it is a Thomas transformed by a new detachment and a greater maturity. Indeed the persona of the poems is distinguished from the 'I' of the prose not through any radical change in character but through the deftness and subtlety by which he is presented.

In the majority of Thomas's poems the speaker is a spectator, a member of the great world wandering through the countryside in search of 'the heart of England' and 'what men call content' (*TCP*, 121). He is just as introspective and self-conscious as the Thomas of the prose, but he has taken on a new strength because, instead of brooding helplessly upon his separation from the world of nature, he now accepts it as a condition of human existence. The distinction appears slight, but it is in fact essential; paradoxically the basic separation opens up possibilities of comparison. He can now place himself in relation to the natural world without either pretentiousness or inadequacy. The landscape is still interpreted in terms of self, and vice versa, but a new tension is achieved within the temporary association. Examples can be found throughout the *Collected Poems*:

> A gate banged in a fence and banged in my head.   (*TCP*, 48)

> The heat, the stir, the sublime vacancy
> Of sky and meadow and forest and my own heart.   (*TCP*, 64)

> And star and I and wind and deer
> Are in the dark together.   (*TCP*, 190)

Landscape and speaker are both seen in terms of opposites – the landscape is divided into 'gleam or gloom' (*TCP*, 32), 'the clouds that are so light, ... the earth that is so dark' (*TCP*, 60), while the speaker is split between 'pleasure and pain' (*TCP*, 148). The negatives and positives discussed in 'As the Team's Headbrass' exist in the speaker as well as in the countryside itself. Like Keats in the 'Ode to Melancholy' he recognizes that opposites can co-exist. In 'October' happiness and melancholy are intertwined; in 'The Unknown Bird' joy and sadness blend. Who can say whether the balance is derived from or read into the world of nature when, in 'Digging,' Thomas imagines that 'the robin sings over again / *Sad* songs of Autumn's *mirth*' (*TCP*, 136, my italics)?

Balance, in fact, seems to be the clue to the superiority of Thomas's verse over his prose. It is not that the weaknesses of the prose are avoided; rather they are faced up to and thereby turned into strengths. For example, he frequently makes the difficulty of connecting with the earth – the topic which was continually intruding to frustrate and weaken the prose – the actual subject of his poetry. The well-known 'October' (*TCP*, 76) provides a convenient instance. It opens with a description which employs details (grass, mushrooms, blackberry, birch) already used in a melancholy autumnal passage in *Beautiful Wales* (*BW*, 185). But there it was only a list; here the focus is upon the effect of the scene on the spectator:

> And now I might
> As happy be as earth is beautiful
> Were I some other or with earth could turn
> In alternation of violet and rose,
> Harebell and snowdrop, at their season due,
> And gorse that has no time not to be gay.

This, indeed, is the kernel of Thomas's melancholy (and, perhaps, of the self-conscious brooding of the later rural tradition). Whereas in his earlier prose the landscape itself and Thomas's subjective responses to it seem to be pulling against each other (where the style clothes the landscape in an artificial patina, and any tension created is continually destroyed by the mordant cynicism of the personal aside), here the two are fused; and both are exalted. The flowers, subtly differentiated in colour as well as time of blossoming, are caught in their essence within the blank verse (like Perdita's in *The Winter's Tale*), whereas the more detailed and exhaustive prose treatment conveys little. Above all, the speaker, in the process of experiencing and articulating the emotion, has gone a long way towards exorcizing his despair:

> But if this be not happiness, – who knows?
> Some day I shall think this a happy day
> And this mood by the name of melancholy
> Shall no more blackened and obscurèd be.

Perhaps the most important element here is concentration. In his commissioned prose Thomas was required to produce a set number of words; he was continually having to eke out his material, was never free to catch his effect as economically as possible and so distil the essence of a given experience. In his poetry, by contrast, he was at liberty to allow the subject to find its own length; hence he could create within the medium of verse 'quintessences of the best parts of [his] prose books.'[35]

Also important, I think, is the intimate connection between the poems and Thomas's concept of a genuine patriotism. I have already pointed out that his earliest attempts at poetry coincided with the outbreak of the First World War. For some months he was debating within himself whether or not to enlist, and much of his best verse was produced at this time: he wrote the rest, after the crucial decision had been made, in military training camps in England. There seems little doubt that the shock of war proved a stimulus to the kind of poetry Thomas attempted. During this period he wrote a number of prose essays, reproduced in *The Last Sheaf*, that explore the contemporary attitudes to war and war conditions, and he was also commissioned to edit an anthology, *This England*. Though repelled by the jingoistic chauvinism of the period, Thomas came to realize, more than ever before, what the word 'England' meant for him. His convictions are well summed up in 'This is No Case of Petty Right or Wrong' (*TCP*, 165), and even more eloquently in Eleanor Farjeon's anecdote in which Thomas, asked what he was fighting for, bent down to pick up handful of earth and replied, 'Literally, for this.'[36]

In one of the essays entitled, simply, 'England,' he writes: 'I take it that England then as now was a place of innumerable holes and corners, and most men loved – or, at any rate, could not do without – some one or two of these and loved all England, but probably seldom said so, because without it the part could not exist. The common man was like a maggot snug in an apple: without apples there are no cores he knew well, nor apples without cores' (*LS*, 103). The richness of Thomas's poetry often consists in the loving delineation of one of these holes and corners. One thinks immediately of 'Tall Nettles' (*TCP*, 70) with its forgotten corner in which lie 'the rusty harrow, the plough / Long worn out, and the roller made of stone,' and his characteristic comment: 'This corner of the farmyard I like most.' Even more to the point, the final insight in 'The Glory' (*TCP*, 64) – 'I cannot bite the day to the core' – is based on the same image. This is, indeed, the 'glory' of all Thomas's poetry, the grudging yet triumphant realization that nature is inexhaustible – grudging because the poet's function is in a sense to bite the day to the core, to preserve the essence of the passing moment, yet triumphant because the richness of nature is a positive that dwarfs even the horrors of human slaughter. Whereas the overall impression of the prose is one of nagging discontent, that of the verse, for all its apparent emphasis on darkness and melancholy, is, I suggest, a muted but palpable acceptance of the whole of the natural life – the shadow along with the sunshine, the pain along with the pleasure.

In Thomas's poetry we experience 'the triumph of earth' (*TCP*, 150) over those who would despoil it, and rejoice in the survival of Lob (in the poem of that name [*TCP*, 54]), the eternal English countryman. It is worth noting that Lob, like the countryside which he represents, is not recognized until he is passed; similarly Thomas's 'happy' days are not acknowledged as such until they are over. But all are recognized ultimately when preserved within the elusively casual art of Thomas's verse. And they are recognized for what they are – not symbols but actualities. In 'Lights Out' (*TCP*, 92) Thomas discovers to his surprise that the silence of the forest needs to be heard and obeyed 'That I may lose my way / And myself.' Paradoxically, as the old mystics knew, to lose oneself in one sense is to find oneself in another. When in 'July' (*TCP*, 144) he learns through the ring-doves the lesson of nature: 'All that the ring-doves say, far leaves among, / Brims my mind with content thus still to lie,' he finds not only content but his second and greater self. The secret is not to fret in the mind, not to impose one's own soreness on the natural world, but simply 'still to lie.' Nature, to adapt T.S. Eliot's phrase, teaches him to sit still. Thomas's victory is recorded, characteristically enough, in a remark that might seem at first sight a casual aside. In 'Digging' [*TCP*, 136], significantly a rural activity, his restless thoughts are transformed into realities – 'To-day I think / Only with scents.' The smell of the bonfire burns up his thoughts along with 'the dead, the waste, the dangerous' and turns all to sweetness. Then, simply and unforced, the final truth is caught: 'It is enough / To smell, to crumble the dark earth.' The perturbed spirit of the earlier Thomas is now at rest.

Thomas had no illusions about the deficiencies of his early prose. He was well aware that the conditions under which he worked were not conducive to the production of masterpieces, and the realization of what he was capable of achieving, if given the opportunity, made his verdicts on most of his work excessively bitter. His correspondence – particularly with Gordon Bottomley – is littered with disparaging references. 'I know so well when I am writing muck,' he insists, and he refers to 'the sham humour which I insert [into the prose] in order to make it clear that my feeble seriousness is as ridiculous to me as to others' (*LGB*, 175, 75). But it is not merely a matter of general dissatisfaction. The Thomas who proved such a responsible and cogent critic of others' work in his reviewing is equally specific in pointing out his own literary faults. No one has put his finger on the weaknesses of *The Icknield Way* so firmly as Thomas himself in the following summing-up: 'Half guide book. The other half diluted me' (*LGB*, 214). Of *The Heart of England* he is even more critical –perhaps hypercritical in this instance; it is 'Borrow & Jefferies sans testicles & guts' (*LGB*, 107), and the unexpected violence of the description indicates how much of his real self is suppressed in his commissioned books.

Above all, he knew that his penchant for fine phrases and elaborate constructions was a hindrance to his success. The following advice about writing which he gave his wife represents an ideal he found difficulty in achieving himself: 'Always write of things that you know. Don't write out of your head, but about something you have experienced, and if you write simply and truthfully it is bound to be interesting.'[37] Oddly enough, the insidious stylistic influence of Pater was finally exorcized when Thomas wrote a book about him. After he had finished this critical study, published in 1913, he remarked to his brother Julian that he wished henceforth to write a prose 'as near akin as possible to that of a

Surrey peasant' (*CET*, 8). As Julian Thomas notes, he clearly had Sturt's Bettesworth in mind.

The results can be seen in *The Childhood of Edward Thomas*, an autobiographical fragment begun late in 1913, and in many of the essays collected posthumously in *The Last Sheaf* – essays which, as H. Coombes has rightly insisted, show Thomas's prose at its simplest and best.[38] It can hardly be accidental that the change coincided, to all intents and purposes, with his turning to poetry. Not only did the discipline of verse bring his best powers to the surface, to the extent that, recalling Pound's phrase about Hardy, we can call his poetry the harvest of his prose, but it freed his prose of the excess ballast of poeticisms. The poem entitled 'The Brook' [*TCP*, 173] is itself an embodiment of the lesson which poetry had taught him. The perfect expression of the scene is provided not by Thomas but by a girl paddling in the stream:

> And then the child's voice raised the dead.
> 'No one's been here before' was what she said
> And what I felt, yet never should have found
> A word for, while I gathered sight and sound.

In his prose he 'gathered sight and sound'; in his verse he learnt the verbal economy and directness that make exact communication possible.

In 1915 he wrote to Eleanor Farjeon concerning his verse: 'I am trying to get rid of the last rags of rhetoric and formality which left my prose so often with a dead rhythm only.'[39] A similar effect may be discerned in the later prose. If we never quite recognize the accents of Bettesworth, at least the directness and unadorned spontaneity which were characteristic of the earlier rural writers are at last regained. Gone is the attempt to transform the natural world into a verbal and symbolic construct which is only a dilution of the original. He has now realized, to quote from *In Pursuit of Spring*, 'the fact that the earth does not belong to man, but man to the earth' (*IPS*, 150). It was a hard lesson, involving the acceptance of nature as the source, not only of his subject matter, but even of his language. It was well and truly learnt by the time he was in a position to write: 'I should use, as the trees and birds did, / A language not to be betrayed' (*TCP*, 100). It is pleasant to record that, despite his untimely death, he had attained his maturity.

ELEVEN

Henry Williamson

b. 1896

People who don't see the earth and sea and stars plainly are spiritually corrupt –
and spiritual corruption begets physical corruption. That is the real cause of the
Great War.[1]

Henry Williamson, in his twenty-first year, had not yet begun to write when
Edward Thomas was killed within a few hundred yards of him at the Battle of
Arras.[2] Not unnaturally the First World War proved to be the crucial experience
of his life, a horror to which he has returned angrily, broodily, ever since.
Moreover he was a participant in the famous Christmas fraternization between the British and German troops in the trenches in 1914,[3] and this event
has remained the central point in his personal and literary life. It was an
inspiring, fleeting testimony to what might have been, and its failure a tragic
and permanent reminder of human folly. Williamson returned from the war a
changed man. Like the Willie Maddison of his novel cycle *The Flax of Dream*,
he was 'haunted by the ghosts of ten million murdered men of his own
generation.'[4] By the end of hostilities he had come close to losing faith in
mankind, and on being demobilized he determined not to be 'crushed into
inanity by civilization' (*DFW*, 70).

The shock of the years 1914–18 must have been all the greater for someone
with Williamson's background and upbringing. 'There was,' he tells us, 'farming blood in me. My mother's family had been farmers; some of them had
farmed the same land under the dukedom of Bedford for more than four
centuries. My father's family had been landowners until comparatively recently, in the Midlands and North of England' (*SNF*, 38). From his early

childhood, moreover, he had been fascinated by natural history in general and bird life in particular. The first two volumes of his *Flax of Dream* tetralogy, *The Beautiful Years* and *Dandelion Days*, though fictional recreation like Jefferies' *Bevis* of a childhood that was in fact less rural and less idyllic, present none the less the essence of Williamson's early life, with its accounts of bird-nesting, fishing expeditions, wild pets, and – an early manifestation of his later talents – a detailed diary of natural observations (part of the original was printed in the 1945 edition of *The Lone Swallows*). 'As a small boy,' he writes, 'I lived a secret life in my grandfather's copies of *Bevis*, *The Amateur Poacher*, and *Wild Life in a Southern Country*.'[5] Like the young Willie Maddison, in looking forward to adult life he 'had dreamed of an existence in the woods and meadows, photographing birds' nests and writing in *The Field* an account of his observations.'[6] As one might expect, this somewhat unusual and naive ambition led to disagreements with his parents. His mother, about whom Williamson has written that 'the link between us, as in the case of D.H. Lawrence and his mother, had been stronger than is normal' (*SNF*, 39) was doubtless sympathetic, but his father (like Thomas's father) saw no practical use for his natural history interests, and as Williamson grew older this led to estrangement and bitterness.

After the war, of course, the clash became even more evident. For all their horror, the war years were 'years of such movement and excitation and comradeship that when they had passed the world had seemed poor and dispirited.'[7] The earlier 'dandelion days' now appeared remote, dead, embalmed in the pages of history; Williamson saw them as 'the Old World, the pre-1914 world.'[8] Yet at the same time it was the one possible world. He came to believe that 'only that secret part of myself that lived for watching wild birds and finding their nests in the fields and woods was an integral harmony in my life.'[9] The more he looked back in an endeavour to isolate the cause of the 1914–18 war, the more he found it in the separation of urban man from the natural life. 'Wars,' he insists, 'are made by the pallid mob-spirit, by mass-escapists from indoor and pavement living; the pale-faced men whose natural instincts are repressed' (*GWC*, 157). It was impossible for Williamson to relax after the armistice; he had begun during the war to feel 'the weight of the whole dark world on one's shoulders' (*LD*, 246), and the immediate post-war period was even more depressing: 'The years 1919 and 1920, their interior or mental life, were lived in a No-man's-land more bitter than that patrolled and crossed during the preceding years, for they were without companionship, and the enemy was world darkness, which must be created into light' (*LD*, 247). Consequently, after an unhappy period as a journalist in London, working for *The Times* and the *Weekly Dispatch*, and after a culminating row with his father, Williamson decided to make his own escape. But, unlike the mass escapes which lead to war, this was to be a solitary escape in quest of peace. Remembering a Devon cottage which he had rented 'on impulse' two years earlier,[10] he set out for the west of England in March 1921.

Basically, of course, this was an escape from the town into the country. Williamson persuaded himself 'that the inspiration of walls and pavements was false, bringing upon men the things of darkness.'[11] Devon was also a retreat where he could 'learn to write' (*SNF*, 37), but it was certainly no escape from the war mentality of 1914–18; there was no question of his forgetting the experiences he had gone through. In writing *The Flax of Dream*, the tetralogy which the war cuts cruelly but neatly into two pieces, Williamson relives the experience of his generation, despite the fact that the actual details of warfare are omitted. During the same period, as H.F. West has noted, he built up an impressive collection of First World War literature, two of the volumes (*The Patriot's Progress* and *The Wet Flanders Plain*) being his own.[12] And even his country books are haunted with memories of the war. The prefatory note to the first edition of *The Lone Swallows* is symbolically dated 11 November 1921, while that of *The Story of a Norfolk Farm* bears the armistice date nineteen years later, at the beginning of yet another war. References recur throughout the books written in the twenties and thirties – even his *Anthology of Modern Nature Writing* is filled with wartime extracts from such writers as Wilfrid Ewart, V.M. Yeates, and Edmund Blunden. All this comes to a culmination, of course, in his ambitious novel cycle *A Chronicle of Ancient Sunlight*, in which five volumes are devoted to the First World War. Thus the Devon journey, if it can legitimately be called an escape at all, was undertaken not in order to forget, but to remember more clearly.

But the Williamson of 1921 was a mystifying, immature, contradictory, and often irritating figure. Even a photograph taken at this time, which appears as the frontispiece to *The Sun in the Sands*, shows an obviously intense and self-conscious young man. He was a romantic idealist, his mind filled with the visions of Blake, Shelley, Jefferies, and Francis Thompson, supremely convinced, on the surface at least, of his literary genius ('I am young and self-confident'[13]), and imagining himself as the much-needed prophet of a newer and better world. 'In those days,' he tells us, 'only one thought moved in my mind: the tragedy of Mankind, and the world's redemption through the truth I would reveal in my work' (*SS*, 10–11). In Willie Maddison, hero of *The Flax of Dream*, Williamson presents his romantic, prophetic self in heightened symbolic form ('He felt himself a stranger, an outcast' [*DFW*, 86]), and in *The Star-Born*, the fantasy which Maddison is supposed to have written and which Williamson himself calls 'a Fifth Gospel,'[14] we find a similar semi- (or pseudo-) mystical version of the pattern. There can be little doubt that he moulded his own life in an attempt to encourage archetypal comparisons. He is the hermit in the wilderness, the visionary poet, the inspired teacher, the prophet without honour in his own country – even, at times, the suffering servant.

There is, however, another, very different side to the portrait of the young Williamson. He can write, with an eloquent gesture, 'I had rejected civilisation just as Jefferies had, I was going to be a hermit' (SS, 35), yet he made the journey from London to Devon on a racing motorcycle, eagerly intent upon setting a record time. Pausing en route to visit Stonehenge, he is soon complaining of 'the big-painted advertisement boards advertising a motor tyre' as a desecration of Salisbury Plain; they are 'offensive, a symbol of that materialism and negation of the spirit that one day would be altered through the Tetralogy about Maddison' (SS, 31). And so, back to what he has already described as his 'beautiful long-stroke, single cylinder Brooklands Road Special Norton' (SS, 12)! (The next time we hear of a visit to Stonehenge, he is himself driving a car; the advertisements are now ignored, and his indignation is reserved for the barbed wire fence and a tea-shop [see LD, 128].) He claims to have settled in the Devonshire countryside 'in order to find peace and quiet,'[15] yet he comes and goes 'at all hours of the day and night' on the motorcycle which, he claims with obvious satisfaction, makes 'a noise like a machine gun' (LL, 99). Despite his love of natural history Williamson belongs to the world of the motor-car which Sturt rails against in his Journals.

It would not be difficult to present the whole of Williamson's life and attitudes as a heap of contradictions. He holds an odi et amo relationship with so much. Despite the numerous passages of prophetic didacticism that clutter his work the reader often finds himself asking, in Auden's phrase, 'which side am I supposed to be on?' Or, to put the point even more crucially, 'which side does Williamson think he is on?' Sometimes, especially in his later work, he is prepared to face up to his own contradictions. On a visit to the north of England, for example, he finds himself bewailing the ugliness of industrialism, but suddenly changes his stance: 'You drive a car, and enjoy its speed; you are of modern life, enjoying its conveniences – so why this attitude because smoke hangs over the factories where your car, and the other things you use and approve, are produced' (LD, 158)? It is the kind of question that many of his readers must have asked years before. Although the older Williamson is often aware of the paradoxes and contradictions, there are only occasional moments when the young man realizes how far he falls short of the artistic prodigy he believes himself to be.

These autobiographical details are necessary here, since Williamson employs his own experience in his writings more than any other rural chronicler with the possible exception of George Borrow. He is continually reliving or rewriting his past, viewing an incident from a different angle or with a different perspective. The same might be said of his countryside. From The Dream of Fair Women to

The Children of Shallowford it is almost invariably north Devon, at first Georgeham and Braunton, later the river Bray around Filleigh; but it is recreated in varying literary genres – in fictional form in *The Dream of Fair Women* and *The Pathway*, in the animal stories such as *Tarka the Otter* and *Salar the Salmon*, in the numerous non-fiction works. The setting remains the same, but the treatment varies with the stance of the speaker, and even the genres tend to dissolve into each other For Williamson also resembles Borrow in the way he mixes his imaginative with his real life so that it is impossible to separate fact from fiction. In *The Dream of Fair Women*, 'neither wholly fiction, nor ... autobiography' (*GWC*, 23–4), instead of insisting, with most novelists, that any resemblance between the characters and living persons is coincidental, Williamson goes out of his way to state that Maddison, 'like all the other characters of the novel, was based on a real person' (*DFW*, 441). On the other hand, *The Village Book*, though apparently non-fiction, is 'an imaginative work which should not be read as the history of any particular village, and certainly not of any man or woman' (*VB*, 9). A careful reading of the books of reminiscence such as *The Children of Shallowford* and *The Story of a Norfolk Farm* reveals sufficient discrepancies to suggest that, consciously or unconsciously, chronology and detail have been altered to increase the effect, while *The Sun in the Sands*, which is ostensibly offered as autobiography, is so well moulded and rounded as to suggest the contrivances of fiction. The description, 'novel autobiography,' to be found on its dust-jacket is appropriate and, one presumes, deliberately ambiguous.

In *Goodbye West Country*, with a profundity that we do not normally associate with him, Williamson has observed: 'All artists, to become real people, have to assume another self, and learn to discard it, lest it envelop them' (*GWC*, 63). Although intended generally, the remark has obvious applicability to his own work. Willie Maddison is clearly a mask, like Lavengro, and 'The Beard' of *The Labouring Life* at least allows for a certain distance between writer and character; but the Williamson of *The Sun in the Sands*, like the Borrow of *Wild Wales*, is problematical. We are never quite sure to what extent we should separate the 'implied author' from what we know of the actual writer. There is an important difference, however, between Williamson and Borrow (whom, by the way, Williamson had apparently not read at this time [see *SNF*, 206]): whereas in *Wild Wales* we are confident that Borrow is aware of the problem and is deliberately exploiting it for his own purpose, with Williamson – and this is true of a number of his 'non-fiction' books, not only *The Sun in the Sands* – we get the uneasy feeling that our judgments and responses are by no means identical with his own. The mask is donned more clumsily by Williamson; we are never fully convinced of the dexterity of the performer; and all sorts of questions therefore become important. Are the elaborate disguises deliberately put on to shield a personality who is basically unsure of himself? Are the contraditions already discussed attributable to the mask or to Williamson himself? How does all this complexity square with his much vaunted ideal of 'clarity'? I propose to consider, though not necessarily to answer, these questions in the ensuing critique. As in the case of Borrow, I shall make no attempt to confine myself to the ostensible non-fiction, since the rigid categories are irrelevant here. Instead I shall try to reveal the evolution of Williamson as a rural writer through an examination of the masks and devices he employs to conceal or reveal his essential self.

The Beautiful Years and *Dandelion Days*, which together chronicle the story of Willie Maddison from childhood to his leaving school on the eve of the First World War, might reasonably be described as presenting a portrait of the naturalist as a young man. In these years are sown the seeds that are to come to a brief and inevitably distorted flowering in the 'lost generation' Willie (the term is Williamson's, as well as Gertrude Stein's and Ernest Hemingway's) of the last two books of the tetralogy. In *The Beautiful Years* we are offered the vision of a potential rural paradise; the countryside around 'Rookhurst' is presented as an ideal environment for the growth of a healthy and harmonious soul. But even at this early stage threatening clouds become visible. Unlike Williamson himself, Willie is motherless and an only child; from the day of his birth he is deprived of the affection to be found in a complete and natural family atmosphere. Unlike Jefferies' Bevis, whose enlightened 'governor' deliberately avoids interfering with his son's self-education in the world of nature, Willie is brought up by a bitter and unsympathetic father who is hopelessly incapable of understanding his child. The climax, in which Willie is accused of trespass and poaching because he has sprung some illegally set traps, brings him for the first time into harsh contact with the prejudice and power of what we have come to call the establishment.

  Dandelion Days, in spite of the idyllic suggestiveness of its title, is a much sadder book than its predecessor.[16] School life, which was peripheral in *The Beautiful Years*, has now become central, and the policy of Colham Grammar School seems to be to stamp out the imaginative spirit which Willie has developed in his natural surroundings. Shades of the prison-house begin to close in upon him. His world is now split, and the main subject of the novel is Willie's desperate attempt to preserve his love for the countryside against the concerted attacks of his father, his girl friend, and most of the boys and masters at the school. As Williamson recalls later, 'my theme was true: the natural development of the boy in the sunshine, contrasted with the unnatural spoliation of the immature mental and nervous tissues when shut away from the sunshine' (SS, 45). As Willie grows up, of course, the problem of human relationships becomes more complex. His boyish, romantic, helpless love for Elsie Norman is, like the rest of life, both beautiful and painful, and its inevitable failure, due not merely, or even primarily, to class differences, but rather to fundamentally opposed attitudes and temperaments, is more shattering to the shy and sensitive Willie than it would be to anyone else. Moreover the breakdown in their relationship takes place on the 'last day' before Willie is to leave Rookhurst and take a job in London. The 'beautiful years' in the countryside are over, though Willie's job at a city desk is almost immediately interrupted by the outbreak of war. 'The summer of 1914,' Maddison is made to write later, 'was to see the apotheosis of ideas and measures which everywhere had crushed the imaginative tissues of childhood' (DFW, 12). His own life provides the archetypal example. It is the end of an era; dandelions are replaced by poppies, the fields of England by those of Flanders. The book ends on a sombre note when in the final sentences of the so-called epigraph we hear of the death in battle of Willie's best friend, Jack Temperley. Willie is now completely on his own.

The war itself, which becomes the focal point in *A Chronicle of Ancient Sunlight*, is not treated here. When we meet Willie again at the opening of *The Dream of Fair Women*, the date is June 1919, and, as the excessively romantic title suggests, the book is concerned with the young man's experiences of love and women in the depressing years of the early twenties. As the novel opens, he is living alone in a hut in north Devon, having exiled himself from a civilization he despises in an attempt to write down his ideas in a ponderous manuscript, modelled on Jefferies' *The Story of My Heart*, and solemnly titled *The Policy of Reconstruction*. But he soon learns that such a hermitlike existence is not only impossible but vain; most of the book is taken up with his unhappy love affair with a married woman, Evelyn Fairfax, and the contrast between his own ideals and the pleasure-seeking but ultimately vacuous society into which his love for Mrs Fairfax leads him. The relevance of this volume to the earlier books – and to the rural tradition – lies in Maddison's apparent inability to find in the post-war world any connection with the dandelion days that seem lost for ever.

In *The Pathway* Willie Maddison finally emerges as a definite if not wholly satisfactory mouthpiece for Williamson's ideas; indeed his function may well remind us of some of the spokesman-figures in D.H. Lawrence's more pugnaciously didactic novels. Wandering about Devon, arguing with anyone who is prepared to listen to him, writing another prophetic book entitled *The Star-Born*, Maddison comes, as it were, into his ministry. His message, like Williamson's, concerns the relation between war and an unnatural life, and he it is who speaks the words that I have chosen as epigraph for this chapter. His despair verges on the misanthropic; only among the wild creatures of the countryside can he find peace. Like Hudson and Thomas before him he finds church-going constricting, and feels closer to God in the open air; unlike Hudson and Thomas he dramatically and ostentatiously walks out of the service. He is at one and the same time passionately sincere and painfully immature, yet Williamson deliberately offers his creation as the way, the truth, and the life – a quotation, incidentally, that he has called 'the most beautiful line in all literature' (SS, 165). Everywhere Maddison goes, of course, he finds selfishness, hate, misunderstanding. Finally, alienated from the family of Mary Ogilvie, whom he loves, he is drowned in a climactic scene that brings together all the romantic archetypes. The manuscript of The Star-Born is burnt as a signal of distress, but, like its message in the world, it is ignored. Maddison drowns, like Shelley, and an attempt is even made to burn his body on the shore, à la Trelawney. At one time Williamson had contemplated a happy ending (see SS, 53–4), but he wisely rejected it. The crusade of a post-war champion of the natural (rural) life, he seems to imply, can only end in failure.

The Flax of Dream is an impressive but infuriating near-masterpiece. Willie Maddison is, of course, a deliberately chosen name with equivocal overtones. Rhythmically it suggests the name of his creator, but at the same time it can readily and neatly be transformed into the undignified 'Mad Willie.' Like 'Stephen Dedalus,' one cannot easily decide whether it is a profound symbol or a complicated joke; unlike A Portrait of the Artist as a Young Man, the tetralogy suffers through Williamson's inability to maintain either a consistent attitude towards, or an appropriate distance from, his leading character. The first two books are acceptable in the sense that the young Willie's absurdities can be attributed to the inexperience of youth; but when in the last two volumes Maddison is in his early twenties and has still not grown up, and when, moreover, Williamson apparently offers his immature simplicity as a virtue rather than a failing, the reader finds it increasingly difficult to view him with the sympathy that is clearly demanded. As a result there is a fatal and undeniable flaw at the centre of the tetralogy which Williamson's drastic alterations and revisions have never been able to overcome. This is all the more unfortunate in view of Williamson's obvious gifts and the admirable boldness of his conception. Had he only been able, like Joyce, to remain 'invisible, refined out of existence, indifferent, paring his fingernails,'[17] he might well have written a comprehensive study not only of the Weltanschauung of the first quarter of this century, but of the uneasy modern relationship between man and the natural world.

The cottage to which Williamson retired in 1921 was in the north Devon village of Georgeham, which he always refers to under its earlier but still surviving name of Ham.[18] It was, in many respects, an ideal spot for one of Williamson's temperament and interests. 'A village of small property owners, without a resident "gennulman,"' as he calls it (*LL*, 474), the whole parish contained at that time a population of a little over eight hundred; still comparatively isolated, it preserved much of the traditional atmosphere of an old world (Williamson would say pre-war) village community. Moreover its environs were varied and scenically spectacular. It was an area rich in bird life, particularly the peregrine-falcons, buzzards, and ravens that Williamson loved. There were badgers in the woods, otters (and salmon) in the rivers, and, since Georgeham lies close to the western extremities of Exmoor, the red deer – Jefferies' red deer, the most imposing wild animals in England – were within easy reach. As for the local flora, Williamson is fond of alluding to the belief of the neighbourhood that every wild flower growing in England can be found on the nearby Santon Burrows (see, e.g., *LD*, 205). Georgeham had not yet been 'discovered' by tourists, and Williamson could explore the moors, wander along the beach with its cliffs and rocky headlands, and never meet another human being. The prospective hermit and follower of Jefferies could hardly ask for a more congenial or artistically stimulating locality.

Georgeham became Williamson's home for the next seven years or so. Here most of *Dandelion Days* and the whole of *The Dream of Fair Women* and *The Pathway* were written, but the *Flax of Dream* tetralogy was only a part of his work at this time, and it cannot even be described as representative. H.F. West forecast in 1932 that 'any future study of Williamson's work will assuredly trace the change from the subjective idealism of *The Flax of Dream* to the objective realism of, for example, *The Labouring Life*.'[19] The very different strands in his writing are obvious – indeed, one can imagine a critical study postulating two Williamsons in much the same way that Williamson has distinguished two Jefferies (see *RJ*, 24–5) – but it would be a mistake to imply any kind of chronological development from one approach to the other. He is at one and the same time Willie Maddison and 'the Ham historian' (*LL*, 84), and the resultant portraits of a village society to be found in his twin volumes *The Village Book* and *The Labouring Life* show him making his own characteristic contribution to the rural tradition in a recognizable 'line' from Jefferies and Sturt.

At one time, apparently, Williamson had plans to write a book called *A Labourer's Life*, an account of 'Revvy' Carter, his next-door neighbour, that was to be 'a marvellous transcription of reality' (*LL*, 100). Unlike most presentations of the agricultural labourer, which are distorted and misleading, this would be 'so true and vivid that William Carter would be a hero for all time' (*LL*, 101). The book was never written, but, making the necessary allowances for Williamson's enthusiastic exaggerations that are yet another manifestation of the writer's mask, one suspects that it would have borne a close resemblance to *The Bettesworth Book*. Interestingly enough, the reasons he gives for abandoning the book are themselves extraordinarily similar to the difficulties that Sturt encountered. Williamson describes the problem as follows:

> What was the theme of Revvy's life? Easy to make it pathetic: a poor man's struggle against rain and rheumatism, a poor man forced by an economic system to remain so poor that on a wet winter's morning he left his cottage with a potato sack over his shoulders, Hodge's usual overcoat. Or to make it dignified: the West Countryman's courtesy and natural charm, and in particular this man's sweetness to his children. How to lead into the story of his prejudices, his sudden bellowings at his children and wife, their taunts at their mother, the general disharmony of those first two years when almost everything that was spoken, and certainly everything that was shouted in bellow and shrill taunt, was heard through the thin lath-and-plaster wall that divided the cottages? Revvy was not a tragic figure; he was a happy man, like most men who work with their arms and muscles and thighs, happy men – except when out-of work.   (LL, 130–1)

Once again the difficulty lies in rendering the complexity of the whole truth, but Williamson was, in fact, in a better position than Sturt to present the realities of the labouring life. Where Sturt was the employer whose experience of Bettesworth was almost always confined to occasions when the old man was 'on duty,' Williamson, though an outsider in the village – a 'foreigner' in the rustic sense, and an eccentric one at that – is able to watch and record the daily routine. He talks to Revvy Carter on the road, in the public house, at church, in the labourer's own garden, not as employer to employee but as man to man. Indeed his enforced overhearing of conversation through the thin walls is reminiscent of that classic example of accurate reporting, J.M. Synge with his ear to the cracked floorboard on the Aran Islands.

But even under these circumstances, which seem almost ideal, Williamson is dissatisfied, and abandons the project in its original form. Little seems to have been lost, however; most of the material appears to be contained in *The Village Book* and *The Labouring Life*, though these books attempt much more besides. They are written (and here, in view of the result, I think we can accept the somewhat exalted authorial statement) 'that the spirit and letter of village life in the decade following the Great War be contained for future students of English country life' (LL, 9). Together they form an impressionistic collage of village events, a *pot-pourri* of descriptions, stories, anecdotes which, though originally separate sketches written for newspapers and magazines, present when united a convincing, rounded picture. Despite the obvious differences of style and treatment we come away from a reading of these books with a feeling of intimate familiarity with the inhabitants not unlike that experienced in *Our Village*.

At first sight, the books seem artless. They are chatty, jagged, uneven, and sometimes repetitious, but, as Williamson is anxious (perhaps too anxious) to point out, this is all part of a conscious design. His own description, '"true but imaginary" local history' (*LL*, 144) is probably the best. Like most rural writers, the closer he comes to actuality, the more reluctant he is to admit it. Carefully worded statements of limited liability abound:

> 'The village of Ham' does not exist in the world of reality, nor are any of the human and other beings described in it necessarily real beings ... I cannot truthfully declare that any baby was buried, that any tract was awarded, that any sermon was preached, in the manner I have written.   (*VB*, 255)

> Even the 'I' and the 'zur' and the 'Mr. Williamson' of certain pages ... are but devices of story-telling.   (*VB*, 9)

> The characters are not meant to represent any living persons; rather are they essences of personalities.   (*LL*, 9)

One can readily appreciate Williamson's reticence in these matters; none the less, the amount of straight reporting is considerable. For example, H. Stevenson Balfour, in his *History of Georgeham and Croyde*, testifies to the essential accuracy of Williamson's hilarious account of the dispute over the new churchyard by inserting a footnote reference to *The Labouring Life*,[20] and his lists of local names indicate that Williamson made few alterations in the interests of 'story-telling.' Moreover H.F. West claims in his memoir to have met 'some of the characters' in *The Village Book*.[21] Above all, whatever he may say about 'Mr. Williamson,' the 'I' of these books admits to being the author of *Tarka the Otter*, *The Pathway*, and *The Old Stag*, and complementary accounts in his other writings point overwhelmingly to biographical foundations. Granting the inevitable 'touching-up,' these books may be accepted as a record that is 'true' in all but the most narrow sense of the word.

None the less, Williamson is here much more than the mere observer. The books are, for instance, painstakingly arranged and constructed. Not only is there a seasonal division, *The Village Book* representing winter and spring, *The Labouring Life* summer and autumn, but within each book the village stories are interspersed with short descriptive essays concerning the non-human world. It is typical of Williamson that the birds and animals are not neglected in favour of the human villagers. Their fortunes continually overlap, but – and this is part of Williamson's point – the outcome is generally fatal. The slow-worm is stoned to death (*VB*, 207), the ackymals (tomtits) are ruthlessly shot by John Kift (*VB*, 273), Billy Goldsworthy's cow dies on the same evening as his mother (*LL*, 406). Moreover those parts of the village in which there are no houses, where the natural inhabitants are buzzards and water ouzels and foxes and stoats, are as relevant to Williamson as Inclefell Manor or 'the Lower House' or the parish church. We are, indeed, offered a human view of the wild life and 'a starling's view of Ham' (*VB*, 52), and it is appropriate that Williamson's Georgeham years resulted not only in these books but in two collections of animal stories, *The Peregrine's Saga* and *The Old Stag*, and the book that is still regarded as his masterpiece, *Tarka the Otter*.

One commentator, Denys Thompson, has complained that there is no indication in *The Village Book* and *The Labouring Life* 'that any particular change has happened to English life in the last hundred years,'[22] but this is hardly fair. It is true that there is no sociological analysis that can compare with Sturt's *Change in the Village*; Williamson, however, is attempting something very different. His is an impressionistic, almost documentary approach, and the evidence of change exists in the very fabric of his anecdotes (which Thompson too hastly dismisses as 'mainly pointless'[23]). Williamson's real subject, we might say, is the extraordinary juxtapositions of modern and ancient in the rural society of the 1920s. The Ham villagers are aware both of age-old superstitions and of the latest scandals in the *News of the World*. The controversy over the new burial ground necessarily involves not only the parish meeting but the urban bureaucracies of the county council and the ministry of health. Means of transportation have, of course, changed completely; attempts are made (not always successfully) to introduce buses and taxicabs, and by the time Williamson writes the second book aeroplanes are 'scarcely heeded' when they fly over the village (*LL*, 460). Even the guillemot that Williamson finds on the beach with its feathers smeared with oil from passing ships (*VB*, 43–4; cf *DFW*, 69; *SS*, 49) is a victim of the modern pollution that some call progress. It is a strange, transitional, uncertain world that Williamson presents here, and 'The Beard' is a suitable commentator to catch the ironies, since he is himself, with his motorcyle and his genuine love for the old England, his passion for the simple life and his weakness for dance-halls and gramophones, a classic embodiment of the pull between old and new. He is a less obvious but in many respects more subtle persona than Willie Maddison. They share many attitudes, and even some adventures, but there is none of the Christ *manqué* about 'the Ham historian' and only occasional traces of Maddison's self-important naiveté. A new type of rural observer, he is looked upon with amused interest and cautious mistrust by the villagers, and , more important, is viewed with a good deal of ironic detachment by Williamson. Moreover he does not play the role of solitary hermit for long. In a few years he acquires a wife and child, symbolically shaves off the beard, and by the end of *The Labouring Life* has left the village and blended imperceptibly into the Henry Williamson of the thirties, the author and broadcaster who rushes about the countryside in the 'Silver Eagle' instead of on the motorbike, and, in books like *The Linhay on the Downs* and *Goodbye West Country*, has apparently dispensed with any mask. Writer and man are now virtually united.

When Georgeham became 'too popular,' and Williamson's increased family and literary profits made a change necessary and possible (*CS*, 25), he moved inland to Shallowford, to 'one of the most secluded villages in England' (*GWC*, 194). The future biographer of Salar the Salmon was, in fact, following the salmon-route from the world of Tarka to the spawning grounds of the river Bray. Here, close to the deer-park of the Fortescues and a 'clear water stream' offering excellent fishing, Williamson lived for seven years in the 1930s. Now established as a novelist and rural writer, winner of the 1928 Hawthornden Prize for *Tarka the Otter*, he is a very different man from the war-scarred 'hermit' of Georgeham, though he is still haunted by the horror of 1914–18 and worried for the future. But experience and maturity have tempered much of the youthful ambition. He is now prepared to see himself not as an inspired prophet but as 'a mere detached observer of animals, for the purposes of amusement and money' (*LD*, 46), 'a minor writer of country things' (*GWC*, 149) – even, in a retrospective memoir of these years, 'an eccentric literary tramp' (*CWS*, 178). He is now sufficiently detached that he can exclaim: 'Thank God I've got away from my pretentious self – it's the devil to one's life' (*GWC*, 63).

None the less, the literary record of these years is unquestionably disappointing. *Salar the Salmon* (1935) is the only work written and published in this period that can confidently be described as up to Williamson's standard. *The Linhay on the Downs* and *Goodbye West Country* both contain excellent writing, but can hardly be regarded as satisfactory wholes. The two pot-boilers *On Foot in Devon* and *Devon Holiday* were disasters, while the notorious 1936 dedication of the one-volume edition of *The Flax of Dream* to Adolf Hitler 'whose symbol is the happy child' might well have proved the last nail in the coffin of a dead reputation.[24] Williamson was himself conscious of a decline in literary quality. As he writes in *The Story of a Norfolk Farm*, 'with the exception of the salmon book, the last three or four books I had published, while as good as most country stuff, were not much good' (*SNF*, 13). Portentousness, his weakness in the early writings, has now been replaced by a cynical flippancy. Thus at the beginning of *On Foot in Devon*, which he accurately describes as a 'sneering, jeering guide,'[25] we find this: 'I don't know if the reader will be interested in these and similar scraps of information; but that's how I intend to write this book; and for those who don't care about following us, there's always a sharrabang round every corner of the main and minor roads. We're going by cliff paths, sheep and deer-tracks, yes, and even rat-runs; we're going in the lowest pubs and by the highest tide-lines, too' (*OFD*, 4). This belligerent, take-it-or-leave-it attitude would be detected as false even if one were not acquainted with Williamson's better work. *Devon Holiday*, we are told at the outset, was written 'in a spirit of slapstick and knock-about,'[26] and the creator of the humourless Willie Maddison is once again out of his depth. He presents himself in the book as 'Henry Williamson,' but has to project the impression of an eccentric – moody, angry, misunderstood; it is all very self-conscious and more than a little silly. One cannot help feeling, however, that the facetious tone, like Thomas's bitter ironies, masks a helpless but genuine despair. The sarcasm against charabancs, litter, main roads (to confine the list to subjects in *On Foot in Devon*) is understandable, but the forced and unsuccessful jocularity surely covers a realization that to them belongs the wave of the future.

Williamson's literary, if not his financial, position had now reached its nadir. One of the reasons, as he was quick to realize, was that he had 'worked out' his Devon material and needed to make a fresh start. Writing of north Devon in *The Linhay on the Downs*, he comments: 'I had exhausted this country, or it had exhausted me. I had stayed here too long' (*LD*, 177). But his dissatisfaction in these years was not confined to the quality of his work; it extended to the very nature of the literary and artistic life. As early as his pamphlet *The Wild Red Deer of Exmoor* (1931) he had claimed that his only real happiness was achieved during 'periods of activity when I was sailing, walking, planting trees, or working with my hands.'[27] The same point is made more positively a little later: 'When I am in good form, that is well and happy, and fishing in the Bray, I enter into another world – the natural world – where senses and instincts are harmonious and co-ordinated to one purpose. The consciousness is no longer a house divided against itself' (*LD*, 215). Several years later in *The Story of a Norfolk Farm*, an account of his radical response to this challenge, he continually reverts to the same argument: 'Writing is not living ... It was unnatural to sit hour after hour, day after day, week after week, getting more and more dyspeptic, while projecting life and vitality into an imaginary world. Much easier to be normal and natural, to go with the tide' (*SNF*, 40, 42).

The last phrase is ironically inappropriate, for Williamson's solution was to go dramatically against the tide of commercial thinking dominant in the 1930s. At a time when, as H.J. Massingham was later to write, 'English agriculture reached the lowest ebb in all its history,'[28] when three hundred acres were going out of cultivation in Britain every day (see *SNF*, 65), Williamson decided to return to the land in the most literal sense of the phrase, and in 1937, without any farming experience, he became owner of a run-down farm near Stiffkey on the north Norfolk coast. While he did not abandon his literary career – he found, indeed, that he had to subsidize his farming venture by articles and broadcast talks prepared after a full day's work in the fields – the land now claimed the centre of his attention. The story, as Williamson tells it, is one of disappointment, frustration, and unending toil – but there is also a sense of achievement, of difficulties overcome, of a creative act more basic and satisfying than that emanating from the study. This is Williamson's answer to the sense of failure so characteristic of later rural writing. The dilemma of Sturt, separated from his wheelwright's shop, finding his own vocation trivial and dilettante compared with the humbler but more natural work of Bettesworth and Will Hammond, the wry despair of Thomas, recognizing the absurdity of producing second-hand imitations of natural experience for readers lacking the means or the desire to gain first-hand experiences for themselves – these situations are avoided by Williamson's return to the realities of the soil. Gradually the sicknesses of civilization are shed, and, despite all the worry and heartache, the basic feeling is a sense of triumph. He writes movingly about the ploughing of his first furrow: 'I felt a warmth of satisfaction coming over me; I was a ploughman, I had found freedom' (SNF, 182).

The Story of a Norfolk Farm is a noble book by virtue of its subject; there can be no more satisfying and appropriate theme in rural literature than the co-operation of man and nature to produce fertility. Throughout it there runs a strong vein of rural patriotism. The whole project is undertaken 'not for my sake, not for profit, directly: but for its own sake, for England's sake' (SNF, 222). When this necessitates a battle against prejudice, irresponsibility, and vested interest, it takes on the qualities of saga. Williamson has some difficulty, however, in adapting himself to the tone of his subject. The earlier pages share many of the faults of the books of the 1930s – in particular, his initial presentation of himself is unsatisfactory. Surely, one feels, he cannot have been as naive and ignorant as he appears, and the series of accidents and misfortunes suggest a contrived comedy of errors. At times, indeed, we seem to be close to the world of Three Men in a Boat, and against such a background it is hard to take the writer's passionately held convictions as seriously as they deserve. As the book progresses, however, and the farm begins to take shape, the inherent dignity of the theme comes to the fore. Perhaps Williamson intended to show himself, as it were, growing up with his subject. At all events, when at the end of the second year he has broken even and what had recently been neglected and run-down is neat and productive, we rejoice in Williamson's achievement.

It is hardly necessary to add, of course, that neither Williamson's sense of achievement nor the achievement itself was long-lasting. Although the 'epigraph' to the book is dated June 1940, Williamson can bring his story to a close on a note of personal optimism. When the Second World War broke out, he comments: 'I knew the end of the final phase of a period of industrialism, with its misery and anguish for so many millions of our people, was come; and I took my eldest son away from the public school which was educating him for a mode

of life which was dead. He spent his fourteenth birthday ploughing his fourteenth acre' (*SNF*, 343). If such a statement appears naive from the viewpoint of
the 1970s, it at least rounds off the narrative with a typical and suitable
challenge. Once again, however, Williamson's hopes were to be disappointed,
and in *The Phasian Bird* (1948), a book which, despite its title, is better
interpreted as a modern parable than as an animal story, he extended the
narrative through the early war years and was thus forced to read the signs of
the times in a new way. The story of the golden pheasant – symbol, like
Lawrence's phoenix, of hope in a new world to be born out of the ashes of the
past and to recreate the best features of that past – is counterpointed by the story
of Wilbo, another of Williamson's masks, upon whose land the Phasian bird
finds shelter. But Wilbo is detained under 18-B like his creator, loses his farm,
and finally, in an ambitious but unconvincing climax, is shot by the local
war-profiteers on the same day as the pheasant. The allegory, though more
complex than it may first appear, revives the tendency towards self-pity which
one hoped Williamson had outgrown. It immediately recalls the death of Willie
Maddison in *The Pathway*, and the 'Father-forgive-them' death-scene is embarrassingly contrived. But the death of the symbolic bird, apparently without
issue, represents a darker ending, and one which is emphasized by the impressive descriptions of a ruined countryside against which the closing events take
place. As a whole, then, the book is annoyingly uneven. The earlier chapters
represent Williamson at his finest; these are, of course, the most objective
chapters, where he is furthest removed from his own personal experience. Yet,
however we respond to the 'moral' of the parable, we cannot help admiring
Williamson's brilliant presentation of the changing countryside in the years
between 1937 and 1944.

It would be possible to trace the development of Williamson's prose style in
much the same way that we traced that of Edward Thomas. A suitable starting-
point would be the opening essay of *The Lone Swallows*, with all its sentimental
clichés and falsities of rhythm, or the notorious sentence from the first draft of
Dandelion Days to which J.D. Beresford objected: 'Sometimes a swallow
rag-tailed and gracile passed through the fine spray upflung by the champèd
waters, descanting on the silver plash and spilth of gold' (*SS*, 145). The
temptation to write bad rural prose seems to have been irresistible in the early
years of this century, but it passed, and Williamson refers later to 'the early and
very precious Henry Williamson and Edward Thomas' (*LD*, 249). It is interesting to note that both writers follow a line of development opposite to that of
their declared hero, Jefferies. Whereas Jefferies moved from straightforward
directness to impassioned complexity (without ever perpetrating the bejewelled
prose of the later period), Thomas and Williamson, beginning with a liking for

lush sentences, end by seeking the greatest accuracy and simplicity. (Both, incidentally, admired Sturt's crisp and untrammelled prose, and were clearly influenced by his example.)

Williamson survived a bad stylistic start to become, if we judge solely by the quality of the prose, one of the purest writers of his time. Certainly of all the contributors to the rural tradition he is the most skilled in treading the middle course between the extremes of inharmonious crudeness and inappropriate elegance. Most remarkable, perhaps, is the sheer effort he puts into his work. *Tarka the Otter*, for example, went through no less than seventeen versions 'not for style but for truth' (*GWC*, 19), and Williamson speaks interestingly of 'rewriting as I saw more clearly, less untruly – the prose arising out of experience, spring, summer, autumn, winter' (*GWC*, 287). 'The prose arising out of experience' seems commonplace enough, but Williamson means it literally and absolutely. For him style is inextricably linked with vision in all the connotations of that word, and both depend upon honesty; by the same token ignorance and stupidity (which Williamson sees as identical) will necessarily be communicated in a muddled prose lacking the all important 'clarity.' Williamson makes the point most forcefully in the introduction to his 'pemmican anthology' of Jefferies:

Here is my belief:
    The base or foundation of a first-class talent is eye-sight. The man who sees more, who perceives quicker than his fellows, is of larger intelligence only by reason of that superior sight. Some people, educated unnaturally, seldom see for themselves ... Wisdom is the essence of observation.   (*RJ*, 21)

Whatever one may think of this as a general theory, its application to his own work is obvious. He makes reference elsewhere to his 'nervous, multi-detailed prose' (*CS*, 234). His continual effort is to suppress the nervousness (a concomitant of weakness) but maintain the multiplicity of detail which is the result of clear vision. For Williamson, then, style is intimately connected with the observing self, and the problem is to omit the unnecessary, whether in the objects seen or in the character of the subject. 'When in doubt, leave out' (*SS*, 146) became his motto. This can be documented by comparing the earlier and later versions of *The Children of Shallowford* (1939 and 1959). It is impossible to decide whether any specific alteration was dictated by considerations of material or of style, since the two are inseparable; in shedding the expendable stylistic excesses he is inevitably altering the 'portrait of the artist' that emerges in the course of the book.

This process has developed considerably in the course of Williamson's long writing life. The irritating aspects of his earlier personae (all the more annoying since they were never integral) have lessened noticeably over the years. None the less, however familiar we may become with his work, Williamson remains a paradox. This results from his being the only full-fledged idealist in the rural tradition – and it leads to all sorts of complexities. Most obvious, perhaps, is the oddity that a romantic artist with high-flown theories concerning his art should present himself as the fervent disciple of Jefferies, for whom such matters were at most peripheral. One finds a similar dichotomy in his attitude to the villagers about whom he writes. At one moment he can complain that 'the entire village life, thought and standard was based on resignation and prejudice' (*SNF*, 191); at another we find him asserting that 'for some time now my criterion of what is true or false, good or bad, has been based on what the ordinary working man, the sociable working man, would think of it, *if he could formulate his thought*. This is the nearest to the natural norm or truth I know' (*GWC*, 283). William- son is aware of this dichotomy in himself; as he notes in the first version of *The Children of Shallowford*, 'the two worlds, of imagination and reality, were irreconcilable, almost hostile, within one human body' (*CS*, 48).

A similar division may be discerned in his writing between the intensely personal, drawing generously on autobiographical experience, and the scrupu- lously objective, in which the writer's own character is effaced. These might be described as the only-sometimes-overlapping worlds of Willie Maddison and Tarka. The former needs no further exemplification here; the latter is less conspicuous but equally important. When Williamson concentrates on the non-human world, his own individual concerns are necessarily excluded. As he remarks of the writing of *Tarka the Otter*: 'My part as writer seemed a small, entirely impersonal part: it was the English countryside that mattered, the trees, the rivers, the birds, the animals, the people. Indeed, I wanted the book to be without the author's name on the title-page' (*CS*, 52). Certainly the em- phasis in these animal stories is on the processes of nature, on the ever- recurring change that lies at the heart of life. Later, in 1943, Williamson can even write: 'The person, as I have long thought, does not matter; it is the use of the talent that is important, the inner, impersonal urge to reveal the truth and glory of the visible world: the colour of corn in wind; the ant hurrying over the hot stone; the startling flame-like translucency of the kestrel's wings against the eastern arc of a cloudless sky ...'[29] The trouble is that Williamson finds a difficulty in practising what he preaches. He can write, as if from his own experience: 'Let one take *all* things easily and lightly, and not curse the wheels or the fumes or the crowds of people or their ideas; otherwise one rivets bands on one's brow' (*OFD*, 32) – but he never learns his own lesson. Similarly, while recognizing in theory the strength of writing that conforms to T.S. Eliot's ideal of 'an escape from personality,' he is continually returning to a nervous, obsessive account of his own quirks and problems.

More than any other rural writer with the exception of Borrow, Williamson is blessed with what John Middleton Murry has called 'the power of retrospective imagination.'[30] Unfortunately, although gifted with a subtler intellect and an infinitely greater stylistic sense, Williamson (and again I am limiting my generalization to his rural writings) has never been able to manipulate this power with any of Borrow's success. He can rarely leave well enough alone. 'The Badger Dig' in *The Village Book* is a case in point. The description is brilliantly realistic, since the viewpoint is at once personal (Williamson is very much 'there'), and at the same time objective (in that the events are chronicled with the minimum of interpretation). The piece centres upon Williamson's own mixed feelings in watching the ritual: 'I felt I had been false to myself, and yet another thought told me that such feelings flourished only in nervous weakness' (*VB*, 32). Similarly, after the kill, his frank acknowledgment of his own involvement – 'With the dried blood stiff on my temples I climbed the hill, cursing the satanic ways of men, yet knowing myself vile' – is excellent, but he spoils it by adding that 'all the tears ... would not wash from my brow the blood of a little brother' (*VB*, 32–3). The last phrase seems so absurdly inadequate – and patronizing – for the badger who has been presented as so much more than that. Williamson makes an unbelievable St Francis, and his lack of verbal tact betrays him into a cheap sentiment that lowers the tone of the whole essay.

It may well be that Williamson is a potentially great writer born too late, into an industrial world which he can never understand (hence his political excesses) and which can never understand him. The man who wanted to become a second Jefferies finds this virtually impossible in his own age, not merely because of the loneliness of such a role (which Williamson is only too ready to equate with the loneliness of the dedicated artist), but because he is himself attracted to the new world (via his motorcycle and gramophone) and finds himself unable to reconcile the two positions. As it is, though his rural writing constitutes an important and substantial part of his total output, Williamson sees his life-work as residing elsewhere – in his novel series, *A Chronicle of Ancient Sunlight*, which focuses on the experience of Phillip Maddison, Willie's urban cousin. The split remains, of course. However, as in the case of Borrow or, more cogently perhaps, of Thomas's poetry, instead of remaining an irritant continually threatening to disrupt the material, the split becomes in itself the subject of attention. It appears no longer as an awkward digression, since it is central. The creative 'wound,' in other words, strengthens rather than destroys the delicately balanced work of art. But, despite the fact that Williamson's development ultimately leads him outside the boundaries of this study, his ideal, no less in *A Chronicle of Ancient Sunlight* than in his earlier writings, remains the same – 'natural man on his natural earth' (*GWC*, 283).

TWELVE

H.J. Massingham

1888-1952

The whole secret of England is her regionalism.[1]

In one of his letters to Edward Garnett Hudson refers to 'young Massingham,' whom he describes as 'a tremendously energetic person ... now fighting for a law to exclude feathers from our markets – in which I'm with him heart and soul' (*HL*, 267). 'Young Massingham,' so designated to distinguish him from his father H.W. Massingham, the well-known liberal journalist and editor, was Harold John Massingham, the subject of this chapter; he became one of Hudson's most fervent disciples during the last four years of the latter's life, wrote eloquently about him at his death, served on the committee that chose Epstein's statue of Rima for the Hudson memorial in Hyde Park, and for a time, indeed, seemed likely to inherit Hudson's mantle as a writer on natural history. In the event he was led into areas of rural life and tradition of which even Hudson knew little, but the older writer had none the less, in Massingham's own words, 'a powerful influence upon me, more so, I think, than that of any other living man I had met' (*MR*, 51). He was inspired by what he has described in another context as Hudson's 'integrated vision'[2] to undertake his steadfast, lonely search for the fundamental qualities of rural culture. His findings, linking such diverse subjects as archaeology, anthropology, religion, agricultural history, geology, topography, and literature, comprise a vast and unified body of rural knowledge that is as impressive as it is unexpected. In what might well be interpreted as the fag-end of the rural tradition, the embers suddenly burst forth into a bright and powerful afterglow.

I have already commented on the unlikelihood of Hudson's developing into an important figure in English rural writing, and the same could be said, though for very different reasons, of Massingham. With Hudson it was primarily a matter of geographical distance; with Massingham upbringing, social position, and the seemingly overwhelming pressures of contemporary events and trends were all involved. His life, in short, was destined to move in obstinate opposition to the current of his times; it entailed a continual struggle against the fashionable grain. In consequence he ran the risk of appearing eccentric, quixotic, even perverse, and, although the tone of disillusioned bitterness which occasionally ruffles the smooth surface of his prose bears witness to the emotional strain, he displays for the most part a remarkable balance and serenity. As the title of one of his books indicates, his was a pilgrimage 'through the wilderness,' and despite his modest verdict, 'Whether I had "gone back" or come out at the other end is not for me to decide' (MR, 90), its successful completion is hardly in doubt. He has told the story (which he characteristically describes as 'a topographical record of the country of my own mind' [MR, v]) quietly, eloquently, convincingly, in his autobiography Remembrance (1942), and he stresses the fact that it is the story of a conversion, of a never-ending quest for wholeness, health, and the good life.

In his later years Massingham came to isolate two important countermovements in the complex, uneasy relationship between town and country that had existed since the close of the eighteenth century. His own time, he writes, saw 'a great migration or exodus from the towns into the country, and this movement is just as significant and symptomatic as the tidal drift a century ago in the opposite direction. The Industrial Revolution was responsible for Exodus I; the fruits of the new system or new chaos for Exodus II.'3 This observation is by no means irrelevant to his own biography. His father, whom he describes as 'a provincial' in origin before his successful move to London (MR, 4), belonged to the first exodus, Massingham (with whom in this context we may associate Thomas and Williamson) to the second. In many respects, indeed, Massingham's early years could be compared to those of Thomas, though the Massinghams occupied a decidedly higher rung of the Victorian social ladder. Born, as he notes, 'within the sound of Bow Bells' (MR, 4), he grew up in a liberal, free-thinking, late Victorian home, earnestly and confidently in the vanguard of the progress that the later Massingham would find himself renouncing and reviling. Being the eldest son, he was sent as a matter of course to Westminster School, where he received the traditional classical education, but this he was likewise to condemn later in life, dismissing it as a grounding in inessentials. 'To think,' he exclaims with indignation from the remoteness of his country retreat, 'that I have lived more than fifty years without recognising a Pilot pea when I see it and that thirty years ago I knew how many ships fought at the Battle of Argusinae!'4 He is well aware that such a remark would be condemned in certain quarters as hopelessly 'provincial,' but for Massingham, as for Sturt, this was by no means a term of reproach.

Westminster was followed in due course by Oxford where, again like Thomas, he went up to read history, though he later transferred to the study of English literature. The influence of both disciplines may be traced in his subsequent work, but once again the later Massingham, impatient of all false starts, declared these years a waste of valuable time. He saw the university as bolstering his shortcomings instead of eradicating them. 'I styled myself a "Free Thinker,"' he recalls, 'a euphemism for not thinking at all but drifting with the tide of current unfaith' (MR, 18). Certainly pre-1914 Oxford was hardly the place to set Massingham upon the road that he had to find painfully and laboriously for himself. Far more valuable was his introduction, during convalescence after a serious illness that coincided with his finals, to 'the society of birds' (MR, 27). To his evident surprise he found himself yielding to the idiosyncrasy of becoming an enthusiastic bird-watcher. It was the first, faint glimmering of his subsequent interests.

Massingham's early journalistic career need not detain us for long. He served on a number of newspapers and journals just before and during the First World War, interspersing his life in London with visits to the countryside whenever he had the opportunity. It was towards the end of the war that he first met Hudson, and the two became friends while Massingham was agitating to get his Plumage Bill through the House of Commons. Hudson was for Massingham 'one of our very few contemporary great artists,'[5] 'the greatest of countrymen,'[6] and his name recurs constantly throughout Massingham's work. The friendship developed at a crucial time for the young writer who has readily acknowledged the extent of Hudson's influence upon him: 'He did more than give a meaning to my pilgrimages into wild places. Through him I was coming to question the whole fabric of "modernism," and that could only lead, as it did lead, to the abandonment of my London life' (MR, 53). But Massingham is anticipating himself; it was some years before the break was finally made. Meanwhile he continued as a free-lance journalist, publishing books on a variety of subjects, though he later dismissed his juvenilia, written while he was 'tainted with Bloomsbury intellectualism,'[7] as 'books that had nothing to do with pub and church and farm and the labour of the fields' (MR, 38). But a few, such as Some Birds of the Countryside (1923) and In Praise of England (1924), derive from Hudson in subject matter, attitude, and even style.

It was probably during this period that Massingham became dissatisfied with his situation as a full-time writer. In the opening pages of his autobiography he expresses a reaction against the literary life that recalls Williamson: 'There seems to me a something unbalanced and nebulous in the life of authorship alone ... If I could have my life over again, it would be with plough-tails in my grasp for the morning, and pen for the evening' (MR, 1, 2). Fortunately he developed in the mid-1920s a new interest which might at first sight seem irrelevant to the present study but was in fact to have unforeseeable consequences. He became attracted to the new 'diffusionist' school of cultural anthropology centred upon London University and the researches of Elliot Smith and W.J. Perry. Soon he was attached to the staff, and set out to apply their general findings to the English evidences of prehistoric man, devoting several books, notably *Downland Man*, to the subject. In travelling widely over southern England to visit prehistoric barrows and encampments, particularly in Wiltshire and the Cotswolds, Massingham not only fell in love with the wolds and downland escarpments but also came to appreciate the historical complexity of the local regions. The variations in earthworks and prehistoric remains according to the geological features of the country, the links between 'primitive' art and later craftsmanship, the continuity of local culture and tradition, the fidelity of the ancient builders to the aesthetic features of the regions in which they settled, all these things gradually coalesced into a discernible pattern, like pieces of a vast jigsaw falling at last into place. The foundations of Massingham's rural knowledge were now firmly laid, and the rootlessness of modern urban living seemed more and more unsatisfactory.

After a year's residence in the Cotswolds, Massingham eventually had a house built in the Chilterns, and settled down to live there permanently. The decision to cut his links with the city, his resolve 'to be off and grow cabbages' (MR, 70), was a momentous one – indeed he describes his 'ultimate disengagement from urbanism' as 'the most important event in [his] life' (MR, 4). Its effect, contrary to the beliefs of his city acquaintances, was not to limit his horizons but to expand them. In *Through the Wilderness* he has told the fascinating story of this period – how his attention was first confined to the home, then spread to the garden, then to the immediate landscape, and then further to include the trackways of prehistoric man that followed the lines of the hills. Massingham was almost obsessively conscious at this time of being 'a unit in a horde of aliens who were descending upon the English country as the plagues descended upon Egypt' (TW, 278–9]. It was not enough merely to reside in the Chilterns; since he could not claim the prerogatives of a native, he must earn his rights by acquainting himself as minutely as possible with the local history, crafts, and customs. This was not an easy process, as his book baldly entitled *Country* (1934) shows, but he gradually developed what he calls 'a kind of land-conscience' (TW, 278), and it could be argued that his numerous books written to explain, justify, and commemorate the rural way of life were offered as tribute for the privilege of becoming (if only by adoption) a true countryman. At this point he had gone beyond Hudson who, though one of the great writers on the countryside, could never be described as himself a man of the country. Massingham had finally escaped from the city, as Hudson had never succeeded in doing, and in later years he was to see his own 'journey of the mind' quite explicitly as 'a journey from Hudson towards Cobbett' (*MR*, 88).

Massingham moved into his new house at Long Crendon, Buckinghamshire, in the early 1930s, got married in 1935 (in fact, for the second time, though he never so much as mentions his earlier marriage in his autobiography), and lived there for the rest of his life. It was from this rural retreat that his finest books were written, and only one subsequent biographical event – serious illness – needs to be recorded. While working outdoors in 1937 he fell over a rusty feeding-trough concealed in long grass; complications set in, and he had to spend the next two years 'between hospital and home' (*MR*, 102). Soon afterwards he suffered another fall which had almost fatal consequences ('During the critical year of 1940, I was a dying man' [*MR*, v]), and resulted in the amputation of one of his legs. Although ultimately less serious than Jefferies' consumption or Sturt's paralysis, the effect of his disability was the same: his active life appeared to be more or less over, though he still wrote and travelled to a surprising extent and lived on until 1952. But his creative energies had to be channelled into narrower bounds. The enforced rest led Massingham to read widely and with profit in areas related to his earlier interests. Once again history and literature were prominent, but more conspicuous was a turning towards religious subjects and a religious attitude. A cynic would doubtless explain this by the fears of increasing age and the shock of his near-fatal accident, but such a neat diagnosis fails to take all the facts into account. Massingham's religious conversion (he was baptized into the Roman Catholic Church) was the culmination of his rural conversion; and the two were intimately related. For Massingham the gospels were 'peasant literature,'[8] and the Jesus in whom he put his faith was the 'Christ of the trades.'[9] The Church which he joined was the Church that had been the focal point of the ancient village communities of the middle ages, for whose God the rural craftsmen had raised the towers and steeples and carved the roodscreens and gargoyles that he loved. Above all Massingham's God was the creator and maintainer of that wholeness which he had at last discovered, a wholeness which was also, he insisted, a holiness.

In Massingham the wheel of rural literature may be said to come full circle. Though there are connections, as I have suggested, with Thomas and Williamson, the differences are far more prominent. Where they brought the town with them when they went into the country – Thomas mentally, Williamson both mentally and physically – Massingham, aware of this tendency as one of the major problems of his time, managed to avoid doing so, since he had no more desire to impose himself on the landscape than to build his house in disregard of its environment. Of all the latter-day country writers Massingham is closest to the tone and attitudes of the earlier members of the rural tradition. Even more remarkable, however, is the development within his own life – from free-thinker to believer, from left-wing liberal to firm conservative ('The sense of continuity led me from a vague and half-hearted Liberalism in the tradition of the 19th century into a Conservatism of a much older tradition' [MR, 62]), and, subsuming all these, from townsman to countryman. Massingham is important not only as a writer but as an example; the pattern of his life is perhaps more impressive than that of his individual books. It would be going too far to suggest that the lost rural paradise had been regained, but at least the direction was pointed out for a fresh start. Where the predominant theme had been the enforced separation of man from the earth, Massingham offers the basis for a new myth: the ability of the resolute individual to put down new roots.

'Broadly speaking,' he writes in his preface to Through the Wilderness, 'my theme is the relationship between man and nature in our own country, its fruitfulness and the disastrous consequences of disturbing it' (TW, vii). This might well be considered the main subject of his whole work. He is certainly no primitivist yearning for rustic solitude. He insists that a quiet countryside is a dead countryside (cf TW, 147), and continually laments the decline in rural population. Nothing could be further from his ideal than a virgin landscape untouched by man. He is explicit on this point: 'In my latter days I do not really care for landscape which is without sign of any co-operation between Nature and Man.'[10] The important word here is 'co-operation'; the relation must never be one of conquest. He is well aware of the extent to which an apparently 'natural' landscape is in fact man-made. His archaeological and historical studies were pursued with the express purpose of tracing this all-important relationship. That is why his particular interest was the civilization that produced the chambered long-barrows: 'With the coming of the megalith-builders, England received her first transformation at the hand of man. It is a remarkable tribute to the first civilization that laid the foundation-stones of the English nation that it left the English country actually more beautiful than it found her.'[11] According to Massingham's reading of history, this civilization set a pattern for subsequent periods which continued virtually unbroken (save for such interludes as the Roman occupation) until towards the end of the eighteenth century. He sees the Industrial Revolution as a disaster which 'destroyed the true England' (FY, 98) precisely because it substituted mechanical conquest for organic co-operation.

Since that time the balance between man and nature has been tragically upset. The needs of the cities, and a commercial, industrialized 'system' by means of which they flourish, have taken increasing priority over the needs of the countryside – except, of course, in times of national crisis when the townsman is rudely reminded that he is dependent upon the farms for his survival. Massingham makes the point firmly in his introduction to *The Fall of the Year*, a diary-style account of the last six months of 1939: 'After a third of the book had been written came the war that, for the first time since 1918, made country England of supreme importance to a mainly urban civilization, and revolutionized the common attitude towards it as scenery for relaxation and ground for building sites rather than as the source of our daily bread and the indispensable foundation of our national well-being' (FY, 9). Massingham's repeated 'message' is that the countryside should always be seen in this way, that it is the neglect of such a view that helps cause the very disasters that enforce remembrance.

Needless to say, Massingham was continually dismissed in his own time as a reactionary. His remarks, as he comments towards the end of his life, were interpreted as 'those of a pointless eccentric, a fiddler with clocks, an idle romanticist, a ruined tower with bats in the belfry,'[12] but he lived long enough to derive a mordant satisfaction from seeing the beginnings of a counter-movement in which his arguments were taken more seriously. Those who dismissed him out of hand were mistaking their man, for Massingham's brand of rural reaction was not based on ignorant prejudice. His attitude to the manorial system of the middle ages has behind it the researches of R.H. Tawney, and the Hammonds, as well as the instinctive response of a Cobbett, and his insistence on the pros of feudalism was the more cogent since it showed full awareness of the cons (see, e.g., ShC, 251, FY, 98). Crucial to his position was the distinction he drew between 'change' and 'progress': 'Change is the law of life, but it is change within a permanence; the "progress" we know is ephemeral by its very nature, superseding itself and plunging deeper and deeper into unreality with no self-protective rind' (FY, 188). Thus husbandry changes 'in details but never in fundamentals,'[13] and Massingham was not impressed by those who criticized him for failing to move with the times. He continually denied the very terms in which such judgments were usually made: 'I have so often been accused of wanting or trying to "put the clock back" – as though the clock-time of the morning train or the factory hooter were the only measurements worth considering' (CT, 11). Preferring a country 'alive in the past' to one 'dead in the present' (ChC, 69), Massingham follows Cobbett in looking to a future that will return to the proved ways of an earlier period. For him the present is an interlude which lacks the necessary qualities for survival. We must learn 'how to progress backwards' (WF, 189), and he sees himself as 'helping to found a new order more advanced because so utterly backward than anything of which our planners ever dreamed' (PE, 95).

Since Massingham renounced any belief in the Victorian cult of progress, one of his favourite literary devices was to interpret the present in terms of the supposedly barbarous past. In the result, conventional assumptions tend to be reversed. Thus he talks of 'the Dark Age of the twentieth century' (CT, 164), and in his early *Downland Man* plays amusingly with the idea that the modern period had revived ancient demons under more sophisticated names. Quoting a news item on unemployment caused by 'the law of supply and demand,' he argues that this law is obviously 'an inexorable demon who demands his quota of human misery exactly like the Moloch of the Tyrians and Carthaginians.'[14] But in later years, as the challenge becomes more acute, the tone of his argument takes on a savage vehemence. This reaches a climax of almost apocalyptic eloquence in *Chiltern Country*, first published in the darkest days of 1940:

> There are people who express surprise at the nature of the world in which we live to-day, who feel that the German violation of Poland and the Low Countries and the Russian of Finland are an inexplicable repudiation of European civilization. They are nothing of the kind; they but carry to their logical extremity the principles of economic expediency set in full motion by the Industrial Revolution and written as visibly ... upon our own native soil as upon the bloody fields of Europe.   (ChC, 70)

Clearly Massingham's protest is not just a sentimental desire to go 'back to the land.'

In fact, he is careful to dissociate himself from the tastes and attitudes of the urban escapists whose rural enthusiasms are divorced from the rural realities. He roundly condemns the 'arts and crafts' movements because they try to preserve the old ways, not as a viable way of life, but as a matter of museum interest. He is suspicious of those whose view of country life is 'something between a pastoral, a lecture hall and a fret-work bench' (WF, 227), and makes an important distinction between 'rural' and 'rustical' (see ChC, 46). Above all, he has no use for what he calls 'a purely ornamental past which has ceased to be in living contact with the present' (MC, 18). A specific example is found in a late book, *The Southern Marches*. Watching the restoration of Tretower Manor, he trusts that it will not become 'an empty shell, a show-place, a museum piece with a turnstile and a notice-board.' He hopes to witness the restoration, not of the building alone, but of the whole way of life which it was built to serve: 'What I should like to see is the ancient manor restored not only to the appearance of its old self but to the reality of usage by relating it once more to the agricultural life of this fertile region, not as a mere storehouse of crops but as the node and pivot of a cluster of local farms, as the old manors always were.'[15] Massingham's reaction, again like Cobbett's, contains a strong streak of radicalism, since its criticisms are not of superficial details, but of the fundamental principles upon which our present civilization is based.

It is difficult to assess Massingham's position objectively, since he separated himself so firmly and finally from the assumptions of modern life. In some respects, however, it is easier now than it was in his own time. Massingham was protesting against the dangers of DDT as early as 1950 (CT, 157), and he continually attacked 'the enormous ramifying vested interests which make their profits out of sprays, fertilizers, insecticides and chemical nostra of one kind and another' (FF, 133). Similarly he took every opportunity to expose the evils of water pollution and the dangers of world famine as a result of uncontrolled commercial speculation in agricultural land. In a world just awakening to the significance of ecology, a subject which might well be described as Massingham's main concern, we are likely to see him as a forerunner rather than one preoccupied with the minutiae of the past. But Massingham goes further than this. He attacks 'the complicated diabolism of international politics and our present economic system which is geared to it' (SM, 60). He refuses to accept an economic reason why 'Australian wool and New Zealand mutton have made a desert of our sheep-walks' (ShC, 31), why 'a nation that supports millions of men in idleness [in the thirties]' will do nothing for 'our own land that is perishing for the need of those workless men' (ShC, 69), why, to give a concrete instance, a Hampshire market-gardener should be forced to send his carrots to Ipswich to be tinned so that they can be returned for sale in his own village at an increased price which goes straight into the pockets of the urban middle-man (see PE, 94), why, 'while Britain is being supplied with Canadian apples, our own lay rotting on the ground or trees' (WF, 204), why the Labour Government of 1945–50, supposedly representing 'the people,' should pursue a 'policy of spending £250 per acre on tearing out the fertility of Africa, and 6d. per acre on rehabilitating the marginal lands of Britain' (FF, 146). If to ask such questions is to qualify as a reactionary, Massingham would accept the title with alacrity. His unending attacks on the absurdities of the contemporary situation again and again recall the heartfelt indignation of Cobbett. In reading Massingham one often gets the feeling that he is a minority of one in favour of sanity.

But we are unjust to him if we concentrate on the things he is against rather than his reasons for being against them. His criticisms of farm-machines stem not from a blind traditionalism but from his considered opinion that they are grossly inefficient and that they do not achieve what is claimed for them. As he remarks in Shepherd's Country, 'I am all for machines on the theory that they minimize drudgery. But the facts are that by eliminating personal skill and communal interest they too often create it' (ShC, 74). Similarly he advocates that the small farm follow the tradition of mixed husbandry not for sentimental reasons but because comparison has convinced him that the best results (in terms of quality and quantity, not of commercial profit) are gained in this way. To see the argument in terms of past and present, traditionalism and originality, orthodoxy and idiosyncracy, is not enough. For Massingham, who is always an advocate of an integrated vision, it extends to include a whole view of human life. The following passage brilliantly sums up his position:

> The real division is between rival philosophies of life. The one believes in exploit-ing natural resources, the other in conserving them; the one in centralized control and the other in regional self-government; the one in conquering and the other in co-operating with nature; the one in chemical and inorganic methods imitated from those of the urban factory and the other in biological and organic ones derived from the observation of nature as a whole; the one in man as a responsible agent with free will to choose between the good and the bad and the other as a unit of production directed from above by an *élite* of technologists and bureaucrats; the one in the divine creation both of man and nature and the other in man as self-sufficient in himself with nature merely as the means for extracting wealth for himself.   (FF, 226–7)

Or, in the memorable remark of an old farmer in Massingham's beloved Chilterns, 'if the new ways won't do, try the old 'uns again' (ChC, 104).

Although Massingham was born late in the day of English rural writing, his knowledge of landscape and scenery is unrivalled. Even Jefferies, whose breadth of interest makes him the most versatile of the rural writers, cannot match Massingham's integrated knowledge of what makes up a harmonious coun-tryside. Edward Thomas modestly admitted that 'it would need a more intellec-tual eye than mine to distinguish county from county by its physical character, its architecture, its people, its unique combination of common elements' (SC, 11), but this is precisely what Massingham was able to do. Encouraged by his early archaeological interests to master the geological factors and so to value 'the structure and anatomy of landscape more than its clothing,'[16] he came to view a particular stretch of country not as a random collection of interesting subjects but as an organic whole in which each feature had its part in the overall design:

> I became a convert to the idea of the region. Regionalism means all the factors of a given region, and each one is woven into the other. The parts, the units, the cells, are not separable, and the unit is what binds them together into a living whole ... A specific quality manifests itself in the complete presentation of a region, in precisely the same way as it does in a work of art. A region thus presented *is* a work of art, achieving its self-sufficiency both by accepting and transcending the limitations of its material, as all such works do that are worthy of the name.   (MR, 81)

In this statement we are offered a vital clue not only to Massingham's approach to his material, but to the way in which it determines the nature of his own writing.

Massingham's most popular (and often his most successful) books take a specific area as their subject, and can qualify as works of art by virtue of the way in which they recreate the unified character of the region. It is ironical, in a sense, that he should have produced a number of books that can be fitted even roughly into the guide-book category, since, with what he calls his 'terror of public playgrounds' (ChC, 41), he is strongly opposed to all that the traditional guide-book stands for. He dislikes being told what to appreciate, and claims to have taken a vow 'never on my journeys to go through a turnstile nor accompany a guide nor consult a guide-book nor visit a beauty-spot.'[17] The idea of a beauty-spot is particularly repugnant to him because it implies a selection, something set aside for a special purpose, an organized tourist centre, a scenic museum. He abominates the obtrusive road signs, phoney tea-shops, and all the commercial degradation seemingly inseparable from such a conception for the simple reason that they are both alien and parasitic, like the tourists to whom they cater. Massingham knows that genuine beauty cannot be imposed on a countryside from without for the benefit of outsiders; it arises when a local impulse is stimulated by a local need.

He is nowhere closer to Cobbett – and, one is tempted to add, to the 'philosophy' of all genuine countrymen – than in this emphasis on the necessary association of beauty and use. 'The principle of beauty-in-use and use-in-beauty' (PE, 240) recurs as a touchstone throughout his work. Although its shortcomings are acknowledged, the traditional open-field system is praised because it obeyed this principle. 'It contributed to the beauty of England as well as to the welfare of the peasantry' (ED, 101). The concentration of post-Industrial Revolution man on commercial utilitarianism divorced from aesthetic considerations has resulted in a catastrophic imbalance reflected in both the aridity of contemporary life and the ugliness of modern landscape. The separation of beauty and utility leads inevitably, Massingham is convinced, to the 'picturesque.' The rise of this term in the romantic period is not, he believes, an accident; it coincides historically with 'a countryside ... no longer occupied with supplying human needs' which therefore 'becomes the arena of sentiment only.'[18] Just as Cobbett saw beauty in a field of ripening corn but found nothing aesthetically pleasing in a tumbledown cottage since it presupposed discomfort on the part of the inhabitants, so Massingham is not to be deceived by artificial prettiness. Beauty is an intrinsic quality, not a varnish that can be overlaid. His linking of beauty with (in the broadest sense of the word) morality is close to Ruskin; 'I have a considered conviction,' he writes, 'that, if a thing is right, it looks right, and, if it has goodness at its heart, beauty goes with it' (WF, 162).

It is hardly surprising, then, that his own topographical writings (a more accurate term than 'guide-books') should prove both unconventional and original. He is, first of all, scrupulous in establishing the natural limits of his subject. His regional books are never determined by the political and therefore artificial boundaries of the modern counties; they remain faithful to the essential geological features – the downland, the Cotswold and Chiltern ranges, the 'southern marches.' Again his ingredients, though necessarily selected, are selected on a new principle. 'We are rather tired,' he writes in the preface to *Chiltern Country*, 'of the repetition of literary anecdotes and the enumeration of local antiquities dissociated from the life of the people' (*ChC*, v). He offers instead his personal impressions based, of course, on his thorough knowledge of the geological and historical nature of the region and of the local specialities of the individual communities. Moreover he refuses to turn a blind eye to contemporary developments. The replacement of thatch by corrugated iron, the takeover of local industries by national or even international combines, the devastation initiated by the Forestry Commission, the relation between the agricultural situation and current governmental policy, all these will be given at least as much attention as the conventional descriptions of church and castle. In short, the region is presented not as a dead repository of history but as a living and developing organism.

Massingham's Cotswold experiences, related in the unfortunately titled *World Without End* (1932), in *Cotswold Country* (1937), and in *Shepherd's Country* (1938), were crucial in impressing upon him the ecological foundation of a unified landscape. He came to discover that 'all things in Cotswold possess a unity whose primary source is the quality and nature of its limestone.'[19] The texture of the stone not only determines the contours of the countryside but affects the building styles. Thus, because 'a modified Gothic is the form best suited to the qualities of the stone,'[20] Gothic features persist in the Cotswolds and tend to impress themselves even upon alien styles. In addition, features used for manor houses and the homes of the rich are adapted for humbler dwellings and so establish a sense of continuity and connection which cuts across time spans and class divisions and so helps to foster a binding sense of community. The following passage, stressing the connection between human life and the natural world, as well as between social and architectural features, is at once an argument for and a demonstration of Massingham's organic vision:

> There is a hierarchy in houses as there is in animate Nature. What the Cotswold mason did was to put his best workmanship into every member of that hierarchy. The result is not only a common relationship between them all, but a multitude of individual beauties and refinements scattered among every type of building and safely preventing conformity to structural type from stiffening into a rigid

formula that would have made one cottage or manor or barn just like every other one. Just as the open field system reconciled personal ownership with communal government by the village, so the loyalty of the Cotswold house to the regional style proved compatible with tens of thousands of individual differences between one house and another. (*ShC*, 206)

Having observed the effects of regional unity in the Cotswolds, Massingham was able to approach other areas with an awareness of all the manifold features that go to make up a landscape. It gave him a clue not only to the appreciation of a countryside but also to the means of writing about it. If he is unique among later rural writers in being untroubled with formal problems, the reason lies in his consciousness of an interrelating pattern in the natural world. He has learnt, in E.M. Forster's term, to 'connect'; since he has reason to disagree with Jefferies' view that nature is 'without design, shape or purpose' (see p. 142 above), he has no need to impose a formal structure from without. The importance of co-operation with, rather than conquest of, nature is for Massingham as relevant to writing as to husbandry. The writer's function is to discover the clues and follow out the revealed pattern. Consequently Massingham's mature writings derive their structural integrity from their successful presentation of his attempt 'to see England as a whole of which her rock, her wild flowers and birds, her megalithic monuments, her Gothic architecture, her poets, her people, and their husbandry, were parts inseparable' (*MR*, 68–9).

Massingham's philosophy of relation (a concept wholly opposed to relativity) is best understood as a trinity generally expressed in terms of God, man, and earth. This has its physical equivalent in the arrangement of the mediaeval village – church, manor, and farm as the points of a containing triangle. In Massingham's own writing, particularly after his accident, his philosophy manifests itself in the related pattern of three major interests – agriculture, craftsmanship, and religion, 'organically one-in-three' (*MR*, 102). In order to appreciate both the consistency and the interconnections of his position it will be necessary to examine all three interests.

Never a farmer himself, Massingham was none the less knowledgeable on agricultural methods, was constantly visiting friends who farmed in various parts of the country, and edited two collections of essays on agriculture, *England and the Farmer* and *The Small Farmer*. His point of departure was the failure of modern agriculture. 'Because we measure falsely,' he maintains, 'our standards have become so low that we fail to understand how badly we farm' (*WF*, 223). He finds the concept of progress nowhere more dramatically contradicted than in agricultural science. Despite the claims of the specialists, he finds, by the simple Cobbett-like process of travelling in the countryside with his eyes open, clear evidence of 'the decline of good farming, the fall in fertility, the depopulation both in men and stocks, the scamped cultivations, the obsolescence of one skill after another and the general disorder of over-mechanized agriculture' (CT, 69). He insists on drawing a distinction between agriculture and 'agri-industry' (CT, 193), and laments the tendency of modern 'agriculturalists' (the very term suggesting to Massingham, as to Cobbett and Jefferies before him, a 'remoteness from practical farming' [WF, 233]) to divorce 'the two halves of the word "agriculture"' (CT, 21). He followed Arnold Toynbee in seeing the large-scale methods of the *latifundia* as a principal cause of the fall of the Roman Empire, and found the parallels with the contemporary situation disturbing in the extreme.

Massingham came to believe strongly that 'the fertility of the earth, on which the existence of mankind depends, cannot be achieved without a self-sufficient economy' (PE, 9), and that this is not possible without a return to intensive husbandry and the encouragement of small farms. Once again it should be emphasized that this is not a matter of blind conservatism or idyllic sentimentalism. He champions small-farming because he sincerely believes that 'small farms all over the world produce more per acre than large' (FF, 144). His later works from *Men of Earth* onwards are full of accounts of individuals who have maintained the principle of mixed husbandry and traditional methods against all the pressures of contemporary vested interest, and who have been justified not only by superior results but by what is more important in Massingham's view – the satisfaction of recreating some of the lost arts of living. Thus of one small farm in Kent he writes: 'They farm in precisely the same way as a poet writes a sonnet or a sculptor carves from the block. They are in the most definite application of the term artists who assemble the materials of their craft into a creative unity.'[21]

At this point, of course, we begin to move from the first to the second element in Massingham's rural trinity. Because agriculture is a basic human activity, it is invariably related to other subjects of primary significance. Because it is eternal, it has obvious connections with art: 'I felt once again that authentic agriculture must always be an art and so that past, present and future have only a minor relevance to it. It is all of them in one' (CT, 172). Agriculture has also been associated from time immemorial with religion, as the imagery of the Bible – especially of the Gospels – makes clear. But Massingham is particularly sensitive of the fact that it is intimately related with craftsmanship. 'Farming is essentially a handcraft, as all crafts are, and that is why extreme mechanisation and standardisation lead only to the literal desert' (MR, 135).

For Massingham craftsmanship is 'the foundation of all civilization in the past' [FF, 58–9], and he considers any way of life that ignores it to be built on sand. Even Sturt is unable to rival Massingham as a champion of the folk crafts. Where Sturt saw all the country skills as rural equivalents of art, for Massingham the crafts are decidedly 'fine' arts. Nowhere, he claims, is the degeneracy of modern existence more evident than in the demonstrable decline in the domestic skills: 'It is a sobering reflection that the arts of living – cookery, making good clothes, chair making, house building, brick making, plastering, textiles, sewing and embroidery, wine and beer and cider making, basketing and other domestic arts – have either vanished or have fallen to their lowest level in history' (CT, 14–15). He quotes with approval Dr Edmund Esdaile's definition of craftsmanship as 'manual literacy' (WMB, 184); by the same token the practical helplessness of the average urban wage-earner might be described as industrialized or even, to point up the irony, educated illiteracy.

What most impresses Massingham about the ancient craftsmen is their versatility (consisting not only in the variety of objects they could make but in their detailed and intimate knowledge of regional materials and local specialities) and their 'natural,' uninstructed good taste. His favourite craftsman, Samuel Rockall the wood-bodger, who appears in a number of books and comes to take on the representative quality of Sturt's Bettesworth, is particularly gifted in this respect. Massingham reports that 'when this peasant-woodman was left to himself to shape his own design [instead of being given an 'art-school' model], he went to the point and made a bowl a bowl, not a piece of ornament' (CT, 13). Yet Rockall had never travelled more than a few miles from his native village, lacked any qualifications that the urban mentality would recognize as 'education,' and would be labelled a provincial, a yokel, or even, like the tradition-proved tools that he used, a 'bygone.'

But Massingham's greatest approval is reserved not so much for the tangible results of this craftsmanship as for the integrity, the satisfaction, and the good life that they foster. He is continually commenting on the sense of honour and honesty displayed by such men. Rockall's chairs, for which he was himself paid a pittance, were 'treated' in the local town and offered, at inflated prices, as antiques, but his own integrity prevented him from asking more than the time-honoured 'just price.' The craftsmen were therefore victims of their own standards. They were used, and then discarded, by factory-style combines pandering to corrupt taste and benefiting from public ignorance of true quality. Massingham does not mince his words about this process; it is 'sheer murder by an evil economics' [ChC, 88]. It is all the more evil since such skill, once blotted out, is irreplaceable: 'The born craftsman is an anachronism to-day, because the tradition of the past which gave an artisan the inherited memory of a predisposition to perfection is broken. Once the tradition is broken the craftsmanship can never be recovered, never while the world lasts, and that is why the Machine Age has beggared human life' (GE, 164).

None the less, for all the sadness that pervades Massingham's presentation of the moribund crafts, the individuals are clearly contented and fulfilled people. They have escaped the rootlessness of the present. Of one family he writes: 'Such cells of organic life are out of present time altogether, and belong not to the past but to the essentials of the sane, whole and goodly life from the days of Adam to the end of the world' (CT, 69). Some readers may find such remarks excessively idealized, but it is probable that they would also fail to understand the attitudes of the craftsmen themselves. One of them, George Greening the master-carpenter of Winchcomb, is recorded to have said: 'My pleasures and hobbies throughout my life have been my work' (CR, 71), and Massingham finds craftsmen almost invariably expressing the same sentiments. That such a statement is obviously inconceivable in the mouths of millions of contemporary factory-workers does not speak well for the achievements of urban 'progress,' even if shorter hours, increased wages, and improved conditions are taken into account. Massingham considers it profoundly significant that 'we have separated work from play and banished God from both' (CR, 71), and this, of course, leads us to the third component of his trinity.

Although the journey from free-thinking agnosticism to an acceptance of Christianity represents by no means an unusual pattern, Massingham's conversion was unusual because, like so much of his life, it involved a struggle against the main stream. He was convinced, indeed, by what might be described as a mirror-image of the same situation that caused so many others to lose their faith. As he documents the process in his autobiography, 'I began to realise God from seeing what the world was like without Him. I came to believe in a purposive universe, because its contrary, as postulated by the Darwinians, seemed to me incredible' (MR, 106). His move from London to the Chilterns assisted the transformation. Massingham came to acknowledge that 'all religions have been born out of an agricultural matrix, just as every movement of rationalism has been urban' (FF, 84). This is not merely a debating-point in the unending controversy between town and country. The religion which Massingham held contained little or no abstract theory. It was more a simple faith than a sophisticated 'position'. He was rarely theological, and never 'preachy'; his chief mentors were not the contemporary divines but such men as William Barnes and Hawker of Morwenstow. For Massingham the harvest festival was no less significant a day in the Church year than Christmas or Easter. Church and farm were equally sacred – he loved 'to see a church built like a barn and a barn like a church.'[22] His was a 'natural' religion that acknowledged the miracle of growth ('When the sun gilds the field of ripening wheat, we are witnessing year by year a symbol of the Incarnation' [TL, 26]), and accepted the gospel of a rural saviour who was born in a stable, grew up in a carpenter's shop, and spread his teaching through examples drawn almost invariably from husbandry.

Massingham came to accept the traditional beliefs not in a spirit of obstinate conservatism but because the circumstances of his time compelled him. His faith was, in fact, a humane one, emphasizing responsibility and therefore free will, but his acute sense of reality did not allow the 'good news' of Christianity to blind him to the sterner principles originating in the Old Testament. 'The Doctrine of the Fall of Man,' he observed, 'is shown by the force of events to be not so much an article of faith as a platitude. The spectacle of modern and economic man confirms the dogma without the need of any theological argument' (TL, 185). Similarly a last judgment is no less final if it comes not through fire and battle but through famine and starvation; and Massingham's last book, *Prophecy of Famine*, written in collaboration with Edward Hyams (1953), which documents the possibility of man's exhausting his food supply, rounds off his work on a suitably apocalyptic note. Massingham's bedrock of faith, we might say, is that 'the Natural Order, when violated, exacts retribution in no uncertain fashion' (SM, 354). To a world that has been irresponsibly misusing its natural resources for over a century the truth is an unpleasant one, but it upholds a principle of justice within the cosmos that Massingham is prepared to call God.

Throughout this discussion I have been obliged continually to compare Massingham to Cobbett, and any summing-up of Massingham's contribution must necessarily focus upon his relations with the earlier writer. A stylistic resemblance is also involved. If, until now, I have neglected any consideration of Massingham as a stylist, the reason lies in his own reluctance, like Cobbett, to concentrate on manner at the expense of matter. He began his working life as a journalist, and, although his early writings are marked by a somewhat self-conscious, and therefore noticeable, imitation of Hudson's colloquially eloquent prose, he soon abandoned this for a direct, straightforward, unostentatious style designed to provide as exact a correspondence as possible between the intention of the writer and the understanding of the reader. He was a prolific author and must have written at speed, apparently caring little for the niceties of stylistic polish. In this respect he is closer to Cobbett and Jefferies than to Hudson. One constantly finds sentences where the substitution of an obvious synonym would have avoided an awkward repetition of syllable or sound. Clearly he wrote for the eye rather than for the ear. He is careless of details, his quotations and references are as inaccurate as Hazlitt's, and in his untiring reiteration of his point of view he can be as repetitious as Cobbett but without Cobbett's power and energy. For Massingham the stylistic virtues are bluntness, clarity, and an avoidance of ambiguity. He mistrusts the contrived artificiality of what he would consider an alien rhetoric. 'Why,' he asks, 'should a country writer dress up his wares in a Bond Street smoothness' (PE, 96)?

Massingham is particularly skilled, like Cobbett, in finding a specific example that takes on symbolic dimension by so perfectly representing a general trend.

Thus during the harsh winter of 1946–7 he notes: 'The Times reported that 'in isolated villages housewives were baking their own bread,' an item of news to blench the hardest heart' (EY, 100). The remark is memorable not so much for its sarcasm, more in sorrow than in anger, but for its quintessential appropriateness in summing up the decline in traditional values. It is strikingly reminiscent of the 'found symbol' of Cobbett ('PARADISE PLACE. Spring guns and steel traps are set here' [RR, 234]). His use of simile is correspondingly skilful. The images, again like Cobbett's, are doubly appropriate in being not only just, but rural in origin. Two examples must suffice:

> Pseudo-Gothic restoration went through [the Cotswold churches] in the nineteenth century as the Black Death went through the village five centuries before.   (ShC, 269)

> Chalfont St. Peter ... had the modern road driven through its entrails as in the old days a stake was driven through the heart of a malefactor.   (ChC, 103)

Such similes are not (or, to be more circumspect, show no trace of being) contrived with ponderous effort in the artist's study; they give every appearance of flowing smoothly from the pen as a natural product of the countryman's thought. Again there is frequently a countryman's humour in the wit, but this is often overshadowed by a sardonic contempt that might be dismissed as gratuitous insult if Massingham had not already convinced us that the points at issue were too crucial for pulled punches. At one point, after commenting on a disturbing increase in rats, Massingham continues in a new paragraph: 'There has been a parallel increase in the ratio of bureaucrats to workers' (EY, 63). Fitfully, but palpably, the indignation of Cobbett is heard once more.

None the less, it is important to question the extent to which an overall comparison with Cobbett can legitimately be made. Massingham certainly considered himself a disciple, praising Cobbett as 'the great Englishman who possessed a genius for looking into the future' (ChC, 35). The comparison is encouraged by Massingham's insistence on reading him as a contemporary: 'I find him – I was going to say the only living author – who understands what has happened to England ... A trifle of proof-correcting, such as financiers for 'fundholders,' wens for 'the Wen,' and here is a great man writing about our own times ... His themes are actually more pertinent to the nineteen thirties than they were to the eighteen twenties, because what Cobbett saw in the grain in the twenties of last century we see come to the ear in the thirties of the next' (FY, 48–9). But, although it is clearly legitimate to view Massingham's writings, particularly the topographical books and such diary-style works as An Englishman's Year and The Curious Traveller, as providing a mid-twentieth-century equivalent of *Rural Rides*, any extended comparison between the two men, though tempting, seems inapposite. One wonders, indeed, if it would be an unqualified compliment to be called a modern Cobbett. Is the chief link between them an unpractical, impossible vision of what might be? And if Cobbett's attitude could not prevail in the nineteenth century, can similar views be taken seriously in the twentieth? We can sympathize with Massingham for preferring 'the parish of Miss Austen to the globe of Mr. Wells' (*GE*, preface), but we may well doubt if such a statement has much relevance for the present stage of human civilization. There are times, indeed, when Massingham seems to have had doubts himself. When, for example, he defines the rules of husbandry and craftsmanship as 'to act by tradition, to prepare for the future, to perform the present need, three in one and one in three' (*PE*, 135), the presumably deliberate echo of Shaw's Father Keegan at the close of *John Bull's Other Island* suggests that he was aware that for many this must appear the dream of a madman.

Clearly comparisons between the two writers can be pushed too far. The differences are considerable, especially in terms of audience and personality. While Cobbett was widely read in his own time, Massingham had to be content with fit audience though few. A regular column in *The Field* is hardly comparable to the proprietorship of the *Political Register*. Cobbett was rightly considered a dangerous enemy of 'the Establishment'; Massingham could safely be discounted as a harmless crank. Even if one ignores the profound differences of historical context, the quiet, retiring Massingham bears little resemblance to the bluff, peppery Cobbett. But such contrasts are inevitably superficial. As we have already seen, Massingham stressed change in details but fixity in fundamentals, and the true relationship with Cobbett lies in a shared heritage of basic principles. In his excellent 'Study of the English Tradition' entitled *The English Countryman* Massingham is able to demonstrate a common attitude between rural people that is all the more impressive for the rich diversity caused by historical period, geographical locality, or social class. It is this common attitude (the *raison d'être*, be it noted, of the present study) which was expressed so forcibly by Cobbett in the 1820s and by Massingham, more quietly but no less cogently, in his own time.

In conclusion, however, I want to stress not what Massingham shared with earlier writers but what made him unique among his contemporaries. This consists, I think, in a viewpoint which manages to avoid both complacency and despair. Although it would be possible to isolate passages in his work which would seem to label him a naive optimist or an unmitigated pessimist, the overall effect conveys a remarkable balance between the two extremes. His strength, indeed, lies in his awareness of complexities. In *The Heritage of Man*, for example, we find an admirable statement of the contemporary rural dilemma: 'It is a melancholy and ironic reflection that the wide distribution for the first time in history of a real love for the country should correspond with a period in which enlightened bodies like the National Trust have to wrest inches of untouched England from the devouring grasp of Progress' (HM, 300). Despite the seriousness of the problem Massingham was not wholly despondent: 'Love of the country is no longer the prerogative of poets, and has indeed so inundated the general run of people that it is partly responsible for rural desecration. People are in the stage of killing the thing they love, but loving is a progressive emotion' (HM, 309; in this context, of course, 'progressive' is being used in an approving sense). This is, admittedly, a comparatively early statement, but the title of one of his latest books, *The Faith of a Fieldsman*, suggests, since it is not concerned with specifically religious faith, that Massingham never gave way to a complete pessimism. Such a position would, in fact, be contrary to the instincts of 'the thinking countryman.' It is indicative of Massingham's central place in the rural tradition that in the following passage we feel that, in addition to offering us a succinct portrait of the countryman for the last two centuries, he is also presenting an accurate summing-up of his own responses:

> The thinking countryman is far less pessimistic than is the intelligentsia of the town ... He is patronised, ignored or despised. Legislation is continually against him; he is the victim of an urban economics built up without reference to him and, so far as his freedom of livelihood is concerned, is no more than a helot ...
>
> Yet he lives not with despair but with nature. He is fortified against the depression imposed upon him because nature is cyclical and a perpetual fount of interest, a perpetual change and a perpetual stability ... He has roots, he lives the organic life and so he can see our urban civilisation in a detachment denied to the urban mind. The wheel of nature and of life predisposes him to accept the Creator in the creation. He is prone to pantheism but not to atheism nor to any form of negation which is the fruit of urbanism and the separated intellect.   (EY, 159–60)

The bedrock of Massingham's faith is a recognition of 'the dependence of short-lived man upon long-lived earth' (PE, 25). That modern man is likely to learn this truth only through the experience of disaster is a corollary that lends bitterness to much of his writing, but a prophet can hardly be blamed for the refusal of the world to heed his message. It is important that we pierce through his denunciatory attacks on urbanism to appreciate the positive quality of his rural vision which, as so often with Massingham, is neatly summed up in the proverbial nutshell of a single sentence: 'Kingdoms fall, but the earth remains' (EY, 160).

THIRTEEN

Conclusion

The example of the English tradition is before us who have become its prodigal son.

H.J. MASSINGHAM[1]

In the preceding chapters I have deliberately confined my attention to a select group of non-fiction rural writers. A more general survey of this kind of literature would prove a lengthy and ambitious undertaking in which quantity would overcome quality and important discriminations of attitude and approach might be lost. The field is too vast. The whole library of angling literature deriving directly or indirectly from Walton would be a major study in itself. Similar important 'lines' could be traced from other writers already considered here – the prose idylls of rural life inspired by Miss Mitford, the free-ranging rural essays and articles derived from Jefferies and Hudson, the numerous sociological studies of the agricultural labourer which elaborate upon, but never surpass, the work of George Sturt. I have been content to isolate the more sustained and artistically successful presentations of rural life. None the less, much has been omitted with regret, and it may be helpful in conclusion to make brief reference to other writings that have not yet received any detailed treatment.

The influence of Gilbert White is worth examining a little more thoroughly, since it is possible to recognize two divergent trends developing out of the work of the Selborne naturalist. The more obvious is, of course, the tradition of local and natural histories. Numerous books can be said to owe their origin to the ultimate success of *The Natural History and Antiquities of Selborne*, but curiously few have any strong claims to qualify as literature. Two of the best-known, J.L. Knapp's *The Journal of a Naturalist* (1829) and Edward Jesse's *Gleanings in Natural History* (1835), were both stimulated by White's example. Knapp remarks that White's book 'early impressed upon my mind an ardent love for all the ways and economy of nature, and I was thereby led to the constant observance of the rural objects around me,'[2] while Jesse (who became one of White's many editors) attributes his own habit of regularly recording local observations to White's recommendations in the 'Advertisement' to his first edition. But White's influence was not confined to his subject-matter; it extended – if only crudely – to his artistic method. Knapp's book imitates White's illusion of spontaneity by being presented as worked-over diary observations roughly classified according to subject, while Jesse's, although ultimately arranged in essaylike sections, 'originally began in a series of letters to [his] daughters.'[3] In both cases, however, the reader is struck by the dullness of these later books when compared to White's own, and it is clear that White's superiority derives less from his material than from the inconspicuous artistry that I have examined in the third chapter. More entertaining reading (though not necessarily more accurate information) is provided by Charles Waterton's *Essays in Natural History* (1837–57), which show no clear influence of White but may well have depended on the interest that White's book created. Once again, however, we have a case of success depending upon a unique and dominant personality, for Waterton was a notorious but genial eccentric, and he possessed a memorable and forthright prose style which, though highly individualistic, has much of the power and pugnacity of Cobbett.

Geoffrey Grigson has recently borne witness to the second possible 'line' in observing that he does not find White 'so different a creature from Dorothy Wordsworth.'[4] This raises the whole subject of the diary writers who have concentrated on recording rural life, the most distinguished of which, after White and Dorothy Wordsworth, was undoubtedly Francis Kilvert. Since White's own *Journals* were not published in any substantial form until 1931, the extent of his influence on later diary writers cannot be pressed too far, but the samples of diary entries in *The Natural History of Selborne* doubtless stimulated later practice. These diarists certainly provide us with invaluable insights into the everyday life of their times. To transform the familiar and ephemeral into the memorable and eternal requires a gift of considerable subtlety. Dorothy Wordsworth's exact and concentrated accounts of weather and her delineations of isolated natural objects are unrivalled; from Kilvert we gain a remarkably comprehensive knowledge of local beliefs and practices, the state of the peasantry in nineteenth-century Radnorshire, and the day-to-day duties and difficulties of a country clergyman. But just as White's *Journals*, fascinating as they are, cannot offer the artistic satisfaction we gain from *The Natural History of Selborne*, so in the diaries of Dorothy Wordsworth and

Kilvert we find, as it were, abundant raw material for unwritten rural books. Such writings raise special problems; for literary-critical purposes this kind of work is best studied within the context of diary literature as a whole.[5]

The closer one approaches the contemporary period, the more difficult selection becomes. The twentieth century has seen a remarkable number of accomplished rural books by knowledgeable and talented authors. Space prevents discussion of the impressive contributions of Rolph Gardiner, John Moore, J.W. Robertson Scott, Sir William Beach Thomas, C. Henry Warren, Alfred Williams, and many others. But some brief comments need to be made about five recent writers whose work is, I believe, of particular interest to the literary-critical approach of this study.

Flora Thompson's trilogy *Lark Rise* (1939), *Over to Candleford* (1941), and *Candleford Green* (1944) has now established itself as a minor classic under the one-volume title *Lark Rise to Candleford*. Unfortunately Flora Thompson has acquired a reputation as a latter-day Mary Mitford (or, to be more precise, as the kind of writer Mary Mitford is popularly believed to be), presenting sentimental recollections of an idealized rural past, whereas her legitimate position is much closer to Sturt. She is, in fact, refreshingly *un*-sentimental, and her recreation of Oxfordshire village life in the 1880s and 1890s maintains an admirable balance between social and cultural loss and gain. The resemblance to Sturt lies not merely in the significant title of her final chapter, 'Change in the Village,' which presumably carries a conscious allusion to Sturt's earlier book and makes a number of related points in her own way; more profoundly, it is to be located in Flora Thompson's carefully contrived viewpoint. While the material is obviously based on autobiographical experience, it is presented as the later reminiscence of Laura, daughter of the village stone-mason, who has moved beyond the confines of the village and can note down her childhood recollections with both sympathy and detachment. Her attitude is chiefly remarkable for a basic cheerfulness combined with honest good sense. While she can be, like Sturt, a distanced spectator – 'Laura Looks On' is a typical chapter-title – she is also representative of the communal life in a way that Sturt, as middle-class inhabitant of the Lower Bourne, was not. What gives *Lark Rise to Candleford* its unique value, beyond the obvious historical interest of the story it has to tell, is the artistic subtlety through which the carefully drawn figure of Laura acts as a filter between the personal reminiscence of Flora Thompson and the discriminating response of the reader.

The work of A.G. Street is remarkable not so much for its intrinsic literary qualities as for the full-blooded and frequently Cobbett-like vigour that stamps almost every sentence with an individual and identifiable intensity. Street stumbled accidentally into writing, with the result that he gives us not merely a rarely articulated viewpoint on the countryside – that of the tenant farmer who is generally too busy to concern himself with the intricate niceties of literature – but also a refreshingly independent stance that, without being ignorant of the rural tradition, is none the less comparatively unaffected by it. Once again individual personality provides the all-important unifying element in the work, and whether he chooses direct non-fiction, as in his first and best-known book *Farmer's Glory* (1931), or ostensible fiction, as in *Strawberry Roan* (1932) and *The Endless Furrow* (1934), we are continually aware of a non-fiction stress on experience and representativeness. Above all Street's bull-headed assertiveness, coming as it did after the quieter, introspective writing of Hudson and Edward Thomas, restored to rural writing the kind of vigorous earthiness which it had not enjoyed since the days of Cobbett and Borrow.

More difficult to characterize is the work of Adrian Bell, whose origins, as his autobiography *My Own Master* (1961) makes clear, associate him with other townsmen-turned-countrymen like Edward Thomas and H.J. Massingham. Best known for his trilogy *Corduroy* (1930), *Silver Ley* (1931), and *The Cherry Tree* (1932), books which give the illusion of non-fiction but which, as comparison with *My Own Master* demonstrates, are radically selected, adapted, and even fictionalized recreations of experience, Bell offers a basically realist view of the modern countryside (his attitude to 'scientific' farming, for example, is less consistent but more practical than Massingham's), combined with a fineness of sensibility which he is able to reconcile with the 'blood-consciousness' of the rural world in a way that escaped Thomas. His unique merit is an ability to elaborate the implications of commonplace incidents until they become filled with meaning and vitality. His true form is the episode, and his best books, like *Apple Acre* (1942; revised 1964) and *The Flower and the Wheel* (1949), consist of collections of brief incidents arranged, often somewhat arbitrarily, into loose chapters. His emphasis is upon simplicity, the humble but fulfilling life of the small-holder upheld, particularly in his later work, by a simple but never naive faith in basic Christian belief and practice. And his prose embodies Henry Williamson's ideal of clarity. Sensitivity to language is, indeed, a constant feature of his writings; this is most evident in an important article, 'English Tradition and Idiom,' originally contributed to *Scrutiny*,[6] but it is also found in the faithful presentation of dialect throughout his books and in the unostentatious precision of his habitual prose which succeeds in combining delicate lucidity with native strength.

Since this is a study emphasizing literary quality and achievement, it is not easy to justify a consideration of George Ewart Evans's recent volumes that aim to preserve a record of folk beliefs and traditional practices too often either unnoticed or neglected by more conventional historians. Evans makes no obvious bid to be appraised as a creative writer, but *Ask the Fellows Who Cut the Hay* (1956), *The Horse in the Furrow* (1960), *The Pattern Under the Plough* (1966), and *Where Beards Wag All* (1970) have considerable value for any broadly cultural examination of village life, and earn a place not far from the writings of George Sturt. Problems of classification present difficulties here, since his work obstinately refuses to fit into the convenient categories of local history, regional sociology, or literary memoir. Like Sturt (and many lesser rural writers), he has been suspected of an idealization of the past, but this is not borne out by a full examination of his text, and the suspicion seems to arise from the uneasy relations that exist between the 'science' of objective recording and the 'art' of human interpretation. Evans approaches the local past with an open mind, always ready to find a nugget of wisdom in beliefs that are generally dismissed, with fashionable prejudice, as irrational superstitions. Humanized sociology might, indeed, be a reasonable description of his method, if only because it seems less misleading than any other.

The same description might well be applied to the last book I shall discuss here, Ronald Blythe's *Akenfield* (1969). This is an appropriate book with which to close this study, since its qualities are intricately connected with the various challenges which, as I demonstrated in the first chapter, have continually recurred throughout the history of the rural tradition in English prose. *Akenfield* purports to be a comprehensive, reliable study in depth of a Suffolk village in the 1960s. It is an initially puzzling but clearly deliberate mixture of styles. After an informative but personal introduction we are confronted with a series of detailed statistics which offer population figures, lists of inhabitants, measurements of agricultural acreage, etc. But the bulk of the book is composed of reproduced interviews with a cross-section of residents who are first described pithily and often wittily by the author and then left to tell their own stories in sections which, we are encouraged to assume, are preserved, like much of George Ewart Evans's information, by means of the tape-recorder.

The book has provoked some curiously extreme critical reactions. Angus Wilson, in a review in the *Observer*, praised Blythe's treatment as 'extraordinarily unprejudiced';[7] Rolf Gardiner, in a follow-up letter, while praising Blythe's 'brilliant reporting,' argued that his 'sympathy with the NUAW [the National Union of Agricultural Workers] 'led him to overstate 'the "bad old times"';[8] yet Jan Marsh, in a shrewdly probing article in the *Cambridge Quarterly*, could write: 'I tend to think that the pastoral images outweigh the unhappy ones, that the overall impression given by the book is that Akenfield is as near Paradise as one is likely to find, rather than a dispassionate conclusion that village life, like most other ways of life, is a mixture of good things and bad things.'[9] I have no intention of attempting any formal adjudication of this controversy; it is essential, however, to stress the significance of the disagreement. In fact, all three views are probably legitimate, since the juxtaposition of these reactions is in itself an illustration of the subjectivity which is likely to influence an individual response.

This subjectivity belongs, of course, to the writer as well as to his readers. Jan Marsh makes the point clearly if a trifle ingenuously: 'Having assumed from his introduction that Blythe's role was simply an enabling one, helping the villagers to express themselves, one suddenly finds that it is a controlling role: it is the village *as Blythe wants it to be presented.*'[10] Precisely, though the opposed reactions I have just quoted show that Blythe is not insisting on his own vision so much as allowing opposed views to co-exist within the framework which he has created. The book is subtitled (as Marsh notes) 'Portrait of an English Village' – and a portrait presupposes a portrait painter. The admission may sound damaging if the book is regarded as sociology, but no scientific inquiry that does not confine itself to raw, uninterpreted statistics can hope to banish the subjective element – nor, indeed, should it presume to do so. Interestingly enough, Angus Wilson has also described *Akenfield* as 'a great social novel,'[11] and this is perhaps just another way of making the same point: *Akenfield* is one of the more important recent contributions to the rural tradition because it is a deliberate artistic construct. Like *The Natural History of Selborne* it is an ostensibly scientific study that depends, to what may be thought a surprising extent, on the individual vision of the writer; like Williamson's *Village Book* it eludes the categories of fiction and non-fiction; and one is tempted to prophecy that, like *Rural Rides*, it will continue to be read when the immediate agricultural situation has passed into history. Ronald Blythe has faced the same general problems that have always confronted the rural writer – the temptation towards nostalgia, the elusiveness of 'essential truth,' and the need to impose a decorous artistic form upon recalcitrant natural material. Like the best of his predecessors he has solved these in his own way and according to the tastes and needs of his own time.

But what of the future? This is no place to indulge in rash and inevitably speculative prophecy, but, since we inhabit an apocalyptic world constantly haunted by the threat of nuclear holocaust, a world in which Massingham's 'kingdoms fall, but the earth remains' (EY, 160) can no longer be regarded as a self-evident assertion, the continuity of the rural tradition may well be brought into question. Is country writing a thing of the past? In an age that can envisage hermetically sealed monster-cities artificially protected from natural phenomena and a polluted atmosphere, that can seriously entertain the possibility that three-quarters of the world's animal species may be extinct by the end of the century, is it feasible to expect the survival of a literature centred upon the countryside and the rural way of life?

Imagination may collapse when faced with such nightmare prospects, but a temperate and considered forecast remains possible. There is little likelihood that rural writing will experience another rich flowering like that enjoyed in the nineteenth and early twentieth centuries, but it is even less likely to wither and die. However citified subsequent generations may become, the 'buried life' of nature is sure to remain a potent force, and will insist on being taken into account. The obstinate 'mutations' that cause Thomas, Williamson, and Massingham to turn against the flowing tide may never become dominant, but on the other hand they are not likely to be eliminated. Rural literature fulfilled a need in the past, and there is no reason to suppose that it will not fulfil a comparable though possibly different need in the future. If D.H. Lawrence is right in asserting that 'the business of art is to reveal the relation between man and his circumambient universe,'[12] rural literature must endure. It therefore seems reasonable to assume that at least a modest continuance of the rural tradition may be taken for granted; indeed its future is in doubt only if, with a decidedly non-rural pessimism, we come to question the survival of mankind as a whole.

NOTES

1 / RURAL LITERATURE AND THE RURAL TRADITION

1 Edward Thomas, *The Country* (London: Batsford, 1913), pp. 22–3.

2 E.M. Forster, *Howards End* [1910] (London: Arnold, 1956), p. 114.

3 See William Empson, *Some Versions of Pastoral* [1935] (London: Chatto & Windus, 1950), p. 6.

4 W.H. Auden, 'Sext,' in *Collected Shorter Poems, 1927–1957* (London: Faber, 1966), p. 327.

5 Alexander Pope, 'A Discourse on Pastoral Poetry,' in *The Poetical Works of Alexander Pope*, ed. A.W. Ward (London: Macmillan, 1956), p. 10.

6 Ibid., p. 11. For useful literary discussions of the whole subject see Peter V. Marinelli, *Pastoral* (London: Methuen, 1971), and Raymond Williams, *The Country and the City* (London: Chatto & Windus, 1973), chap. 3.

7 See Empson, op. cit., pp. 11–12.

8 Joseph Addison, 'An Essay on Virgil's Georgics,' in *The Miscellaneous Works of Joseph Addison*, ed. A.C. Guthkelch, 2 vols. (London: Bell, 1914), II, 4.

9 Marie Loretto Lilly, *The Georgic* (Baltimore: Johns Hopkins University Press, 1919), p. 170. The best study of its influence on the English poetic tradition is John Chalker's *The English Georgic* (London: Routledge & Kegan Paul, 1969).

10 Robert Herrick, 'A Country Life: To his Brother, Master Thomas Herrick,' l. 4; Alfred Tennyson, *In Memoriam*, lxxxix.

11 Thomas Hardy, *Tess of the D'Urbervilles* [1891] (London: Macmillan [St Martin's Library], 1957), p. 270.

12 Stephen Duck, 'The Thresher's Labour' (1730); Richard Jefferies, *The*

Toilers of the Field (London: Long-mans, 1892), p. 127.

13 William Wordsworth, 'Of the Princi-ples of Poetry and the "Lyrical Ballads,"' in *The Prose Works of William Wordsworth*, ed. Rev. A.B. Grosart, 3 vols. (London: Moxon, 1876), II, 83.

14 Raymond Williams, 'Thomas Hardy,' in R.O. Preyer, ed., *Victorian Litera-ture* (New York: Harper, 1966), pp. 220–1.

15 John Galsworthy, *The Man of Prop-erty* [1906] (New York: Scribner's, 1949), p. 16.

16 H. Rider Haggard, *Rural England*, 2 vols. (London: Longmans, 1902), I, 2.

17 Quoted in E.W. Martin, *The Secret People* (London: Phoenix House, 1954), p. 37.

18 *The Life and Letters of Mary Russell Mitford*, ed. Rev. A.G. L'Estrange, 2 vols. (New York: Harper, 1870), II, 149.

19 Quoted in Amelia Defries, *Sheep and Turnips: Being the Life and Times of Arthur Young, F.R.S.* (London: Methuen, 1938), p. 204–5.

20 Quoted in *Joseph Arch: The Story of His Life, Told by Himself*, ed. the Countess of Warwick (London: Hutch-inson, 1898), p. 263. The bill was defeated by a large majority, and the rural worker was not enfranchised until 1884.

21 Alfred Williams, *A Wiltshire Village* (London: Duckworth, 1912), p. 163.

22 W.E. Houghton, *The Victorian Frame of Mind* (New Haven: Yale University Press, 1957), p. 79.

23 Richard Jefferies, *Field and Hedgerow* [1889] (London: Lutterworth, 1948), pp. 179–80.

24 Forster, pp. 121–2.

25 See C.E.M. Joad, *The Untutored Townsman's Invasion of the Coun-tryside* (London: Faber, 1946).

26 Wordsworth, 'Kendal and Winder-mere Railway: Two Letters reprinted from the *Morning Post*,' in *The Prose of William Wordsworth*, II, 330.

27 Aldous Huxley, *Point Counter Point* [1928] (Harmondsworth: Penguin, 1965), p. 245.

28 Llewelyn Powys, *Dorset Essays* (Lon-don: Bodley Head, 1953), p. 50.

29 George Eliot, *Scenes from Clerical Life* [1858] (London: Dent, 1932), p. 1.

30 Raymond Williams, 'Literature and Rural Society,' *Listener*, 16 November 1957, p. 630.

31 Ibid.

32 George Borrow, *The Zincali*, in *The Works of George Borrow*, ed. Clement Shorter, 16 vols. (London: Constable, 1923), X, 28.

33 Tennyson, *In Memoriam*, XXIV.

34 *The Journals of George Sturt (1890–1927)*, ed E.D. Mackerness, 2 vols (Cambridge: University Press, 1967), p. 227.

35 George Sturt ('George Bourne'), *Change in the Village* [1912] (London: Duckworth, 1920), p. 97.

36 Ibid., p. 308.

37 *The Journals of George Sturt*, pp. 671–2.

38 Edward Thomas, *The South Country* (London: Dent, 1909), p. 125.

39 Richard Jefferies, *Round About a*

Great Estate [1880] (London: Eyre &
Spottiswoode, 1948), p. xvi.

40 Richard Jefferies, *The Life of the Fields*
[1884] (London: Lutterworth, 1948),
p. 151.

41 Forster, p. 127.

42 Arnold Kettle, *An Introduction to the
English Novel*, 2 vols. (New York:
Harper, 1960), II, 49.

43 Dorothy Van Ghent, *The English
Novel: Form and Function* (New York:
Harper, 1961), p. 205.

44 Oliver Goldsmith, Dedication to *The
Deserted Village*, in *The Works of
Oliver Goldsmith*, ed. Peter Cunning-
ham, 4 vols. (London: Murray, 1854),
I, 37.

45 George Crabbe, *The Village*, I, 5–6,
53–4.

46 Thomas Hardy, 'General Preface to the
Novels and Poems,' in *Thomas
Hardy's Personal Writings*, ed. Harold
Orel (Lawrence: University of Kansas
Press, 1966), p. 46.

47 George Eliot, *Adam Bede* [1859] (London: Dent, 1951), pp. 172–3.

48 J.W. Robertson Scott, *England's
Green and Pleasant Land* [1925], rev.
ed. (Harmondsworth: Penguin, 1947),
p. 165.

49 Edward Thomas, *A Literary Pilgrim in
England* [1917] (London: Cape, 1928),
p. 227.

50 *The Autobiography of John Britton*
(London: privately printed for the
'Britton Testimonial,' 1850), p. 59n.

51 W.H. Hudson, *A foot in England*
[1909] (London: Dent, 1923), p. 116.

52 W.H. Hudson, *The Land's End* [1908]
(London: Dent, 1923), pp. 30–1.

53 Robertson Scott, p. 18.

54 Hardy, 'The Dorsetshire Labourer,' in
Thomas Hardy's Personal Writings,
pp. 172–3.

55 Mary Russell Mitford, *Our Village*
[1824–32], 2 vols. (London: Bohn,
1848), I, 20.

56 Robertson Scott, p. 80.

57 Richard Jefferies, *The Open Air* [1885]
(London: Eyre & Spottiswoode, 1948),
p. 90.

58 Thomas, *The Country*, p. 31.

59 James Thomson, *The Seasons*, 'Summer,' l. 486, quoted from *Thomson's
Poetical Works*, ed. Rev. George
Gilfillan (Edinburgh: Nichol, 1853),
p. 51.

60 John Henry Newman, 'Discourses on
University Education,' In *Newman:
Prose and Poetry*, ed. Geoffrey Tillot-
son (London: Hart-Davis, 1957),
p. 485.

61 Hudson, *The Land's End*, p. 35.

62 Both these examples are quoted from
Douglas Grant, *James Thomson, Poet
of 'The Seasons'* (London: Cresset,
1951), p. 115.

63 Ibid. For a more positive view of the
poem see Ralph Cohen, *The Unfolding
of 'The Seasons'* (London: Routledge &
Kegan Paul, 1970).

64 John Ruskin, *The Stones of Venice*, in
The Works of Ruskin, ed. E.T. Cook,
and Alexander Wedderburn, 38 vols.
(London: Allen, 1904), X, 217.

65 George Crabbe, 'The Learned Boy'
(*Tales, 1812*), ll. 319–20.

66 Quoted in Vera Watson, *Mary Russell
Mitford* (London: Evans, [1949]),
p. 307.

67 Thomas Hughes, *The Scouring of the White Horse* [1858] (London: Macmillan, 1899), p. xv.

68 Quoted in Robert L. Chamberlain, *George Crabbe* (New York: Twayne, 1965), p. 108.

69 Quoted in *Nature Studies from Ruskin*, ed. Rose Porter (Boston: Dana Estes, 1900), p. 21.

70 Edmund Blunden, *Nature in English Literature* (London: Hogarth Press, 1929), p. 32.

71 Robertson Scott, p. 164.

72 John Burroughs, 'Gilbert White Again,' in *Literary Values* [1902] (New York: Wise, 1924), p. 170.

73 D.H. Lawrence, 'Tourists,' in *The Complete Poems of D.H. Lawrence*, ed. V. de Sola Pinto and W. Roberts, 2 vols. (New York: Viking, 1964), p. 660.

74 Mary Russell Mitford, *Belford Regis*, 3 vols. (London: Bentley, 1835), I, viii.

75 See Walter Pater, 'Style,' in *Appreciations* (1889).

76 Travis R. Merritt, 'Taste, Opinion, and Theory in the Rise of Victorian Prose Stylism,' in George Levine and William Madden, eds., *The Art of Victorian Prose* (New York: Oxford University Press, 1968), p. 18.

77 Richard E. Haymaker, *From Pampas to Hedgerows and Downs: A Study of W.H. Hudson* (New York: Bookman, 1954), p. 154.

2 / IZAAK WALTON

1 Izaak Walton, *The Compleat Angler*, World's Classics edition (London: Oxford University Press, 1960), p. 8. Hereafter cited in text as *CA*.

2 See Gerald Eades Bentley, ed., *The Arte of Angling (1577)* (Princeton: University Press, 1958).

3 John R. Cooper, *The Art of 'The Compleat Angler'* (Durham, NC: Duke University Press, 1968), p. 160.

4 Ibid., p. 181.

5 Douglas Bush, *English Literature in the Earlier Seventeenth Century*, 2nd ed., rev. (Oxford: Clarendon Press, 1962), p. 238.

6 Mary Russell Mitford, *Recollections of a Literary Life* [1852] (London: Bentley, 1883), p. 187.

7 William Cowper, *The Task*, I, 749.

8 William Wordsworth, *The Prelude* (1850 text), I, 6–9.

9 Cooper, p. 94.

10 Leslie Stephen, 'Country Books,' in *Hours in a Library*, 3 vols. (London: Murray, 1919), III, 176.

11 Peter Oliver, *A New Chronicle of 'The Compleat Angler'* (New York: Paisley, 1936), p. ix.

12 B.D. Greenslade, 'The Compleat Angler and the Sequestered Clergy,' *Review of English Studies*, n.s. 5 (1954), 365.

13 Stephen, III, 176.

14 From *Love and Truth* and the *Life of Sanderson* respectively, quoted in Margaret Bottrall, *Izaak Walton*, Writers and Their Work series (London: Longmans, 1955), pp. 15, 17.

15 Quoted in Cooper, p. 25.

16 Ibid., p. 47.

17 Stapleton Martin, *Izaak Walton and his Friends* (London: Chapman & Hall, 1904), pp. 22.

18 Greenslade, p. 364.

19 Bush, p. 239.

20 William Cobbett, *Rural Rides*, ed. G.D.H. and Margaret Cole, 3 vols. (London: Davies, 1930), pp. 434, 33.

21 Edward Thomas, *The Last Sheaf* (London: Cape, 1928), p. 109.

22 Edward Thomas, ed., *This England* (London: Oxford University Press, 1915), pp. iii.

23 Bottrall, p. 24.

24 Cooper, pp. 62–3.

25 Ibid., p. 64.

26 John Cowper Powys, *Autobiography* (London: Bodley Head, 1934), p. 398.

27 Stephen, III, 178.

28 H.J. Massingham, *Chiltern Country* [1940] (London: Batsford, 1949), p. 97.

29 Walter de la Mare, 'Izaak Walton', in *Selected Poems* (London: Faber, 1954), p. 137.

30 H.J. Oliver, 'Izaak Walton's Prose Style,' *Review of English Studies*, 21 (1945), 281, 282.

31 Ibid., 287.

32 James Russell Lowell, 'Walton,' in *Latest Literary Essays and Addresses* (Boston: Houghton Mifflin, 1893), p. 90.

33 Cooper, p. 112.

34 Stephen, III, 178.

35 Cooper, pp. 124–5.

36 Lowell, p. 64.

37 I write 'apparent' in view of the interesting discussion of this matter in Cooper, pp. 92–3.

38 H.J. Oliver, 'The Composition and Revisions of *The Compleat Angler*,' *Modern Language Review*, 42 (1947), 298.

39 Bottrall, p. 27.

40 Northrop Frye, *The Anatomy of Criticism* (Princeton: University Press, 1957), p. 312.

41 Cooper, p. 12

42 Ibid., p. 83.

43 See R.B. Marston, *Walton and Some Earlier Writers on Fish and Fishing* (London: Stock, 1894), p. 2.

44 I am indebted to my colleague, Professor Michael Kirkham, for this observation.

45 Stephen, III, 175.

3 / GILBERT WHITE

1 Gilbert White, *The Natural History of Selborne*, ed. E.M. Nicholson (New York: Dutton, [1929]), letter xx to Thomas Pennant. Hereafter cited in text as *NHS*, with (*P*) indicating the letters to Pennant and (*B*) those to the Hon. Daines Barrington. Page references given without either initial are to Nicholson's introduction; Roman numerals refer to letter numbers.

2 James Russell Lowell, 'Walton,' in *Latest Literary Essays and Addresses* (Boston: Houghton Mifflin, 1893), p. 88.

3 Ibid., pp. 88–90.

4 *The Life and Letters of Gilbert White of Selborne*, ed. Rashleigh Holt-White, 2 vols. (London: Murray, 1901), II, 255. Hereafter cited in text as *WLL*.

5 H.J. Massingham, *The English Countryman* (London: Batsford, 1942), p. 110.

6 H.J. Massingham, *Untrodden Ways* (London: Fisher Unwin, 1923), p. 229.

7 Quoted in Dwight L. Durling, *Georgic Tradition in English Poetry* (New York: Columbia University Press, 1935), pp. 146–7.

8 Quoted in Loren Eiseley, *Darwin's Century* (New York: Doubleday, 1961), p. 17.

9 *The Letters to Gilbert White of Selborne from his intimate friend and contemporary The Rev. John Mulso*, ed. Rashleigh Holt-White (London: Porter, [1907]), p. 266.

10 Walter Johnson, *Gilbert White: Pioneer, Poet and Stylist* (London: Murray, 1928), p. 3.

11 Richard E. Haymaker, *From Pampas to Hedgerows and Downs: A Study of W.H. Hudson* (New York: Bookman, 1954), p. 61.

12 From the advertisement to the first edition of *NHS*, not reprinted by Nicholson. I quote here from the recently published facsimile of the first edition (Menston: Scolar Press, 1970), p. iii.

13 *The Heart of Thoreau's Journals*, ed. Odell Shepard (Boston: Houghton Mifflin, 1927), p. 188.

14 C.S. Emden, *Gilbert White in His Village* (London: Oxford University Press, 1956), p. 9.

15 W.H. Hudson, *Hampshire Days* [1903] (London: Dent, 1923), p. 169.

16 Quoted in *The Age of Johnson: Essays Presented to Chauncy Brewster Tinker* (New Haven: Yale University Press, 1949), p. 378.

17 William Cobbett, *Rural Rides*, ed. G.D.H. and Margaret Cole, 3 vols. (London: Davies, 1930), p. 651.

18 Quoted in Eiseley, p. 15.

19 Johnson, p. 12.

20 See Edward A. Martin, *A Bibliography of Gilbert White* (London: Halton, 1934), p. 33.

21 Henry C. Shelley, *Gilbert White of Selborne* (London: Laurie, 1909), p. 92

22 James Fisher, introduction to *NHS* (Harmondsworth: Penguin, 1941), p. vii.

23 Richard Jefferies, *Field and Hedgerow* [1889] (London: Lutterworth, 1948), p. 44.

24 John Burroughs, 'Gilbert White Again,' in *Literary Values* [1902] (New York: Wise, 1924), p. 175.

25 R.M. Lockley, *Gilbert White* (London: Witherby, 1954), p. 22.

26 Emden, p. 107.

27 Cobbett, *Rural Rides*, pp. 134–5.

28 Richard Jefferies, introduction to *NHS* (London: Scott, n.d.), p. ix.

29 James Fisher, introduction to *NHS* (London: Cresset, 1947), p. xiii.

30 Lockley, p. 122.

31 John Henry Newman, 'Literature. A Lecture in the School of Philosophy and Letters,' reprinted in Martin J. Svaglic, ed., *The Idea of a University* (New York: Rinehart, 1964), pp. 206–7.

32 W.H. Hudson, *Far Away and Long Ago* [1918] (London: Dent, 1923), p. 339.

33 Jefferies, introduction to *NHS*, p. vii.

34 Quoted in Martin, p. 27.

35 Shelley, p. 65.

36 Virginia Woolf, 'White's Selborne,' in *The Captain's Death Bed* (London: Hogarth Press, 1950), p. 20.

37 Johnson, p. 302.
38 John Burroughs, 'Gilbert White's Book,' in *Indoor Studies* [1889] (New York: Wise, 1924), p. 166.
39 Woolf, p. 19.
40 Burroughs, *Indoor Studies*, p. 163.
41 Grant Allen, introduction to *NHS* (London: Bodley Head, n.d.), p. xxxi.
42 Shelley, p. xiii.
43 Quoted in E.D.H. Johnson, ed., *The Poetry of Earth* (New York: Athenaeum, 1963), p. 3.
44 Woolf, p. 23.
45 Burroughs, *Literary Values*, p. 169.
46 Jefferies, introduction to *NHS*, pp. xi–xii.
47 George Sturt ('George Bourne'), *Lucy Bettesworth* [1913] (London: Duckworth, 1918), pp. 213–14.
48 *The Life and Letters of Mary Russell Mitford*, ed. Rev. A.G. L'Estrange, 2 vols. (New York: Harper, 1870), I, 148.
49 George Sturt ('George Bourne'), *The Bettesworth Book* [1901] (London: Duckworth, 1911), p. 278.
50 Ibid., p. 180.
51 *The Journals of George Sturt (1890–1927)*, ed. E.D. Mackerness, 2 vols. (Cambridge: University Press, 1967), p. 786.
52 Woolf, p. 22.
53 E.V. Bovill, *English Country Life, 1780–1830* (London: Oxford University Press, 1962), p. 19.
54 Cobbett, *Rural Rides* p. 189.
55 See Hudson, *Hampshire Days*, pp. 206–7, 217, and J.L. and Barbara Hammond, *The Village Labourer, 1760–1832*, new ed. (London: Long-

mans, 1920), p. 236. See also L. Sutherland, ed., *Trouble at Selborne* [1946] (Selborne: B.B. Paton, Queen's Hotel, 1967).

4 / WILLIAM COBBETT

1 William Cobbett, *The Opinions of William Cobbett*, ed. G.D.H. and Margaret Cole (London: Cobbett Publishing Co., 1944), p. 41. Hereafter cited in text as *OWC*.
2 William Cobbett, *A Legacy to Labourers* [1835] (London: Griffin, 1872); p. 3. Hereafter cited in text as *CLL*.
3 William Cobbett, *The Autobiography of William Cobbett*, ed. William Reitzel (London: Faber, 1967), p. 92. Hereafter cited in text as *AWC*.
4 William Cobbett, *Rural Rides*, ed. G.D.H. and Margaret Cole, 3 vols. (London: Davies, 1930), p. 357. Hereafter cited in text as *RR*.
5 William Cobbett, *Advice to Young Men* [1830] (London: Davies, 1926), p. 15.
6 *The Prose of Edward Thomas*, ed. Roland Gant (London: Falcon, 1948), p. 200.
7 William Cobbett, *Cottage Economy* [1821–2] (London: Davies, 1926), p. 144. Hereafter cited in text as *CE*.
8 Edward Thomas, *In Pursuit of Spring* (London: Nelson, 1914), p. 81.
9 G.K. Chesterton, *William Cobbett* (London: Hodder & Stoughton, [1926]), p. 61.
10 John W. Osborne, *William Cobbett: His Thought and his Times* (New

Brunswick, NJ: Rutgers University Press, 1966), p. 18.

11 Quoted in Edward I. Carlile, *William Cobbett* (London: Constable, 1904), p. 5.

12 Mary Russell Mitford, *Recollections of a Literary Life* [1852] (London: Bentley, 1883), p. 200.

13 Quoted in Edward Smith, *William Cobbett: A Biography*, 2 vols. (London: Sampson Low, 1878), II, 44n.

14 William Cobbett, *The Woodlands* (London: William Cobbett, 1825–8 [issued in parts]), para. 32.

15 G.D.H. Cole, *Life of William Cobbett*, 3rd ed. rev. (London: Home & Van Thal, 1947), p. 134.

16 Alexander Somerville, *The Whistler at the Plough* (Manchester: Ainsworth, 1852), p. 263.

17 Chesterton, p. 73.

18 Ibid., pp. 82–3.

19 Quoted in Cole, *Life of William Cobbett*, p. 129.

20 *The Friendships of Mary Russell Mitford*, ed. Rev. A.G. L'Estrange (New York: Harper, 1882), p. 27.

21 Chesterton, p. 270.

22 William Cobbett, *Twelve Sermons* (London: William Cobbett, 1828), p. 73).

23 Quoted in W. Baring Pemberton, *William Cobbett* (Harmondsworth: Penguin, 1949), p. 183.

24 Ibid., p. 87.

25 Quoted in Osborne, p. 49.

26 Ibid.

27 Quoted in Cole, *Life of William Cobbett*, p. 129.

28 *The Friendships of Mary Russell Mitford*, pp. 28–9.

29 Quoted from the Everyman edition of *Rural Rides*, 2 vols. (London: Dent, 1957), I, 159, not included in Cole edition.

30 H.J. Massingham, *The English Countryman* (London: Batsford, 1942), p. 7.

31 *Selections from Cobbett's Political Works*, ed. John M. and James P. Cobbett, 6 vols. (London: Ann Cobbett, 1835–7), V, 12. Hereafter cited in text as *CPW*.

32 Chesterton, p. 190.

33 See Cole, *Life of William Cobbett*, p. 320.

34 Mitford, *Recollections of a Literary Life*, p. 201.

35 H.J. Massingham, *Chiltern Country* [1940] (London: Batsford, 1948), p. 91.

36 William Cobbett, *The English Gardener* [1828] (London: Ann Cobbett, 1838), p. 260.

37 *William Morris: Selected Writings and Designs*, ed. Asa Briggs (Harmondsworth: Penguin, 1962), p. 245.

38 George Woodcock, introduction to *Rural Rides* (Harmondsworth: Penguin, 1967), p. 16.

39 See ibid., p. 289.

40 G.D.H. Cole, *Persons and Periods* (Harmondsworth: Penguin, 1945), p. 120.

41 See, e.g., Deut. 7:26, Joshua 6:17–18.

42 Chesterton, pp. 228–9.

43 Ibid., p. 4.

44 William Cobbett, *A Grammar of the English Language* [1818] (London: Griffin, n.d.), pp. 121, 192, 195, 197, 198.

45 *The Prose of Edward Thomas*, p. 201.

46 Cole, *Persons and Periods*, p. 126.

47 *The Prose of Edward Thomas*, p. 201.

48 Quoted in Pemberton, p. 113.

49 H.J. Massingham, *The Wisdom of the Fields* (London: Collins, 1945), p. 252.

50 Cole, *Life of William Cobbett*, p. 423.

51 Osborne, p. 87.

52 *The Journals of George Sturt, 1890–1927*, ed. E.D. Mackerness, 2 vols. (Cambridge: University Press, 1967), pp. 621–2.

5 / MARY RUSSELL MITFORD

1 Mary Russell Mitford, *The Friendships of Mary Russell Mitford*, ed. Rev. A.G. L'Estrange (New York: Harper, 1882), p. 2. Hereafter cited in text as *FM*.

2 Quoted in Marjorie Astin, *Mary Russell Mitford: Her Circle and her Books* (London: Douglas, 1930), p. 4.

3 Mary Russell Mitford, *Recollections of a Literary Life* [1852] (London: Bentley, 1883), p. 345. Hereafter cited in text as *RLL*.

4 Quoted in W.J. Roberts, *The Life and Friendships of Mary Russell Mitford* (London: Melrose, 1913), p. 137.

5 Mary Russell Mitford, *The Life and Letters of Mary Russell Mitford*, ed. Rev. A.G. L'Estrange, 2 vols. (New York: Harper, 1870), I, 263–4. Hereafter cited in text as *MLL*.

6 Mary Russell Mitford, *Atherton, and Other Tales* (Boston: Ticknor, 1854), p. 283. Hereafter cited in text as *ATH*.

7 Mary Russell Mitford, *Letters of Mary Russell Mitford, Second Series*, ed. Henry Chorley, 2 vols. (London: Bent-

ley, 1872), I, 86. Hereafter cited in text as *LMM*.

8 Mary Russell Mitford, *Our Village: Sketches of Rural Character and Scenery* [1824–32], 2 vols. (London: Bohn, 1848), I, 260. Hereafter cited in text as *OV*.

9 Mary Russell Mitford, *Mary Russell Mitford: Correspondence with Charles Boner and John Ruskin*, ed. Elizabeth Lee (London: Unwin, 1914), p. 268.

10 W.H. Hudson, *Afoot in England* [1909] (London: Dent, 1923), p. 73.

11 Leslie Stephen, 'Country Books,' in *Hours in a Library*, 3 vols. (London: Murray, 1919), III, 166.

12 Quoted in Vera Watson, *Mary Russell Mitford* (London: Evans, [1949]), p. 162.

13 See William Howitt, 'A Visit to Our Village,' *Athenaeum*, 8 August 1835, pp. 600–3, and the letters of Mary Howitt reprinted in *FM*.

14 Jane Austen, quoted from J.E. Austen-Leigh's *Memoir of Jane Austen*, included in *Persuasion* (Harmondsworth: Penguin, 1968), p. 380. G.K. Chesterton, *William Cobbett* (London: Hodder & Stoughton, [1926]), p. 188.

15 Quoted in Watson, p. 162.

16 Quoted in Astin, p. 4.

17 Mary Russell Mitford, *Belford Regis*, 3 vols. (London: Bentley, 1835), I, ix. Hereafter cited in text as *BR*.

18 *The Autobiography of John Britton* (London: privately printed for the 'Britton Testimonial,' 1850), pp. 26–7.

19 *The Prose of John Clare*, ed. John and Anne Tibble (London: Routledge, 1951), p. 34.

20 Quoted in Watson, p. 211.
21 William Howitt, *The Rural Life of England* [1838] (London: Longmans, 1844), p. 483.
22 Quoted in Roberts, p. 135.
23 Mary Russell Mitford, *Country Stories* [1837] (London: Simms & M'Intyre, 1850), p. 126. Hereafter cited in text as *CS*.
24 Roberts, p. 243.
25 Hudson, p. 70.
26 Quoted in Watson, p. 307.
27 Hudson, p. 75.
28 Ibid., p. 72.
29 Ibid., p. 73.

6/ GEORGE BORROW

1 *Wild Wales*, II, 296. Quotations from Borrow are taken from the Norwich edition of his works, ed. Clement Shorter, 16 vols. (London: Constable, 1923–4). The following abbreviations are used in the text: *WW* for *Wild Wales*: *LAV* for *Lavengro*; *RYE* for *The Romany Rye*; *BS* for *The Bible in Spain*; *BZ* for *The Zincali*.
2 Seton Dearden, *The Gipsy Gentleman* (London: Murray and Barker, 1939), p. 78.
3 Edward Thomas, *George Borrow: The Man and his Books* (London: Chapman & Hall, 1913), pp. 213, 228–9.
4 Edward Thomas, *A Literary Pilgrim in England* [1917] (London: Cape, 1928), p. 237.
5 See J.H. Shorthouse, 'The Successor of Monsieur Le Sage,' in *The Literary Remains of J.H. Shorthouse*, ed. by his wife (London: Macmillan, 1905), p. 79.

6 Quoted in Herbert Jenkins, *The Life of George Borrow* (London: Murray, 1912), p. 451.
7 Theodore Watts-Dunton, *Old Familiar Faces* (New York: Dutton, 1916), p. 288.
8 R.A.J. Walling, *George Borrow: The Man and his Work* (London: Cassell, 1908), p. 303.
9 Brian Vesey-Fitzgerald, *Gypsy Borrow* (London: Dobson, 1953), p. 42.
10 Quoted in Clement Shorter, *George Borrow and his Circle* (London: Hodder & Stoughton, 1913), p. 234.
11 Arthur Rickett, 'George Borrow,' in *The Vagabond in Literature* (London: Dent, 1906), p. 62.
12 Quoted in W.I. Knapp, *The Life, Writings and Correspondence of George Borrow*, 2 vols. (London: Murray, 1899), I, 361.
13 Martin Armstrong, *George Borrow* (London: Barker, 1950), p. 83.
14 Alfred Tennyson, *In Memoriam*, cxi.
15 Quoted in Walling, p. 169.
16 Quoted in Armstrong, p. 27.
17 Eileen Bigland, *In the Steps of George Borrow* (London: Rich & Cowan, 1951), p. 36.
18 Quoted in Shorter, p. 317.
19 See J.E. Tilford, 'Contemporary Criticisms of *Lavengro*: A Re-examination,' *Studies in Philology*, 41 (July 1944), 442–6.
20 Quoted in Knapp, II, 174.
21 R.R. Meyers, *George Borrow* (New York: Twayne, 1966), p. 43.
22 Quoted in Knapp, II, 29–30.
23 Quoted in Shorter, p. 281.
24 Quoted in Knapp, II, 159.
25 Jessie Chambers, *D.H. Lawrence: A*

Personal Record [1935] (London: Cass 1965), pp. 109–10.

26 Northrop Frye, *The Anatomy of Criticism* (Princeton: University Press, 1957), p. 303.

27 Quoted in Armstrong, p. 82.

28 Knapp, I, 110.

29 Quoted in Bigland, p. 290.

30 Quoted in Jenkins, p. 396.

31 See J.E. Tilford, 'The Critical Approach to *Lavengro-Romany Rye*,' *Studies in Philology*, 46 (January 1949), 79–96.

32 Thomas, *George Borrow: The Man and his Books*, pp. 188–9.

33 Quoted in John Moore, *Life and Letters of Edward Thomas* (London: Heinemann, 1939), p. 316.

34 Leslie Stephen, 'Country Books,' in *Hours in a Library*, 3 vols. (London: Murray, 1919), III, 190.

35 Walling, p. 304.

36 Tilford, 'The Critical Approach to *Lavengro–Romany Rye*,' p. 88.

37 See Knapp, I, 102, and Walling, p. 27.

38 Quoted in Knapp, II, 11.

39 Rickett, p. 67.

40 *PMLA*, 44 (June 1949), 369–84.

41 Quoted in Knapp, II, 11.

42 Quoted in Shorter, p. 285.

43 Armstrong, p. 96.

44 Two notebooks covering Borrow's visit to the Isle of Man are printed in Knapp, II, 121–57. Another MS, 'An Expedition to the Isle of Man,' together with 'A Tour in Scotland,' is printed in vol. XVI of the Norwich edition. For a notebook concerning a trip to Belfast see Knapp, II, 368.

45 Vesey-Fitzgerald, p. xii.

46 Watts-Dunton, p. 38.

47 Quoted in Knapp, II, 163.

48 Shorter, p. 341.

49 René Fréchet, *George Borrow, vagabond, polyglotte, agent biblique – écrivain* (Paris: Didier, 1956), p. 302.

7 / RICHARD JEFFERIES

1 Richard Jefferies, *The Story of My Heart* [1883], ed. Samuel J. Looker (London: Constable, 1947), p. 47. Hereafter cited in text as *SH*.

2 Edward Thomas, *Richard Jefferies, His Life and Work* (London: Hutchinson, 1909), p. 320.

3 E.W. Martin, *The Secret People* (London: Phoenix House, 1954), p. 247.

4 Richard Jefferies, *Field and Hedgerow* [1889] (London: Lutterworth, 1948), p. 360. Hereafter cited in text as *FH*.

5 Richard Jefferies, *The Life of the Fields* [1884] (London: Lutterworth, 1948), p. 62. Hereafter cited in text as *LF*.

6 Richard Jefferies, *Wild Life in a Southern County* [1879] (London: Lutterworth, 1949), p. 201. Hereafter cited in text as *WLSC*.

7 E.M. Forster, *The Longest Journey* [1907] (London: Arnold, 1955), p. 146.

8 Thomas, p. 1.

9 Richard Jefferies, *The Toilers of the Field* (London: Longmans, 1892), pp. 211–212. Hereafter cited in text as *TF*.

10 Richard E. Haymaker, *From Pampas to Hedgerows and Downs: A Study of W.H. Hudson* (New York: Bookman, 1954), p. 126.

11 Q.D. Leavis, 'Lives and Works of Richard Jefferies,' in F.R. Leavis, ed., *A Selection from 'Scrutiny,'* 2 vols.

(Cambridge: University Press, 1968), II, 206.

12 W.E. Henley, *Views and Reviews* (London: Nutt, 1890), p. 180.

13 Richard Jefferies, quoted in Samuel J. Looker and Crichton Porteous, *Richard Jefferies, Man of the Fields* (London: Baker, 1965), p. 204.

14 Richard Jefferies, *The Old House at Coate*, ed. Samuel J. Looker (London: Lutterworth, 1948), p. 131.

15 Richard Jefferies, *Nature Near London* (London: Chatto & Windus, 1883), p. 48. Hereafter cited in text as *NNL*.

16 Richard Jefferies, *The Gamekeeper at Home* [1878] (London: Smith Elder, 1896), pp. 85–6. Hereafter cited in text as *GH*.

17 Richard Jefferies, *The Open Air* [1885] (London: Eyre & Spottiswoode, 1948), pp. 178–9. Hereafter cited in text as *OA*.

18 Richard Jefferies, *Chronicles of the Hedges*, ed. Samuel J. Looker (London: Phoenix House, 1948), p. 141. Hereafter cited in text as *CH*.

19 Thomas, p. 127.

20 Richard Jefferies, *Hodge and His Masters* [1880] (London: Eyre & Spottiswoode, 1948), p. 99.

21 Quoted in Looker and Porteous, p. 122.

22 Richard Jefferies, *The Amateur Poacher* (London: Smith Elder, 1879), p. 238. Hereafter cited in text as *AP*.

23 Henry Williamson, *The Pathway* [1928] (London: Faber, 1969), pp. 48–9. Compare also Williamson's anthology, *Richard Jefferies* (London: Faber, 1937), pp. 24–5, and his 'Some Nature Writers and Civilization,' in

Essays by Divers Hands, xxx (London: Oxford University Press, 1960), p. 6.

24 Mary Webb, *The House in Dormer Forest* [1920] (London: Cape, 1931), p. 278.

25 Henry Williamson, *A Clear Water Stream* (London: Faber, 1958), p. 46.

26 See Marghanita Laski, *Ecstasy* (London: Cresset, 1961).

27 *The Prose of John Clare*, ed. J.W. and Anne Tibble (London: Routledge, 1951), p. 32.

28 See Jerome Buckley, *Tennyson: The Growth of a Poet* (Boston: Houghton Mifflin, 1965), p. 1, and Tennyson's *The Two Voices*, l. 399.

29 Quoted in Looker and Porteus, p. 121.

30 Quoted in Morley Roberts, *W.H. Hudson: A Portrait* (London: Eveleigh, Nash & Grayson, 1924), p. 206. Chapter ii of Hudson's *Nature in Downland*, where he discusses the sense of exhilaration felt on the Downs, is also relevant to *SH*.

31 See chapter v of Mill's *Autobiography* and Arnold's 'Memorial Verses,' ll. 48–57.

32 *The Poetical Works of William Wordsworth*, Oxford Standard Authors (London: Oxford University Press, 1960), p. 590.

33 D.H. Lawrence, *Apocalypse* [1931] (New York: Viking, 1966), p. 200.

34 Ibid., p. 43.

35 Llewelyn Powys, *Impassioned Clay* (London: Longmans, 1931), p. 7.

36 See *The Nature Diaries and Note-Books of Richard Jefferies*, ed. Samuel J. Looker (London: Grey Walls, 1948), pp. 129 ff. Hereafter cited in text as *JN*.

37 See Powys, *Impassioned Clay*, p. 8,
and his *Love and Death* [1939] (New
York: Simon and Schuster, 1941), p. 1.
38 H.J. Massingham, *The English Countryman* (London: Batsford, 1942),
p. 130.
39 See Thomas, pp. 189–90.
40 See W.H. Hudson, *Nature in Downland* [1900] (London: Dent, 1923),
p. 14.
41 Q.D. Leavis, II, 203.
42 See W.J. Keith, *Richard Jefferies: A
Critical Study* (Toronto: University of
Toronto Press, 1965), pp. 151–2, 169.

8 / GEORGE STURT / 'GEORGE BOURNE'

1 George Sturt, *Lucy Bettesworth* [1913]
(London: Duckworth, 1918), p. 268.
Hereafter cited in text as *LB*.
2 George Sturt, *The Journals of George
Sturt (1890–1927)*, ed. E.D. Mackerness, 2 vols. (Cambridge: University
Press, 1967), p. 132. Hereafter cited in
text as *J(M)*. Not to be confused with
the Grigson edition (see n. 10 below).
3 George Sturt, *The Wheelwright's Shop*
[1923] (Cambridge: University Press,
1963), p. v. Hereafter cited in text as
WS.
4 George Sturt, *A Small Boy in the Sixties* (Cambridge: University Press,
1927), p. 3. Hereafter cited in text as
SBS.
5 The astuteness and the irony are both
explained if John Fraser is right in his
belief that this review in the *Academy*
was written by Sturt's friend Arnold
Bennett. See Fraser's article 'George

Sturt's Apprenticeship,' *Review of English Literature*, 5 (January 1964), 48.
6 George Sturt, *Change in the Village*
[1912] (London: Duckworth, 1920),
p. 12. Hereafter cited in text as *CV*.
7 George Sturt, *The Bettesworth Book*
[1901] (London: Duckworth, 1911),
pp. 4–5. Hereafter cited in text as *BB*.
8 George Sturt, *A Farmer's Life* (London: Cape, 1922), p. 174. Hereafter
cited in text as *FL*.
9 George Sturt, *Memoirs of a Surrey
Labourer* (London: Duckworth, 1907),
p. 61. Hereafter cited in text as *MSL*.
10 George Sturt, *The Journals of George
Sturt ('George Bourne'), 1890–1902*,
ed. Geoffrey Grigson (London: Cresset, 1941), p. 76. Hereafter cited in text
as *J(G)*. Not to be confused with the
Mackerness edition (see n. 2 above).
11 See W.A. Ward, 'Poor old Grover,'
Cambridge Quarterly, 3 (Winter
1967–8), 87.
12 *Thomas Hardy's Personal Writings*,
ed. Harold Orel (Lawrence: University
of Kansas Press, 1966), p. 168.
13 See Francis Brett Young, *Portrait of a
Village* (London: Heinemann, 1937),
p. 44.
14 See John Fraser, 'George Sturt and
Rural Labouring Life,' unpublished
PH D thesis, University of Minnesota,
1961, p. 176.
15 George Sturt, *William Smith, Potter
and Farmer* (London: Chatto & Windus, 1919), p. v. Hereafter cited in text
as *PF*.
16 John Fraser, 'Sturt and Class: The Bettesworth Book,' *English Studies in Africa*, 10 (September 1967), 146.

9/ W.H. HUDSON

1 W.H. Hudson, *Hampshire Days*, p. 154. Quotations from Hudson are taken from the collected edition of his works, 24 vols. (London: Dent, 1922–3). The following abbreviations are used in the text: *AAB* for *Adventures Among Birds*; *AIE* for *Afoot in England*; *BL* for *Birds in London*; *BM* for *Birds and Man*; *BN* for *The Book of a Naturalist*; *BTV* for *Birds in Town and Village*; *DMP* for *Dead Man's Plack*; *FAR* for *Far Away and Long Ago*; *HBB* for *British Birds*; *HD* for *Hampshire Days*; *HPR* for *A Hind in Richmond Park*; *IDP* for *Idle Days in Patagonia*; *LE* for *The Land's End*; *ND* for *Nature in Downland*; *SL* for *A Shepherd's Life*; *TLT* for *A Traveller in Little Things*.

2 H.F. West, *For a Hudson Biographer* (Hanover, NH: Westholm Publications, 1958), p. 33.

3 See ibid., p. 8.

4 Basil Willey, *The Eighteenth Century Background* (Harmondsworth: Penguin, 1962), p. 261n.

5 See Richard E. Haymaker, *From Pampas to Hedgerows and Downs: A Study of W.H. Hudson* (New York: Bookman, 1954), p. 23.

6 W.H. Hudson, *Men, Books and Birds* (Hudson's letters to Roberts), ed. Morley Roberts (London: Eveleigh Nash & Grayson, 1925), p. 61. Hereafter cited in text as *MBB*.

7 See Ruth Tomalin, *W.H. Hudson* (London: Witherby, 1954), p. 112.

8 Edward Thomas, *A Literary Pilgrim in England* [1917] (London: Cape, 1928), p. 188.

9 W.H. Hudson, *Letters from W.H. Hudson, 1901–1922*, ed. Edward Garnett (New York: Dutton, 1923), p. 142. Hereafter cited in text as *HL*.

10 Haymaker, p. 124.

11 See Tomalin, chap. III.

12 W.H. Hudson, *Birds in a Village* (London: Chapman & Hall, 1893), p. 195. This volume was later revised as *Birds in Town and Village*. Quotations from the original version are hereafter cited in text as *BV*.

13 D.H. Lawrence, *Phoenix II*, ed. Warren Roberts and Harry T. Moore (London: Heinemann, 1968), p. 391.

14 Quoted in David R. Dewar, 'Afoot in England with Hudson,' in *W.H. Hudson: A Tribute by Various Writers*, ed. Samuel J. Looker (Worthing: Aldridge Brothers, 1947), p. 53.

15 Edward Thomas, *In Pursuit of Spring* (London: Nelson, 1914), p. 249.

16 Ford Madox Ford, *Joseph Conrad: A Personal Reminiscence* (London: Duckworth, 1924), p. 197.

17 Q.D. Leavis, 'Lives and Works of Richard Jefferies,' in F.R. Leavis, ed., *A Selection from 'Scrutiny,'* 2 vols. (Cambridge: University Press, 1968), II, 206.

18 Thomas, *In Pursuit of Spring*, pp. 249–50.

19 William Wordsworth, *The Prelude* (1850 text), II, 221.

20 *The Complete Writings of William Blake*, ed. Geoffrey Keynes (London: Nonesuch, 1957), p. 818.

21 H.J. Massingham, *Untrodden Ways*

(London: Unwin, 1923), p. 21.

22 See Morley Roberts, *W.H. Hudson: A Portrait* (London: Eveleigh Nash & Grayson, 1924), p. 201.

10/ EDWARD THOMAS

1 Edward Thomas, *Horae Solitariae* (London: Duckworth, 1902), p. 108. Hereafter cited in text as *HS*.

2 Edward Thomas, *Cloud Castle, and Other Papers* (London: Duckworth, 1922), p. v. Hereafter cited in text as *CC*.

3 Quoted in John Moore, *The Life and Letters of Edward Thomas* (London: Heinemann, 1939), p. 277.

4 Edward Thomas, *The South Country* (London: Dent, 1909), p. 107. Hereafter cited in text as *SC*.

5 Herbert G. Wright, 'Edward Thomas,' in *Studies in Contemporary Literature* (Bangor: Jarvis & Foster, 1918), p. 81.

6 Edward Thomas, *The Childhood of Edward Thomas* (London: Faber, 1938), p. 14. Hereafter cited in text as *CET*.

7 Moore, p. 17.

8 Edward Thomas, *The Last Sheaf* (London: Cape, 1928), p. 17. Hereafter cited in text as *LS*.

9 Helen Thomas, *World Without End* (London: Heinemann, 1931), p. 90. In this memoir by his widow, and in its predecessor *As It Was*, Edward Thomas is called David throughout.

10 Edward Thomas, *Letters from Edward Thomas to Gordon Bottomley*, ed. R. George Thomas (London: Oxford University Press, 1968), p. 135. Hereafter cited in text as *LGB*.

11 Edward Thomas, *In Pursuit of Spring* (London: Nelson, 1914), pp. 44–5. Hereafter cited in text as *IPS*.

12 Edward Thomas, *The Happy-Go-Lucky Morgans* (London: Duckworth, 1913), pp. 226–7.

13 Helen Thomas, *As It Was* (London: Heinemann, 1926), pp. 20, 22. See n. 9 above.

14 Edward Thomas, *The Country* (London: Batsford, 1913), p. 36. Hereafter cited in text as *TC*.

15 Helen Thomas, *World Without End*, p. 151.

16 William Wordsworth, *The Prelude* (1850 text), III, 34–5.

17 Edward Thomas, *The Heart of England* (London: Dent, 1906), p. 65. Hereafter cited in text as *HE*. Also, *TC*, p. 19.

18 See Moore, p. 202.

19 Edward Thomas, *The Icknield Way* (London: Constable, 1913), p. 29. Hereafter cited in text as *IW*.

20 Edward Thomas, *Beautiful Wales* (London: Black, 1905), p. 7. Hereafter cited in text as *BW*.

21 Edward Thomas, *The Woodland Life* (Edinburgh: Blackwood, 1897), p. 4. Hereafter cited in text as *WL*.

22 Moore, p. 78.

23 See ibid.

24 See ibid., p. 154.

25 Wright, p. 84. The passage quoted is from *HE*, p. 57.

26 Edward Garnett, 'Some Letters of Edward Thomas,' *Athenaeum*, 16 April 1920, p. 501.

27 Edward Thomas, *Rest and Unrest*

(London: Duckworth, 1910), p. 151.
Hereafter cited in text as *RU*.

28 See H. Coombes, *Edward Thomas* (London: Chatto & Windus, 1956), p. 220.

29 Edward Thomas, *Richard Jefferies: His Life and Work* (London: Hutchinson, 1909), p. 106.

30 See William Cooke, *Edward Thomas: A Critical Biography* (London: Faber, 1970), p. 73.

31 See ibid., p. 243.

32 John F. Lynen, *The Pastoral Art of Robert Frost* (New Haven: Yale University Press, 1967), p. 9.

33 Edward Thomas, *Collected Poems* (London: Faber, 1956), pp. 29–30. Hereafter cited as *TCP*.

34 See Eleanor Farjeon, *Edward Thomas: The Last Four Years* (London: Oxford University Press, 1958), p. 144.

35 Quoted in Moore, p. 326.

36 Farjeon, p. 154.

37 See Helen Thomas, *World Without End*, p. 77.

38 See Coombes, p. 48.

39 Quoted in Farjeon, p. 110.

11 / HENRY WILLIAMSON

1 Henry Williamson, *The Pathway* [1928] (London: Faber, 1969), p. 110.

2 See Henry Williamson, *The Linhay on the Downs* [1934] (London: Cape, 1938), p. 129. Hereafter cited in text as *LD*.

3 See, for example, Henry Williamson, *The Story of a Norfolk Farm* [1941] (London: Readers' Union, by arrange-

ment with Faber, 1942), pp. 186–9. Hereafter cited in text as *SNF*.

4 Henry Williamson, *The Dream of Fair Women* [1924] (London: Faber, 1968), p. 440. Hereafter cited in text as *DFW*.

5 *Richard Jefferies: Selections of His Work, with details of his Life and Circumstances, his Death and Immortality*, ed. Henry Williamson (London: Faber, 1937), p. 417. Hereafter cited in text as *RJ*.

6 Henry Williamson, *Dandelion Days* [1922] (London: Faber, 1966), p. 151. Hereafter cited in text as *DD*.

7 Henry Williamson, *A Clear Water Stream* (London: Faber, 1958), pp. 20–1. Hereafter cited in text as *CWS*.

8 Henry Williamson, *The Children of Shallowford* (London: Faber, 1939), p. 265. Hereafter cited in text as *CS*.

9 Henry Williamson, *Goodbye West Country* [1937] (Boston: Little, Brown, 1938), p. 107. Hereafter cited in text as *GWC*.

10 Henry Williamson, *The Sun in the Sands* (London: Faber, 1945), p. 27. Hereafter cited in text as *SS*.

11 Henry Williamson, *The Village Book* (London: Cape, 1930), p. 150. Hereafter cited in text as *VB*.

12 See H.F. West, *The Dreamer of Devon: An Essay on Henry Williamson* (London: Ulysses Press, 1932), p. 9.

13 Henry Williamson, *The Lone Swallows* (London: Collins, 1922), p. 51.

14 See West, p. 19, and compare *SS*, p. 19.

15 Henry Williamson, *The Labouring Life* (London: Cape, 1932), p. 294.

Hereafter cited in text as *LL*.

16 I am referring here to the revised text of the book. The whole question of the revisions of the *Flax of Dream* tetralogy is a complex one, and outside the scope of this book. All critical statements on the novel cycle are based on the later versions.

17 James Joyce, *A Portrait of the Artist as a Young Man* [1916] (New York: Viking, 1962), p. 216.

18 See H. Stevenson Balfour, *The History of Georgeham and Croyde* (Privately printed for the author, n.d.), p. 33.

19 West, p. 29.

20 Balfour, p. 26n.

21 West, p. 33.

22 Denys Thompson, 'A Cure for Amnesia,' in F.R. Leavis, ed., *A Selection from 'Scrutiny'*, 2 vols. (Cambridge: University Press, 1968), II, 219.

23 Ibid.

24 The vexed question of Williamson's admiration for Hitler during the 1930s, though apparently outside the concern of this study, is so conspicuous a feature within his whole career that it would be critically irresponsible to ignore it. From the perspective of the 1970s, of course, it neither requires any formal condemnation nor merits any defence. None the less, it is worth noting here that Williamson's enthusiasm was derived from Hitler's plan 'based on every man owning, in a trustee-to-nation sense, his own bit of land, and fulfilling himself in living a natural life' (*GWC*, 229). While deploring the catastrophic misreading of Hitler's intentions that is involved, we may at least acknowledge that Williamson's motives, however naive, had more respectable origins than most of the literary-intellectual flirtations with fascism at that time.

25 Henry Williamson, *On Foot in Devon* (London: Maclehose, 1933), p. 32. Hereafter cited as *OFD*.

26 Henry Williamson, *Devon Holiday* (London: Cape, 1935), p. 7.

27 Henry Williamson, *The Wild Red Deer of Exmoor* (London: Faber, 1931), p. 54.

28 H.J. Massingham, *The Wisdom of the Fields* (London: Collins, 1945), p. 35.

29 Lilias Rider Haggard and Henry Williamson, *Norfolk Life* (London: Faber, 1943), pp. 11–12.

30 John Middleton Murry, 'The Novels of Henry Williamson,' in *Katherine Mansfield, and Other Literary Studies* (London: Constable, 1959), p. 161.

12 / H.J. MASSINGHAM

1 H.J. Massingham, *Remembrance* (London: Batsford, 1942), p. 50. Hereafter cited in text as *MR*.

2 H.J. Massingham, *The Fall of the Year* (London: Chapman & Hall, 1941), p. 47. Hereafter cited in text as *FY*.

3 H.J. Massingham *Through the Wilderness* (London: Cobden-Sanderson, 1935), p. 111. Hereafter cited in text as *TW*.

4 H.J. Massingham, *Country* (London: Cobden-Sanderson, 1934), p. 145. Hereafter cited in text as *MC*.

5 H.J. Massingham, *People and Things*

[1919] (London: Swarthmore Press, 1920), p. 182.

6 H.J. Massingham, *The Wisdom of the Fields* (London: Collins, 1945), p. 169. Hereafter cited in text as *WF*.

7 H.J. Massingham, *Chiltern Country* [1940] (London: Batsford, 1949), p. 18. Hereafter cited in text as *ChC*.

8 H.J. Massingham, *This Plot of Earth* (London: Collins, 1944), p. 270. Hereafter cited in text as *PE*.

9 H.J. Massingham, *The Tree of Life* (London: Chapman & Hall, 1943), p. 29. Hereafter cited in text as *TL*.

10 H.J. Massingham, *Shepherd's Country* (London: Chapman & Hall, 1938), p. 299. Hereafter cited in text as *ShC*.

11 H.J. Massingham, *The Heritage of Man* (London: Cape, 1929), p. 294. Hereafter cited in text as *HM*.

12 H.J. Massingham, *The Faith of a Fieldsman* (London: Museum Press, 1951), p. 134. Hereafter cited in text as *FF*.

13 H.J. Massingham, *The Curious Traveller* (London: Collins, 1950), p. 59. Hereafter cited in text as *CT*.

14 H.J. Massingham, *Downland Man* (London: Cape, 1926), p. 397.

15 H.J. Massingham, *The Southern Marches* (London: Hale, 1952), pp. 96–97. Hereafter cited in text as *SM*.

16 H.J. Massingham, *Genius of England* (London: Chapman & Hall, 1937), p. 122. Hereafter cited in text as *GE*.

17 H.J. Massingham, *English Downland* [1936] (London: Batsford, 1949), p. 40. Hereafter cited in text as *ED*.

18 H.J. Massingham, *Where Man Belongs* (London: Collins, 1946), p. 83.

Hereafter cited in text as *WMB*.

19 H.J. Massingham, *World Without End* (London: Cobden-Sanderson, 1932), p. 290.

20 H.J. Massingham, *Country Relics* (Cambridge: University Press, 1939), p. 17. Hereafter cited in text as *CR*.

21 H.J. Massingham, *An Englishman's Year* (London: Collins, 1948), p. 143. Hereafter cited in text as *EY*.

22 H.J. Massingham, *Cotswold Country* [1937] (London: Batsford, 1946), p. 81.

13/CONCLUSION

1 H.J. Massingham, *The English Countryman* (London: Batsford, 1942), p. 135.

2 J.L. Knapp, *The Journal of a Naturalist* [1829] (Buffalo: Phinney, 1853), p. v.

3 Edward Jesse, *Gleanings in Natural History* (London: Murray, 1835), p. v.

4 *The English Year from Diaries and Letters*, compiled by Geoffrey Grigson (London: Oxford University Press, 1967), p. xiv.

5 Kilvert has attracted little critical attention, but H.J. Massingham devotes a good chapter to him in *The Southern Marches*. For an excellent pioneering study of the neglected subject of diary literature see Robert A. Fothergill's *Private Chronicles*, to be published by Oxford University Press.

6 First published in *Scrutiny* (1933), reprinted in F.R. Leavis, ed., *A Selection from 'Scrutiny'* (Cambridge: University Press, 1968), II, 211–15.

7 Angus Wilson, 'East Anglian Attitudes,' *Observer* (London), 1 June 1969.

8 Rolf Gardiner, 'Fled is that Music,' *Observer* (London), 15 June 1969.

9 Jan Marsh, 'A Miraculous Relic?' *Cambridge Quarterly*, 6 (July 1972), 73.

10 Ibid.

11 In a television broadcast, quoted in ibid., p. 71.

12 D.H. Lawrence, *Phoenix* [1936] (London: Heinemann, 1961), p. 527.

BIBLIOGRAPHY

It should be noted that this bibliography confines itself to the specifically rural writings of the authors concerned.

Izaak Walton

WORKS

The Compleat Angler, first published in 1653, went through five editions in Walton's lifetime, and considerable revisions and additions were made. The work has now been reprinted over three hundred times. Most modern reprints follow the text of the enlarged fifth edition (1676), but not all include the second part written by Charles Cotton. Notable editions include those by Sir H. Nicholas, 2 vols. (1836), G.W. Bethune (1847), and R.B. Marston, 2 vols. (1888). Since 1960 the World's Classics edition (London: Oxford University Press) has included not only the texts of Walton and Cotton but also *The Arte of Angling* (1577), an earlier work, apparently by William Samuel, that influenced Walton.

BIBLIOGRAPHY

The most recent and most detailed bibliography is Bernard S. Horne's *The Compleat Angler, 1653–1967: A New Bibliography* (Pittsburgh: University Press, 1970), though Peter Oliver's *A New Chronicle of 'The Compleat Angler'* (New York: Paisley Press, 1936) remains useful.

SELECTED CRITICISM

Easily the best treatment of the book is John R. Cooper's *The Art of 'The Compleat Angler'* (Durham, NC: Duke University Press, 1968). The following criticism is useful:

Bottrall, Margaret. *Izaak Walton*. London: Longmans, 1955. British Council 'Writers and Their Work' pamphlet

Goldman, Marcus S. 'Izaak Walton and *The Arte of Angling*, 1577,' in *Studies in Honor of T.W. Baldwin*. Urbana: University of Illinois Press, 1958

Greenslade, B.D. '*The Compleat Angler* and the Sequestered Clergy,' *Review of English Studies*, n.s. 5 (1954), 361–6

Lowell, James Russell. 'Walton,' in *Latest Literary Essays and Addresses*. Boston: Houghton Mifflin, 1893

Marston, R.B. *Walton and Some Earlier Writers on Fish and Fishing*. London: Stock, 1894

Oliver, H.J. 'Izaak Walton's Prose Style,' *Review of English Studies*, 21 (1945), 280–8

– 'The Composition and Revisions of *The Compleat Angler*,' *Modern Language Review*, 42 (1947), 293–313

Williamson, Henry. 'Izaak Walton,' in *The Linhay on the Downs* [1934]. London: Cape, 1938

MISCELLANEOUS

Also of interest are the facsimile edition of *The Arte of Angling*, edited by Gerald Eades Bentley with an introduction by Carl Otto von Kienbusch (Princeton: University Press, 1956); and J. Milton French's edition of *Three Books on Fishing Associated with 'The Compleat Angler'* (Gainesville, Florida: Scholars' Facsimiles and Reprints, 1962). The latter reprints *A New Booke of Good Husbandry* (1599) by Jan Dubravius, *The Pleasures of Princes* (1614) by Gervase Markham, and *Barker's Delight* (1659) by Thomas Barker.

Gilbert White

WORKS

The Natural History and Antiquities of Selborne was first published in 1789 and has gone through numerous editions since. More often than not, however, the *Antiquities* have been omitted from later reprints. The best edition from the literary student's viewpoint is by E.M. Nicholson (London: Butterworth / New

York: Dutton, [1929]); this does not, however, include the *Antiquities*. Other notable editions include those by R. Bowdler Sharpe, 2 vols. (1900), L.C. Miall and W. Warde Fowler (1901) and H.J. Massingham (1938). A facsimile of the first edition has recently been issued (Menston: Scolar Press, 1970). Many of the letters from which the book was originally adapted, together with White's journals, are in the British Museum.

Also of interest are *The Journals of Gilbert White* (London: Routledge, 1931) and *The Poems of Gilbert White* (London: S.P.C.K., 1919), both edited by Walter Johnson.

BIBLIOGRAPHY

The standard bibliography is Edward A. Martin's *A Bibliography of Gilbert White*, rev. ed. (London: Halton, 1934).

BIOGRAPHY

The most detailed and thorough biography is Rashleigh Holt-White's *The Life and Letters of Gilbert White of Selborne*, 2 vols. (London: Murray, 1901).

SELECTED CRITICISM

No criticism of White can be considered outstanding. The following list includes the more significant items:

Blunden, Edmund. 'The Selbornian,' in *Nature in English Literature*. London: Hogarth Press, 1929

Burroughs, John. 'Gilbert White's Book,' in *Indoor Studies* [1899]. New York: Wise, 1924

– 'Gilbert White Again,' in *Literary Values* [1902] New York: Wise, 1924

Emden, C.S. *Gilbert White in his Village*. London: Oxford University Press, 1956

Hammond, L.V. 'Gilbert White, Poetizer of the Commonplace,' in *The Age of Johnson: Essays Presented to Chauncy Brewster Tinker*. New Haven: Yale University Press, 1949

Hudson, W.H. 'Selborne,' in his *Birds and Man* [1901]. London: Dent, 1923

Johnson, Walter. *Gilbert White: Pioneer, Poet, and Stylist*. London: Murray, 1928

Lockley, R.M. *Gilbert White*. London: Witherby, 1954

Massingham, H.J. 'Gilbert White and Selborne,' in *Some Birds of the Countryside*. London: Unwin, 1921

Rye, Anthony. *Gilbert White and His Selborne*. London: Kimber, 1970

Scott, Walter S. *White of Selborne and his Times*. London: Westhouse, 1946
Shelley, Henry C. *Gilbert White and Selborne*. London: Werner Laurie, 1909
Thomas, Edward. 'Gilbert White,' in *A Literary Pilgrim in England* [1917]. London: Cape, 1928
Woolf, Virginia. 'White's Selborne,' in *The Captain's Death Bed*. London: Hogarth Press, 1950

MISCELLANEOUS

Herbert W. Tompkins' *Selborne* (London: Dent, 1905) is a useful topographical guide to White's village. Rashleigh Holt-White has also edited *The Letters to Gilbert White of Selborne from his intimate friend and contemporary, the Rev. John Mulso* (London: Porter, [1907]).

William Cobbett

WORKS

The original and artistically superior text of *Rural Rides* (1830) has recently been reprinted by George Woodcock in his edition for the Penguin English Library (1967). Most modern reprints follow the enlarged edition of James Paul Cobbett (London: Ann Cobbett, 1853). The most elaborate edition, enlarged again and with extensive and admirable critical notes, is by G.D.H. and Margaret Cole, 3 vols. (London: Davies, 1930).

Cobbett's autobiographical writings have been skilfully arranged and edited by William Reitzel in *The Progress of a Ploughboy* (London: Faber, 1933), recently reissued by the same publishers as *The Autobiography of William Cobbett* (1967).

A useful abridgment of Cobbett's writings for *The Political Register*, etc., many of which are relevant to the rural situation, will be found in *Selections from Cobbett's Political Works*, edited by John M. and James P. Cobbett, 6 vols. (London: Ann Cobbett, 1835–7). A more modest but well-selected anthology is *The Opinions of William Cobbett*, edited by G.D.H. and Margaret Cole (London: Cobbett Publishing Company, 1944).

Other relevant Cobbett writings include:

Cottage Economy [1821–2]. London: Davies, 1926
The Woodlands. London: William Cobbett, 1825–8 [issued in parts at irregular intervals]
The English Gardener [1828]. London: Ann Cobbett, 1838

Advice to Young Men [1830]. London: Davies, 1926
A Legacy to Labourers [1835]. London: Griffin, 1872
A Legacy to Parsons [1835]. London: Griffin, 1872
    Cobbett also edited Jethro Tull's *Horse-Hoeing Husbandry* (1822).

BIBLIOGRAPHY

The standard bibliography is M.L. Pearl, *William Cobbett: A Bibliographical Account of his Life and Times* (London: Oxford University Press, 1953).

BIOGRAPHY

The most detailed and scholarly biography is G.D.H. Cole's *Life of William Cobbett* [1924], 3rd ed. rev. (London: Home & Van Thal, 1947). For a balanced view of Cobbett, however, this sober study is ideally complemented by G.K. Chesterton's impressionistic, opinionated, but extremely lively 'intimate biography,' *William Cobbett* (London: Hodder & Stoughton, [1926]). Other biographical studies include:

Briggs, Asa. *William Cobbett*. London: Oxford University Press, 1967. Clarendon Biographies pamphlet
Carlile, Edward I. *William Cobbett*. London: Constable, 1904
Melville, Lewis. *Life and Letters of William Cobbett in England and America*. 2 vols. London: Bodley Head, 1913
Pemberton, W. Baring. *William Cobbett*. Harmondsworth: Penguin, 1949
Smith, Edward. *William Cobbett: A Biography*. 2 vols. London: Sampson Low, 1878

SELECTED CRITICISM

Cole, G.D.H. 'William Cobbett,' in *Persons and Periods* [1938]. Harmondsworth: Penguin, 1945
Hazlitt, William. 'Character of Cobbett,' in *Table-Talk* [1821], *The Complete Works of William Hazlitt*, ed. P.P. Howe (London: Dent: 1931), vol. VIII
Heath, Richard. 'William Cobbett,' in *The English Peasant*. London: Fisher Unwin, 1893
Massingham, H.J. 'Rider of the Shires,' in *The Wisdom of the Fields*. London: Collins, 1945
Osborne, John W. *William Cobbett: His Thought and his Times*. New Brunswick, NJ: Rutgers University Press, 1966
Thomas, Edward. Introduction to *Rural Rides* [1912], reprinted in *The Prose of*

Edward Thomas, ed. Roland Gant. London: Falcon, 1948.
- 'William Cobbett,' in *A Literary Pilgrim in England* [1917]. London: Cape, 1928
Williams, Raymond. 'Contrasts, 1: Edmund Burke and William Cobbett,' in *Culture and Society, 1780–1950*. London: Chatto & Windus, 1958

Mary Russell Mitford

WORKS

Our Village: Sketches of Rural Character and Scenery was published in five series at two-year intervals between 1824 and 1832. The Bohn edition (2 vols., 1848) contains all but two of the original sketches. All subsequent editions consist of selections. Other rural writings of Miss Mitford include:
Belford Regis: Sketches of a Country Town. 3 vols. London: Bentley, 1835
Country Stories [1837]. London: Simms & M'Intyre, 1850.
Recollections of a Literary Life [1852]. London: Bentley, 1883.
Atherton, and Other Tales. Boston: Ticknor, 1854.

BIBLIOGRAPHY

No full bibliography of Miss Mitford exists, but the following items will be found useful:
Phillips, J.D. *Mary Russell Mitford, 1787–1855* [Catalogue of an Exhibition]. Reading: Public Libraries, [1955]
Coles, William A. 'Magazine and Other Contributions by Mary Russell Mitford and Thomas Noon Talfourd,' in Fredson Bowers, ed. *Studies in Bibliography*, vol. 12. Charlottesville, Va: Bibliographical Society of the University of Virginia, 1959

BIOGRAPHY AND LETTERS

Rev. A.G. L'Estrange's *The Life and Letters of Mary Russell Mitford*, 2 vols. (New York: Harper, 1870) and a related volume edited by Henry Chorley entitled, rather clumsily, *Letters of Mary Russell Mitford, Second Series*, 2 vols. (London: Bentley, 1872) provide the main biographical material. Rev. L'Estrange's other volume, *The Friendships of Mary Russell Mitford* (New York: Harper, 1882), consists mainly of letters written to Miss Mitford, but is also useful

Of later biographies, the best is Vera Watson's *Mary Russell Mitford* (London: Evans, [1949]). Others include:

Astin, Majorie. *Mary Russell Mitford: Her Circle and Her Books*. London: Douglas, 1930

Hill, Constance. *Mary Russell Mitford and her Surroundings*. London: Lane, 1920.

Roberts, W.J. *The Life and Friendships of Mary Russell Mitford: The Tragedy of a Blue Stocking*. London: Melrose, 1913

Later collections of letters include:

Lee, Elizabeth, ed. *Mary Russell Mitford: Correspondence with Charles Boner and John Ruskin*. London: Unwin, 1914

Johnson, R. Brimley, ed. *Letters of Mary Russell Mitford*. London: Lane, 1925

'Her Geraniums and Her Dog: New Letters from Miss Mitford,' in J.W. Robertson Scott, ed., *The Countryman Book*. London: Odhams, 1948

Duncan-Jones, Caroline M., ed. *Miss Mitford and Mr. Harness: Records of a Friendship*. London: S.P.C.K., 1955

In addition, the letters of Elizabeth Barrett Browning to Miss Mitford have been edited by Betty Miller (London: Murray, 1954).

CRITICISM

Most of the attention that Miss Mitford has attracted has been biographical. The following, however, may be found useful:

Agate, James. 'Mary Russell Mitford,' in Leonard Russell, ed. *English Wits*. London: Hutchinson, 1940

Howitt, William. 'A Visit to Our Village,' *Athenaeum*, 8 August 1835, pp. 600–3

Hudson, W.H. 'By Swallowfield,' in *Afoot in England* [1909]. London: Dent, 1923

George Borrow

WORKS

The works of Borrow that primarily concern us here are *Lavengro* (1851), *The Romany Rye* (1857), *Wild Wales* (1862). All these are to be found in the collected 'Norwich Edition' of Borrow's works, edited by Clement Shorter, 16 vols. (London: Constable, 1923–4). This edition, which contains passages from these books not appearing in the original editions, also includes previously unpublished material, of which 'An Expedition to the Isle of Man' and 'A Tour in Scotland' (both in vol. XVI) are of special interest here.

BIBLIOGRAPHY

The standard bibliography is T.J. Wise, *A Bibliography of the Writings in Prose and Verse of George Henry Borrow* (London: privately printed, 1914); this has recently been reissued (London: Dawsons, 1966).

BIOGRAPHY AND CRITICISM

In Borrow's case these two cannot be separated. Dominating all biographical scholarship on Borrow is the monumental work of W.I. Knapp, *The Life, Writings and Correspondence of George Borrow*, 2 vols. (London: Murray / New York: Putnam, 1899). The most useful of subsequent biographies are Herbert Jenkins, *The Life of George Borrow* (London: Murray, 1912) and Clement Shorter, *George Borrow and his Circle* (London: Hodder & Stoughton, 1913). The most comprehensive study, covering both biography and criticism, is René Fréchet's *George Borrow, vagabond, polyglotte, agent biblique – écrivain* (Paris: Didier, 1956). The following is a selected list of the more useful criticism:

Armstrong, Martin. *George Borrow*. London: Barker, 1950

Bigland, Eileen. *In the Steps of George Borrow*. London: Rich & Cowan, 1951

Boyle, A. 'Portraiture in *Lavengro*,' *Notes and Queries*. A series of nine articles published between 12 May 1951 and 13 September 1952.

Dearden, Seton. *The Gypsy Gentleman: A Study of George Borrow*. London: Murray & Barker, 1939

Dutt, William A. *George Borrow in East Anglia*. London: Nutt, 1896

Herbert, Lucille. 'George Borrow and the Forms of Self-Reflection,' *University of Toronto Quarterly*, 40 (Winter 1971), 152–67

Meyers, R.R. *George Borrow*. New York: Twayne, 1966

Rickett, Arthur. 'George Borrow,' in *The Vagabond in Literature*. London: Dent, 1906

Thomas, Edward. *George Borrow: The Man and his Books*. London: Chapman & Hall, 1912

– 'George Borrow,' in *A Literary Pilgrim in England* [1917]. London: Cape, 1928

Thompson, Thomas William. 'Borrow's Gypsies,' *Journal of the Gypsy Lore Society*, n.s. 3 (January 1910), 162–74

Tilford, J.E. 'Contemporary Criticism of *Lavengro*: A re-examination,' *Studies in Philology*, 41 (July 1944), 442–6

– 'The Critical Approach to *Lavengro-Romany Rye*,' *Studies in Philology*, 46 (January 1949), 79–96
– 'The Formal Artistry of *Lavengro-Romany Rye*,' *PMLA*, 44 (June 1949), 369–84
Vesey-Fitzgerald, Brian. *Gypsy Borrow*. London: Dobson, 1953
Walling, R.A.J. *George Borrow: The Man and his Work*. London: Cassell, 1908
Watts-Dunton, Theodore. 'George Borrow,' in *Old Familiar Faces*. New York: Dutton, 1916

Richard Jefferies

WORKS

There is no collected edition of Jefferies, though Lutterworth Press and Eyre & Spottiswoode both initiated never completed editions in 1948. The following are Jefferies' specifically rural works:
The Gamekeeper at Home; or, Sketches of Natural History and Rural Life [1878]. London: Smith Elder, 1896
Wild Life in a Southern County [1879]. London: Lutterworth, 1949
The Amateur Poacher. London: Smith Elder, 1879
Greene Ferne Farm. London: Smith Elder, 1880. Fiction
Hodge and His Masters [1880]. London: Eyre & Spottiswoode, 1948
Round About a Great Estate [1880]. London: Eyre & Spottiswoode, 1948
Bevis: The Story of a Boy [1882]. London: Cape, 1932. Fiction
Nature Near London. London: Chatto & Windus, 1883
The Story of My Heart: My Autobiography [1883]. Edited by Samuel J. Looker. London: Constable, 1947
Red Deer. London: Longmans, 1884
The Life of the Fields. [1884]. London: Lutterworth, 1948
The Dewy Morn. 2 vols. London: Bentley, 1884. Fiction
The Open Air [1885]. London: Eyre & Spottiswoode, 1948
Amaryllis at the Fair. London: Sampson Low, 1887. Fiction
Field and Hedgerow [1889]. London: Lutterworth, 1948
The Toilers of the Field. London: Longmans, 1892
Jefferies' Land: A History of Swindon and its Environs. Edited by Grace Toplis. London: Simpkin, Marshall, 1896
The Hills and the Vale. Edited by Edward Thomas. London: Duckworth, 1909
The Old House at Coate. Edited by Samuel J. Looker. London: Lutterworth, 1948

The Nature Diaries and Note-Books of Richard Jefferies. Edited by Samuel J.
Looker. London: Grey Walls, 1948
Chronicles of the Hedges. Edited by Samuel J. Looker. London: Phoenix
House, 1948
Field and Farm. Edited by Samuel J. Looker. London: Phoenix House, 1957

BIBLIOGRAPHY

No full-scale formal bibliography of Jefferies exists. Some useful bibliographical information will be found in the first edition of Samuel J. Looker's anthology, *Jefferies' England* (London: Constable, 1937). The most up-to-date and
accurate general bibliography, including a checklist of articles, is in my *Richard
Jefferies: A Critical Study* (see under 'Selected Criticism' below).

BIOGRAPHY

The best biography is still Edward Thomas's *Richard Jefferies: His Life and
Work* (London: Hutchinson, 1909). This should be supplemented with *Richard
Jefferies: Man of the Fields* by Samuel J. Looker and Crichton Porteous (Lon-
don: Baker, 1965). Neither is trustworthy about details. Walter Besant's *The
Eulogy of Richard Jefferies* (London: Chatto & Windus, 1888) is best charac-
terized by its title.

SELECTED CRITICISM

The most detailed study of Jefferies' work is my *Richard Jefferies: A Critical
Study* (Toronto: University of Toronto Press / London: Oxford University
Press, 1965), which also contains an all-but-complete list of secondary sources
up to the time of publication. The following items will be found useful:

Blench, J.W. 'The Fiction of Richard Jefferies,' *Cambridge Journal*, 7 (March
1954), 361–77
Drew, Philip. 'Richard Jefferies and the English Countryside,' *Victorian
Studies*, 11 (December 1967), 181–206
Hyde, William J. 'Richard Jefferies and the Naturalistic Peasant,' *Nineteenth
Century Fiction*, 11 (December 1956), 207–17
Leavis, Q.D. 'Lives and Works of Richard Jefferies' [1938], in F.R. Leavis, ed., *A
Selection from 'Scrutiny.'* 2 vols. Cambridge: University Press, 1968
Looker, S.J., ed. *Richard Jefferies: A Tribute by Various Writers.* Worthing:
Aldridge Brothers, 1946
Perry, P.J. 'An Agricultural Journalist on the "Great Depression": Richard
Jefferies,' *Journal of British Studies*, 9 (May 1970), 126–40

Salt, H.S. *Richard Jefferies: A Study*. London: Sonnenschein, 1894.
Williamson, Henry. 'Some Nature Writers and Civilization' (Jefferies and Hudson), in *Essays by Divers Hands*, xxx. London: Oxford University Press, 1960

George Sturt / 'George Bourne'

WORKS

The following works by Sturt are relevant here, the first six being originally published under the pseudonym of 'George Bourne':
The Bettesworth Book [1901]. London: Duckworth, 1911
Memoirs of a Surrey Labourer. London: Duckworth, 1907
Change in the Village [1912]. London: Duckworth, 1920
Lucy Bettesworth [1913]. London: Duckworth, 1918
William Smith, Potter and Farmer. London: Chatto & Windus, 1919
A Farmer's Life. London: Cape, 1922
The Wheelwright's Shop [1923]. Cambridge: University Press, 1963
A Small Boy in the Sixties. Cambridge: University Press, 1927
Journals of George Sturt ('George Bourne'), 1890–1902. Edited by Geoffrey Grigson. London: Cresset, 1941
Journals of George Sturt, 1890–1927. Edited by E.D. Mackerness. 2 vols. Cambridge: University Press, 1967

SECONDARY MATERIAL

Critical treatments of Sturt are few, the most detailed being an unpublished PH D. thesis by John Fraser, 'George Sturt and Rural Labouring Life' (University of Minnesota, 1961). Articles include the following:
Fraser, John. 'George Sturt's Apprenticeship,' *Review of English Literature*, 5 (January 1964), 35–50
– 'Sturt and Class: *The Bettesworth Book*,' *English Studies in Africa*, 10 (September 1967), 129–46
Mackerness, E.D. 'The Early Career of George Sturt (1863–1927),' *Notes and Queries*, n.s. 8 (March 1961), 104–6
– 'George Sturt and the English Humanitarian Tradition,' in *Essays and Studies*, n.s. xxii. London: Murray, 1969.
Thompson, Denys. 'A Cure for Amnesia' [1933], in F.R. Leavis, ed., *A Selection from 'Scrutiny.'* 2 vols. Cambridge: University Press, 1968

Most of the surviving correspondence between Sturt and Arnold Bennett is published in the second volume of *The Letters of Arnold Bennett*, edited by James Hepburn (London: Oxford University Press, 1968).

W.H. Hudson

WORKS

The collected works of Hudson were published in twenty-four volumes by Dent in 1922–3. They include the following: *British Birds* (1895), *Birds in London* (1898), *Nature in Downland* (1900), *Birds and Man* (1901), *Hampshire Days* (1903), *The Land's End* (1908), *Afoot in England* (1909), *A Shepherd's Life* (1910), *Adventures Among Birds* (1913), *Far Away and Long Ago* (1918), *Birds in Town and Village* (1919, a revised version of *Birds in a Village* [London: Chapman & Hall, 1893]), *The Book of a Naturalist* (1919), *Dead Man's Plack and An Old Thorn* (1920), *A Traveller in Little Things* (1921) *A Hind in Richmond Park* (1922). The following works have appeared since:

Rare, Vanishing and Lost British Birds. Edited by Linda Gardiner. London: Dent, 1923

153 Letters from W.H. Hudson. Edited by Edward Garnett. London: Nonesuch, 1923. Published in New York under the tital *Letters from W.H. Hudson, 1901–1922*

Men, Books and Birds. Edited by Morley Roberts. London: Eveleigh Nash, Grayson, 1925

W.H. Hudson's Letters to R.B. Cunninghame Graham. Edited by Richard Curle. London: Golden Cockerel Press, 1941

BIBLIOGRAPHY

The standard work is G.F. Wilson's *A Bibliography of the Writings of W.H. Hudson* (London: Bookman's Journal, 1922). Also relevant are C.F. Wells, *The G.M. Adams–W.H. Hudson Collection* Bulletin of the Clements Library, no. 39 (Ann Arbor: 1943), and Sidonia C. Rosenbaum, 'William Henry Hudson, Bibliografía,' *Revista Hispánica Moderna*, 10 (1944), 222–30

BIOGRAPHY

No full biography of Hudson exists. The closest to a biographical study is Ruth

Tomalin's *W.H. Hudson* (London: Witherby, 1954). Morley Roberts, *W.H. Hudson: A Portrait* (London: Eveleigh Nash & Grayson, 1924) is a significant memoir. H.F. West's *For a Hudson Biographer* (Hanover, NH: Westholm Publications, 1958) also contains useful biographical information.

SELECTED CRITICISM

The best general study of Hudson is Richard E. Haymaker's *From Pampas to Hedgerows and Downs: A Study of W.H. Hudson* (New York: Bookman, 1954). The following will also be found useful:
Charles, R.H. 'The Writings of W.H. Hudson,' in *Essays and Studies*, xx. Oxford: Clarendon Press, 1935
Hamilton, Robert. *W.H. Hudson: The Vision of Earth*. London: Dent, 1946
Looker, S.J., ed. *W.H. Hudson: A Tribute by Various Writers*. Worthing: Aldridge Brothers, 1947
Massingham, H.J. 'W.H. Hudson,' in *Untrodden Ways*. London: Unwin, 1923
– 'W.H. Hudson,' in Derek Hudson, ed., *English Critical Essays, Twentieth Century, Second Series*. London: Oxford University Press, 1958
Thomas, Edward. 'W.H. Hudson,' in *A Literary Pilgrim in England* [1917]. London: Cape, 1928
Williamson, Henry. 'Some Nature Writers and Civilization' (Jefferies and Hudson), in *Essays by Divers Hands*, xxx. London: Oxford University Press, 1960

Edward Thomas

WORKS

Thomas's rural writings consist of the following:
The Woodland Life. Edinburgh: Blackwood, 1897
Horae Solitariae. London: Duckworth, 1902
Rose Acre Papers. London: Brown Langham, 1904. The 1910 volume of the same name (London: Duckworth) is a collection drawn from this volume and from *Horae Solitariae*.
Beautiful Wales. London: Black, 1905
The Heart of England. London: Dent, 1906
Richard Jefferies: His Life and Work. London: Hutchinson, 1909
The South Country. London: Dent, 1909
Rest and Unrest. London: Duckworth, 1910

The Isle of Wight. London: Black, 1911
Light and Twilight. London: Duckworth, 1911
George Borrow: The Man and his Books. London: Chapman & Hall, 1912
The Icknield Way. London: Constable, 1913
The Country. London: Batsford, 1913
The Happy-Go-Lucky Morgans. London: Duckworth, 1913. Fiction
In Pursuit of Spring. London: Nelson, 1914
A Literary Pilgrim in England [1917]. London: Cape, 1928
Cloud Castle, and Other Papers. London: Duckworth, 1922
The Last Sheaf. London: Cape, 1928
The Childhood of Edward Thomas. London: Faber, 1938
Collected Poems of Edward Thomas. London: Faber, 1949. Only this and subsequent impressions are complete.

Thomas also edited a number of volumes, including *This England* (London: Oxford University Press, 1915).

BIBLIOGRAPHY, BIOGRAPHY, AND LETTERS

Robert P. Eckert's *Edward Thomas: A Biography and Bibliography* (London: Dent, 1937) was an excellent pioneering work, and has only recently been superseded biographically by William Cooke's *Edward Thomas: A Critical Biography* (London: Faber, 1970). For bibliographical information Cooke also brings Eckert's work up to date, but the latter remains standard. John Moore's *The Life and Letters of Edward Thomas* (London: Heinemann, 1939) should also be consulted. Helen Thomas's memoirs, *As It Was* (London: Heinemann, 1926) and *World Without End* (London: Heinemann, 1931), are moving personal accounts. Eleanor Farjeon's *Edward Thomas: The Last Four Years* (London: Oxford University Press, 1958) is also a memoir, and prints some two hundred of Thomas's letters.

The chief collection of letters, apart from those of Moore and Farjeon, is *Letters from Edward Thomas to Gordon Bottomley*, edited by R. George Thomas (London: Oxford University Press, 1968). This volume also contains a useful year-by-year chronology of Thomas's life. Other collections of letters are:

Garnett, Edward, ed. 'Some Letters of Edward Thomas,' *Athenaeum* 16 and 23
　　April 1920, pp. 501–3, 534–6
Guthrie, James, ed. 'Edward Thomas's Letters to W.H. Hudson,' *London*
　　Mercury, 2 (August 1920), 434–42

SELECTED CRITICISM

The most detailed critical study of Thomas's work is H. Coombes' *Edward*

Thomas (London: Chatto & Windus, 1956). The following will be found useful:

Keith, W.J. 'The Present State of Edward Thomas Studies,' *University of Toronto Quarterly*, 41 (Autumn 1971), 74–7

Lewis, C. Day. 'The Poetry of Edward Thomas,' in *Essays by Divers Hands*, XXVIII. London: Oxford University Press, 1956

Murry, John Middleton. 'The Poety of Edward Thomas,' in *Aspects of Literature*. London: Collins, 1920

Scannell, Vernon. *Edward Thomas*. London: Longmans, 1963. British Council 'Writers and Their Work' pamphlet

Wright, Herbert G. 'Edward Thomas,' in *Studies of Contemporary Literature*. Bangor: Jarvis & Foster, 1918. This volume also contains 'Notes on the Life and Ancestry of Edward Thomas by his Father.'

Henry Williamson

WORKS

The following writings are relevant here:

The Beautiful Years (Part I of *The Flax of Dream*) [1921]. London: Faber, 1967

Dandelion Days (Part II of *The Flax of Dream*) [1922]. London: Faber, 1966.

The Lone Swallows. London: Collins, 1922. Revised edition, London: Putnam, 1945

The Peregrine's Saga [1923]. London: Putnam, 1934

The Dream of Fair Women (Part III of *The Flax of Dream*) [1924]. London: Faber, 1968

The Old Stag [1926]. London: Putnam, 1933

Tarka the Otter. London: Putnam, 1927

The Pathway (Part IV of *The Flax of Dream*) [1928]. London: Faber, 1969

The Village Book. London: Cape, 1930*

The Wild Red Deer of Exmoor. London: Faber, 1931

The Labouring Life. London: Cape, 1932*

On Foot in Devon. London: Maclehose, 1933

The Linhay on the Downs [1934]. London: Cape, 1938

Salar the Salmon [1935]. London: Faber, 1959

Devon Holiday. London: Cape, 1935

Goodbye West Country [1937]. Boston: Little, Brown, 1938

The Children of Shallowford. London: Faber, 1939. Revised edition, 1959

---

* *Life in a Devon Village* and *Tales of a Devon Village*, both published by Faber in 1945, are drawn from the sketches in these earlier volumes.

The Story of a Norfolk Farm [1941]. London: Readers' Union, by arrangement with Faber, 1942
Norfolk Life, with Lilias Rider Haggard. London: Faber, 1943
The Sun in the Sands. London: Faber, 1945
The Phasian Bird. London: Faber, 1948
Tales of Moorland and Estuary. London: Macdonald, 1953
A Clear Water Stream. London: Faber, 1958
In the Woods. Llandeilo: St. Albert's Press, 1961
    Books edited by Williamson include the following:
An Anthology of Modern Nature Writing. London: Nelson, 1936
Richard Jefferies: Selections of his Work, with details of his Life and Circumstances, his Death and Immortality. London: Faber, 1937
Jefferies, Richard. *Hodge and His Masters*, revised by Henry Williamson. London: Methuen, 1937. A later revision, published by Faber in 1946, was entitled *A Classic of English Farming*.

BIBLIOGRAPHY

I.W. Girwan's *A Bibliography and Critical Survey of the Works of Henry Williamson* (Chipping Campden: Alcuin Press, 1931) is inevitably limited because of its date. Far more useful is the annotated book-catalogue devoted to Williamson recently issued by Alan Hancox (Cheltenham, 1973).

CRITICISM

The *Aylesford Review* has published a special issue (2: 2 [Winter 1957–8]) devoted to Henry Williamson. The following items will also be found useful:
Murry, John Middleton. 'The Novels of Henry Williamson,' in *Katherine Mansfield and Other Literary Studies*. London: Constable, 1959
West, H.F. *The Dreamer of Devon: An Essay on Henry Williamson*. London: Ulysses Press, 1932
Wilson, Colin. 'Henry Williamson,' *Aylesford Review*, 4 (Autumn 1961), 131–3

H.J. Massingham

WORKS

The following works by Massingham are most relevant here:
Some Birds of the Countryside. London: Unwin, 1921
Untrodden Ways. London: Unwin, 1923

In Praise of England. London: Methuen, 1924
Downland Man. London: Cape, 1926
The Heritage of Man. London: Cape, 1929
Birds of the Seashore. London: Werner Laurie, 1931
Wold Without End. London: Cobden-Sanderson, 1932
Country. London: Cobden-Sanderson, 1934
Through the Wilderness. London: Cobden-Sanderson, 1935
English Downland [1936]. London: Batsford, 1949
Genius of England. London: Chapman & Hall, 1937
Cotswold Country [1937]. London: Batsford, 1946
Shepherd's Country: A Record of the Crafts and People of the Hills. London:
    Chapman & Hall, 1938
A Countryman's Journal. London: Chapman & Hall, 1939
Country Relics. Cambridge: University Press, 1939
The Sweet of the Year. London: Chapman & Hall. 1939
Chiltern Country [1940]. London: Batsford, 1949
The Fall of the Year. London: Chapman & Hall, 1941
Remembrance: An Autobiography. London: Batsford, 1942
The English Countryman: A Study of the English Tradition. London: Batsford,
    1942
The Tree of Life. London: Chapman & Hall, 1943
Men of Earth. London: Chapman & Hall, 1943
This Plot of Earth: A Gardener's Chronicle. London: Collins, 1944
The Wisdom of the Fields. London: Collins, 1945
Where Man Belongs. London: Collins, 1946
An Englishman's Year. London: Collins, 1948
The Curious Traveller. London: Collins, 1950
The Faith of a Fieldsman. London: Museum Press, 1951
The Southern Marches. London: Hale, 1952
    Massingham has also edited, among other works, the following:
English Country. London: Wishart, 1934
England and the Farmer. London: Batsford, 1941
The Small Farmer. London: Collins, 1947

BIOGRAPHY AND CRITICISM

Apart from reviews, there are no biographical or critical studies of Massingham.
The Midwinter 1952 number of *Wessex Letters from Springhead* (issued by
Rolf Gardiner at Fontmell Magna, Dorset) was entitled 'In Memoriam Harold
John Massingham' and included short tributes by Arthur Bryant, Adrian Bell,

Edmund Blunden, Rolf Gardiner, J.E. Hoskin, The Earl of Portsmouth, and C. Henry Warren. The issue also contains a 'Bibliography of the Works of H.J. Massingham' by John Sherwood. A more detailed but unpublished check-list of Massingham's work, a copy of which is in my possession, has recently been compiled by Marvin Hays (1971).

INDEX

This book
was designed by
WILLIAM RUETER
under the direction of
ALLAN FLEMING
and was printed by
University of
Toronto
Press